The Cambridge Companio

John Dryden, Poet Laureate to Charles II and James II, was one of the great literary figures of the late seventeenth century. This Companion provides a fresh look at Dryden's tactics and triumphs in negotiating the extraordinary political and cultural revolutions of his time. The newly commissioned essays introduce readers to the full range of his work as a poet, as a writer of innovative plays and operas, as a purveyor of contemporary notions of empire, and most of all as a man intimate with the opportunities of aristocratic patronage as well as the emerging market for literary gossip, slander and polemic. Dryden's works are examined in the context of seventeenth-century politics, publishing and ideas of authorship. A valuable resource for students and scholars, the Companion includes a full chronology of Dryden's life and works and a detailed guide to further reading.

STEVEN N. ZWICKER is Stanley Elkin Professor of Humanities at Washington University, St. Louis and Professor of English. He is the editor of *The Cambridge Companion to English Literature, 1650–1740* (Cambridge, 1998), *Reading, Society, and Politics in Early Modern England*, ed. with Kevin Sharpe (Cambridge, 2003), *John Dryden: Selected Poems* (2001), *Refiguring Revolutions*, ed. with Kevin Sharpe (1998), *Lines of Authority* (1993), *Politics of Discourse*, ed. with Kevin Sharpe (1987) and *Politics and Language in Dryden's Poetry* (1984).

THE CAMBRIDGE
COMPANION TO
JOHN DRYDEN

EDITED BY

STEVEN N. ZWICKER

Washington University, St. Louis

CAMBRIDGE
UNIVERSITY PRESS

PUBLISHED BY THE PRESS SYNDICATE OF THE UNIVERSITY OF CAMBRIDGE
The Pitt Building, Trumpington Street, Cambridge, United Kingdom

CAMBRIDGE UNIVERSITY PRESS
The Edinburgh Building, Cambridge, CB2 2RU, UK
40 West 20th Street, New York, NY 10011–4211, USA
477 Williamstown Road, Port Melbourne, VIC 3207, Australia
Ruiz de Alarcón 13, 28014 Madrid, Spain
Dock House, The Waterfront, Cape Town 8001, South Africa

http://www.cambridge.org

First published 2004

Printed in the United Kingdom at the University Press, Cambridge

Typeface Sabon 10/13 pt.   *System* LATEX 2$_\varepsilon$ [TB]

A catalogue record for this book is available from the British Library

ISBN 0 521 82427 3 hardback
ISBN 0 521 53144 6 paperback

CONTENTS

CONTRIBUTORS

JOHN BARNARD   Leeds University

LAURA BROWN   Cornell University

ANNE COTTERILL   Rutgers University

PAUL DAVIS   University College, University of London

KATSUHIRO ENGETSU   Doshisha University

PAULINA KEWES   Jesus College, University of Oxford

HAROLD LOVE   Monash University

JOHN MULLAN   University College, University of London

ANNABEL PATTERSON   Yale University

RONALD PAULSON   Johns Hopkins University

CHRISTOPHER RICKS   Boston University

STUART SHERMAN   Fordham University

JOHN SPURR   University of Wales, Swansea

STEVEN N. ZWICKER   Washington University, St. Louis

CHRONOLOGY

1631   Born in Aldwinckle, Northamptonshire, 9 August.

1644   Admitted as a King's Scholar to Westminster School.

1649   *Upon the death of the Lord Hastings* published in *Lachrymae Musarum* sometime after 24 June, the date of Hastings's death.

1650   Admitted to Trinity College, Cambridge 11 May.
To his friend the Author, on his divine Epigrams, published in John Hoddesdon's *Sion and Parnassus*, licensed 7 June.

1654   BA, Trinity College, Cambridge, January.

1659   *Heroic Stanzas* published in *Three poems to the happy memory of the most renowned Oliver*, January.

1660   *To my Honored Friend, Sr. Robert Howard, On his Excellent Poems* published in Howard's *Poems*, advertised in June.
Astraea Redux, Thomason's copy marked 19 June.

1661   *To His Sacred Majesty*, Thomason's copy marked 23 April.

1662   *To my Lord Chancellor, Presented on New-years day.*
To my Honored Friend, Dr. Charleton, commendatory verse to Charleton's *Chorea Gigantum*, licensed on 11 September, imprint date of 1663.
Proposed for membership in the Royal Society on 12 November by Walter Charleton.

1663   *The Wild Gallant* first performed 5 February; published in 1669.
Marriage to Lady Elizabeth Howard on 1 December.

1664   *The Indian Queen* (with Sir Robert Howard); Pepys saw the play on 27 January, published in March 1665.
The Rival Ladies performed early in 1664, published that fall with a dedication to Roger Boyle, Earl of Orrery.

1665   *The Indian Emperor* first performed *c.* April, published in October 1667 with a dedication to Anne Scott, Duchess of Monmouth, and again in 1668 together with "A Defence of an Essay of Dramatic Poesy."

Dryden leaves London in midsummer for Charleton, Wiltshire; during next eighteen months he writes *Annus Mirabilis*, published early in 1667 with a dedication to "The City of London"; *An Essay Of Dramatic Poesy*, published 1667 with a dedication to Charles Sackville, Lord Buckhurst who became the Earl of Dorset in 1677; and *Secret Love*, which Charles II "graced . . . with the title of His Play," performed in March of 1667, and published the same month.

1666   Dryden's first son, Charles, born 27 August.

1667   *Annus Mirabilis*; Pepys read the poem on 2 February.
      Sir Martin Mar-All (with William Cavendish, Duke of Newcastle) first performed in August, published 1668.
      The Tempest, adaptation by Dryden and Sir William Davenant, performed 7 November, published in 1670.

1668   Dryden's second son, John, born.
      Created Poet Laureate 13 April by royal warrant.
      An Evening's Love first performed 12 June, published 1671 with a dedication to William Cavendish and a preface on the nature of comedy.
      A Defense of "An Essay of Dramatic Poesy" prefixed to the second edition of the *Indian Emperor*, published before 20 September when Pepys had a copy.

1669   Dryden's third son, Erasmus-Henry, born 2 May.
      Tyrannick Love, or the Royal Martyr first performed *c.* June 1669, published in the fall of 1670 with a dedication to James Scott, Duke of Monmouth.

1670   Made Historiographer Royal 18 August.
      The Conquest of Granada, Part 1, first performed December, published together with Part 2 in 1672 with a dedication to James, Duke of York, the prefatory "Of Heroic Plays. An Essay," and a concluding "Defence of the Epilogue. Or, An Essay on the Dramatic Poetry of the last Age."

1671   *The Conquest of Granada*, Part 2, first performed in January, published 5 February 1672.
      Marriage A-la-Mode first performance *c.* November, published in 1673 with a dedication to John Wilmot, Earl of Rochester.
      Buckingham's *Rehearsal* first performed 7 December; here Dryden is first satirized as "Mr. Bayes."

1672   *The Assignation, or Love in a Nunnery* first performed in the summer or fall; published in June 1673 with a dedication to Sir Charles Sedley.

1673   *Amboyna* perhaps first performed *c.* June, published that fall with a dedication to Thomas, Lord Clifford of Chudleigh.

       The State of Innocence, possibly written for the wedding festivities of the Duke of York and Mary of Modena celebrated 21 November; published in February 1677 with a dedication to Mary of Modena, Duchess of York, and "The Author's Apology for Heroic Poetry and Poetic Licence."

1674   *Notes and Observations on the Empress of Morocco*, an attack on Elkanah Settle, written together with John Crowne and Thomas Shadwell.

1675   *Aureng-Zebe*, the last of Dryden's heroic plays, acted on 17 November, published early in 1676 with a dedication to John Sheffield, Earl of Mulgrave, whom Dryden commemorates as "Sharp judging Adriel" in *Absalom and Achitophel*.

1677   *All for Love* first performed in early December, published in the spring of 1678 with a dedication to Thomas Osborne, Earl of Danby.

1678   *MacFlecknoe* in manuscript circulation by 1678; probably written *c.* 1676.

       The Kind Keeper first performed 11 March, published in late in 1679 (imprint date of 1680) with a dedication to John, Lord Vaughan.

       Oedipus (with Nathaniel Lee) first performed late 1678, published in March 1679.

1679   *Troilus and Cressida* first performed in the spring and published later the same year by Jacob Tonson with a dedication to Robert Spencer, Earl of Sunderland; this is the first association between Tonson and Dryden.

       Rose Alley beating of Dryden 18 December, perhaps provoked by his association with the Earl of Mulgrave's *Essay upon Satyr*, verse which circulated in manuscript in 1679, and possibly instigated by the Earl of Rochester or the Duchess of Portsmouth.

1680   *Ovid's Epistles, Translated by Several Hands*; Dryden wrote the Preface and translated two epistles, "Canace to Macareus" and "Dido to Aeneas"; the book was advertised 6 February.

       The Spanish Friar first performed in the fall, published in March 1681 with a dedication to John Holles, Lord Haughton.

1681   *His Majesty's Declaration Defended*, published in June.

       Absalom and Achitophel; Luttrell's copy marked 17 November.

1682   *The Medal*; Luttrell's copy marked 16 March.

       MacFlecknoe published in an unauthorized edition; Luttrell's copy marked 4 October.

The Second Part of Absalom and Achitophel (with Nahum Tate),
Luttrell's copy marked 10 November.
Religio Laici; Luttrell's copy marked 28 November.
The Duke of Guise (with Nathaniel Lee) first performed
28 November, published in February of 1683 with a dedication to
Laurence Hyde, Earl of Rochester.

1683   "Life of Plutarch" written for Tonson's edition of *Plutarch's Lives*,
published in early May with Dryden's dedication to the Duke of
Ormonde.
The Art of Poetry, a translation of Boileau's *L'Art Poetique*, made
collaboratively by William Soame and Dryden.

1684   *Miscellany Poems*; includes twenty-six poems by Dryden; the book
was advertised 2 February.
Albion and Albanius likely performed 29 May and published in
1685; Luttrell's copy marked 6 June.
Maimbourg's *History of the League*, translated by Dryden,
published in late July with Dryden's dedication of the book to
Charles II.
*To the Earl of Roscommon on his Excellent Essay on Translated
Verse* published *c.* summer.
To the Memory of Mr. Oldham published in *Remains of Mr. John
Oldham c.* fall.
King Arthur finished *c.* fall, performed in 1691.

1685   *Sylvae*; includes seventeen poems by Dryden, among them
translations of Lucretius, Virgil, Theocritus, and Horace, published
January.
Threnodia Augustalis; British Museum copy marked 9 March.
Revised version of *Albion and Albanius* first publicly performed
3 June, published soon after.
To Mr. Northleigh, Dryden's commendatory verse published in
Northleigh's *Triumph of Our Monarchy c.* June.
To the Pious Memory of Mrs. Anne Killigrew published in *Poems by
Mrs. Anne Killigrew*, advertised in November and published with a
1686 imprint date.

1686   Dryden's conversion to Roman Catholicism, *c.* 1685–6; John Evelyn
notes his going to mass on 19 January 1686.

1687   *The Hind and the Panther* published *c.* May.
To My Ingenious Friend, Mr. Henry Higden, published in Higden's
Modern Essay on the Tenth Satire of Juvenal, c. summer.
A Song for St. Cecilia's Day performed 22 November.

On the Marriage of Anastasia Stafford, likely to have been written in December.

1688   *Paradise Lost*, fourth edition, which includes the first printing of Dryden's *Lines on Milton*.

Britania Rediviva licensed 19 June.

Dryden's translation of Dominique Bouhours's *The Life of St. Francis Xavier* advertised in July, published with a dedication to Mary of Modena.

1689   *Don Sebastian* first performed 4 December, published in January 1690 with a dedication to Philip Sidney, Third Earl of Leicester.

1690   *Amphitryon* first performed October, advertised for publication late that month and published with a dedication to Sir William Leveson-Gower.

1691   *King Arthur* first performed June and published soon after with a dedication to George Savile, Marquis of Halifax.

1692   *Eleonora*; Luttrell's copy marked 7 March.

"The Character of Polybius" mentioned in *The Gentleman's Journal* in April, published in 1693 prefatory to *The History of Polybius*.

Cleomenes first performed in April and published in May, with a dedication to Laurence Hyde, Earl of Rochester.

The Satires of Juvenal and Persius published in October with an imprint date of 1693 and with a dedication, the "Discourse Concerning Satire," to Charles Sackville, Sixth Earl of Dorset; Dryden translated Juvenal's Satires 1, 3, 6, 10, and 16 and all the Persius.

1693   *Examen Poeticum* containing new translations from Ovid's *Metamorphoses*, published in the summer with Dryden's dedication to Edward Lord Radclyffe.

Congreve's *The Double Dealer* published in December including Dryden's *To my Dear Friend Mr. Congreve*; imprint date, 1694.

1694   *Love Triumphant* first performed in January, advertised for sale in March and published with a dedication to James Cecil, Fourth Earl of Salisbury.

Contract between Dryden and Tonson for *The Works of Virgil* signed 15 June.

The Annual Miscellany for the year 1694; the book was advertised in July and printed for the first time as *The Third Book of the Georgics*, and *To Sir Godfrey Kneller*.

1695   Dryden's translation of Du Fresnoy's *De Arte Graphica* with Dryden's "Parallel, of Poetry and Painting"; advertised in late June.

1696   *An Ode on the Death of Mr. Henry Purcell* published in the spring.
Dryden writes the "The Life of Lucian," published prefatory to *The Works of Lucian* in 1711.

1697   *The Works of Virgil* advertised in June; publication probably late July or early August, with dedications to Hugh, Lord Clifford (*Pastorals*); Philip Stanhope, Earl of Chesterfield (*Georgics*); and John Sheffield, Earl of Mulgrave and Marquis of Normanby (*Aeneis*), and two sets of subscriptions.
Dryden translates Ovid's *Art of Love*, Book 1, summer; published 1709.
Alexander's Feast performed 22 November (St. Cecilia's Day) and published by December.

1698   *To Mr. Granville*, published with the first edition of Granville's *Heroic Love*, advertised in February.
To my Friend, the Author, published in Peter Motteux's *Beauty in Distress* 20 June.
The Annals and History of Cornelius Tacitus ... Made English by Several Hands published *c.* 30 June; Dryden translated Book 1, vol. 1 of the *Annals*.

1700   *Fables Ancient and Modern* advertised for sale in March, with a dedication to James Butler, Second Duke of Ormonde; includes *To the Duchess of Ormond* and *To My Honored Kinsman*.
Dies 1 May.
The Secular Masque published in Fletcher's *The Pilgrim*, for sale in June.

ABBREVIATIONS

Evelyn   John Evelyn (1620–1706), diarist and founding member of the
          Royal Society. Evelyn's *Diary* covers almost eight decades and
          is a remarkable source for students of seventeenth-century
          history and literature. The *Diary* was edited by E. S. De Beer,
          6 vols. (Oxford, 1955).

Luttrell Narcissus Luttrell (1657–1732), book collector, diarist, and
          parliamentarian. Luttrell marked his copies of pamphlets and
          books with the price of the item and its date of publication,
          often the date of his purchase. Luttrell items are now owned
          by, among others, the Henry E. Huntington Library and the
          Folger Shakespeare Library including *Absalom and
          Achitophel* (HEH) and *Religio Laici* (Folger).

Pepys   Samuel Pepys (1633–1703), civil servant and collector whose
          Diary (1 January 1660 to 31 May 1669) is a storehouse of
          information for the first decade of the Restoration. The *Diary*
          was edited by Robert Latham and William Mathews, 10 vols.
          (Berkeley and Los Angeles, 1970–83).

Thomason George Thomason (1602–66), bookseller and collector of
          pamphlets, tracts, newssheets, and books (1640–61).
          Thomason marked many of his purchases with the publication
          date and attributions of authorship. The Thomason Tracts are
          housed in the British Library; their *Catalogue* was edited by
          G. K. Fortescue, 2 vols. (London, 1908).

Works   All citations to Dryden's work, unless otherwise indicated, are
          to the California edition, *The Works of John Dryden*, ed. E. N.
          Hooker and H. T. Swedenberg, Jr. *et al.*, 20 vols. (Berkeley and
          Los Angeles, 1956–2002), abbreviated as *Works*. Poems are
          cited by volume, page, and line number; plays by act, scene,
          and line numbers; and prose by volume and page number.

I

PLEASURES OF THE IMAGINATION

1

STEVEN N. ZWICKER

Composing a literary life: introduction

John Dryden has come down to us through the exemplary practices of literary editing: a large number of uniform volumes, learnedly prefaced, packed with history and explanatory notes. Who first thought of *The Works of John Dryden*? Not, I think, the poet himself. During his long writing life Dryden showed little interest in collecting or revising his work; neither he nor apparently anyone else kept his manuscripts; and Dryden seldom wrote of, or even seems to have imagined, a coherent and progressive literary career of the kind that was often on Spenser's or Milton's mind. Of course, the idea of collected works would have been obvious to Dryden from the humanist editions of classical authors, from *The Works* of Ben Jonson or the Shakespeare folios, or from collected editions even closer to hand – Cowley, Cleveland, and Suckling. Dryden himself contributed an elegy to John Oldham's *Remains*, and he knew too of the *Œuvres* of Corneille and Racine. His shrewd publisher Jacob Tonson made an effort at such collection in the 1690s, but the sustained impulse to collect "the works" began after Dryden's death, first with Tonson's various compilations of poems and plays, then at the end of the eighteenth century with Edmond Malone's edition of Dryden's prose. Sir Walter Scott's monumental edition in eighteen volumes appeared in 1808, to be revised late in the nineteenth century by George Saintsbury, and in the early 1950s planning began for what would, half a century later, become *The Works of John Dryden*, complete in twenty volumes that bind together, apparatus and all, close to ten thousand pages.

Neither Dryden nor his first readers could have quite imagined the way in which his works would later be presented, especially work that was written, as it were, on the run. Not that Dryden wrote only on the run, but the rapidity with which he turned out his work, its original daring, and the sense of entrepreneurship and experiment that informed much of it – these are difficult to imagine from within the solid uniformity of *The Works*. It might seem churlish to complain of the labor that has unlocked so much of a world that is now lost to us without scholarship, and yet there is something lost as well in these monumentalizing editions, and not only of the rapidity and fluency with which Dryden managed the thousands of pages of verse and prose – prologues, epilogues, and plays; songs, satires, state poems, and panegyrics; commendatory verse and elegies; epitaphs, epistles, odes, essays, dedications, prefaces, biographies, and a raft of translations from ancient and modern languages – but also of the contingent, combative, and improvisatory atmosphere in which a good deal of the work was at first imagined and written. Lost too in the habits of editing monumentally, of tracing sources and influences, is the collusive character of much of early modern writing, how responsive that writing was not just to occasion and not just to the long shadow of the classical and vernacular past, but to the exactly contemporary texts, conditions, and communities within, and against, which it was read and circulated through adaptation and allusion, and even plagiary, and through mockery and scornful imitation.

What set a good deal of Dryden's work in motion was competition and combat, the spinning together of interest and vindication, and this while the poet wrote with an eye on the commerce of the stage and print and on the favor of patronage. But merely to identify commerce and patronage as the most important institutional circumstances of this career is to conjure too stable and homogeneous a world, for print and patronage were themselves volatile and sinuously complex institutions, at one moment proffering glamor and privilege, at the next humiliation and scorn. And the larger civic structures to which Dryden sought to attach himself – the crown, its instruments and ministers, its programs and prerogatives – were not much more fixed or stable than were taste and favor. The civil wars, their persistent shadow, and the repeated crises of the later seventeenth century taught the fragility of institutions and the uncertainty of fortune. From the beginning of his career to its end, Dryden operated in a mercurial political environment and in a fiercely competitive market, even while reforming letters, fashioning a new theatre, and inventing a place for himself in the pantheon of letters, as well as in the trade of books.

How then should we imagine the poet in negotiation with all the varied and volatile circumstances of his work? Neither Dryden nor his readers understood this career as the first move in the creation of Augustan literature or as the farewell of print commerce to aristocratic patronage and Renaissance humanism. Retrospectively the career allows both constructions, but as Dryden got that career underway – and rather late, near the age of thirty – he must have seen himself as elbowing his way into a crowded writerly field opened by such occasions as the death of the Lord Protector, the restoration of monarchy, and the revival of the theatre. When Dryden's first important verse was published – an elegy on the death of Oliver Cromwell – the poem was part of a nervously contrived effort at commemoration with a last-minute change of publishers and substitution of verse; and when he turned from republican eulogy to Stuart restoration, Dryden entered a field of play in which his verse had to jostle for recognition with a hundred other entrepreneurial offerings. How then did Dryden as poet laureate, historiographer royal, and finally inventor of Restoration literature emerge from such competition?

Partly, of course, the emergence is retrospective, the clearing of a crowded field of texts in the interest of admiration and anthology, and in the securing of lines of inheritance – Milton yielding Thomson, Blake, and Shelley; Dryden yielding Swift, Pope, and Byron. In the busy workshop of early Restoration literature, Dryden's emergence was not so certain, though by the end of the first decade of his career, it seems to have been decisive. He wrote buoyantly on his own behalf, in prefaces and dedications, in prologues, epilogues, and free-standing criticism, and not only of his own projects and patrons, but of the world of letters, ancient and modern, English and continental, that he meant to join.

In achieving that ambition, Dryden had a certain amount of luck and some personal connections; effort and proximity pushed him into visibility. Member of a minor branch of a distinguished Northamptonshire family, educated at Westminster School and at Cambridge, Dryden went down to London in his mid-twenties, worked in some minor capacity for the Protectorate government, then met and lodged with the volatile and opinionated Sir Robert Howard, an aristocrat interested in politics, theatre, and self-display. After his first occasional pieces for the new regime – poems on the Restoration and coronation of the king, and a celebration of the lord chancellor – Dryden married Lady Elizabeth Howard, Sir Robert's sister, joined the newly formed Royal Society, and began to write for the theatre. In the summer of 1665, with the theatres closed and the plague raging in London, Dryden retreated to the country estate of his father-in-law, the Earl of Berkshire. There he wrote two extremely ambitious pieces in which he invented himself as a man of letters – entrepreneurial, articulate, self-conscious, perhaps a touch shy or diffident (like his counterpart Neander in *An Essay of Dramatic Poesy*), and certainly opinionated – and there he mastered a subtle and dexterous prose style with which to set in motion a wide range of opinions on a variety of literary topics.

The verse that Dryden created from his country retreat was a city poem called *Annus Mirabilis* (1667); his prose was *An Essay of Dramatic Poesy* (1668). In its range of learning, its contrapuntal form, its mastery of vernacular dramatic traditions, and its ability to articulate and balance contradictory points of view, all the while arranging the vindication of English theatre – its mixtures, flexibility, and capaciousness of form – the *Essay* is the masterpiece of Dryden's first decade as author. By contrast, *Annus Mirabilis* – Dryden's poem on the Anglo-Dutch wars and the Great Fire of London – seems a display of brilliant amateurism with a breathless variety of scenes: naval battles and the appetites of trade, a city laid low by fire and plague, the colors of heroism, the plangent notes of despair. Dryden displays an impressive ability to think strategically and polemically in *Annus Mirabilis*, but the verse is effortful and the learning self-conscious, the poet anxious at once to register erudition and not to irritate with learning: "In some places, where either the fancy, or the words, were [Virgil's] or any others, I have noted it in the Margin, that I might not seem a Plagiary; in others, I have neglected it, to avoid as well the tediousness, as the affectation of doing it too often" (*Works* 1: 56). A guileless admission, but when Dryden has fully mastered this medium, the anxiety will get folded completely into the verse and the poet will disappear behind the veil of his art, as he does so immaculately in the *Essay of Dramatic Poesy*, where he makes a piece of theatre out of the eagerness to please and impress that he cannot quite control in *Annus Mirabilis*.

When Dryden returned to London in the fall of 1666 it was to the theatre and theatrical controversy, and to the enterprise of fashioning, theorizing, and defending heroic drama. That work thrust Dryden fully into the world of Restoration theatricality with its controversies, critiques, and tart opinions. In the quickened pace of pamphleteering that swirled around the theatre of the 1660s and 1670s, there emerged not only a delight in slander and abuse but as well a taste for opinion and, more broadly, for aesthetic responsiveness. With greater clarity and certainty than ever before, criticism – though not always by that name – became one of the formative contexts for the conduct of literature, and Dryden's great achievement in the early years of his career was to operate simultaneously as poet, playwright, and critic, at times theorizing on behalf of his own work, at times writing more disinterestedly within – and by that act helping to create – an emergent discourse of literary criticism.

From the varied strands of literary controversy and conversation, what emerges, quite distinctively, in the late 1660s is the figure of John Dryden – Poet Laureate and Historiographer Royal, apologist for the great, dramatic theorist, and theatrical innovator. For a decade after his return to London, Dryden wrote almost exclusively for the theatre; he had become a shareholder in the King's Company and was contracted with them for three plays a year. By the time he had published his great verse satires in the early 1680s, Dryden had written nearly two dozen plays in a variety of genres: comedy, tragedy, tragicomedy, and, most innovatively, heroic drama – the form that he was most closely identified with, and so much so that the heroic style, and

Dryden as its chief agent, became bywords for elevation and for flattering excess. Nor is it difficult to see why when we read Dryden's address to the Duke of York in the Dedication to *Conquest of Granada*:

> Since . . . the world is govern'd by precept and Example; and both these can onely have influence from those persons who are above us, that kind of Poesy which excites to virtue the greatest men, is of the greatest use to humankind. 'Tis from this consideration, that I have presum'd to dedicate to your Royal Highness these faint representations of your own worth and valor in Hero-ique poetry: or, to speak more properly, not to dedicate, but to restore to you those Ideas, which, in the more perfect part of my characters, I have taken from you . . . And certainly, if ever Nation were oblig'd either by the conduct, the personal valour, or the good fortune of a Leader, the English are acknowl-edging, in all of them, to your Royal Highness. Your whole life has been a continu'd series of Heroique Actions.　　　　　　　　　　　　　　(*Works* XI: 3)

The play was published in 1672, shortly before the duke's public display of his conversion to Rome, but already when he was much suspected and reviled. With the *Conquest of Granada*, Dryden moved into the center of political factionalism and professional envy, a broad cultural discourse in which heroic drama was indelibly typed by its underwriting of the personal grandeur and absolutist ambitions of Stuart monarchy. The critique was con-ducted through pamphlets and tracts, but nowhere to better effect than in *The Rehearsal*, a skit by the Duke of Buckingham and a coterie of aristo-crats and literary amateurs who mocked the heroic drama by ridiculing the stylistic excesses, the personality, and the political ideals of its chief agent. By the early 1670s Dryden had emerged fully into public view, and there would be no retreat from that publicity. Critical, personal, and political engagement became, inextricably and indisputably, the context not only for Dryden's theatre but for all his work, and most artfully for the satires that Dryden began to write in the late 1670s, poems spun from a mix of gossip, news, literary polemics, and political argument. When we read *MacFlecknoe* (c. 1676), *Absalom and Achitophel* (1681), *The Medal* (1681), or the prefaces to works like *Religio Laici* (1682) and *The Hind and the Panther* (1687), it seems remarkable that it took Dryden twenty years to figure out that satire, with all its registers of irony and innuendo, would indisputably be his form. He remarked in the 1690s, with a touch of impersonality and diffidence, that others had noticed his art – "They say my Talent is Satyre; if it be so, 'tis a Fruitful Age" – but even by the late 1670s he had developed a buoyant confidence in his satiric stride (*Works* III: 234).

　　MacFlecknoe is the first of the great verse satires. The motives for its creation, the modes of its circulation, even its subject, are still in dispute;

what is not in dispute is Dryden's satiric mastery, his glancing way of imagining his contemporaries, veiled but easily identified, and of orchestrating together personal invective, artistic principles, political ideals, and flattery, and humiliation, of the great. Of course, Dryden did not invent the complex entertainments of satire; those he learned from the great Roman satirists Horace, Juvenal, and Persius – poets he had translated as a schoolboy and to whom he would later return. But to the themes and idioms of classical satire – the correction of vice and folly, the mingling of irony, elegance and derision – Dryden added the sheen of his own vernacular style of insult and innuendo, privileging the high style, but deftly mixing it with the buzz of personal malice and local gossip and rumor.

In *MacFlecknoe* Dryden is in superb control of satire's armory and energy – assault and attack, and scorn. But where Dryden most fully shines as satirist is in *Absalom and Achitophel* (1681), his rendering of the Exclusion Crisis – the parliamentary effort to block the Duke of York's succession to the throne – as biblical history. Here satire's devices of injury and exposure are mixed with a broad range of topics and tonalities. His rogues' gallery is full of literary pleasure, but Dryden also plays admiration against enmity and his little elegy for the Earl of Ossory, the complex and funny rescue operation that he mounts in his portrait of Charles II, his mixed address to the Duke of Monmouth as the king's beautiful, favored, foolish, and illegitimate son, and his edgy indictment of the Earl of Shaftesbury display subtleties of argument and psychology that allow Dryden's capacity for assault to emerge as only one effect within a much broader imaginative field. It is not simply that range and mixture allowed Dryden to baffle and heighten insult with other literary effects, it is that Dryden's capacity to sustain argument through image, rhythm, and rhyme is itself broadened by the reach of satire into other kinds of work: the constitution of political community, the admiration for dexterity and defense, the mourning for lost opportunity. In *Absalom and Achitophel* everything came together for Dryden: his assurance, his self-understanding, his capacity to be simultaneously client and author, protégé of the great and fully his own person. Here Dryden worked under great pressure and with superb economy; his verse moves in a number of different, even contradictory ways.

Something of the same counterpoint and contrary movement is achieved at other points in this career and always to wonderful effect. In the elegy for John Oldham, Dryden uses Virgil simultaneously to express sorrow and acknowledge ambition; and later, in his address to the Duchess of Ormond, Dryden manages a range of tones and arguments that allows him, in the midst of praise and celebration, to imagine absence and longing, suffering and sorrow. He darkens and extends panegyric in new, seemingly contradictory ways; and yet as the poem unveils cultural compromises and personal disappointments, it projects the duchess's life as a fully imagined, coherent, and poignant whole.

In *The Medal*, Dryden worked on a narrower scheme than in *Absalom and Achitophel*, a design suggested, some said, by the king himself. The poem looks like a move to the side in Dryden's career, a simpler, angrier enterprise suited to the personal attacks that followed the pseudonymous publication of *Absalom and Achitophel* and to the backlash against the crown's triumphs over Exclusion. Dryden's tone in *The Medal* conjures the world of canting and libeling; he responds vigorously to the affronts and reproaches that now greeted his every move. But Dryden's poems of religious confession – first an Anglican apologia, *Religio Laici*, and then his remarkable, nearly impenetrable, script of Roman Catholic conversion, *The Hind and the Panther* – demonstrate that the subtle and ironic public posturing and the complexity of feeling and self-understanding that Dryden had achieved in *Absalom and Achitophel* could be renegotiated on new terrain. And religion certainly represented a new terrain for Dryden, unless we count the scandalously dismissive address to priests and priestcraft in *Absalom and Achitophel* as part of the poet's spiritual directory. But in *Religio Laici* Dryden had reason to recalibrate his address to the spiritual, or so it might seem from the preface to this poem where he adopts a beguiling deference, a bland confession of his simple faith and charity, spiritual amateurism, and reverence for authority. At the same time, Dryden manages to suggest that he has something in mind quite different from mere deference, and as the Preface unfolds Dryden strikes contrapuntally at a variety of targets, on the one hand whispering deference and charity, on the other cutting sharply against a variety of religious dogmatisms from the rigidity of dissent and the intolerance of high-flyers to the arrogance of Rome. Dryden weaves carefully between the argumentative extremes that he himself has arranged in order to emerge the cool skeptic, the private man less concerned with spiritual precision than generosity of spirit, a spokesman, but only in his privacy, for the traditional virtues of charity and harmony, for toleration and civic quiet. Rather a surprising stance for the poet laureate as civic satirist, and yet Dryden means to speak directly into and against the contemporary clamor over religion stirred not only by the "Popish Plot" – a supposed effort by Catholics to poison Charles II and install the Duke of York on the throne – and by the Exclusion Crisis, but also by Charles II's sustained campaign to achieve religious toleration simply by declaring the charity of Indulgence, a move opposed at various points both by dissenters and by the established church.

Why does Dryden insist on the privacy of *Religio Laici* when the poem's themes and arguments make it perfectly clear that he means to participate in the public controversies over religion? Perhaps the question contains its own answer, for the private convictions of the laureate would necessarily have been read as public relations by his contemporaries. In the wake of poems like *Absalom and Achitophel* and *The Medal*, nothing of the laureate's religious convictions could have been read outside the sphere of public debate. When we see Dryden's claims of privacy as a way of privileging the conscience as its own domain, of opening space for personal belief in the midst of an overwhelmingly public controversy over religious politics, it becomes easier to de-personalize the personal, to understand privacy as one of the rhetorics of religious confession, and an authenticating one at that. After all, no group had made more noise over privacy and personal inspiration than the dissenters – and their Whiggish allies – who now clamored against the crown; for the king's laureate to take their idioms in defense of the king's Indulgence meant that Dryden could colonize and hence disarm the factions that Charles II aimed to defeat in his efforts to impose comprehension and toleration. Recognizing the impersonality of this self-styled confession of faith allows us not only to situate *Religio Laici* fully within the rhetorical whirlwind of late seventeenth-century religious controversy but to situate the poet's spiritual life fully within the public sphere – that site of pamphleteering and sermonizing, of literary satire and parliamentary debate – to which it most surely belonged.

To turn from Dryden's confession of Anglican faith to the Roman Catholic identity he suddenly assumed in 1686 and published the next year in *The Hind and the Panther* comes as something of a surprise if we think of his poetry of religious confession as a record of personal identity rather than public policy. James II, a Roman Catholic convert, had assumed the throne in 1685, and prizes were rumored for Dryden, and pressure exerted, so that the laureate might see his way to a spiritual awakening, a conversion to the religion of kings, and a campaign on behalf of his new co-religionists. It is also true that members of Dryden's family were Roman Catholics so that this conversion might be understood not only as part of a very public program of religious politics but also in its private and domestic circumstance, and in that setting it might not seem the stunning contradiction that it appears in light of *Religio Laici* and of Dryden's sustained abuse of the Roman Catholic clergy. Yet the alarm of venality and apostasy was immediately sounded with the publication of *The Hind and the Panther*, and these accusations were hardly anachronistic. Men and women living in the early modern world understood, as much as we do – though not necessarily in quite the same terms – the meaning of integrity and authenticity. What Dryden's enemies were unwilling to allow was the fully public and political position of these poems, and of this rhetoric of spiritual autobiography. Dryden had chosen his stance in order to endow the public realm with the authority of private conviction and confession, and he was now to be held to, and pilloried by, the standards of his own rhetoric. *Absalom and Achitophel* and *The Medal* suggest that Dryden gave as good as he got, but we ought to acknowledge just how much and how often he got.

It is one thing to outline the conditions in which Restoration writers practiced their art, it is another to be drenched in their idioms of insult and injury, to be subject to the publicity in which they conducted their literary lives and the verbal, even physical, violence that often defined the life of letters in late seventeenth-century London. By the time the Glorious Revolution put an end to James II's Catholic kingship, Dryden must have tired of defensive strategies, and when we turn to the last phase of his career – his work after the Revolution of 1688 as principled adherent to the hapless cause of Stuart loyalism – we can sense not only the costs of sustaining a public career in an atmosphere of partisan rancor and literary vindictiveness, but perhaps too the relief that the poet must have felt as he accepted and then made a weary triumph out of the posture of political defeat. After the Revolution, Dryden was removed from pension and public office, forced back to the theatre and to translation as means of marketing his literary talents, and though complaint and lament are laced through his writing after 1688, they cast only a shadow over the literary riches of his last decade: plays and operas like *Don Sebastian* (1690), *Amphytrion* (1690), *King Arthur* (1691), and *Love Triumphant* (1694); the *Works of Virgil* (1697), a masterful translation and a poignant rendering of the costs of empire; and a last miscellany, *Fables* (1700), where Dryden seems to be utterly at his literary ease, choosing to translate just those poems of antiquity and modernity that most pleased him, and writing an essay of literary appreciation and self-display that better than any other text gives us a sense of how Dryden reflected back on what had become, by the late 1690s, a remarkable life of letters:

> 'Tis with a Poet, as with a Man who designs to build, and is very exact, as he supposes, in casting up the Cost beforehand: But, generally speaking, he is mistaken in his Account, and reckons short of the Expence he first intended: He alters his Mind as the Work proceeds, and will have this or that Convenience more, of which he had not thought when he began. So has it hapned to me; I have built a House, where I intended but a lodge: Yet with better success than a certain Nobleman, who beginning with a Dog-kennel, never lived to finish the Palace he had contriv'd. (*Works* VII: 24)

The image of poetry as improvisation and architecture is meant to apply to the creation of *Fables*, but equally it is an allegory for the life of writing over the forty years of Dryden's career, with all its expenses, alterations, and conveniences. Perhaps the poet tells us more than he might consciously allow of costs and compromises. And yet, superbly self-conscious as ever about the language of writing, Dryden would, I think, willingly acknowledge the constructedness and the improvisatory character of writing, the naïveté of an ambition that could not have reckoned all the expenses of a life of letters in the Restoration, and the deep satisfactions of having made a living structure of his work. But the allegory of literary art as architecture does not quite end on that elevated note. The ironies that Dryden indulges at his own expense at the beginning of the paragraph are turned sharply outwards at its close as Dryden contrasts the modesty, taste, and, by implication, the eternity of his own contrivance with the ambitions and devices of "a certain Nobleman, who beginning with a Dog-kennel, never lived to finish the Palace he had contriv'd."

The target is Dryden's old enemy, the Duke of Buckingham, who had mocked him in that witty contrivance, *The Rehearsal*. The juxtaposition of dog kennel and palace debases grandiosity, ridicules failed ambition, and suggests that the proper measure of Buckingham's talents might be taken not only by contrasting his finished work, the dog kennel at Cliveden (and I think Dryden would also have us apply that image to *The Rehearsal*), with the country estate of which Buckingham had dreamed, but as well with the home, and the eternity, that Dryden realized through the poetry that Buckingham had once aimed to debase. What makes Dryden's prose shine is the tremendous efficiency of its ironies, its ability to work simultaneously as personal memoir, literary history, and caustic satiric engagement. For his translation of Virgil, Dryden had developed a model of the way Virgil worked – simultaneously with an eye on eternity and on business at hand; Virgil wrote Augustus Caesar and the Roman empire into the eternity of verse, and yet he was not so busy with eternity as to forget that there were scores to settle in the present. Dryden wrote exactly in this manner; indeed it would have been difficult for him to conceive one part of his writing life without the other. He had little interest in mere lampoon; and yet no matter how distant and elevated the idioms and landscapes in which he allowed his imagination to work, Dryden invariably anchored his writing in the spaces and relations of late seventeenth-century London – site of court and capital, of patronage networks and political associations, of street theatre and riot as well as literary club and coffee house, and of a cornucopia of manuscript and print: handwritten squibs and miscellanies, printed broadsides and pamphlets, octavos and quartos, playbooks and folios. Dryden had entered that market in 1659 on the pages of a hastily printed, crowded quarto; he bid farewell on the beautiful folio pages of *Fables* with its elegant typeface and wide margins. Between lay a world of print and imagination, and all the complex financial, professional, and personal institutions and relations that made possible this incomparable literary career.

We began with questions about the experience of reading Dryden in the learned and ample uniformity of the modern collected edition. We cannot of course do without those editions; in estimating Dryden's debts to antiquity, his love for and constant use of Virgil, his admiration for Horace and Juvenal, his keen appropriation of Ovid – these editions and that perspective are indispensable. And who would willingly forgo the experience of reading individual poems, plays, or essays within the body of a "collected works," or abandon the full chronology of a writer's career with its story of development and dissolution? And yet when Dryden's texts are surrounded only by the aura of learning and fixity that such editions convey, it is difficult to credit the uncertainty and volatility in which these works were imagined, to conjure the atmosphere of contingency and improvisation that so marks Dryden's work, or to feel the energy with which Dryden conducted the complex, often partisan and interested, negotiations with past and with present. That Dryden's learning was considerable, there is no question, but I suspect that few of Dryden's contemporary readers would have experienced that learning as intimidation. He aimed at quick comprehension; he intended to caress patrons and annihilate enemies; he wrote into the busy marketplace of texts, and he was superbly equipped to participate in its counterpoint of challenge and exchange. While he often claimed to be above the fray – too elevated to bother answering envy and assault – such elevation was merely a convenience for striking obliquely, and with a high hand, at those who would challenge his motives or his preeminence. Dryden cultivated the idea of literature and literary eternity, especially in his last years; for him, his true peers were not Shadwell and Flecknoe or Blackmore and Collier, they were Shakespeare, Spenser, and Jonson, and Ovid, Horace, and Virgil. But Dryden was bound to the tumult of contemporary print, and he knew better than most how to work there. He was caught between transience and literary immortality, and his texts occupy a position both in the marketplace of print and in the pantheon of letters – pamphlets and books that were, first of all, merchandise, then polemic, and only then art and eternity. Fully to understand that position we need to cultivate an openness to all the ways in which literature functioned and continues to function in the social world – its traffic with ephemera, ambition, and argument – and in the realm of the aesthetic that Dryden thought of as transcendent, and to the intricate traffic between the two. This volume of essays aims to serve as a companion to the pleasures and challenges of Dryden's work, its theatrical and satirical energies, its location in the scenes and sites and sociability of Restoration London and in the marketplace of books and ideas, its conjuring of empire and embrace of the Roman analogy. Here too readers will discover the implication of Dryden's work in the elaborate system of aristocratic patronage, the perplexities of his political and religious identities and allegiances, and the last blossoming of Dryden's career in the 1690s as he became poet and translator of empire and exile, and of elevation and eternity.

2

STUART SHERMAN

Dryden and the theatrical imagination

Dryden's most enduring early work as dramatist is not a play, but an essay that reads like one. In *An Essay of Dramatic Poesy* (1667), four speakers take up in turn the questions of the drama that would preoccupy Dryden throughout his theatrical career. Of the four, Neander, endorsing modern over ancient, English over French, tragicomedy over modes more mannerly and less mixed, and rhyme over blank verse, gets the most space, the best lines, and the last word. But the *Essay* accords each contradictory position its own energy and heft. "It will not be easy," Samuel Johnson wrote in his "Life of Dryden," "to find in all the opulence of our language a treatise so artfully variegated with successive representations of opposite probabilities . . ."[1]

The successive representation of opposite probabilities is the playwright's stock in trade, and one of Dryden's chief accomplishments as dramatist was to devise new ways of crafting this commodity and of purveying it to audiences peculiarly situated to savor them. The *Essay* provides abundant foretaste of his technique. Though Neander appears to prevail, or at least preponderate, Dryden stages the entire conversation in such a way as to call the very notion of prevailing into question. He sets the dialogue at a historical moment two years before the *Essay* first appeared: "It was that memorable day, in the first Summer of the late War, when our Navy ingag'd the *Dutch*." The day was 3 June 1665, the engagement was the Battle of Lowestoft, and Dryden spends some sentences conjuring up a memory both auditory and communal, as "the noise of the Cannon from both Navies reach'd our Ears about the City" and "every one" listened attentively, until the noise's recession signaled English victory and Dutch retreat.[2] But by August 1667, when the *Essay* first appeared, the memory of this moment would be distinctly mixed. The seeming victory at Lowestoft had given way, over the ensuing two years, to the triple depredations of plague, fire, and, just last June, the retaliatory Dutch invasion of the Medway and destruction of the fleet's best ships. The dramatic moment of *An Essay of Dramatic Poesy* must have evoked in its initial audience an almost ineluctable double vision, of triumph and disgrace.[3] Doubleness inheres too in the textures of the *Essay*'s prose, as when Dryden, describing the all-important sound of the cannon, supplies two different similes: "like the noise of distant Thunder, or of Swallows in a Chimney . . ." (9). The "or" that links the two comparisons makes a quiet argument of its own: that representations, if they are to be precise and powerful, demand a layered attention from author and auditor, a careful reckoning and rendering of alterations, of the ways things change over distance, over time.

The doubled moment, the paired similes, the dialogic sequence of opposing probabilities – these elements of the *Essay* afford a small sampling of all the instruments of pivot that Dryden would devise for his dramas. Twice in the *Essay*, Neander expresses his pleasure in what he calls the "quick turns" of drama, construing them as both a criterion for good plays – the "quick turns and counterturns of Plot" (57) – and a defining national propensity: "the quick turns and graces of our *English* stage" (45). Both formulations respond at least in part to the variegated succession of opposite probabilities that had shaped English political experience throughout the seventeenth century. Dryden and his audience had survived such pressing moments of choice, had traversed such arduous political and cultural changes of mind over time, from monarchy to Commonwealth to Restoration to crisis to Revolution, that many or most, including the playwright himself, could recall however reluctantly moments when, out of conviction or self-interest or some barely assessable combination of the two, they occupied the opposite stance from the one they now assumed.

Both Dryden's preeminence as dramatist in his own time, and the marked occlusion of his plays from his otherwise abiding canon in the time since, have much to do with his masterly allegiance to the arts of the quick turn, and his near obsessive immersion in them. There were of course, as his detractors never tired of noting, the shifts in faith, stance, and condition that marked his whole career, from Puritan to Anglican to Catholic, from young Cromwellian to loyal laureate to injured and insistent Jacobite. "As I am a Man, I must be changeable," Dryden declares in his dedication to *Aureng-Zebe* – then promptly cites Montaigne, whom he often took as touchstone both for the inevitability of change and the value of attending closely to its operations and effects (*Works* XII: 157).[4]

As crafter of plays, prefaces, and poems, Dryden construed mutability as not merely necessity but prerogative; he made it the occasion of his art. Throughout his theatrical career, he would often, as he had in the *Essay*, write to the political moments that he and his audience presently inhabited: the inaugural phases of colonialism and empire (*The Indian Queen, The Indian Emperor, Amboyna*); the recurrent questionings of succession (*Secret Love, The Conquest of Granada, Marriage A-la-Mode, Aureng-Zebe, The Spanish Friar*); the aftermaths of the 1688 Revolution (*Don Sebastian, Amphitryon*). Recent historical and cultural studies of these contexts have rendered many of these plays deeply intelligible for the first time in centuries.[5] But the emphasis on topicality can sometimes obscure the deliberate densities and intensities of dramatic texture. Dryden insistently structures his dramas, as in the *Essay* he triggers the mixed memories of Lowestoft and Medway, so as to draw his audience almost helplessly, often perhaps subliminally, into a complex collation of opposing probabilities that even the conclusion will not wholly resolve. Within his plays – in the structure of the plots, in the pacing of the action, in the motions of verse or prose, and even in the shifts and volatilities of his prefaces – Dryden stages moments governed, like the *Essay*'s figures of the thunder and the swallows, by the authorial *or*. He makes it his business and his boast to ratchet up to their highest imaginable pitch the moments of choice and change: to effect an increase in their number, a new rapidity in their rate, and an intensifying of their language. What Dryden most conspicuously offered his audiences was a sequence of quick turns among opposite probabilities, wherein what was often most hypnotic was not the choice but the choosing.

The results of such an approach were both copious and variable. "I wish," Johnson writes with ominous reluctance near the beginning of the "Life," "that there were no necessity of following the progress of [Dryden's] theatrical fame, or tracing the meanders of his mind through the whole series of his dramatick performances . . ."[6] Here there is no such necessity, nor might so methodical an approach prove particularly companionable. Yet the labors of language and thought which produced the twenty-eight plays that now fill nine of the California Dryden's twenty volumes encompass, as Johnson promptly affirms, "too much of a poetical life to be omitted." In the pages that follow, I will look at just seven of the plays, arranged not quite chronologically but in clusters centered on some of the devices – compression, doubling, change – by which Dryden repeatedly accomplishes his densities and intensities. I will suggest throughout that Johnson, however reluctantly he assays his larger task, gets quickly and characteristically to its core. The meanders of the mind, heightened, pointed, and quickened by the demands of drama, are key to the poetical life the plays possess. They are what engaged Dryden most as playwright, and what meshed him most intimately with his first audience.

Compressions

In one of his earliest prefaces, Dryden commends that component of playcraft he calls "the compression of the Accidents," by which the author "crowds together" in the narrow "compass" of the play's few hours as many events and quick turns as possible; such density, he argues, "produces more variety, and consequently more pleasure to the Audience" (*Works* IX: 21). Dryden attained his early ascendancy in the Restoration theatre, particularly in the heroic drama of which he quickly became foremost practitioner, by making himself a master of compression. By his plots, in all their (sometimes stupefying) plenitude, he aimed, as Johnson remarked, to "glut the publick with dramatick wonders."[7] His ambitions toward that end underwrite his most compact and canvassed assertion about the new kind of drama he was endeavoring to create, "that an Heroick Play ought to be an imitation, in little of an Heroick Poem" – an epic compassed in an evening (*Works* XI: 10). By his relentless advocacy of the rhymed heroic couplet Dryden was serving the same end. Compression – the dense packing, the lucid, expressive arranging, of information, image, thought – is the couplet's core trick. In *An Essay of Dramatic Poesy*, Neander depicts rhymed repartee – the rapid-fire backtalk between contending characters – as a near delirium of compounded, compacted verbal effects: "[T]here is . . . the quick and poynant brevity of it . . . and this joyn'd with the cadency and sweetness of the Rhyme, leaves nothing in the soul of the hearer to desire . . . the care and labour [entailed in the making] of the Rhyme is carry'd from us, or at least drown'd in its own sweetness, as Bees are sometimes bury'd in their Honey" (*Works* XVII: 77). This is the language of ravishment, deployed to describe the experience of not only the audience but the author too. For Dryden, the models of epic and romance assure compression of plot and pace; the couplet makes compression a matter of the moment.

Dryden's most audacious experiment in heroic compression produced the paradoxical countereffect of expansion. *The Conquest of Granada* (1670, 1671) is so crammed with incident that it extends over two evenings and ten acts. Granada, like most of Dryden's heroic settings, is a site for symmetrical conflicts (a civil war between two Moorish factions; an ongoing attack by Spanish forces), geometrical passions (a heroine adored by two men, a villainess pursued by two others), rapid-fire reversals, and poetic pyrotechnics. In the arc of Dryden's early career, the play functioned both as winning hand for the author ("I have already swept the stakes," Dryden boasts in the preface [*Works* XI: 18]) and as lightning rod for the audience. No play since the Restoration had attracted so much attention or excited so much scorn, in pamphlets, in parodies, and even on the selfsame stage, where Buckingham's *Rehearsal* appeared to enthusiastic applause about a year after the *Conquest*'s premiere, brilliantly and successfully pillorying its pretensions.

What made the play a source of both triumph and travesty was the outsized character, the breathtaking self-assertion, of its hero Almanzor, who memorably declares his own uniqueness early on. He defies Granada's King Boabdelin, whom he has already aided and irritated, in a couplet that quickly became a catchphrase for audacity, both heroic and comic:

> Obey'd as Soveraign by thy Subjects be,
> But know, that I alone am King of me.
>
> (I. i. 205–6)

This compact self-anointing establishes two of the play's core terms. Over the ensuing nine acts, the plot will investigate, like so many play-plots at this historical moment, questions of kingship, authority, and succession, while the text will tease out the implications of that initially less striking term, *alone*. Until the play's last moments, Almanzor is not king but kingmaker. He knows nothing of his own origins or status, but possesses such might that whatever figure he supports – king, insurgent, invader – attains ascendancy for the moment. The plot tracks the quick turns of his allegiance; "he moves excentrique," notes another character, "like a wandring star" (v. i. 208). Though the play's early detractors found such shifts preposterous in a hero, Susan Staves has suggested that the protagonists of heroic romance, Almanzor chief among them, proffered the audience a kind of wish-fulfillment. "They always behave well and always preserve honor intact under kaleidoscopically shifting circumstances – and are thus quite unlike the vast majority of real royalists in the audience" – who could recall their own less comfortable, more compromised shifts, from Commonwealth back to kingship, over the preceding decades.[8]

Almanzor's actual conduct, though, may complicate this reckoning. Subject to none, and momentarily loyal to several in succession, he can hardly serve as an exemplary royalist. Whenever he deems himself insulted or injured by his current client, he shifts allegiance out of not principle but pride. In the play's dedication to James, Duke of York, Dryden eagerly if defensively confesses that his hero does *not* always behave well, cataloguing some of the qualities that comprise his "excentrique vertue . . . not wholly exempted from [human] frailties": "a roughness of Character, impatient of injuries," "a confidence of himself, almost approaching to an arrogance," and "above all, an inviolable faith in his affection" (*Works* XI: 6–7). That confidence in the truth and force of his own feelings renders Almanzor eccentric even by the extravagant standards of the heroic drama. In William Cartwright's play *The Royal Slave* (1636), the hero Cratander, choosing between rebellion and self-restraint, describes his predicament in a simile that, as Arthur C. Kirsch remarks, epitomizes the instances of heroic choice omnipresent in Cavalier and Restoration drama:

> Like to the doubtfull Needle 'twixt two Loadstones
> At once inclining unto both, and neither![9]

Such moments of articulate immobility constituted the high points in many a heroic play. Almanzor, though, never really lingers between the lodestones; he pauses just long enough to declare their powerlessness over him before taking the next quick turn. What may have appealed to "old royalists" in the audience was not the steadfastness with which Almanzor navigates dilemmas but the rapidity, the utter self-certainty, with which he dissolves them. A self-anointed "King," identified explicitly with James and implicitly with Charles, he makes it possible for the audience to reconcile a whole-hearted identification with royalty (who in the play would they rather be?) with the less comfortable memory of their own oscillations. He makes quick turns and erratic motions look majestic.

Throughout the play, though, Dryden implies that Almanzor's "inviolable faith in his own affection" may entail a near-paradoxical cost in isolation. When the hero decrees that "I alone am King of me," he is stipulating first for autonomy – I alone govern my actions – and second (as though in connivance with his creator Dryden) for uniqueness – I alone among the people of this play (and of others) can lay claim to this degree of freedom from law and convention. As the plot advances, though, the solitude latent in "I alone" becomes less splendid, more fraught. Almanzor's isolation comes to seem to him at times an index of debility, as when, late in the play's eighth act, the ghost of his mother, in a tantalizingly brief visitation, hints at the secret of his origins but does not explain it, despite his entreaties that she stay. Alone on stage for the first time in the play, Almanzor extrapolates his ignorance into a universal isolation and helplessness:

> Thus, like a Captive in an Isle confin'd,
> Man walks at large, a Pris'ner of the Mind:
> (*Conquest* 2 IV. iii. 147–8)

There may be echoes here of Hamlet ("Denmark's a prison") and of Aeneas, endeavoring in vain and in tears to embrace his elusive goddess-mother before lamenting his aloneness. Almanzor's sense of debility deepens in his next (and last) soliloquy where, with echoes of Othello, he succumbs for a moment to the conviction that his beloved has bedded another man:

> She was as faithless as her Sex could be:
> And now I am alone, she's so to me.
>
> (v. i. 3–4)

Here, at the very start of the final act, *alone* cues desolation; a little later, near play's end, the same word will almost paradoxically herald reconnection and revelation. After the final battle, in which the Spanish forces retake Granada, their leader the Duke of Arcos tells how he confronted Almanzor "alone" in single combat (v. iii. 183), only to recognize him, by the bracelet on his arm, as his own long-lost son. But the dramatic resolution that follows recognition leaves Almanzor in a curiously suspended predicament. Though betrothed to his beloved Almahide, whose monarch-husband has been killed in the battle, he must wait a year to wed her while she mourns her loss; at play's end she gives only the most muted assent to her betrothal. Almanzor is King of Granada, but tributary too to Spain, though also heir to Arcos. There are echoes here of the royal brother James, the play's dedicatee: heir apparent, duke not king, whose allegiances (Protestant? Catholic? English? French?) were soon to undergo their first vexed public interrogation. There is an alertness also, in this final moment and throughout the play which has led to it, to the vulnerability inherent in solitary magnificence.

Perhaps also to its comedy, its bafflements. Early in the play, as respite from warfare, the court listens to the performance of a love song that seems at first one of the most preposterous incongruities in all drama. The song's narrator describes how, frustrated in waking life by his mistress's resistance, he slept and dreamed in detail of her surrender and of his, then

> waked, and straight I knew
> I lov'd so well it made my dream prove true:
> Fancy, the kinder Mistress of the two,
> Fancy had done what *Phillis* wou'd not do!
>
> (*Conquest* 1 III. i. 228–31)

And so he concludes by exulting over his mistress in the waking world:

> Ah, Cruel Nymph, cease your disdain,
> While I can dream you scorn in vain;
> Asleep or waking you must ease my pain.
>
> (232–4)

What this onanistic love song purports to proclaim is quite audacious: absolute erotic supremacy. What it actually performs is less grand: somnolent masturbation. What is registered in the gap between the two is the possibility of self-delusion. In its willful abrogation of power, the song's argument from a wet dream echoes Almanzor's self-anointing "King of me," uttered less than a half hour earlier, and anticipates the speech with which he will close the play, solacing himself for Almahide's forthcoming yearlong absence by promising that "dreams of love shall drive my nights away" (*Conquest* 2 v. iii. 344). Such inviolable faith in one's own affection may conceivably, so the song's comedy suggests, lead a lover astray. The king of me may not, after all, turn out to be king of much else – including even his absent or reluctant mistress.

Tragicomedy was always one of Dryden's favorite modes of combination and compression, but the proportion of the comic in the more straight-forward heroic plays has been variously calculated, and may be ultimately incalculable. The gap between the ideal and the real which Derek Hughes persuasively locates at the core of Dryden's heroic plays provides enormous room for variance in the response of individual readers and spectators.[10] The same Theatre Royal audience that had made the double-length *Conquest* a major hit was laughing long and loud, less than a year later, to see its features resurface in Buckingham's brilliant parody: a preening playwright who asserts complacently that "the variety of all the several accidents . . . are, you know, the things in Nature that make up the grand refinement of a Play";[11] a brazen braggart-hero named Drawcansir; and the town-sized monarchy of Brentford in which two kings amicably and mysteriously occupy the same throne. By that last masterstroke, Buckingham was partly parodying a play by Henry Howard, but also making fun of a particular form of compression already conspicuous in Dryden's drama: his fascination with elaborate symmetries of situation, with packing two characters into a space where other playwrights might deem that one would do.

Doublings

To admirers of Shakespeare's *Tempest*, Dryden's and Davenant's 1669 revision will look a little overpopulated. "The effect produced by the conjunction of these two powerful minds," Johnson remarks drily, "was that to Shakespeare's monster Caliban is added a sister-monster Sicorax; and a woman, who, in the original play, had never seen a man, is in this brought acquainted with a man that had never seen a woman."[12] For Dryden, though, the pleasures of such doubling seem to have been the project's chief attraction. In the play's preface he recalls that when Davenant approached him with the suggestion that there "might be added to the Design of *Shakespear*" the "excellent contrivance" of "a Man who had never seen a Woman . . . I confess that from the very first moment it so pleas'd me, that I never writ any thing with more delight" (*Works* x: 4). Nor did the doubling stop there. Miranda, the only child of Shakespeare's Prospero, acquires a sister here; Shakespeare's two inebriates Stephano and Trinculo team up with a second clownish pair; and even Ariel, solitary sprite, is paired off with his true love Milcha, who makes her first appearance in the play's last lines.

Dryden's delight in the dramatic payoffs of such doubling remains conspicuous throughout his theatrical career. It suffuses the design not only of the collaborative *Tempest*, but also of his subtlest early comedy, *Marriage A-la-Mode* (1671), and of his greatest late one, *Amphitryon* (1690), where he does with earlier plays by Molière and Plautus what he and Davenant had long ago done with Shakespeare's *Tempest*: increases the number of the couples. The comic payoff of such multiplicity is clear and familiar enough. The plenitude of potential pairings intensifies the intricacy of search and surmise, plotted by the playwright and tracked by the audience, whereby an overlapping assortment of romantic triangles gradually re-sort themselves into grids and rectangles half-predictable from the start: couples sturdily paired off in parallel, en route to marriage banns and bed. Increasingly, though, Dryden calls the sturdiness into question. In his love comedies the multiplicities and geometries, which can seem schematic at first glance, end up imaging the problematic plenitude of the real world, the near-infinite complexity of desire and choice, and the consequent uncertainties that can suffuse the choices finally made, the seeming stabilities of the plot's final moments. And since both *Marriage* and *Amphitryon* – like so many of Dryden's plays, and of the period's – stage a restoration, the recovery of a throne from a usurper by the rightful possessor, Dryden makes the problem of multiplicity also a question of power: how does abundance impinge on control?

In *Marriage A-la-Mode* the doublings are less profuse than in *The Tempest*, but the interactions are more complex. The marriage-plot to which the title alludes entails two couples: Doralice and Rhodophil, a wife and husband married two years, and bored (as they repeatedly avow) near death; Palamede, an unmarried courtier, just returned from long travels and betrothed by his father to Melantha, a woman he has not yet met. The two men are old friends but the plot sets them working, though at first they don't realize it, at cross purposes. In the play's first act, the unmarried Palamede tries to initiate an intrigue with Doralice, unaware that she's his friend's wife; the bored husband Rhodophil has commenced pursuit of his friend's as yet unseen fiancée. From the start, then, the copular rectangle underwritten by conventional rectitude – marriage, betrothal – is schematically criss-crossed by adulterous desire, the man in each couple pursuing the woman in the other. And why not, as Dryden asks in the opening lines of the song that all but commences the play:

> Why should a foolish Marriage Vow
> Which long ago was made,
> Oblige us to each other now
> When Passion is decay'd?
>
> (I. i. 3–6)

The answer, for much of the play and for many of the characters, would seem to be that the marriage vow can't, and perhaps shouldn't, impose such obligation. For them, desire's default mode consists in variety and multiplicity. Rhodophil grimly assures his wife that in the labors of their marriage bed, "I have fanci'd thee all the fine women in the Town, to help me out. But now there's none left for me to think on, my imagination is quite jaded" (III. i. 79–81). Melantha repeatedly regrets that she must ultimately choose between her "fine" but married "Gentleman" and her betrothed "gallant *homme*" (II. i. 29); and Palamede conjectures that, were the rectangle to resolve itself into a *ménage à quatre*, the women would savor the new doubling more adroitly than the men: "If their necessities and ours were known, / They have more need of two, then we of one" (III. ii. 147–8). Dryden conjures an amorous round robin, where lover displaces lover – in imagination if not reality – with almost orgiastic ease. He does so from the outset, by the curious way he stages the opening song. As the curtain rises, Doralice enters with her attendant just long enough to request the song, whereupon both of them "*go in*" to an arbor where, at least partly concealed from view, the servant plays and the lady sings. The audience, then, hears the song while gazing on an all but empty stage, as though to reinforce the point that the wayward passions implicitly affirmed by the song's rhetorical question attach themselves to no person in particular; they are the outbreak of insistent, arbitrary desire. At song's end, Palamede promptly enters, Doralice emerges from the arbor, and the play's intrigues commence.

Doralice, who sings the song and poses the question, turns out to be the most knowing, nuanced explorer of its implications. Throughout the plot's many intricacies – an early convergence where all four begin to recognize their reciprocal deceptions; an ill-timed double tryst by night in a grotto, where mutual suspicions keep ardor in check just short of consummation; a subsequent convocation of the four at a tavern, wherein the two women have disguised themselves as boys in order to balk and tease their wooers – Doralice consistently displays the deepest perception and the fullest control. In the transvestite scene, for example, she sees through Melantha's boy-disguise, but no one sees through hers. By such small touches, Dryden endows her with some portion of the double-perspective that myth attributes to Teiresias – the understanding that arises from having viewed love from the vantage of both genders. She limits the scope of her liaison from the first, and later, disguised as a boy, taunts her wooer by describing, precisely but indetectably, what she is doing at the moment: "If I were [your mistress], I would disguise [myself] on purpose to try your wit; and come to my servant like a Riddle, Read me, and take me" (IV. iii. 51–3). She remains alert, above all, to an ineluctability of the self-as-riddle, to the limits on the knowing, the reading, and the taking. Near play's end, when she calls the bluff on all its amorous intrigues, seeing clearly that they cannot come to consummation, that conventional rectitude will instead reassert the rectangle, she boldly tells her husband that he must take her fidelity on faith: "Consider, if I have play'd false, you can never find it by any experiment you can make upon me" (V. i. 338–9). And Dryden accords her, with her less witty wooer Palamede, a gorgeous valedictory dialogue in which they guess at the long-term effects of their unconsummated ardor. "'Tis better as 'tis," Doralice suggests. "We have drawn off already as much of our Love as would run clear; after possessing, the rest is but jealousies, and disquiets, and quarrelling, and piecing [i.e., making up]" (V. i. 260–2). Palamede eventually concurs; as a result of present restraint, "I shall have a warmth for you, and an eagerness, every time I see you; and if I chance to out-live *Melantha* – " (V. i. 275–6). The exchange between the two is in many ways the most intimate of the play; Rhodophil, coming upon them, is convinced – momentarily, mistakenly, but understandably – that he has at last "confirm'd" his betrayal by both wife and friend (V. i. 290). The pair's affectionate jokes are tinged with melancholy, even with intimations of mortality. Desire will persist after action is renounced. Death proffers a tenuous hope ("if I chance to out-live *Melantha*"), but also a deadline past which desire is impracticable.

The play's upper plot turns on questions not of adultery but of identity. It too involves two pairs, whose ultimate combination is at first far less predictable: Amalthea and Argaleon, an aristocratic sister and brother reared at court; and Palmyra and Leonidas, a young woman and man raised in the country as upright rustics, who love each other and who at play's end will turn out to be the daughter of the present usurper, and the son of the late, deposed, and rightful king. En route to that resolution, though, the covert prince and princess are amorously pursued by the courtly sister and brother, and Amalthea's love for Leonidas is the play's most poignant, volatile crux. He asks Amalthea to help him gain access to his true love; oblivious to her feelings for him, he is nonetheless alert to the agitation with which she conceals them:

These often failings, sighs, and interruptions,
Make me imagine you have grief like mine:
Have you ne'er lov'd?
Amal.   I? never.   (IV. i. 62–4)

Dryden recapitulates this near-recognition in the play's closing lines, when Amalthea, seeing her beloved united with his own, assures him,

I have all I hope,
And all I now must wish; I see you happy.
Those hours I have to live, which Heav'n in pity
Will make but few, I vow to spend with Vestals:
(V. i. 522–5)

In one of the play's quietest, richest pieces of structural counterpoint, Dryden has from the first linked the emotional life of Amalthea with that of Doralice, who announces in the opening line that the song she is about to sing is one that "*Amalthea* bad me learn" (I. i. 2). By play's end, this little link pays off in complicated ways. If the opening song partly voices Amalthea's own interests, then her steadfast, futile love throughout the play must somehow occupy the same constellation of feeling as the wayward, fleeting passions the song affirms; in different ways, these two modes of love are elusive, even fantastical. For Amalthea, as not for Doralice, there will be no righting of the amorous triangle; multiplicity resolves not to monogamy but to isolation. For her, love's stage will be abidingly empty, as it was only momentarily and provisionally when Doralice sang at the start of the play. And for her, the intimations of imminent mortality ("Those hours I have to live") are not a matter of teasing and communion, as they were for Doralice and her paramour, but of determination and despair. By these near-subliminal contrasts, Dryden cultivates in his audience an intense sympathy for Amalthea at play's end, and a consequent alienation from the new-found king Leonidas, whose response to her, in an aside at the start of the play's closing speech, seems hardly adequate:

Too well I understand her secret grief,
But dare not seem to know it. – [*To* Palmyra] Come my fairest,
Beyond my Crown, I have one joy in store;
To give that Crown to her whom I adore.   (V. i. 529–32)

This time, recognition is not aborted but repressed, oblivion not accidentally sustained, but deliberately and deceptively reinstated. The crown the new king celebrates is thereby partly compromised. He who has dared much – defiance of a usurper, leadership of a rebellion – dares not do this: "seem to know" the feelings that would complicate the play's rectangular resolutions by doubling his affinities. With "Come my fairest," he closes the doubling down. In *Marriage A-la-Mode* the agitations of amorous multiplicity make for dissonance with the complacencies of recovered power.

In *Amphitryon*, nineteen years later, Dryden turned much of *Marriage* inside-out. Here the wife Alcmena, whose husband is away at war, laments in her first lines the burden of her marriage, as does Doralice in the earlier play – but from precisely the opposite vantage, of ardor, not ennui.

> Why was I marri'd to the Man I love!
> For, had he been indifferent to my choice,
> Or had been hated, absence had been pleasure:
> But now I fear for my *Amphitryon*'s life:
>
> (I. ii. 1–4)

The problem this time is not waywardness but steadfastness, a monogamous longing so intense as to be momentarily wished away. The plot, ostensibly comic, will thwart her longing by fulfilling it; tonight Jupiter will arrive disguised as her husband, and thereby inveigle this faithful wife into passionate, unknowing adultery.

Like *Marriage A-la-Mode*, this later play is dubbed a comedy on its title page but gestures towards the tragic too, the more emphatically because here adultery is not just contemplated but consummated. The play's full title, *Amphitryon; or the Two Socias*, sketches the vectors of the affective double-pull. In a subplot appropriated from Plautus and Molière, Dryden shows the servant Socia divinely doubled too, and in his predicament, in his baffled colloquies with the "other" Socia – actually Mercury in disguise – consists most of the play's hilarity. But in the plight of Amphitryon, and especially of Alcmena, Dryden explores the human solitudes that the divine doublings lay bare. Once Jupiter has revealed his trick, Alcmena reckons its cost as a combination of abiding uncertainty and terrible conviction:

> I know not what to hope, nor what to fear.
> A simple Errour, is a real Crime;
> And unconsenting Innocence is lost.
>
> (v. i. 390–2)

Moments later, the observant Mercury utters, as an aside, a line that amounts to a poignant stage direction: "*Amphitryon* and *Alcmena*, both stand mute, and know not how to take it" (v. i. 409–10). The penalty of this not knowing is partly isolation: the silence, which will persist through the end of the play, of loving spouses too stunned to speak, who may now wish, as Alcmena voiced it in her first lines, for an anodyne indifference they cannot master. Socia's earlier pun, when he describes himself as "unsociated" because his clone has stolen his identity (III. i. 232), speaks in a way for all the alienations that permeate the play. The comedy is sustained partly through the sense that these goings-on are mere myth and magic, transpiring long ago and far away. But Dryden handles his doublings here in such a way as to collapse distance, and make the play's preposterous doings at times uncomfortably proximate to ordinary life. For Jupiter's dupes and victims, the divine doublings play out as manifestations of familiar human inconsistency, as capricious changes of mood, manner, and commitment. Dryden contrives to touch on such shifts at many moments and in many registers. They underwrite the play's Jacobite satire, for example, in the running parallel between Jupiter and William III, usurpers wreaking cruel domestic havoc, and in the servant Phaedra's denunciation of her mercenary wooer the local magistrate: "Thou Weather-cock of Government: that when the Wind blows for the Subject, point'st to Priviledge; and when it changes for the Soveraign, veers to Prerogative" (V. i. 13–16). Intimacies veer too. When Jupiter urges Alcmena, partly out of prudence and partly out of pride, to pretend that he is not her "yawning Husband" but her ardent lover, he is savoring the secret knowledge that these two personages actually occupy, at the moment, two separate persons (II. ii. 94); but the audience knows that they can also alternate in one. And when Alcmena, confronted by the two incarnations of her husband and urged to choose between them, declares confidently that "my Heart will guide my Eyes / To point, and tremble to its proper choice" (V. i. 257–8), she nonetheless chooses wrong, because the real Amphitryon's real anger, never witnessed by her before, convinces her that he must be the counterfeit. As god and mortal occupy the stage by turns until the final, cruelly clarifying confrontation, Dryden ensures that the extraordinary alternation of the plot will mirror the ordinary alterations of the world, in which neither heart nor eye prove adequate to assess human volatilities, or to forestall the possibilities, in the words of Alcmena's last mournful speech, of "simple Errour," "real Crime," and irrecoverable loss. In *Marriage A-la-Mode*, Dryden's doublings indexed insatiable human appetites. In *Amphitryon* they point instead, and more poignantly, to ineluctable mutabilities.

Change

In the prologue to *Aureng-Zebe* Dryden depicts himself as "betwixt two Ages cast" (*Works* XI: 159), and in the play's dedication he limns the changes imminent in his own art: he is disenchanted with comedy and weary of rhyme, and it is here too that, invoking Montaigne, he declares that "as I am a Man, I must be changeable." The play itself, as Derek Hughes has argued well, offers a running critique of hubristic fixity: those characters who deny their own "weakness and volatility," dwelling instead in dreams of "heroic magnificence, transcendence of time," and imperviousness to change, all come to wretched ends.[13] The two protagonist-survivors, Aureng-Zebe and Indamora, distinguish themselves partly by something like capaciousness. In the tragedy's last quick turns, they are both forced to absorb a sudden shock: that Indamora, though professedly in love with Aureng-Zebe, has nonetheless offered comfort and affection to his villainous rival at the moment of his dying. By play's close, though, she and Aureng-Zebe have both accepted what Leonidas, at the end of *Marriage A-la-Mode*, "dare[d] not seem to know": the plot-confounding complexity, multiplicity, and mutability of human attachments. For Dryden, as for his much-invoked Montaigne, the inconstancy of human actions has in it the appearance of a fault, but the force of an inevitability, and often, if sufficiently and properly attended to, the value of a virtue: rightly studied, richly worded, it can yield truth, complexity, audacity, surprise, pleasure, and discovery. Among Dryden's dramatizations of such argument, *Aureng-Zebe* does mark a cusp. His last rhymed heroic play, it intimates in its paratexts (prologue, dedication) innovations that will shape the tragic masterpieces of his later phase, *All for Love* (1678) and *Don Sebastian* (1690), as well as that complex comedy *Amphitryon*: a shift both in the kinds of change that Dryden tracks, and in the means by which he tracks them.

All for Love is *sui generis*. Dryden drops many of the features that had most conspicuously marked his drama heretofore: heroic couplets, epic compressions, doubled plots, amorous geometries, tragicomic minglings, and quick turns. For Neander in *Essay of Dramatick Poesy*, as for Johnson a century later, Shakespeare's *Antony and Cleopatra* served as the strikingly successful poster-play for anti-neoclassical sprawl; in defiance of the unities of time and place, it spans many years, and much of the Mediterranean. Dryden, eager in *All for Love* to imitate the "Stile" of "the Divine *Shakespeare*" (*Works* XIII: 18), is interested also in altering his structure. The play unfolds in a single place, Alexandria, and on a single day that starts just after Antony and Cleopatra's defeat at Actium and ends in their double suicide. The result of these diminutions is not compression but a new spaciousness. With blank verse replacing rhyme, the repartee of intimacy or combat that Dryden always prized acquires a new music, of verse lines split and shared by the two speakers as if in ongoing duet, as in this early passage where the Roman Ventidius undertakes to convince Antony to abandon Cleopatra and take up arms again against Caesar:

> *Ven.* Are you Antony?
> I'm liker what I was, than you to him
> I left you last.
> *Ant.*   I'm angry.
> *Vent.*   So am I.
> *Ant.* I would be private: leave me.
> *Ven.*   Sir, I love you,
> And therefore will not leave you.   (I. i. 246–50)

Ventidius interrogates change ("Are you *Antony*?") in hopes of effecting change. By the mingling of closeness and contest, registered in the cut and thrust mix of replication ("So am I") and revision ("leave me"/ "love you"), which Dryden had doubtless absorbed from his recent careful reading of Euripides, Ventidius achieves his goal at the end of the first act, when Antony announces that he will leave Cleopatra. By the end of the second, though, Cleopatra, speaking to Antony in the same stichomythic music, will have persuaded him to stay.

These shifts, and the few that follow, are not quick turns but slow. As Judith Milhous and Robert D. Hume have beautifully argued, the play is not so much about choice – since after Actium there are really no choices left – as about self-recognition.[14] Antony oscillates slowly between the claims of Rome and Egypt, the image of himself as on the one hand dutiful soldier, husband, father, and on the other, passionate lover, only to discover, upon receiving the false news of Cleopatra's death, what the play's full title has affirmed from the first: that he has long been all for love, and by that reckoning can count the world well lost. The exquisite love-elegy he speaks to Cleopatra on the verge of death serves also as an epitome of the play's focused, passionate design:

> Think we have had a clear and glorious day;
> And Heav'n did kindly to delay the storm
> Just till our close of ev'ning. Ten years love,
> And not a moment lost, but all improv'd
> To th' utmost joys: What Ages have we lived!
>   (V. i. 389–93)

Ten years as one day: the retroactive conflation of time all but erases oscillation, as though in seeming to have shifted from one position to another – lover to husband, soldier to sybarite – Antony was always, fundamentally the same, possessed of the passion that suffuses this moment and by expansion the whole decade. The last change now is that he knows it.

Change works more speedily in *Don Sebastian*, produced in 1690 after Dryden's long hiatus from the playhouse. Here the playwright resumed some of his old familiar plenitudes, "crowding" the piece, as he confesses in his preface, with so many "Characters and Incidents" that it was as though, "through long disuse of writing," he had "forgot the usual compass of a Play." The first-night audience found it "insupportably too long," and only the removal of some 1,200 lines, "judiciously lopt" by Thomas Betterton, ensured the impressive success of subsequent performances (*Works* xv: 65, 66). Dryden chose, though, to print the play in all its original profusion, so that readers could savor its "Descriptions, Images, Similitudes, and Moral Sentences" (*Works* xv: 66), as well as all the narrative intricacies that, even at the playhouse, Betterton's judicious lopping had left intact: the tragic and comic parallel plots, the densely convergent triangles of passion and power, and perhaps the most controversial quick turn in Dryden's theatrical career – the sudden reconciliation of the violently alienated former friends Dorax and Sebastian. Walter Scott would later deem this scene the playwright's lifelong masterstroke, surpassing even Shakespeare: "had it been the only one ever Dryden wrote, [it] would have been sufficient to ensure his immortality."[15] Some members of the original audience, though, regarded the abrupt shift of feeling more skeptically, as Dryden makes huffily clear in his preface, where he derides that "ignorant sort of Creatures" who

> maintain that the Character of *Dorax*, is not only unnatural, but inconsistent with it self; let them read the Play and think again, and if yet they are not satisfied, cast their eyes on that Chapter of the Wise *Montaigne*, which is intituled *de l'Inconstance des actiones humaines*. (*Works* xv: 70)

Dryden here invokes in defense of Dorax's quick turns the same scripture he had often cited in favor of his own. "If I speak variously of my self," Montaigne had written in the essay Dryden urges upon his detractors, "it is, because I consider my self variously. All contrarieties are there to be found, in one corner or another, or after one manner or another."[16] Here, as so often in both writers, inconsistency becomes not merely credible but inevitable, productive of both truth and copiousness ("*all* contrarieties") – more perhaps, than can be comfortably contained in "the compass of a Play." Yet throughout this preface Dryden argues more proudly, pointedly, even aggressively for the fundamental "uniformity of design" in the play that follows – a unity that derives in part from the patterning of images and similitudes he brings to bear on the delineation of rapid human change.

The scene which Scott celebrated and detractors decried is notable primarily for what does not happen. Dorax, goaded by years of resentment and dreams of revenge, challenges Sebastian to a duel but never fights it. Instead the two men talk their way, alternately combative and hesitant, furious and forgiving, toward reconciliation. One of the most striking things about the scene is the change it registers in Dryden's handling of the moment of heroic choice. Dorax has just rescued his former friend from death at the hands of other enemies, solely in order to exact his own long-contemplated vengeance for an injury suffered long ago, when as Sebastian's closest aide and most devoted friend, he saw himself displaced in both capacities by a new and "hated Rivall" (IV. iii. 556):

> By me thy greatness grew; thy years grew with it,
> But thy Ingratitude outgrew 'em both.
>
> (IV. iii. 463–4)

Sebastian argues, though, that to fight the accuser who has just rescued him would be to confirm the accusation:

> To fight thee, after this, what were it else,
> Than owning that Ingratitude thou urgest?
> That Isthmus stands betwixt two rushing Seas;
> Which, mounting, view each other from afar;
> And strive in vain to meet.   (IV. iii. 531–5)

The image is complex, and Dryden will do much with it both here and in the play's last moments. It differs strikingly from Cartwright's lodestone-metaphor cited earlier, in which the protagonist is the needle between two magnets, and the play's next change will depend on his next move, in the rapid-fire mode that Dryden developed and Buckingham mocked. Sebastian's image of the "Isthmus" turns things inside out. Here, the human agents stand on either side. What drives them, like the "rushing Seas," is not the necessity of choice but the desire to converge. For the moment, Sebastian and Dorax both construe that convergence as combat, but the aquatic imagery and the closing verb "to meet" prove expressively ambiguous, mingling the antagonistic with the amorous. "I'le cut that Isthmus," Dorax retorts, intent on making convergence imminent (IV. iii. 536). And so he will, but not in the way he here imagines. Over the ensuing dialogue he and Sebastian "meet" not in a swordfight but in a flood of reciprocal revelation and forgiveness, in which the antagonists air the whole history of their alienation, each repenting quick misjudgments and long resentments. The "rushing Seas" don't clash; they merge.

In the play's closing moments Dryden brings back the image of the isthmus, no longer as metaphor but as stage picture. The Portuguese king Sebastian and the African queen Almeyda, the play's central lovers, who have consummated their marriage only the night before, now stand at the verge of exit on opposite sides of the stage, having accepted that they must part forever. Dorax moves to join the comic couple Antonio and Morayma, as the final stage direction carefully specifies, in "*the Middle of the Stage*." There he speaks the closing lines, in which, Dryden insists in the preface (*Works* xv: 71), the play's "*general Moral*" is explicitly ensconced:

> . . . let *Sebastian* and *Almeyda*'s Fate,
> This dreadful Sentence to the World relate,
> That unrepented Crimes of Parents dead,
> Are justly punish'd on their Childrens head.
>
> (v. i. 724–7)

The parents' crime is adultery, the children's punishment is incest. Almeyda and Sebastian have just learned that she is the child of an adulterous liaison between her mother and his father. The lovers are also siblings, and so must part. Dryden's plotting of the incest, as Earl Miner argues, is unique (*Works* xv: 395); it breaks with dramatic precedents ancient and modern. In other tragedies of brother–sister incest, the siblings know their true relation before they consummate; only in *Don Sebastian* is the sequence reversed. The innovation allows Dryden plenty of time to develop between Sebastian and Almeyda the mode of amorous fusion, intense and thwarted, that interested him throughout his later phase, from *All for Love* to *Amphitryon*. Though he apprises his audience of the incest early on by signs (prophecies, misgivings) that the lovers can't yet read, he shows the couple savoring fully their "Sympathy of Souls," and hurtling headlong toward what seems a happy ending, before they abruptly understand, in a quick final turn played out as expressive duet, their sympathy's "Sinfull" source (v. i. 586):

> *Seb.* Nay then there's Incest in our very Souls,
>   For we were form'd too like.
> *Alm.*   Too like indeed,
>   And yet not for each other.   (v. i. 589–91)

The exchange, with its intimate echoic sharing and splitting of the middle line, enacts the deep unity of the play's design and the harsh logic of its plot, expressing a fusion so complete as to compass the necessity of its own sundering.

At play's end then, when Dryden recapitulates the image of the isthmus, he runs it in reverse. Poised at opposite exits, the lovers re-enact Sebastian's earlier simile as ardor rather than enmity. *They* are the "two rushing Seas" that "strive in vain to meet"; Dorax, who has gently helped them absorb the shock of revelation and the necessity of separation, is here the isthmus that keeps them sundered. Throughout the play, Dryden has assimilated Dorax almost entirely into the system of excessive "likeness" that governs the incest theme. Like Sebastian, like Almeyda, Dorax swaggers through the scenes repeatedly declaring his autonomy, his defiance of the authorities (the Muslim emperor, priest, conspirators) who would exploit him. It is as though the play were populated by three Almanzors, each of whom, out of reciprocal, ineluctable sympathy of soul with the other two, proves ultimately incapable of the original's absolutist, isolationist insistence on the primacy of "I alone." The last stage moment isolates all three, but completes also their densely convergent trajectories, the "uniformity of design" that Dryden boasts of in his preface. The image of the isthmus, with its volatile conflation of ardor and antagonism, union and division, has defined the play's two pivotal relationships, but has played out differently in each: as a move from enmity to amity between Dorax and Don Sebastian; from passion to prohibition between Sebastian and Almeyda. By positioning Dorax himself as isthmus at the end, Dryden compresses into the play's closing moment all the dynamics that make *Don Sebastian* perhaps the most dazzling of his dramas: a "crowding" of "Characters and Incidents" so plentiful as to overrun "the usual compass of a Play," but so adroitly managed as to make the crucial reversals reverse each other, quick turns that measure out abiding, tender, and tragic attachments.

"'Tis with a poet," Dryden wrote in the endlessly re-quotable opening of his preface to the *Fables*, "as with a Man who designs to build, and is very exact, as he supposes, in casting up the Cost beforehand: But, generally speaking, he is mistaken in his Account, and reckons short of the Expence he first intended: He alters his Mind as the Work proceeds, and will have this or that Convenience more, of which he had not thought when he began" (*Works* VII: 24). What held true of the poet in this final volume had held true too of the playwright over the course of his career. As his work proceeded on plays and prefaces, Dryden ended up altering his mind – often more than once – on nearly every one of the dramatic-poetical convictions he voiced through Neander in his early *Essay*. The only principle to which he remained comparatively steadfast was the importance of alteration itself. In the dedication of his last full-length play, *Love Triumphant* (1694), he stipulates, like Neander long ago, that the English "love variety" in their drama "more than any other Nation" – though he allows that if they were to change their taste, he "cou'd be content to change my Method" in order to match it (*Works* XVI: 171).

In his last work of all, the tiny, lapidary *Secular Masque* (1700) wedged into the Fletcher/Vanbrugh comedy *The Pilgrim* a few weeks before his death, Dryden offers a final staging of vicissitude, as well as a last look back over the tumults of his own career. Janus enters first, heralding the new century and initiating a survey of the old. It will be a short sequence of speech and song, witnessed also by weary Chronos and laughing Momus, in which three divinities, Diana, Mars, and Venus, embody in turn the successive, variegated preoccupations of the period: the innocent and "unthinking" pursuits (hunting, dancing, drinking, laughing) of "Merry" England under Elizabeth and James I (XVI, 271, lines 39–40); the violence of the civil wars; the amorous intrigues of the Restoration court. In this final rite, as over the whole arc of Dryden's posthumous reputation, the satiric voice comes to dominate, with Momus commenting acerbically at every turn. Momus, though, is surely not the sole self-portrait embedded in this gleaming miniature. Steven N. Zwicker has argued well for Chronos, as an image of Dryden's fascination, at life's end, with the dissolution of things.[17] Janus too may merit nomination. With twinned faces turned in opposite directions, perpetually cast betwixt two ages as though by virtue of his very constitution, he is the incarnation of the doubled moment. In the *Masque*, as perhaps in the career, he is the sole figure to occupy the stage from first to last.

NOTES

1. Samuel Johnson, *Lives of the Poets*, ed. G. B. Hill, 3 vols. (Oxford, 1905), vol. I, p. 412.
2. *Works* XVII: 8.
3. For a reading of the *Essay*'s political context see M. Thale, "The Framework of Dryden's *An Essay of Dramatick Poesie*," *Papers in Language and Literature*, 12, 2 (1976), 363–9.
4. On Montaigne as touchstone, see James A. Winn, *John Dryden and His World* (New Haven, 1987), pp. 13, 439.
5. On Dryden's drama and colonialism, see James Thompson, "Dryden's *Conquest of Granada* and the Dutch Wars," *The Eighteenth Century: Theory and Interpretation* 31, 3 (1990), 211–26; Robert Markley, "Violence and Profits on the Restoration Stage: Trade, Nationalism, and Insecurity in Dryden's *Amboyna*," *Eighteenth-Century Life* 22, 1 (February 1998), 2–17; Bridget Orr, *Empire on the English Stage 1660–1714* (Cambridge, 2001), and Bridget Orr, "Poetic Plate-Fleets and Universal Monarchy: The Heroic Plays and Empire in the Restoration," in *John Dryden: A Tercentenary Miscellany*, ed. Susan Green and Steven N. Zwicker (San Marino, 2001), pp. 71–97. On Dryden's drama in the wake of 1688, see David Bywaters, *Dryden in Revolutionary England* (Berkeley, 1991); and Richard Kroll, "The Double Logic of *Don Sebastian*," in *Dryden: A Tercentenary Miscellany*, ed. Green and Zwicker, pp. 47–69.
6. Johnson, *Lives*, vol. I, p. 336.
7. Ibid., pp. 348–9.
8. Susan Staves, *Players' Scepters* (Lincoln, 1979), p. 52.
9. William Cartwright, *The Plays and Poems of William Cartwright*, ed. G. Blakemore Evans (Madison, 1951), p. 221; quoted in Arthur C. Kirsch, *Dryden's Heroic Drama* (Princeton, 1965), p. 71.

10. Derek Hughes, *Dryden's Heroic Plays* (London, 1981), pp. 1–21 and *passim*.
11. George Villiers, Duke of Buckingham, *The Rehearsal*, ed. D. E. L. Crane (Durham, 1976), I. i. 230–2.
12. Johnson, *Lives*, vol. I, p. 341.
13. Hughes, *Dryden's Heroic Plays*, p. 119.
14. Judith Milhous and Robert D. Hume, *Producible Interpretation: Eight English Plays 1675–1707* (Carbondale, 1985), pp. 107–40.
15. John Dryden, *The Works of John Dryden*, ed. Walter Scott and George Saintsbury (1882–93); quoted in *Works* XV: 516.
16. Montaigne, *Essays*, translated by Charles Cotton the Younger, 2 vols. (London, 1686), vol. II, p. 9; quoted in *Works* XV: 416.
17. Steven N. Zwicker, "Dryden and the Dissolution of Things: The Decay of Structures in Dryden's Later Writing," in *John Dryden: Tercentenary Essays*, ed. Paul Hammond and David Hopkins (Oxford, 2000), pp. 308–29.

3

RONALD PAULSON

Dryden and the energies of satire

In the twenty volumes of the standard edition of Dryden's works there are only three major satires. This is strange considering that his reputation today is primarily as a satirist, the father of Augustan satire (Swift, Pope, Gay, and Fielding). *MacFlecknoe* (1676) and *Absalom and Achitophel* (1681) were the two satires he singled out in his "Discourse concerning the original and progress of Satire" (1693), and, besides these, there were only *The Medal* (1682) and the characters of Doeg and Og in *Absalom and Achitophel* Part II (1682). Thereafter satire in his poetry was incidental, most fully utilized in the bestiary and beast fables of *The Hind and the Panther* (1687), a poem whose end was not ostensibly satiric. Satire remained fragmentary, as in the Horatian imitations he wrote at the end of his life. And yet running through the whole of Dryden's *oeuvre* we can detect the energies of satire.

In "A Discourse concerning . . . Satire," which is still the best essay in English on the nature of satire, Dryden notes two derivations: from the Greek *satyra* and the Latin *satura*, the first essentially a tone, the second a form (*Works* IV: 3–90).[1] The first, supposedly drawing on the nature of satyrs (rough hairy beasts, man to the waist and goat below), is characteristically crude demotic language of a sort that reveals satire's ritual origins in the curse addressed to drought, worms, parasites, and the forces of sterility, which balanced prayers and praise addressed to the sun and rain, the forces of fertility. Dryden prefers the Latin etymology from *satura*, filled with food or sated; *satura lanx* was a festival platter filled to overflowing with meats chopped fine and, recovering a more savory version of the *satyra* tone, heavily seasoned. He cites approvingly the rhetorician Quintilian's dictum, "Satura [as opposed to other literary forms, epic, panegyric, elegy, pastoral] tota nostra est," satire is wholly ours, wholly Roman. The prototypical Roman satirists were Horace and Juvenal, whose formal verse satires were mixtures of many things, subjects, and examples, but (Dryden makes the important point) they maintain the unity of a single theme, one vice tying together the multitudinous examples (*Works* IV: 79).

In the case of Horace, his *satura*, which he modestly called a *sermo* (a conversation), uses the *exemplum*, an anecdote or telling example, to illustrate opposite extremes such as avarice and prodigality, deviations from a "golden mean" which, Horace implies, lies between. (Horace's *Epistles*, on the other hand, foreground a recommended course of action or way of life, against which deviations are contrasted and condemned.) Horace wrote in the age of Augustus, as a member of the imperial inner circle, which also included the epic poet Virgil. The alternative prototype was Juvenal, who lived in the time of the "bad" emperors, and in whose satires a corrupt present (a Rome no longer Roman) is contrasted with an ideal lost in the distant (republican, even pre-Horatian) past. The mode is no longer a conversation among like-thinking equals but the savage indignation of a lone survivor.

In the 1690s Dryden translated the satires of Juvenal and Persius, to which he attached his "Discourse concerning . . . Satire." He ends with a comparison of Horace and Juvenal, coming finally down on the side of the second. Juvenal's vision of imperial Rome in the time of Domitian (rather than Horace's in the Augustan age) is the implicit vehicle for Dryden's feelings about England in the reign of William III when he wrote his "Discourse." Dryden wrote, however, Horatian epistles, and his ideal of satiric practice, described in the most famous passage of the "Discourse," retains the *savoir faire* of Horace, who "writ according to the Politeness of *Rome*, under the Reign of *Augustus Caesar*" (*Works* IV: 78):

> Yet there is still a vast difference betwixt the slovenly Butchering of a Man, and the fineness of a stroak that separates the Head from the body, and leaves it standing in its place. A man may be capable, as *Jack Ketch's* Wife said of his servant, of a plain piece of Work, a bare Hanging; but to make a Malefactor die sweetly, was only belonging to her husband.   (*Works* IV: 71)

"I wish I cou'd apply it to myself," he adds, citing the character of Zimri (the Duke of Buckingham) in *Absalom and Achitophel*. The duke, he claims, "was too witty to resent it as an injury. If I had rail'd, I might have suffer'd for it justly" (*Works* IV: 71). The reference is back to 1681 and the reign of Charles II, when Dryden was Poet Laureate; but the words could apply as well to a satirist writing in a time of censorship.[2]

The Restoration was the beginning of an age (*the* age) of English satire, defined by its historical situation following a decade of disastrous civil war and Puritan commonwealth. Cavalier satire represented the Puritan "Saint" as a speaker of pious words that masked sexual desire and economic interest, summed up in mock forms based on impersonation, in fact on masquerade: a plebeian rebel/enthusiast claims (pretends to be, thinks he is) something he is not, ultimately the head of state. In the example given by the influential

French satirist-theorist, Nicolas Boileau, the fishwife talks as if she were Queen Dido, thus satirizing the social pretensions or the seditious inclination of the lower orders – the outsiders who want to get in or replace the insiders.[3] (A model was Horace's *Sermones*, his verse satires, especially i.ix, but the particular case of the mock form appears only in *Epode 2*, a lyric in which praise of the country life turns out to be delivered by a usurer.) On the other hand, if Queen Dido talks the language of a fishwife she reveals the low bodily reality under the royal trappings. The model this time was travesty, enjoyed by the French in Scarron's *Virgile travestie* (1648) and carried over into English by Charles Cotton in his *Scarronides* (1663). The Cavaliers (later the Court Wits) first satirized the Puritan hypocrite by revealing his true lust and greed, and then, in the 1670s following disillusionment with the Restoration (or the shifting political winds), satirized the king by exposing the sexual urge – the scepter that is only a penis, controlled by his mistresses – at the bottom of his policies-of-state. The mock heroic (the fishwife thinks she is Dido) served the court party satirizing its opponents, and travesty (Dido revealed to be no more than a fishwife) served the opposition. Dryden, patronized by the Duke of York (and implicitly by his brother the king, who made him poet laureate), took the court's position and wrote mock-heroic satire.

What Dryden did not write was the primitive *satyra* based on the curse and the medical and penal metaphors of cure and punishment, of phlebotomy and purgation, scourging and pillorying, not to mention burning, biting, piercing, and blistering – the satire practiced by his predecessors and illustrated by his contemporary John Oldham, whose *Satyres upon the Jesuits* appeared in 1680, shortly before *Absalom and Achitophel*:

> All this urge on my rank envenom'd spleen,
> And with keen Satyr edge my stabbing Pen:
> That its each home-set thrust their blood may draw,
> Each drop of Ink like *Aquafortis* gnaw.[4]

Oldham's diction is Elizabethan (when Juvenalian satire was understood as primarily invective). With his example of Jack Ketch, Dryden preserves the punishment metaphor,[5] but beheading is carried out with such style that the victim is not immediately aware that he has lost his head. Even looking back from the 1690s when he is himself an outsider and Juvenalian "rebel," Dryden calls for an ideal of civility and politeness commensurate with the dignity he attributed to a royal poet – a version of politeness the Whigs Addison and Steele in the 1700s would adapt to an ethos of their own, which condemned Dryden's natural successors, Pope and Swift, as writers of crude slanders and lampoons.

Dryden began as a poet of praise, whether of Cromwell or Charles II, but implicit in the genre was a space for satire. In 1649 young Lord Hastings dies of the smallpox, which is compared to the uprising of the rebels who killed, about the same time, their king, Charles I. Hastings is praised, the rebels condemned. Praise is the form that dominates both Dryden's *Heroic Stanzas* on the death of Cromwell and *Astrea Redux* on Charles II's Restoration, and praise remains a constant in his dedications, prefaces, prologues, and epilogues, as well as in his major works, the heroic plays to which they were attached. The model for Dryden's poems of praise was the classical panegyric, "a Speech deliver'd before a solemn and general Assembly of People, especially in praise of a great Prince," that is, in praise of a Cromwell or a Charles II, as opposed to the subject of an encomium, which was *any* person.[6] In one of the models of panegyric, Pliny's address to the Emperor Trajan, the form was neither biography nor catalogue of virtues but a series of contrasts between good and evil: an almost Juvenalian enumeration of the irresponsibility, effeminacy, triviality, weakness, and licentiousness of previous emperors and, in the present, the piety, abstinence, and fortitude of Trajan.

Sir William Davenant – poet, dramatist, and, in the 1650s, Royalist in exile – in his preface to *Gondibert* (1650) had argued that the panegyric historically subsumed the greatest of genres, the epic. He made the point that princes admire and emulate the epic hero and so become worthy of such admiration themselves. Dryden followed Davenant's theory (and his practice in *The Siege of Rhodes*) by making his own heroic plays the celebration of heroes, contrasting the heroic individualism of Almanzor with the solipsism of Lyndaraxa, the weakness of the king Boabdalin, and the treachery (guided by sexual passion) of his brother Abdalla. One character is interrelated with another, producing a dramatic version of extremes, opposites, and contrasts, but always with implicit an ideal or normative figure. The panegyric, in short, offered Dryden room for contrasting portraits, which eventually he developed into the portraits in *Absalom and Achitophel* of David, Barzillai, and the "loyal few" set against the traitors Achitophel, Zimri, Corah, and their rebel legions.

The basic unit on which Dryden builds all his satires (as well as his panegyrics) is the portrait or "character," that succinct summation of a personality developed to a fine art by his contemporaries Halifax, Burnet, and Clarendon (whose satiric progenitors in the previous age were Earl, Hall, and Overbury). The character, like satire itself, was based on classical models, in particular the histories of Tacitus and the comparative and contrasting portraits of Plutarch in his *Lives*. In *Absalom and Achitophel* the character is based most pertinently on the epic catalogues of heroes and on Milton's parody of these in his portraits of the rebel angels in Book 1 of *Paradise*

Lost. (To judge by Dryden's admiration for Chaucer, the prologue to *The Canterbury Tales* provided another model.)

In Pliny's panegyric on Trajan the contrast is most prominently between the past and the present (*prius* and *nunc*): the vicious past is, or we hope will be, superseded by the virtuous present. In Davenant's preface to *Gondibert* he argues that the theme of epic comes from "elder times," whereas panegyric deals directly with the present. Virgil's *Aeneid* showed Dryden how in an epic the past can serve as an analogue for the present, the emphasis less on the story than on the placing of our present society beside that of the past. Contemporary "society" is the common subject of Virgil's epic and Dryden's major satires.

The nucleus of Dryden's satire is the epic simile, specifically Virgil's. In the famous Neptune simile (*Aeneid* 1. 148) the storm disrupting Aeneas' pilgrimage to found Rome is compared to a contemporary Roman crowd, which is brought back to order by Neptune, who is compared to a Roman orator. The simile not only extends the reference outward to the world of nature, using nature and natural phenomena to illustrate human behavior and emotions, but to "one man" who within the text is Aeneas and without, in Rome, Octavius. The simile comparing the storm to the out-of-control Roman crowd is a microcosm of the larger analogy between Aeneas then and Octavius now, Troy Novant (London) and contemporary Rome (*prius* and *nunc*) – a case of propaganda justifying the Empire with which Octavius was replacing the Republic.

The comparison of past and present dominates Dryden's early Horatian epistle "To My Honored Friend, Dr. Charleton" (1663), where the bad past is corrected by the Restoration: Aristotle (a priori reasoning) is contrasted with and temporally replaced by Christopher Columbus and his discovery of the new world, as well as by English empirical philosophy and science; Oliver Cromwell is replaced by Charles II, and thus the "Torrid Zone . . . fevrish aire" of civil war and theocracy by the Stuart Restoration: "Temp'rate . . . zone . . . fann'd by a cooling breez" (*Works* 1: 43, lines 10–11). Inigo Jones's former identification of Stonehenge with a temple is now replaced by Dr. Charleton's "restoration" of it as a throne (it was also a refuge for the fleeing Charles II after his defeat at Worcester). Only a shift of emphasis would be necessary – quantitative rather than qualitative – to turn the panegyric into a satire. One needs only imagine the poem is not about Charleton but Aristotle and Inigo Jones's "temple," with Columbus locked away like Galileo by the Inquisition – and imagine that Cromwell did not die and George Monck, Duke of Albermarle had no way of restoring Charles II. This possibility is always implicit in Dryden's panegyrics, for generic reasons and perhaps also for reasons of a basically satiric temperament.[7]

When Dryden's similes do not connect past and present they suggest that one eye is always on politics. In his prologues and epilogues (attached to his own and the plays of others), which were his chief experimental ground for formal verse satire in the 1660s and 1670s, the similes most often compare the stage and England, acting and politics, the playwright/poet and the monarch, and the critics of plays and dissident Whigs. One half of the comparison is poetry-drama, the other politics; the tenor and vehicle are usually balanced (as in the "Charleton" epistle), but with the Popish Plot in 1679–80 the emphasis shifts toward politics. In the prologues and epilogues written for performance at Oxford, the university is contrasted with London, places where poets are more and less respected, critics more and less good, and past glory with present urban values. Depending on whether value is placed on the side of the tenor or the vehicle, these poems are panegyric or satire.[8]

In *Annus Mirabilis* (1667), the conventional simile governs the first part about the Dutch naval battles (the English fleet "like maimed fowl" or "Some falcon"), but in the second part, on the Plague and Fire, the simile takes the form of *this* historical event is like – or rather anticipates or fulfills – *that* historical event. Alan Roper, discussing *Annus Mirabilis*, has called this strategy analogy,[9] a term under which Dr. George Cheyne in the eighteenth century subsumed typology: "Analogy and its Appendages, Type, Allusion, Similitude, Parable, Hieroglyphic and Allegory (all more remote or nearer Approaches to Analogy) is the only natural Language the Deity can speak to us at present, under our Degeneracy and Lapse."[10] Divine analogy related microcosm and macrocosm – God and king; the spirit and body; religion, politics, and art. But Christian typology, as in *Annus Mirabilis*, was analogy based on history. The Great Fire of London is like an insurrection, specifically that of the usurper Cromwell ("As when some dire usurper heav'n provides / To scourge his country with a lawless sway"):

> Till fully ripe his swelling fate breaks out
>   And hurries him to mighty mischiefs on;
> His prince, surprised at first, no ill could doubt
>   And wants the pow'r to meet it when 'tis known.
> . . . .
> Such was the rise of this prodigious fire,
>   Which in mean buildings first obscurely bred,
> From thence did soon to open streets aspire,
>   And straight to palaces and temples spread.
>   (*Works* 1: 91–3, lines 849–52, 857–60)

The Great Fire is also like a purgation or atonement in the 1660s for the sin of rebellion against the monarch in the 1640s. The words Dryden puts into

Charles II's mouth allude to Isaiah's Suffering Servant, the type of Christ: "If mercy be a precept of thy will, / Return that mercy on thy servant's head . . . On me alone thy just displeasure lay, / But take thy judgements from this mourning land" (*Works* 1: 99, lines 1055–6, 1059–60). As simile, the fire is like the Christian Atonement for the sin of rebellion (Eve's original disobedience), from which only the king (God/his Son) can "redeem" his nation. As typology, the 1640s foreshadow the 1660s – or the latter fulfill the former. Dryden uses typology to explain and justify a catastrophe, showing that it is not, as the opposition party would have it, punishment for a sinful court in the 1660s but rather atonement for the opposition's sin of rebellion in the 1640s, being repeated now in the 1660s.[11]

Dryden does not employ allegory. In *Absalom and Achitophel*, describing Achitophel's conception of his son, which is *like* the conception of rebellion, he alludes to Satan's "conception" of rebellion which, allegorically, shows him producing the offspring Sin. But Achitophel is not Temptation or Evil; he is typologically Satan tempting Absalom by persuading him that he is the "Son," Christ; in the 1680s he is typologically the First Earl of Shaftesbury and Charles's bastard, the Duke of Monmouth. These are all "discernible, historically authentic particulars," not allegorical representations.[12] If Virgil used the past to glorify the present – connecting Augustus with Aeneas, Rome with its humble origins – Christian typology offered the present (the antitype) as a corrective of the past, which frees man from the Old Testament Law, indicating his redemption or "restoration." The Old Testament is the negative pole, the New the positive; this as opposed to the Juvenalian structure (especially Satire III, but evident in all the satires) of value embodied in a past now lost and subverted.

Part of Dryden's running argument in the 1660s and 1670s (as in Neander's speeches in the *Essay of Dramatic Poesy*) was that contemporary poets improved on the works of the giants of the Elizabethan-Jacobean age. The present "has the advantage of knowing more, and better than the former" age.[13] In the "Battle of the Ancients and Moderns" the present improved on the past because it benefited from the past's mistakes as well as its discoveries. In the art of translation into English (one of Dryden's greatest accomplishments), the poet absorbed the classical into the national culture, and the original object from the past was revalidated if not superseded by its new Englishness.

In the plot of comedy an older generation tries to block a younger and more vigorous one, preventing its love affairs – as, for example, the Townleys and Woodvilles of Etherege's *Man of Mode* (1676). But, as Etherege shows, there is also a sense of loss: Lady Woodville's sentimental view of love in the past (Petrarchan or Cavalier) corresponded to the words of Rochester's

Artemiza in "An Epistle from Artemiza in the City to Chloe in the Country," who recalls a time when love was not perverted into a "business" or into affectation (literally *aping*) or mere custom. In Rochester's satires love and right reason (based on the senses) are ideals, no longer attainable except as memories of the past. In the libertine terms of Rochester and Etherege, they are unattainable because of our fallen (Hobbesian) state of nature, in which we can only seek change and are driven, at bottom, by fear. When love *is* supposedly present, as in Rochester's "Imperfect Enjoyment," the ordinarily potent rake (potent with whores) becomes incapable of consummation – and so is incapable of producing offspring such as, in the macrocosm, a royal heir.

Dryden's identification with the libertine tradition was through the idealization of wit. His argument for the Moderns, as the present correcting the past, pitted a comedy of wit (and witty conversation) against a comedy of humors and humor characters. In his preface to *An Evening's Love* (1671) he distinguishes wit from humor: "The first works on the judgment and fancy; the latter on the fancy alone: there is more of satisfaction in the former kind of laughter, and in the latter more of scorn" (*Works* x: 203). Since both obviously share the end of comedy (as argued by critics from Aristotle to Hobbes and Dennis) as "scorn," the first, he writes, "entertains us with the imperfections of humane nature," the second "with what is monstrous and chimerical." The distinction recalls the Jonsonian dramatic satire, *Everyman Out of His Humour* or, at its highest reach, *Volpone*: humor characters (characters distorted into monsters by the preponderance of one humor) must be de-humored by a satirist, in a discourse roughly that of Oldham's *Satyrs upon the Jesuits*.[14]

In his earliest writings on wit, Dryden devalues humor and with it satire against wit and comedy. When one "writes humour he makes folly ridiculous," but "when wit, he moves you, if not always to laughter, yet to a pleasure that is more noble" (*Works* x: 202), and this is because humor (adapting Aristotle) represents "conversation with the vulgar," thus demonstrating "much of ill nature in the observation of their follies"; while Dryden associates wit with the aristocratic conversation of the Restoration, which, he argues, made this age more polished than the last (Horace over Lucilius, the Empire over the Republic). Dryden cites the conversation of courtiers and, the ultimate model, the monarch himself, the epitome of witty conversation; that is, he equates wit, polite discourse, aristocracy, and monarchy. Jonsonian humor has by the 1670s come to be represented by Jonson's imitator, the "true-blue Whig," and Dryden's comedic rival, Thomas Shadwell. In his own comedies, and in the higher register of his heroic plays, Dryden uses witty conversation as his valuative norm. He employs humor characters like Lyndaraxa and Abdalla as the far end of a spectrum of "the imperfections of humane nature."

By arguing for wit over humor Dryden identified himself with the Earl of Rochester and the aristocratic Court Wits: he was, after all, a country gentleman, the brother-in-law of Sir Robert Howard, and by 1688 the king's poet laureate. He dedicated *Marriage A-la-Mode* (1671) to Rochester with an appreciative essay, acknowledging his patronage, suggestions, and perhaps even contributions. The libertine premise in *Marriage A-la-Mode* is the inability of natural men and women to continue living within the constraints of the institution of marriage, and included are two libertine lyrics, the second a Drydenian (softened) version of Rochester's "Imperfect Enjoyment."[15]

In his "Allusion to Horace" of *c.* 1675, Rochester distinguished himself from Dryden as a genteel Horace correcting his crude precursor Lucilius, and on the grounds of class disqualified Dryden from practicing wit. Dryden is a drudging professional, addressing the ignorant masses with his plays (a position Dryden had defended in his preface to *An Evening's Love*). To be witty Dryden can only cry "cunt." The break between Dryden and Rochester was a result of the polarizing of parties and the increased criticism of the monarch – and especially his brother, the Catholic heir, Dryden's patron. As Rochester wrote his "Allusion to Horace" he was also reducing the monarch's Body Politic to his body private and the illusion of what Dryden was to call "godlike" to the gross reality of his sexual apparatus.

The first salvo was the Duke of Buckingham's *Rehearsal* (1671), which reduced Dryden's heroic love/honor conflicts to the putting on and taking off of boots.[16] Proving that Dryden's employment of couplets, however skilled, was not suited to any conceivable form of genuinely heroic drama, Buckingham and his collaborators recommended that Bayes turn to satire, which was, as Dryden had made clear, a step down from comedy, as humor was from wit. It was Buckingham, attacking Dryden for political as well as aesthetic reasons, who drew Dryden's attention to the satiric utility of his couplet, at the same time that he stimulated Dryden to respond in kind. Within his "perception about the potential for unintended comedy in rhymed drama," Dryden came to realize that couplets are most effectively used for a mock-heroic satire to correct Whig travesty.[17]

In Dryden's first major satire, *MacFlecknoe*, Shadwell and the shabbier parts of London are compared (as by a simile) to Rome, the emperor, Virgil, and Aeneas – as well as to John the Baptist. *MacFlecknoe* shows the poetaster aspiring to the laurel, the seditious rebel aspiring to the throne.[18] The mock epic was available to Dryden not only in Boileau's *Lutrin* but in the work of one of his favorite poets, Chaucer, whom Dryden recovered in the 1690s in his metaphrase of "The Nun's Priest's Tale" in *Fables*. In one of Dryden's additions to Chaucer's text, Chanticleer, the strutting rooster (reversing the beast-admiring premise of Rochester's "Satyr against Reason and Mankind"), says that he "with pleasure see[s] / Man strutting on two Legs and aping me!" (*Works* VII: 313, lines 459–60). In *MacFlecknoe* the poetaster sees himself as superior to real poets as Chanticleer does to his human master and mistress. In the terms of past-present, the past is the memory of Augustus and Virgil, and so the present of Flecknoe and Shadwell is a degeneration, but, in the 1670s, it is only a subculture within a classical culture and not yet dominant. *MacFlecknoe* is not yet Juvenalian but rather a mock-heroic satire on the ridiculous pretensions of the poetasters and their political analogues, the out-of-place Whigs.

MacFlecknoe is also a defense of wit against humor. With wit Dryden attacks Shadwell's humor, his farcical "humor characters." Shadwell declares his lineage from Jonson, but Jonson's satire of humor characters has by now degenerated into Shadwell's meaningless laughter, laughter for its own sake, at their farcical japes. With Rochester Dryden presumes that wit operates more efficiently on these figures than the mere representation of "the follies and extravagances of *Bedlam*." He makes wit normative in a satire of humor; the poet's wit provides the "bite" that Shadwell's humor so notably lacks. The measured, solemn voice of Dryden notices the resemblance between Flecknoe and Augustus, based on the common element of succession (poetic *and* royal). To connect Shadwell and Jonson is witty in that Dryden discovers a likeness: not only does Shadwell imitate Jonson and think he is Jonson's heir, he physically resembles him (both are fat); and yet, what *Dryden* notes in this witty similitude is the difference – how unlike they are in value; and this is judgment, a quality superior to wit. If Dryden supplies the "bite" that Shadwell lacks, he also adds to this the judgment that he felt Rochester and Buckingham lacked.[19] With the word "Nonsense" he detects the difference between Flecknoe and Augustus, which in effect adds to Rochester's irresponsible wit the correction of judgment – replacing the mere fancy of the libertine aristocrat with the the authority of the true satirist.

In his post-Rochester phase, Dryden would have agreed with Archbishop Tillotson that "Wit is a very commendable quality, but then a wise man should always have the keeping of it. It is a sharp weapon, as apt for mischief as for good purposes if it be not well manag'd."[20] Dryden has absorbed Hobbes's contrast in *Leviathan* (1650) between wit and judgment (anticipating Locke's in his *Essay* of 1690), whose locus is "conversation and business":

those that observe their similitudes, in case they be such as are but rarely observed by others, are said to have a *good wit*; by which, in this occasion, is meant a *good fancy*. But they that observe their differences, and dissimitudes; which is called *distinguishing*, and *discerning*, and *judging* between thing and thing; in case, such discerning be not easy, are said to have a *good judgment . . .* The former, that is, fancy, without the help of judgment, is not commended as a virtue: but the latter which is judgment, and discretion, is commended for itself, without the help of fancy.[21]

Dryden employs both: wit, which finds similarities between the most dissimilar objects, is corrected by judgment, which distinguishes the difference elided by wit – raising satire above the comedy of aristocratic libertine conversation to a nobler, more just, more dignified art, as Dryden now conceived it. In the "Discourse Concerning . . . Satire" the image of shaking the head which, unnoticed by the object of satire, has been cut off, suggests the operation of wit upon an oblivious humor character of the sort Jonson and Shadwell created, and applied in *Absalom and Achitophel* to the great wit Buckingham himself ("too witty to resent it as an injury").[22] Dryden's animus against the aristocratic libertine rebel fits with his invocation of Jack Ketch, who beheaded the king's enemies, guilty of treason; beheading was for precisely those aristocratic traitors like the Duke of Buckingham or the Earl of Shaftesbury (not for the plebeians, who were hanged, drawn, and quartered).[23] In *Absalom and Achitophel* Rochester's libertine wit, politicized in Whiggery, unleashed in fancy and religious enthusiasm, is transferred to Shaftesbury-Achitophel, and is now "to madness near allied" (line 163), who even begets his son "while his soul did huddled notions [i.e., subversive plots] try," thus producing "a shapeless lump, like anarchy" (lines 171–2) – that is, treason.

The two most celebrated and influential mock-heroic satires of the seventeenth century were Dryden's *MacFlecknoe* and *Absalom and Achitophel*, but the mode operates very differently in each. In *MacFlecknoe* a subject is made ridiculous by comparing it to an elevated type (Shadwell to Roman emperors and poets), seeming to say that Shadwell *thinks of himself* as Roman, but the contrast shows wherein his greatness really lies (he rules not Rome but the kingdom of Nonsense). *MacFlecknoe* served (by way of Samuel Garth's *Dispensary* of 1699) as model for Pope's mock-epic *Dunciad* (1728ff.); that is, the characters whose humor is to aspire to a higher status, to which they are ludicrously ill suited. For Swift and Pope mock heroic diction is used to characterize virtually all their objects of satire as affected, deluded, and seditious. Dryden continues to write what is essentially witty conversation (supplemented by judgment), and Pope does much the same; but Swift takes seriously the element of pretension and delusion (ultimately madness). He, returning to Jonsonian mimesis, turns the mock heroic discourse into impersonation of the humor character, who exposes himself out of his own mouth.

In *Absalom and Achitophel*, on the other hand, a contemporary event is elevated by comparing it with the story in 2 Samuel of David and Absalom.[24] Dryden himself makes the valid connection between Charles II and David, with the common element fecundity and adultery. The true importance of the event is shown – not only how important it really is but exactly how to interpret it, negatively and positively. In *Absalom and Achitophel* no one is simply mocked by the analogy, though some are severely condemned. With the Old Testament typology and the allusions to *Paradise Lost* (in subject and diction), even the evil characters, are made to seem of the greatest importance – and threat. The poor crippled Shaftesbury becomes the ominous Satanic figure of the Great Tempter, and Absalom becomes not only the truly beloved son but a pseudo-Christ in the desert, a role imposed upon him by Achitophel (who calls him "saviour").[25]

Dryden's overtly political poems are in the mock-heroic mode, which permits him to deflate the plebeian pretensions of the Whigs (and their poets) but also to take them seriously. (Rochester's travesty did not take Charles seriously; he made him a fool only, and essentially "humorous.") The fiction of *Absalom and Achitophel*, where a contemporary subject is elevated by comparison with the Old Testament, its true importance shown, led to the mock epic of John Phillips's *Splendid Shilling* (1701) and Pope's *Rape of the Lock* (1712–14). There a shilling or a lock of hair, by being heroicized, is mocked; but attention is also drawn to its beauty and its special qualities, which may transcend the heroic stereotypes of an earlier time, certainly draw attention to the anachronism of those heroic standards in 1700s London.

When in the "Discourse concerning . . . Satire" Dryden mentions his own satires, *MacFlecknoe* and *Absolom and Achitophel*, he classifies them as Varronian – that is, according to his definition, a mixture of styles (verse and prose, different voices or levels of style), including "Tales or Stories of [the satirist's] own invention."[26] Dryden's *The Hind and the Panther* (1687) was his most obviously Varronian work. The structure is Lucianic, a dialogue of contrasting voices: that of the narrator, the more personal voice of Dryden himself (talking about himself), the voices of the Hind and the Panther in conversation, of each telling her fable, and of characters within the fables; and so dialogue, monologue, narrative, and speech permit Dryden, for example in the Panther's fable, to satirize the sparrows and the Martin for their respective folly and knavery, while qualifying the truth of the tale by the character of the teller, noted for the "malice of her tale."[27]

A significant characteristic of Varronian satire is imitation or parody – the juxtaposition of texts, ancient and modern: Varro "often quoted the Verses of *Homer* and the Tragick Poets, and turn'd their serious meaning into something that was Ridiculous" – as in Seneca's "Mock Deification of *Claudius*" and Erasmus's *Praise of Folly* (IV: 47–8). Thus the mock-heroic diction of *MacFlecknoe* combines the epic or heroic drama with demotic lowlife and farce; *Absalom and Achitophel* combines biblical parody with contemporary history, juxtaposing different characters and voices. *Absalom and Achitophel*, like Varronian satire, is not formally satiric; its form is closer to that of the court masque, where at the end the king reasserted order over a world of threatening chaos. Charles's reassertion of order also recalls the ending of *The Conquest of Granada* or one of Dryden's comedies – or, indeed, Molière's *Tartuffe*, where Tartuffe's total victory is canceled by the intervention of none other than Louis XIV. What keeps the ending satiric rather than comic is the fact that Achitophel, Absalom, and Tartuffe are not, as in comedy, reabsorbed into the social order. One might say that *Absalom and Achitophel* is satire disguised as a miniature epic or a court masque. Although about the triumph of David-Charles, its main energy is satiric rather than panegyric. (So also the real aim of *The Hind and the Panther* is denigration of the beasts who threaten the Hind.)

The imitation (going back, perhaps, to Rochester's "Imitation of Horace") became the basis for Dryden's mature satire. His translations, more often (to use his own terminology) "metaphrases," were often "imitations" in that he worked variations upon the original, bringing it up to date; and this included not only parallels but recognizable deviations, discrepant and ironic analogies, based on a strategy of allusion. *Absalom and Achitophel* alludes to *Paradise Lost* by invoking the *gravitas* of the Miltonic diction and adapting the Miltonic plot to the story of David and Absalom. Dryden learned from *Paradise Lost* how to use elevated and sacred parody: Milton's Satan is a mock Aeneas, leaving the ruins of Troy to refound his empire in Italy; he transplants his empire to God's newly created earth. Satan, Sin, and Death are a Satanic parody of the Trinity, and their building of the bridge connecting Chaos and earth parodies God's Creation.

The satiric fiction of Dryden's satires derives from *Paradise Lost*: a cast of characters, Satan, Adam, and the crowd of unreliable, restless, and fallen angels (Dryden's backsliding Israelites); a story of temptation and fall, based on a lie (Satan is the Prince of Liars, or, in the *Aeneid*, Sinon), a plot invented by the tempter.[28] The consequence is an image of chaos: Milton's Chaos; in the *Aeneid* the unruly crowd of Virgil's storm simile, or better, the Greek soldiers who emerge from the horse and in the darkness burn and blindly kill each other as well as the Greeks. The vocabulary Dryden employs throughout all his poems is of monarch, rebel, usurper, and so on – as in the prologues and epilogues, each a little story of order and disorder (a small court masque): politically, monarchy vs. commonwealth, hereditary ruler vs. democracy.

The religious, political, and literary subjects coincide: God, a rightful monarch, a true poet, and (as in *Religio Laici*) a textual authority, with their negations. The terms, moral and religious, are sin and evil, the first divine, the second civic. On the theological level, the sin (original and thereafter) is disobedience, Eve's denial of God's order, and so a negation; on the level of civil society, the sin is treason, rebellion, and usurpation – the denial or replacement of the monarch (reflecting the first Commandments that there be no other, no false gods); and so the evil, from the Genesis story to *Paradise Lost*, is temptation to disobedience – the original temptation by the serpent Satan, which was based on a lie (that eating of the Tree of Knowledge brought godhead). Finally, evil in the theological sense (as in the Problem of Evil) is death, disease, pain, and labor; and for Dryden this is the direct consequence of temptation and rebellion in a Commonwealth. Democracy and chaos are always self-defeating (in *The Medal* the inevitable falling out between the elitist libertine Shaftesbury and his mob of enthusiast followers), and variously take the form of degeneration, decline, flux, entropy, and loss – or a return to Hobbes's state of nature, "nasty, brutish, and short."

Theological sin and evil both are the absence of good. The evil represented in *MacFlecknoe* accords with the Christian definition – an absence or denial or perversion of the good, which is everything created. There can be no evil in a world created by God (that is, not a Manichean world of equal powers of good and evil); and so the evil here is *not*-Augustus, *not*-Virgil, and *not*-Christ, not sense but only nonsense (as in *The Dunciad* it will be anti-creation). Among other things, it is Satan's parody of God, or, as in "But S— 's genuine night admits no ray," it is darkness, night, the absence of light, implicitly opposed to the Light of John 1: 5ff. and the First Epistle 1: 5–7. In political terms, therefore, evil was the denial of the monarch, revolt and regicide – and in practice the many against (a degeneration, fragmentation of) the one.

Swift's satire also derives from Varronian satire – from the paradoxical encomium and Erasmus's *Praise of Folly*. As in *MacFlecknoe*, the affected tone of praise conceals a mock panegyric. Irony would be basic to Swift's satires – blame by praise. Swift and Dryden both rely upon the discrepancy between what a text appears to say and what it says; but Swift's depends on the discrepancy between what it *appears* to be and what it *is*; Swift embodies irony in a deluded speaker, and the reader is intended to believe, up to a point, that it is Folly speaking and not Erasmus or Swift. The words of Gulliver, Isaac Bickerstaff, the Grub Street Hack, and the Modest Proposer are passed off in printed texts whose apparent authenticity deceives and thereby implicates the unwary reader. Therefore the lie (the successful lie, whether of Satan or Sinon) is the primary focus of Swift's satire – a simulated almanac, a Modest Proposal, an Argument against abolishing Christianity, even the dying speech of a criminal on his way to the gallows (summed up in his essay on lies in *The Examiner*). The "plot," the form the lie took for Dryden, a donnée of the Popish Plot scare, becomes Swift's project or proposal aimed at tempting the unwary.

In Dryden's satire irony is incidental and seldom sustained, never extended to "black journalism" or satiric impersonation. Even in the prologues and epilogues the speakers are only mouth-pieces – Horatian speakers, often supplemented by an adversarius; and these are poets or actors playing out the similes that dominate the poems. In *MacFlecknoe* the dramatic voice of Flecknoe is simply a mock-epic diction parallel to Dryden's. Only in the plays does Dryden have a basis for mimicry. In Lyndaraxa's speeches in *Conquest of Granada* or Morat's in *Aureng-Zebe* he puts the words of rebels and usurpers into the mouth of Swiftean villains, who expose themselves in what we might think of as distantly Varronian satire. *Absalom and Achitophel*, a genuinely Varronian satire, uses the speeches of the heroic plays to recall the speakers in *Paradise Lost*.

But in both *MacFlecknoe* and *Absalom and Achitophel* Dryden uses a normative poet's voice, similar to Pope's though with the authority of a poet laureate and representative of the crown – until 1689 when both Dryden and his patron, James II, were deprived of office – and the result is normative discourse. Dryden's Horatian imitations laid the ground for Pope's Horatian–Juvenalian satires and epistles of the 1730s and 1740s, and so for Samuel Johnson, Dryden's true heir (and greatest admirer), in "London" and "The Vanity of Human Wishes." Swift's poems, which are travesties, poetry of the out-of-office, follow not from Dryden's poetry but from Rochester's.

The Medal, Dryden's third satire, is mock heroic only in so far as the head of Shaftesbury on the medal struck to celebrate his acquittal is contrasted with the royal head on a true coin of the realm. It shows Achitophel, acquitted of treason by Whiggish London juries, elevated by the crowd into a false idol, his face usurping the king's. *The Medal* is, however, a discursive satire, its diction Juvenalian denunciation. Even the Shaftesbury medal recalls Juvenal's use of a central image – a giant fish (which he treats mock-heroically), a dinner party, the relationship of a patron and a client that has degenerated into that of knave and fool, or a Rome repopulated by un-Roman immigrants, or a Rome in which gender roles have been reversed.

If, however, we accept Phillip Harth's interpretation, *The Medal* follows from Charles's successful restoration of order in *Absalom and Achitophel* and shows Shaftesbury and his Whigs, however victorious momentarily, now reduced to a small enclave within the City of London,[29] analogous to the kingdom of Nonsense in *MacFlecknoe*, a contained cancer within the Body Politic of England. The lord mayor's (or Shaftesbury's crippled) body replaces the king's, the body poxed replaces the Body Politic. Swift picks up from *The Medal* not its form, for it lacks anything approaching a Swiftean impersonation, but its melange of metaphors, which build piecemeal into an image of the body politic with disease working within it and seeking an outlet; this Swift uses as a unifying image in *A Tale of a Tub*.

In his Juvenal translations, Dryden gives himself more freedom to express indignation of the sort used in *The Medal* and his portraits of Doeg and Og. But, given the 1690s, and within the context of Juvenal's savage indignation, he uses innuendo, and so he chooses Juvenal's Satires I and III. From Satire I he takes the satirist's need in bad times to evade the censor, using past history to write about the present; and from Satire III he takes the image of Rome overrun by foreigners, with the Greeks now William III's Dutch friends (which Johnson, in his "London" of 1739, replaces with the French): loss, foreign invasion, and, among other forms of degeneration (another favorite Juvenalian subject), that of gender divisions, for which read William III's minions. Umbricius leaves present-day Rome for the country and the distant past – back to Cumae, where Aeneas first landed and consulted the Sybil.

Dryden's satire in the 1690s appears in the suggestive parallels of Juvenal's satires, his revisions of *The Aeneid* (Aeneas now an imperialist invader, a Panther to Latium's Hind), and his additions to Chaucer's "Nun's Priest's Tale," which emphasize Chanticleer's hubris, the clerical hypocrisy of the fox, the moral disaster of flattery, and the vocabulary of usurpation – the fox is "th'artificer of lies" (Satan), and "loyal subjects often seize their prince, / Forced (for his good) to seeming violence" and "treason" (lines 776, 790–2, 808).[30]

In the Horatian "Epistles" he wrote in the 1690s Dryden returns to the panegyrics of the 1660s, but now the counter examples are situated in a present contrasted with a nostalgic past. In "To my dear Friend Mr. Congreve" he writes a passage that places himself and Congreve in the position of Flecknoe and Shadwell in *MacFlecknoe*. The world is turned upside down, and they are now the lone bearers of value in a society governed by Shadwells and Rymers:

> Oh that your Brows my Lawrel had sustain'd,
> Well had I been depos'd, if You had rein'd!
> The Father had descended for the Son;
> For only You are lineal to the Throne.
> . . . .
> But now, not I, but Poetry is curs'd;
> For *Tom* the Second reigns like *Tom* the first.
>   (*Works* IV: 433, lines 41–4, 46–7)

In "To My Honour'd Kinsman, John Driden of Chesterton" (1700) the Horatian epistle serves as a vehicle for satire on an adversarial England of hunt-loving and bloodthirsty "princes," murderous physicians, and greedy apothecaries, which sets off the true old-fashioned Englishman, the poet's Cousin Driden.

Dryden's satire becomes ostensibly Juvenalian only after the fall of James II in 1688 – and the loss of his laureateship. Juvenalian satire uses the past to denigrate the present, showing how it has fallen away from the ideal in the past. Instead of a fulfillment of a long, divinely ordained process (as in Christian typology or Virgilian epic), the present is a perversion, a parody. The significance of the past for Dryden shifts from the bad past of the 1640s and 1650s redeemed by the Stuart Restoration (when he talked of how we are now better poets than the Elizabethans and Jacobeans) to the 1670s and nostalgia for the Restoration and the innocent 1660s, now corrupt with politics and dissent, and finally to the 1690s.

There is a sense in which Dryden always wrote Juvenalian satire (whether in the reign of Charles II, James II, or William III). *Religio Laici* (1684) pretends to be a Horatian epistle on the subject of religious belief, which posits a mean between extremes. The "mean" is a Latitudinarian belief in a few basic unarguable truths, and where disagreement persists one should follow the tradition of the Church Fathers. But in *Religio Laici* the middle way fudges the fact that Dryden is really opposing the authority of the Fathers to the combined extremes of aristocratic atheism and plebeian religious enthusiasm. *Religio Laici* followed soon after *The Medal*, and the deviations reflect the dissensions among Shaftesbury Whigs, with which Dryden ended *The Medal*; that is, the readings of Shaftesbury the deist and the City mob of religious enthusiasts are together opposed to a proper reading of the Bible. In the prologues and epilogues, though they sound like Horatian *sermones*, the satire was based on sheer contrast. The contrast between monarchy and commonwealth is at the bottom of all his satires, the Juvenalian convention only becoming more emphatic as the first recedes into the past and is replaced by the second. Imitation itself involves the contrast between past and present, as an ideal and the real (the text made viable for contemporary English men and women), the primitive and the modern.

Dryden's use of Juvenal illustrates the close relationship between satire and elegy. In *Alexander's Feast*[31] the bard Timotheus, a sort of poet laureate (in this sense, both Tom One – Thomas Shadwell – and Tom Two – Thomas Rymer), flatters Alexander (William III) with memories of his great victories, urging him on to relive them in more bloodshed, and eventually to burn the city of Persepolis.[32] But Timotheus is also the poet who elegizes the defeated king Darius (James II), now deserted by friends and followers.

When in *The Hind and the Panther* Dryden writes, "Here let my sorrow give my satire place, / To raise new blushes on my British race," he is conflating elegy and satire. Panegyric subsumes elegy, extending from "Upon the death of the Lord Hastings" (1649) to the elegies of the 1690s. There are even elements of elegy in the mourning for Barzilai's son (contrasted with the monstrous birth of Shaftesbury's son) in *Absalom and Achitophel*, and of Absalom himself; and again in the panegyric of the Duchess of Ormonde (wife of Barzilai's grandson the Second Duke of Ormonde). Finally, "The Secular Masque," recalling the court masque and the golden time before the civil war, suggests that the last decade of the century has rendered civil war, Restoration, life public and private, all meaningless – and now the past, finally discredited, can only be bettered by something new. The mourning of elegy suits a poet writing Juvenalian satire, which judges the degenerate present by comparison with an idealized, lost past, first in 1649, then again in the 1690s.

This mode informs Dryden's most successful dramatic effort, his "tragedy" *All for Love* (1678): Antony and Cleopatra – heroic grandeur and love – are survivors of the Flood (read, civil wars) which sweeps away the anachronistic figures of Antony and Cleopatra, as described by Serapion in the opening lines of the play:

> Here monstrous phocae panted on the shore;
> Forsaken dolphins there, with their broad tails,
> Lay lashing the departing waves: hard by 'em,
> Sea-horses flound'ring in the slimy mud,
> Tossed up their heads, and dashed the ooze about 'em.
> *Enter* ALEXAS *behind them.*
> (*Works* XIII: I.i. 11–15)

The appearance of Alexas, the eunuch, heralds the new age. As the play opens the battle of Actium is already past and lost. The tone, from Serapion's opening speech to the final words, is elegiac; and the prologue and epilogue show, on the comic level, similarly ambivalent feelings about the past.[33]

The heroic energies and splendors of *The Conquest of Granada* have been replaced and are now memories in the unheroic world of Alexas and Octavius that is engulfing Antony and Cleopatra.

Laura Brown has said of the final simile, "See, see how th'lovers sit in state together, / As they were giving laws to half mankind!" (v. i. 507–8): "As a lost and ruined lover and a poor, weak woman, the 'real' Antony and Cleopatra give no laws, direct no fates, and attain no glory. They are only like the monarchs whose names they bear."[34] In so far as these are characters who only make it appear that empires and eternal glory are at stake, the simile is a sentimental version of the satiric mock-heroic of *MacFlecknoe*, and the tragedy of Antony and Cleopatra is the other side of the satire of Flecknoe and Shadwell.

"Venom" (as in the last line of Dryden's translation of Juvenal III) is the added ingredient of satire – and (again, as in the translation of Juvenal into English) indirection. *All for Love* (with its preface attacking Rochester and the aristocratic, libertine, Whig ethos), written in the disillusionment and the political fragmentation of the 1670s, represents the coming age with Octavius, who never appears on stage and is only seen through Antony's eyes – as cold, a youth ("'tis the coldest youth . . . so tame"), no soldier, all energy directed toward power, whose symbol within the dramatis personae is the other survivor, the eunuch Alexas.[35] *All for Love* comes after *MacFlecknoe* and before *Absalom and Achitophel* and the Popish Plot. It seems out of place with the optimism of these satires; it rather anticipates the elegiac satire of the 1690s. It might be argued that the elegy expresses Dryden's characteristic, and satiric, stance.

Classical satire offered Dryden two models: Horace contrasted opposite extremes and indicated as an ideal (or only a norm) a middle way between them; while Juvenal contrasted good and evil, as past and present, basing the contrast on a principle of degeneration – the present is a corruption of the past (Horace's satire supposed a dialectical progress). Horace wrote about folly (in the *sermones* but not, always, in the *epodes*), which usually affects only oneself and was, moreover, as he explained, correctible. Although it could spread like a stain to implicate others, it was essentially self-absorbed. Juvenal's evil reached out, engrossing, damaging, and destroying others – as in Dryden's figures of the tempter and usurper. The Christian idea of evil was similar to that of Juvenal, who influenced the grimmer Church Fathers (Jerome, Tertullian, Irenaeus): it was a falling away from, a degeneration or merely a bad parody of, most generally an absence of, the good. Elegy, based on Pauline love, served as the Christianizing of Juvenal's satire, mourning where Juvenal condemned; its mood was sadness where Juvenal's was anger and indignation. Finally, Varronian satire completed Dryden's picture by feigning a tone of mourning, as in *Absalom and Achitophel* – or of praise in *MacFlecknoe*; thus recalling the Varronian sense of this genre versus that, this text versus that, this time and that.

NOTES

1. For a useful discussion of the "Discourse," see Howard Weinbrot, *Eighteenth-century Satire: Essays on Text and Context from Dryden to Peter Pindar* (Cambridge, 1988), pp. 1–20. With Weinbrot's sections on Dryden, the reader should also consult Dustin Griffin, *Satire: A Critical Reintroduction* (Lexington, 1994). For background on the theory of satire, see Ronald Paulson, ed., *Satire: Modern Essays in Criticism* (Englewood Cliffs, NJ, 1971).
2. Cf. the preface to *Absalom and Achitophel*: "For there's a sweetness in good verse, which Tickles even while it hurts" (*Works* II: 3).
3. Boileau, *Le Lutrin* (1674, 1683), "Au lecteur," in *Œuvres* (1702), 1006.
4. Oldham, *Satires upon the Jesuits*, Prologue, lines 57–60, in *The Poems of John Oldham*, ed. Harold F. Brooks (Oxford, 1987), 6. In his elegy, "To the Memory of Mr. Oldham" (1684), Dryden compares Oldham and himself: Oldham wrote a kind of satire that dispensed with the decorum of the heroic couplet, "the numbers of thy native tongue." "But satire," Dryden adds, "needs not those, and wit will shine / Through the harsh cadence of a rugged line" (*Works* II: 175, lines 14–16). He employs a metaphor of organic growth: Oldham died before coming to full, "mellow," civilized growth (before Dryden wrote *Absalom and Achitophel*), and in fact represented the old, satyr-satire of the Elizabethans Jonson, Marston, and Hall.
5. He refers to the medical metaphor (preface to *Absalom and Achitophel*, *Works* II: 5) but does not use it except indirectly in *The Medal*, where he presents us with a poxed Body Politic.
6. See James D. Garrison, *Dryden and the Tradition of Panegyric* (Berkeley and Los Angeles, 1975).
7. On Dryden's "temper," see the preface to *An Evening's Love*, *Works* X: 202.
8. As critics have noticed, whenever Dryden writes about literature, he is writing also about religion and politics. See, e.g., Earl Miner, *Dryden's Poetry* (Bloomington, 1967) and Earl R. Wasserman, *The Subtler Language: Critical Readings of Neoclassical and Romantic Poems* (Baltimore, 1959).
9. Roper points out that in its first half, the English–Dutch war, *Annus Mirabilis* is primarily a series of epic similes (*Dryden's Poetic Kingdoms* [London, 1961], pp. 15–34, 74–86).
10. Cheyne, *An Essay on Regimen* [London, 1740], p. 228; see Earl R. Wasserman, "Nature Moralized: The Divine Analogy in the Eighteenth Century," *ELH* 20 (1953), 39–76.
11. See Michael McKeon, *Politics and Poetry in Restoration England: The Case of Dryden's Annus Mirabilis* (Cambridge, 1975).
12. See Edward Rosenheim, *Swift and the Satirist's Art* (Chicago, 1963), p. 25.
13. "Defense of the Epilogue," *Works* XI: 204.
14. See Alvin Kernan, *The Cankered Muse* (New Haven, 1959).

15. The obsession with the problem of marriage persisted with Dryden long after his libertine phase (as in "To My Honoured Kinsman, John Driden").

16. *The Rehearsal*, III. v. Buckingham also makes much of Dryden's obsession with the "new" (both in the sense of his having superseded the Elizabethans and of introducing whatever is new and strange into his heroic dramas) and his reliance on fantastic similes (II. i.; I. ii. and III. i.).

17. See James Anderson Winn, *John Dryden and his World* (New Haven, 1987), p. 261, and more generally, on the sources of *MacFlecknoe*, pp. 290–8; also, supplementing Winn, Howard Erskine-Hill, "MacFlecknoe, Heir of Augustus," in *John Dryden: Tercentenary Essays*, ed. Paul Hammond and David Hopkins (Oxford, 2000), pp. 15–31.

18. Even the first MS version of *MacFlecknoe* with its plot of "royal" succession reflects the political crisis, evident by 1676 (Charles could have no children and the heir was therefore his Roman Catholic brother James), which was exacerbated by the exclusions bills and the Popish Plot that intervened before publication in 1682.

19. Rochester also explored the negative aspects of wit, but with irony: wits are distrusted as whores are because they leave behind the fear of infection. See "Artemiza to Chloe" and "Satyr against Reason and Mankind."

20. John Tillotson, "The Folly of Scoffing at Religion," *Works* (1696), pp. 40–1.

21. Hobbes, *Leviathan*, I. viii, ed. Michael Oakeshott (Oxford, 1960), p. 43. Cf. Locke, *Essay concerning Human Understanding*, II. xi. 2.

22. Dryden could also have been recalling the "huge, great hangman" Buckingham has cut off Bayes's head in *The Rehearsal* (I. ii.).

23. Cf. Dryden's remarks in "Defense of the Epilogue," *Works* XI: 213: "all Poetry being imitation, that of Folly is a lower exercise of fancy, though perhaps as difficult as the other: for 'tis a kind of looking downward in the poet; and representing that part of Mankind which is below him." Jonson's excelling lay in his representation of "low Characters of Vice and Folly" – as opposed to Dryden's, which in *Absalom and Achitophel* are high.

24. See Weinbrot, *Eighteenth-Century Satire*, pp. 80–99.

25. On the political nuances of *Absalom and Achitophel*, see Harth, *Pen for a Party: Dryden's Tory Propaganda in its Contexts* (Princeton, 1993), pp. 120–1; and, further, pp. 161, 173–5.

26. "Discourse concerning . . . Satire," *Works* IV: 46–8.

27. See Steven N. Zwicker, *Politics and Language in Dryden's Poetry* (Princeton, 1984), pp. 146–58.

28. See Bernard Schilling, *Dryden and the Conservative Myth: A Reading of "Absalom and Achitophel"* (New Haven, 1961); and Ronald Paulson, *The Fictions of Satire* (New Haven, 1967), pp. 120–8.

29. Harth, *Pen for a Party*, pp. 172–7.

30. See Zwicker, *Politics and Language*, chapter 6.

31. On Dryden's linking in his *Fables* of the "Epistle to the Duchess of Ormond" and his translation of Chaucer's "Palemon and Arcite" to William III's wars in Ireland, see Miner, *Dryden's Poetry*, pp. 293–4.

32. Cf. the epistle "To . . . John Driden," where Dryden directs an innuendo at William III, whose wars seemed never-ending:

> When once the *Persian* king was put to flight,
> The weary *Macedons* refused to fight:
> Themselves their own Mortality confess'd;
> And left the son of *Jove* to quarrel for the rest.
>
> (lines 160–3)

33. R. J. Kaufman sees this as exemplary of the "terminal tragedy" of all Dryden's heroic plays. As Kaufman has noted, tragedy divides into two aspects – the satiric technique for analyzing human faults ("for satirizing deluded motivation") and "the sense of human greatness actively transforming its world" (89). Jacobean tragedy had been of this sort: satire was conveyed by a Vendice, Bosola, or Malevole. See R. J. Kaufmann, "On the Poetics of Terminal Tragedy: Dryden's *All for Love*," in *Dryden: A Collection of Critical Essays*, ed. Bernard Schilling (Englewood Cliffs, NJ, 1963), pp. 86–94.

34. Brown, *English Dramatic Form, 1660–1760* (New Haven, 1981), p. 85.

35. The satiric structure of *All for Love* is best seen looking back from its burlesque in John Gay's *Beggar's Opera* (1728). Honor, Ventidius, and the Roman Antony, declined into the Egyptian Antony, now reemerges as Gay's Captain Macheath – and, worse, the "honor" of Jenny and Jemmy Twitcher. Duty has degenerated from the imperial Octavius to the mercantile Peachum. Love has slipped from Antony–Cleopatra down to Macheath–Polly and the romances he feeds her.

4

LAURA BROWN

Dryden and the imperial imagination

Imperial rivalry and *An Essay of Dramatic Poesy*

The political and economic processes that generated England's first era of imperial expansion might seem distant from the literary culture of Dryden's age, in which we often think of aesthetic questions such as the status of classical literature or the problem of the imitation of "Nature" as more prominent in contemporary debate. But even Dryden's most influential work on aesthetics, *An Essay of Dramatic Poesy* (1668), often considered the pioneering instance of modern literary criticism, gives us a clear signal of the intersection of historical events with Dryden's literary production. Written in the form of an extended debate on contemporary literature among a group of friends – Eugenius, Crites, Lisideius, and Neander – the essay *Of Dramatic Poesy* compares classical and modern drama, and contemporary French and English drama, exploring topics like the effects of formal rules, the qualities of plot and character, the relative importance of aesthetic pleasure and moral instruction, the nature of tragedy and comedy, and the roles of passion, taste, and prosody. But Dryden gives his literary essay a specific historical setting. According to the opening story that explains the occasion for the debate, the group of friends assembles on a barge on the Thames, on 3 June 1665, where they have gone in order to hear more clearly the "distant thunder" of the cannon from the encounter of the English and Dutch fleets in the English Channel, engaged in the battle of Lowestoft, which ultimately saw an English victory under the Duke of York. Their literary debate is represented as a means of passing time while awaiting the outcome of the battle. At least in the frame tale of the *Essay*, imperial history takes precedence over literature, providing the significant occasion against which the literary debate is set.

Dryden's imaginary literary discussants were the witnesses of a major battle in the second Anglo-Dutch war, an instance of the long-term rivalry between England, the Netherlands, and France for imperial power over the global networks of commerce – a rivalry that marked the first age of European imperialism. The war between England and the Netherlands began during the Protectorate in 1652 and concluded in 1678 with the effectual replacement of the Netherlands by France and England as the major imperial powers of Europe. At stake for all three nations was the lucrative trade with East India, West Africa, and the new world. The second Anglo-Dutch war had begun with the English capture of Dutch possessions in West Africa and New York. Its settlement at the Treaty of Breda in 1667, a few weeks before the publication of *An Essay of Dramatic Poesy*, gave the English those territorial conquests, in exchange for a modification of English trade laws. But the commercial power of the Dutch was already extensively undermined. The opening lines of Dryden's essay, then, lay claim to a particular historical moment, to a distinctive international rivalry, and to a specific national destiny:

> It was that memorable day, in the first Summer of the late war, when our Navy engag'd the Dutch: a day wherein the two most mighty and best appointed Fleets which any age had ever seen, disputed the command of the greater half of the Globe, the commerce of Nations, and the riches of the Universe.
>
> (*Works* XVII: 8)

The "riches of the Universe" spread themselves before the English imagination, even in these early decades of imperial rivalry, and even in the context of this comparatist aesthetic tract. In fact, Dryden's preamble encourages us to connect this aesthetic debate with "the commerce of Nations," and the inception of the mode of discourse and the discipline that we now understand as literary criticism, with the imperial imagination. The comparison of "Ancient" or classical with "Modern" or contemporary poetry, with which the *Essay* begins, sets up a detailed analytical apparatus. The contestants utilize specific critical applications of ideas about formal rules and plot structure, linguistic usage and social custom, imitation and originality, delight and instruction, characters and character types, wit and passion. This apparatus is then brought to bear, in the middle of the *Essay*, on the nationalist question of the superiority of English to French drama. Lisideius prefaces this second phase of the debate with a clear allusion to the historical rivalry of the two nations: "I am at all times ready to defend the honour of my Countrey against the *French*, and to maintain, we are as well able to vanquish them with our Pens as our Ancestors have been with their swords" (*Works* XVII: 33). The "Pens" of today stand in the place of English imperial power, which is seen in a continuum – from the Hundred Years War and Henry V's victory over the French at the Battle of Agincourt, to the contemporary contest of imperial powers in Europe. In Dryden's imperial imagination, the literary rivalry with France, which is at the center of the essay *Of Dramatic Poesy*, is the equivalent of the literal battle with the Dutch, which gives the essay its frame.

As the argument in support of the English drama against the French takes shape in the second half of the essay, broader lines are drawn, that connect international rivalry with corollary historical changes. English writing is represented as the equivalent of English imperial expansion, and both are seen to be built upon the major shifts in philosophical and scientific thinking that mark this era. Eugenius defines this position by taking up Crites's notion of the "perfection" of modern thought and applying it to both arts and sciences together. Crites has asked:

> is it not evident in these last hundred years . . . that almost a new Nature has been reveal'd to us? that . . . more useful Experiments in Philosophy have been made, more Noble Secrets in Optics, Medicine, Anatomy, Astronomy discover'd, than in all those credulous and doting ages from *Aristotle* to us? so true it is, that nothing spreads more fast than Science, when rightly and generally cultivated. (*Works* XVII: 15)

For Eugenius, then, "it follows that Poesie and other Arts may with the same pains, arrive still neerer to perfection" (*Works* XVII: 22). The "perfection" that Eugenius defends is the comprehensive perfection of modernity, of which imperial expansion was the geographical manifestation. The detailed and sustained critical analysis that follows in Dryden's essay is unique at this stage in the history of European writing about imaginative literature; and it is marshaled to support the aesthetic equivalent of an imperial rivalry.

Dryden's treatment of the English relation to mercantile capitalist expansion, and his projection of a national imperial destiny that was to become a nearly unanimous topic of literary celebration in the first half of the eighteenth century, is apparent at various moments and in various modes elsewhere in his poetic and dramatic production. These aspects of Dryden's corpus demonstrate the ways in which the self-conscious literary artist engaged with early ideas of the prospect of English imperial power, but they can also show us the complex unconscious rationalizations for and anxieties about empire that mark the formation of the imperialist imagination in its early stages, and that shaped the structures of imperialist ideology as it came to prominence in the literary culture of England in the first decades of the eighteenth century. In other words, Dryden's corpus can give us a glimpse of the ways in which a new understanding of national identity entered into and emanated from literary culture.

A poetry of national expansion

Much of Dryden's poetic production, especially before the Revolution of 1688, could be described as topical political poetry, which engaged directly with the major figures and events of the day. Dryden's career began almost simultaneously with the Restoration of King Charles II in 1660, an event that could be seen as the penultimate stage in the century-long English revolution, in which absolutist monarchy was replaced by parliamentary rule, and an isolationist foreign policy by economic imperialism. Dryden's poems on the death of Oliver Cromwell, the return and coronation of Charles II, the Popish Plot, the Duke of Monmouth, and other contemporary figures and events, make assumptions and projections about a global future for the English nation that become part of the story that English imaginative literature invents and promulgates throughout the first period of British imperial expansion, from the Restoration to the mid-eighteenth century. In his poems on Charles II, for instance, Dryden praises King Charles for a special relationship to the sea – the contemporary medium of mercantile expansion. For example, in *To His Sacred Maiesty, A Panegyrick on His Coronation* (1661), King Charles is, according to Dryden, "Born to command the Mistress of the Seas," a "blue Empire" over which his thoughts, like his power, is seen to extend (*Works* 1: 35, lines 99–100). In the last verse paragraph of *Astrea Redux* (1660), celebrating the king's return to England in 1660, Dryden projects a prosperous future for Charles II specifically through the evocation of mercantile capitalist expansion:

> Abroad your Empire shall no Limits know,
> But like the Sea in boundless Circles flow.
> Your much lov'd fleet shall with a wide Command
> Besiege the petty Monarchs of the Land:
> And as Old Time his Off-spring swallow'd down
> Our Ocean in its depths all Seas shall drown.
> (*Works* 1: 30, lines 298–303)

Here we can see in Dryden's image of "Our Ocean" an early form of the theme that becomes an insistent chorus in the poetry on the English nation of the first half of the eighteenth century, that of the "British ocean," a figure that "drowns" or subsumes all other seas, and that confers upon Britain the effectual ownership of international shipping, along with the profit and power that increasingly accrued to that economic sector. In his works on the reign of Charles II, Dryden projected an imperial future that was taken up in the poetry of the early eighteenth century by Alexander Pope, Thomas Tickell, James Thomson, Edward Young, and others.[1] Some of the central rhetorical aspects of the imperialist panegyric of the eighteenth century are built upon the foundations laid in Dryden's poetry of the 1660s.

The very prominent image of a benevolent "empire of the seas" that later comes to characterize England's imperial power evokes the same figures of "circling" and "command," and the same celebration of a limitless "watery" empire that Dryden describes for Charles II. For instance, in Thomas Tickell's poem on the Peace of Utrecht, *On the Prospect of Peace* (1712), we can see how Dryden's language is subsequently developed and extended:

> From Albion's cliffs thy [Queen Anne's] wide-extended hand
> Shall o'er the main to far Peru command;
> So vast a tract whose wide domain shall run,
> Its circling skies shall see no setting sun.
> . . . .
> Round the vast ball thy new dominions chain
> Thy watery kingdoms, and control the main;
> . . . .
> On either bank the land its master knows,
> And in the midst the subject ocean flows.[2]

The most famous and long-lived example of this very figure, of course, is the familiar couplet from James Thomson's poem: "Rule Britannia! Britannia rules the waves! / Britons never shall be slaves."[3]

Dryden's early poetry on the monarchy thus suggests an imaginative precedent for a powerful ideological formation that becomes central to British imperialist thought. But ironically, the Stuart monarchs who were the focus of Dryden's poetic praise and political allegiance during the period from 1660 to 1688 were weak and reactionary figures, whose attempts to recreate a prior absolutist era impeded rather than promoted the national trajectory toward empire, a trajectory that finally found firmer footing after the final stage of the English revolution, the deposing of James II in 1688 in favor of William of Orange. In this sense, Dryden's role as the harbinger of the major subgenre of celebratory nationalist poetry is strangely paradoxical.[4] We can trace a similar paradox in his major poem on the English nation, *Annus Mirabilis*.

The imperial prospect of *Annus Mirabilis*

Dryden's imperialist imagination is most strongly projected in *Annus Mirabilis. The Year of Wonders, 1666* (1667), a long poem on the topic of the Anglo-Dutch war and the Great Fire that destroyed a large part of the City of London in the same period. The evident aim of this poem is to redefine empire in terms of benevolent economic expansion, in contrast with the selfish and monopolistic Dutch trade policies.[5] Dryden thus begins with a criticism of Dutch trade monopoly: "Trade, which like bloud should circularly flow, / Stop'd in their Channels, found its freedom lost" (*Works* I: 59, lines 5–6) – in other words, the natural freedom of a benevolent system of trade was destroyed when the Dutch asserted monopolistic control. As a result, the various riches of the world were diverted to a single consumer:

> For them [the Dutch] alone the Heav'ns had kindly heat,
>   In Eastern Quarries ripening precious Dew:
> For them the *Idumæan* Balm did sweat,
>   And in hot *Ceilon* Spicy Forrests grew.[6]
>
> The Sun but seem'd the Lab'rer of their Year;
>   Each wexing Moon suppli'd her watry store,
> To swell those Tides, which from the Line did bear
>   Their brim-full Vessels to the *Belg'an* shore.
>   (*Works* I: 60, lines 9–16)

These stanzas argue that the "watery empire" that should be British is occupied by Dutch ships, whose movements only "to the Belgian shore" are a sign of a violation of natural order and freedom. The poem describes English enterprise, scientific progress, and benevolent trade as an antidote to these violations, and a sign of the advancement of learning and civilization, sponsored by the British imperialism:

> Of all who since have us'd the open Sea,
>   Than the bold *English* none more fame have won:
> Beyond the Year, and out of Heav'n's high-way,
>   They make discoveries where they see no Sun.
>   (*Works* I: 83–4, lines 637–40)

These English "discoveries," in the new era of British imperial dominance, will be used generously to benefit other nations, in a contrast to the selfish monopoly of the Dutch:

> But what so long in vain, and yet unknown,
>   By poor man-kind's benighted wit is sought,
> Shall in this Age to *Britain* first be shown,
>   And hence be to admiring Nations taught.
>
> The Ebbs of Tydes and their mysterious flow,
>   We, as Arts' Elements, shall understand:
> And as by Line upon the Ocean go,
>   Whose paths shall be familiar as the Land.
> . . . .

Then, we upon our Globes last verge shall go,
And view the Ocean leaning on the sky:
From thence our rolling Neighbors we shall know,
And on the Lunar world securely pry.
(*Works* 1: 84, lines 641–8, 653–6)

In these stanzas, Dryden evokes the advances in empirical science sponsored by the Royal Society, especially the work on astronomy, chronometry, and navigation that led to the precise calculation of latitude. According to Dryden, these new discoveries, consequences of English mercantile prowess, will be taught to an "admiring" European audience. But more important, and more broadly, Dryden takes a further step, extending his fantasy of English benevolence beyond the European nations to the world at large:

Instructed ships shall sail to quick Commerce,
By which remotest Regions are alli'd:
Which makes one City of the Universe;
Where some may gain, and all may be suppli'd.
(*Works* 1: 84, lines 649–52)

Everyone engaged with the British merchant marine is imagined to participate in this benevolent imperialist fantasy, by which the world is united, and commerce is redefined as a generous exchange of goods that evens out the wealth of the globe. The ideology enunciated here by Dryden is a prominent dimension of English imperialist thought in the first half of the eighteenth century. One of its most explicit spokesmen is George Lillo, who eloquently describes the same fantasy over half a century later, in his popular middle class drama, *The London Merchant* (1731):

the method of merchandise . . . is founded in reason and the nature of things . . . it has promoted humanity . . . arts, industry, peace, and plenty; by mutual benefits diffusing mutual love from pole to pole . . . those countries where trade is promoted and encouraged do not make discoveries to destroy but to improve mankind – by love and friendship to tame the fierce and polish the most savage; to teach them the advantages of honest traffic by taking from them, with their own consent, their useless superfluities, and giving them in return what, from their ignorance in manual arts, their situation, or some other accident, they stand in need of . . . The populous East, luxuriant, abounds with glittering gems, bright pearls, aromatic spices, and health-restoring drugs. The late found western world glows with unnumbered veins of gold and silver ore. On every climate and on every country Heaven has bestowed some good peculiar to itself. It is the industrious merchant's business to collect the various blessings of each soil and climate and, with the product of the whole, to enrich his native country.[7]

Dryden's early development of these images of benevolent commerce focus on the City of London, in a way that also presages later literature. Though he claims in *Annus Mirabilis* that commerce will make "one City of the Universe," that "one City" looks suspiciously like the British capital. In fact the strange superimposition of an imaginary global city upon the very real City of London is also typical of imperialist apologia as the tradition emerges partly through Dryden's early adumbration. For Alexander Pope, in the best-known imperialist poem of the early eighteenth century, *Windsor Forest* (1713), the port of the Thames becomes a gathering place for the peoples of the world who "launch forth" toward London:

> The Time shall come, when free as Seas or Wind
> Unbounded *Thames* shall flow for all Mankind,
> Whole Nations enter with each swelling Tyde,
> And Seas but join the Regions they divide;
> Earth's distant Ends our Glory shall behold,
> And the new World launch forth to seek the Old,
> Then Ships of uncouth Form shall stem the Tyde,
> And Feather'd People crowd my wealthy Side,
> And naked Youths and painted Chiefs admire
> Our Speech, our Colour, and our strange Attire![8]

In this global fiction, the "new world" comes to the old, and all the nations engaged with British trade crowd the imperial city. "Admiration" – with its sense of wonder as well as approval – results and is attributed not only to the European nations, but to the world at large. London has become the world and Dryden's evocation of the "admiring nations" has become a global tribute to British power.

For Dryden's *Annus Mirabilis*, then, London is the geographical and ideological centerpiece. The poem envisages a new imperial City of London, rising from the ashes of the Great Fire, that will be the center of a commercial empire as great in its humanity and benevolence as that of the Dutch was in its selfishness and cruelty:

> More great than humane, now, and more *August,*
>   New deifi'd she from her fires does rise:
> Her widening streets on new foundations trust,
>   And, opening, into larger parts she flies.
>
> Before, she like some Shepherdess did show,
>   Who sate to bathe her by a River's side;
> Not answering to her fame, but rude and low,
>   Nor taught the beauteous Arts of Modern pride.

> Now, like a Maiden Queen, she will behold,
> From her high Turrets, hourly Sutors come:
> The East with Incense, and the West with Gold,
> Will stand, like Suppliants, to receive her doom.
> (*Works* 1: 103–4, lines 1177–88)

As the proud center of a global network, the modern City of London is for Dryden the site of a fantasy of accumulation, to which goods from a global economic system flow and personified exotic figures – the "East" and "West" – submit to British power.

The next step in Dryden's construction of the ideology of British trade supremacy is the claim that the voluntarism of the new economic system will bring world peace; here he helps to promulgate the idea of the *pax britannica* – a neoclassical equivalent to the *pax romana* and a prominent catchword in the imperialist apologia of the early eighteenth century:

> Our pow'rful Navy shall no longer meet,
> The wealth of *France* or *Holland* to invade:
> The beauty of this Town, without a Fleet,
> From all the world shall vindicate her Trade.
> (*Works* 1: 104, lines 1201–4)

Britain will need no naval force, since the world will come voluntarily to London. And even the merchants themselves, drawn to the beauty of the imperial power center, will remain in this new cosmopolitan city, using it as the sole destination of their trading circuit, and then presumably awaiting the "suppliants" bearing their exotic merchandise:

> The vent'rous Merchant, who design'd more far,
> And touches on our hospitable shore:
> Charm'd with the splendour of this Northern Star,
> Shall here unlade him, and depart no more.
> (*Works* 1: 104, lines 1197–1200)

The idea that the metropolitan center will serve as a kind of microcosm for or projection of the global trade network that generates British imperial power and prosperity involves a contradiction for Dryden and for the numerous imperialist poets who followed him, a contradiction in which the claim of global peace is just the most obvious component. Of course the extension of British imperial power to the new world, the exploitation of the slave trade, and the settlement of the Caribbean and the American colonies were not peaceable enterprises. But the image of a metropolis in which all the material desires of an expansionist culture are met *in situ*, without the need for travel or movement, is another peculiar aspect of this ideological structure, which Dryden helps to generate in *Annus Mirabilis*. In this period to "rule the waves" could also mean, paradoxically, never to leave English shores, as if England had actually become the world. Joseph Addison supports this fantasy in his image of British prosperity in a periodical essay on this topic in the *Spectator*: "whilst we enjoy the remotest Products of the North and South, we are free from those Extremities of Weather which gave them Birth; That our Eyes are refreshed with the green Fields of *Britain*, at the same time that our Palates are feasted with Fruits that rise between the Tropicks."[9] Pope's *Windsor Forest* exploits the same idea when it describes the arrival in London of the various peoples of the globe, "Feather'd," "naked," and "painted" in a way that brings the vividness and variety of the human form to be admired by an English eye.

Another fundamental paradox structures the imperialist imagination. Dryden's *Annus Mirabilis* provides an early example of an anxiety about the fate of empire that also becomes prominent in early eighteenth-century poetry. For Dryden this anxiety is implicit in the evocation of danger and risk that accompanies his representation of the new expansionist mode:

> Already we have conquer'd half the War,
>   And the less dang'rous part is left behind:
> Our trouble now is but to make them dare,
>   And not so great to vanquish as to find.
>
> Thus to the Eastern wealth through storms we go;
>   But now, the Cape once doubled, fear no more:
> A constant Trade-wind will securely blow,
>   And gently lay us on the Spicy shore.
>   (*Works* I: 104–5, lines 1209–16)

England has already "conquer'd half the War," so only the "less dang'rous part" is still left to pursue: the search and destroy missions of the English against the Dutch fleet. But "danger" is evoked here with an insistence that disturbs the tranquil success that Dryden seems to claim for the future. And in the next stanza, the last of the poem, Dryden compares England's progress toward imperial power to the merchant's voyage around the Cape of Good Hope, weathering the storms of that dangerous passage until the ship reaches the calm seas of the Indian Ocean. This image directly equates the progress of the merchant with the progress of the nation, mercantile expansion with national identity. But also it suggests an uneasiness about this future. The merchant's voyage is a dangerous and uncertain one, and the naming of the notorious geographical locale of its uncertainty – the Cape of Good Hope – creates a rhetorical resonance that would have been powerful in the period, and that became a trope in the later imperialist poetry of the eighteenth century.[10] The Cape of Good Hope embodied the risk of early modern mercantile adventurism; and though "hope" remains implicit in this passage, the evocation of the "Cape" would certainly have brought that idea to mind for contemporary readers. In counterposing the most dangerous passage for contemporary shipping with the image of a secure destination, this stanza subtly generates a rhetorical paradox between "fear" and "hope," a paradox that was typical of many poems on British imperial expansion after Dryden. For Edward Young, for instance, in *Ocean: An Ode* (1728), "all are tost" and "most are lost" on the "restless seas" of British imperial supremacy, but amidst that danger he wishes for "a noiseless shore, unruffled homes."[11] In fact, at the time of Dryden's composition of *Annus Mirabilis*, England's imperial future was not guaranteed. The wars with the Dutch continued until 1678, and the contest with France lasted throughout the eighteenth century. But even when England's power seemed more secure, the ambivalence about British imperial destiny, or the unconscious paradox in its representation, remained a component of imperialist poetry throughout the first half of the eighteenth century. Dryden gave this paradox one of its earliest expressions.

A drama of imperial nostalgia

Dryden's imperial imagination found a very different form in the theatre. In the decade of the 1660s, Dryden wrote a group of plays that made him the preeminent dramatist of a unique subgenre, the heroic drama, a form distinctive to the culture of the Restoration. These stylized, proto-operatic works were performed with elaborate stage machinery before a coterie elite audience. Plays like Dryden's *Indian Queen* (1664), *Indian Emperor* (1665), and *Aureng-Zebe* (1675), William Davenant's *Siege of Rhodes* (1656, 1661) and *The Cruelty of the Spaniards in Peru* (1658), Elkanah Settle's *Empress of Morocco* (1673) and *Conquest of China* (1676), Aphra Behn's *Abdelazer* (1676) and *Widow Ranter* (1689), Mary Pix's *Ibrahim* (1696), and Delarivier Manley's *Royal Mischief* (1696), among others, are notable for their engagement with a global imagination. These plays typically portrayed exotic characters and scenes – from India, Moorish Spain, and Morocco, to Mexico, the Caribbean, and China – and often treated the topic of lost, decaying, or declining empires. Though the period of their original composition was short-lived, and though they tend to be associated with the political and cultural reaction of the Restoration, some of these plays remained in the theatrical repertory through the first half of the eighteenth century, and their depiction of distant lands influenced the representation of exotic peoples in English literary culture beyond the Restoration.

The prominence of a global setting in this subgenre is not easy to explain. The exotic sites and characters, especially in the new world, are sometimes used as a way of attacking Dutch and Spanish colonialism, by dramatizing its cruelties and contrasting the benevolent motives of the British. The representations of political power and the challenges to monarchy serve in many instances as an allusion to contemporary English politics and the problematic situation of Charles II's anachronistic absolutist court. But on other occasions, the elaborately staged representation of the exotic in these plays must have served simply as an escape from the complexities and anxieties of recent English history.[12] Dryden, however, does not use his major heroic plays solely to escape from history. These works engage with questions of empire through the affective route of heroic nostalgia, an indirect but peculiarly powerful imaginative encounter with imperialism.

Dryden's major works of heroic drama include *The Indian Queen* (1664), *The Indian Emperor* (1665), *Tyrannic Love* (1669), *The Conquest of Granada* (1670), *Aureng-Zebe* (1675), and *All for Love* (1677). Though these plays do not focus on British imperial expansion, they are dominated by representations of imperial rivalry, stage warfare, and, perhaps most notably, the tragic ends of empires – themes that were, in this period, the common parlance of the historical imagination. *The Conquest of Granada* stages the last phase in the expulsion of Muslim power from Europe. *All for Love* retells Shakespeare's *Antony and Cleopatra*, the story of the demise of Egypt and its queen and the victory of Octavius Caesar over Mark Antony. And *The Indian Emperor* describes the last days of the "flourishing Empire" of Mexico (*Works* IX: 27), when the European invaders, Cortez the "Spanish General" and his "Commanders," Vasquez and Pizarro, conquer the heroic Montezuma.

In all these plays, the conventional opposition of love and honor, central to the mode of heroic romance, serves as the formal and rhetorical framework for a repeated evocation of imperial loss. The love and honor paradigm that dominates this subgenre poses a simple structure of rules for exemplary behavior that tends to generate a paradox for the primary characters and a crisis for the plot: honor requires the strict performance of duty to friend, father, king, or country, and love demands unqualified allegiance to a lover and at the same time a perfect record of honor. Thus, when love and honor are at odds, the choice of honor results in the loss of love – because of the failure of allegiance to the lover, but that failure can itself constitute a loss of honor. Similarly, the choice of love results in the loss of honor – because of the failure of duty to friend, father, king, or country, but that loss of honor in itself entails the loss of love. In other words, in the peculiar formal paradox that characterizes this drama, the choice of honor can result in the loss of honor, and the choice of love in the loss of love.

This paradox is the core of the heroic drama's nostalgic affect, as it structures a situation from which its protagonist has no exit, personal or historical. Antony in *All for Love* is caught between the claims of empire and his love for Cleopatra. Alternately, he pursues a "brave Roman fate" (*Works* XIII: v. 180), presenting himself as an honorable soldier in battle against Octavius and defending his hold on the Roman empire and Cleopatra's Egypt together, and, on the other hand, he repudiates these pursuits in the name of love:

> Faith, Honour, Virtue, all good things forbid,
> That I should go from her, who sets my love
> Above the price of Kingdoms! Give, you Gods,
> Give to your Boy, your *Cæsar*,
> This Rattle of a Globe to play withal,
> This Gew-gau World, and put him cheaply off:
> I'll not be pleas'd with less than *Cleopatra*.
>
> (II. 441–7)

The paradox of Antony's personal dilemma, and the crisis of the plot, is felt throughout the play in the continual evocation of historical loss – both of Rome and of Egypt: Antony's battle for the Roman empire is "past recovery" (I.50), and

> *Ægypt* has been; our latest hour has come:
> The Queen of Nations, from her ancient seat,
> Is sunk forever in the dark Abyss:
> Time has unrolled her glories to the last,
> And now closed up the Volume.
>
> (V. 71–5).

The rhetoric of imperial loss directly parallels that which describes the protagonists' love crisis, which achieves an identical nostalgia: "But now 'tis past" (II. 28), "Now 'tis past forever" (II. 217), "What ages have we lived!" (V. 393).

This same heroic nostalgia characterizes Dryden's earlier *Indian Emperor*, in which a more diverse cast of characters enacts a more complex and intersecting series of love and honor paradoxes, which, nevertheless, mirror the play's affective representation of imperial loss and regret. Cortez and Montezuma are parallel heroic figures, of different cultures, whose honor is bound up with their respective historical empires. In *The Indian Emperor*, the fall of Mexico is technically brought about by the direct military actions of the unscrupulous and cruel Spanish characters, Vasquez and Pizarro, who act to instigate battles without the direct permission of the admirable Cortez, when accident and oversight remove them from his direct supervision. Cortez's sympathies lie with the Mexicans, both because of his natural heroic affinity with Montezuma, and because of his love for Montezuma's daughter, Cydaria. Thus the trope of the torture of Montezuma and his pagan "priest," so prominent in the historical accounts of the time, is represented in this play as a kind of vigilante action by Pizarro, who is halted in the act and reprimanded by Cortez for his cruelty. In the logic of the play, the real plot crises are generated by the love and honor paradoxes, which play out in a series of rivalries centered on the two heroic protagonists: Montezuma loves Almeria, but she loves Cortez; Cortez loves Cydaria, but she is also loved by Orbellan.

These paradoxes produce Montezuma's death and the conquest of Mexico, and they are represented through the same affective rhetoric that characterizes Antony's end. The familiar refrain, "'Tis past!" (*Works* IX: v. ii. 239), recurs in the last scene of *The Indian Emperor*, as the crucial Mexican characters kill themselves and their empire passes away. Montezuma stabs himself, upon losing Almeria and his empire to Cortez, and dies with the words, "Already mine is past" (v. ii. 242). His death, though it is staged as a consequence of the love conflicts of the play, is strongly represented as an imperial loss. To Cortez's offer of Spanish clemency, he replies:

> No, *Spaniard*, know, he who to Empire born,
> Lives to be less, deserves the Victor's scorn:
> Kings and their Crowns have but one Destiny:
> Power is their Life, when that expires they dye.
>
> (v. i. 226–9)

As a martyred king, Montezuma clearly evokes the royal martyrdom of immediate English history, the execution of Charles I in 1649. When Cortez rescues Montezuma from the rack, he lays claim to the same patient suffering that was popularly attributed to Charles at his death:

> Am I so low that you should pity bring,
> And give an Infants Comfort to a King?
> Ask these if I have once unmanly groan'd;
> Or ought have done deserving to be moan'd.
>
> (v. ii. 119–22)

Charles, too, was said to have "suffered as an Heroick Champion . . . by his patient enduring the many insolent affronts of this subtile, false, cruel, and most implacable Generation."[13] The parallel between Charles I and Montezuma serves to bring heroic nostalgia home to England, and shows us

72

that the loss and regret so powerfully evoked in these plays is not as distant as their exotic settings might make it appear.

The paradox of the imperial imagination

We could see in these heroic plays that other side of the coin of Dryden's imperial imagination, which we glimpsed in *Annus Mirabilis*, where the connection of hope with fear seems to reflect an anxiety about imperial destiny, or even an ambivalence about the peace and benevolism that accompanied the imperialist apologia of the period. Dryden's major heroic plays figure empire not as a secure and peaceful future, but as a contingent and transitory stage in a self-limiting process that leads to inevitable loss. This evocation of loss reflects the early modern engagement with the histories of past empires, both classical and modern. The celebration of ancient imperial cultures led directly to an analysis of their failures and their fall. In fact, neoclassical writers were struck by both the power and the transitory character of the great ancient empires. From the biblical tradition, they were aware of the rise and fall of Egypt, Assyria, and Babylonia. From more narrowly classical sources, they could read about Persia, Greece, Egypt again, Carthage, and above all Rome. It was Rome, the city of Caesar and St. Peter, that provided the dominant cultural model from the early Middle Ages through at least the end of the nineteenth century. And this fascination was more than a curiosity of intellectual history. Other empires, before and after, had dominated much of the Mediterranean. It was Rome, most strikingly in the conquests of Julius Caesar, that had drawn the inland regions of the west into the orbit of the universal empire and thus paved the way for the emergence of Europe – culturally, economically, and linguistically. Yet that profound legacy made the collapse of the founding political system all the more sobering. In this sense, imperial demise is a central subtext of Renaissance classicism and eighteenth-century neoclassicism. Dryden's plays show how that subtext informs the imperial imagination, even on its upward trajectory in the Restoration and early eighteenth century, as England moves toward a position of dominance among the European imperial nations.

Dryden's works reflect the contradictions of contemporary imperialist ideology with a special sensitivity that arises, in part, from Dryden's own paradoxical relationship to the historical and cultural forces of his time. Dryden was a self-supporting author in an age of patronage; a proponent of the new science but a student of classicism; a Stuart loyalist who accepted the Restoration settlement; a defender of the old metaphysics but an advocate of a private faith; a proponent of past ideals whose thinking was bound to a present reality; and a conservative who invariably looked to the future.

The complexity of Dryden's representation of empire is of a piece with the paradoxes of his personal historical situation. But those complexities – especially the evocation of anxiety, fear, and loss – give us an insight into future images of empire, and a way of uncovering the ambivalence even in the celebrations of empire in the literature of the first half of the eighteenth century. John Dryden helps to shape the literary praise of empire that characterizes England's first age of expansion, but he also provides a paradigm for its critique.

NOTES

1. See C. A. Moore, "Whig Panegyric Verse, 1700–1760," *PMLA* 41 (1926), 362–401. David S. Shields describes a group of poems focusing specifically on the British "empire of the seas" in *Oracles of Empire: Poetry, Politics, and Commerce in British America, 1690–1750* (Chicago, 1990), p. 25.
2. Thomas Tickell, *On the Prospect of Peace*, in *The Works of the English Poets* (London, 1810), vol I, p. 105.
3. From the masque *Alfred*, by James Thomson and David Mallet (1740).
4. Steven N. Zwicker provides a close reading of the "technique of denial and misrepresentation" that for him defines Dryden's poetic form as well as his characterization of the Stuart monarchy in these works. See *Politics and Language in Dryden's Poetry: The Arts of Disguise* (Princeton, 1984), esp. pp. 39–43.
5. Michael McKeon's essential study of *Annus Mirabilis* provides an account of the poem's ideological function in supporting national unity and commercial power despite the political debates of the day. *Politics and Poetry in Restoration England: The Case of Dryden's "Annus Mirabilis"* (Cambridge, 1975).
6. Dryden's note: "*In Eastern Quarries, &c. Precious Stones at first are Dew, condens'd and harden'd by the warmth of the Sun, or subteranean Fires.*"
7. George Lillo, *The London Merchant*, ed. William H. McBurney (Lincoln, 1965), III. i. 1–28.
8. Alexander Pope, *Windsor Forest*, in *Poetry and Prose of Alexander Pope*, ed. Aubrey Williams (Boston, 1969), lines 397–406.
9. Joseph Addison, *The Spectator*, no. 69 (19 May 1711), ed. Donald F. Bond (Oxford, 1965), vol. I, p. 296. See James H. Bunn, "The Aesthetics of British Mercantilism," *New Literary History* 11 (1980), 303–21 for a fuller account of idea of the location of world trade on English soil.
10. See Laura Brown, *Fables of Modernity: Literature and Culture in the English Eighteenth Century* (Ithaca, 2001), chapter 2.
11. Edward Young, *The Poetical Works of Edward Young* (London: Bell and Daldy, 1866), vol. II, p. 165.
12. On the exotic subjects of heroic drama, see Bridget Orr, *Empire on the English Stage, 1660–1714* (Cambridge, 2001).
13. William Dugdale, *A Short View of the Late Troubles in England* (Oxford, 1681), pp. 371–5.

5

PAUL DAVIS

Dryden and the invention of Augustan culture

The idea that between the Restoration and the middle of the eighteenth century England enjoyed an "Augustan age" may soon be a thing of the past. Historians were the first to jettison the concept, and by and large literary critics have now followed suit: twenty years ago there would have been a *Cambridge Companion to Augustan Literature*; today we have the *Cambridge Companion to English Literature, 1650–1740*. Some have flung off the term Augustan like a straitjacket, delighted to be free at last to stress tendencies in the culture of Restoration and early eighteenth-century England which might be thought of as un- or even anti-Augustan: the persistence of a republican idiom; the development of a rhetoric of sublimity; the rise of British literature (though, as we shall see, the first two of these fall within the pale of what Dryden understood by Augustanism).[1] Others have abandoned it more reluctantly like a favorite item of clothing now sadly rather moth-eaten and unpresentable, knowing it to be true that the careers of a number of the central writers of the period were shaped by their engagements with the culture of Augustan Rome, but fearing that to point out as much may be to give these writers the kiss of death where modern readers are concerned. First, there is the sheer look of the word: "august" is something only the headmasters of old-fashioned boarding-schools want to be. Then there are the pejorative connotations which have attached themselves to it like foul-smelling fungus: of dreary backward-lookingness; of aesthetic conservatism; of toadying to royalty. No wonder the contributors to the volume of essays published to commemorate the tercentenary of Dryden's death in the year 2000 mostly drew a veil over his Augustan affiliations, concentrating instead on such matters as his "creative allegiances" to Latin poets of the post-Augustan age, his relations with Homer and Milton, those twin pillars of anti-Augustan poetics, and his self-fashioning after un-Augustan prototypes of the poet as a figure of "amoral, manipulative" power.[2]

This chapter aims to rehabilitate Augustanism as a framework for understanding Dryden's mentality and career; to show that Augustan culture as

Dryden understood and mediated it was a complex and radical invention. As well as being amongst the most historically minded of our first-rank poets – Charles II and James II chose wisely in appointing him not only Poet Laureate but also Historiographer Royal – Dryden was the last of them to make a sustained effort to live up to the ideal of the poet as shaper of his national culture which had been promulgated by the Renaissance humanists. In seeking to interpret what he termed the "giddy turns" of his age, that prolonged series of after-shocks of the Civil War we somewhat inaptly call the Restoration, his principal resource was comparison with the post-civil-war era in Roman culture, the epochal period in which Augustus transformed Rome from republic to principate. But Dryden did not use that resource unthinkingly or tendentiously, failing to notice or else screening out the individuating characteristics of each culture. He did not seek to clone Augustan Rome in Restoration England. On the contrary, his sense of the relatedness between the two cultures was informed by the principles of dynamism and plurality which had been laid down in classical (not least Augustan) and Renaissance theories of poetic imitation.[3] The passages of Horace's *Ars Poetica*, the bible of Augustan poetics, which inculcate such principles were among those Dryden most liked to quote in his critical essays.[4] And he practiced what he preached from the first in his Augustan thinking and writing: if the poems Dryden wrote during the first half of his Augustan career (1660–88) were intended to justify the ways of the Stuarts to their subjects, they do not, as we shall see, any more than Milton's justification of God in *Paradise Lost*, function with the blinkered, monolithic efficiency of propaganda. But it was in the second half of that career (1688–1700), when Dryden was no longer the official mouthpiece of Stuart power but a kind of internal émigré from Williamite England, that the subtlety and severalness of his Augustan vision became increasingly apparent.

During these years, Dryden's contacts with Augustan culture mostly took the form of translation. This dimension of Dryden's Augustanism receives fuller treatment here than it has done in previous surveys of the subject, because Dryden's strongest claim to have invented Augustan culture in England rests on it. When Dryden hailed Charles II as a reincarnation of Augustus destined to preside over a golden age of arts and arms, he was doing nothing new: earlier English poets had said the same of Charles I, James I and even (despite her gender!) Elizabeth I. However, no previous English poet of Dryden's standing had translated so much of the work of Horace, Virgil, and Ovid, been so well-placed to shape English readers' understandings of the voices of the three primary poets of the Augustan age. And for Dryden it was emphatically voices plural: he never worked on one Augustan poet in isolation, but on a pair (Virgil and Ovid in the early

1690s) or else all three (in the early 1680s) concurrently; and he encouraged his readers to adopt a similarly pluralist outlook on Augustan culture by publishing many of the resulting translations in verse miscellanies, Virgilian eclogues beside Ovidian love elegies, Horatian odes alongside episodes from the *Aeneid*, and by distinguishing carefully between the styles of the three poets (as well as between theirs and those of pre- or post-Augustan poets like Lucretius and Claudian) in the series of prefaces he wrote for those miscellanies. Out of these translations, particularly those from Virgil in whose poems Dryden heard the entire variousness of Augustan culture sounded, emerges an Augustanism altogether more nuanced and radical than any of Dryden's contemporaries elaborated (and, one might add, than that promulgated by anti-Augustan critics today).[5] So much so in fact that the poets and commentators who followed Dryden proved in the main able or willing to sustain only selected portions of that vision: in a sense, Augustan culture, as invented by Dryden, died with Dryden.

On 22 April 1661, the eve of his coronation, Charles II processed through London from the Tower to Whitehall, passing beneath a series of triumphal arches encrusted with Virgilian mottoes identifying him as a new Augustus, and prophesying that the Restoration would be a second Augustan age. But he was not the first ruler of England in Dryden's lifetime to take up his power against a backdrop of Augustan pageantry. His father's executioner-in-chief Oliver Cromwell was. Significantly, Cromwell's rebirth as Augustus involved major complications. Dryden probably witnessed Cromwell's formal entry into London to be installed as Lord Protector on 8 February 1654; he certainly would have kept up with the storm of controversy it provoked about Augustus and Augustanism. The eye of this storm was Edmund Waller's *A Panegyrick to my Lord Protector* (1655) which, citing Augustan precedent, welcomed Cromwell's assumption of executive authority as a necessary means of restoring peace and security to the English polity after a period of virtual anarchy caused by divisions between the Army and parliament. This version of events was attacked on two fronts. Supporters of the Stuarts disputed Cromwell's Augustan pedigree, looking back to Charles I as the true English Augustus, and to the "halcyon days" of the personal rule between 1628 and 1640 as England's true Augustan peace. Meanwhile, republicans readily conceded Cromwell's title to the Augustan succession, but used it to bury rather than praise him: by concentrating power in his own hands and elevating himself over the legislature, like Augustus before him, Cromwell had, like Augustus before him, betrayed the cause of liberty. All sides in this debate were drawing on venerable traditions of commentary on the Augustan age: a panegyric tradition, deriving from certain passages of Horace and Virgil, which credited Augustus with having led Rome out of chaos into unparalleled stability and prosperity, thereby enabling the production of its culture's most golden achievements; and a tradition of invective, rooted in the writings of the historian Tacitus, which blamed Augustus for curtailing the freedoms which Romans had enjoyed under the republic, thereby sowing the seeds of their culture's decline toward decadence. Both traditions had long since been naturalized within the learned enclaves of English culture, mediated in particular through Renaissance commentaries on Virgil and humanist treatises of political philosophy like Bodin's *Six Livres de la Republique* (1576) and Lipsius's *De Constantia* (1584).[6] Now they locked horns in the nascent public sphere, the open arena of popular debate whose emergence following the collapse of censorship in the 1640s Milton had celebrated in *Areopagitica* (1644).

Even as Dryden was setting out on his poetic career, then, English culture was losing its innocence about the Augustan age. The readers of his first Augustan poems, *Astraea Redux* (1660) and *Annus Mirabilis* (1666), could not be counted on to consume their rhetoric passively. At first glance, Dryden might be accused of forgetting that fact. *Astraea Redux* has as its epigraph Virgil's prophecy of a coming golden age in the Fourth Eclogue, and concludes with an echo of the paean to Augustus from Book VI of the *Aeneid*, as if Dryden hoped by stationing these two bulwarks of Virgilian Augustanism at either end of the poem to establish a firewall around its panegyric narrative of the Restoration, to prevent that narrative from being hacked into by dissenting republican voices. But in fact the assured look of the Augustan allusions in Dryden's early public poems is somewhat deceptive. A curious reader, tracing those allusions back to their sources, would soon have discovered that the accolades they implied were provisional, as Renaissance critical theory insisted poetic accolades should be.[7] In *Annus Mirabilis*, when the English engage the Dutch fleet "And seeming to be stronger makes them so" (*Works* 1: 88, line 760), a note supplied by Dryden points out that the line imitates Virgil's phrase "Possunt quia posse videntur"; but that phrase occurs in Book V of the *Aeneid*, where it applies to the courage of the future Romans not in the heat of an actual sea fight but in the phony war of the boat-race during the funeral games for Anchises. Virgil's description of those games is shot through with a plangent sense of the disparity between such artificial joustings and the real battles which await Aeneas and his men in Italy. By extension, then, war with the (notoriously cowardly) Dutch is no more than a gentle prelude to the more intractable obstacles the English will have to surmount if they are to realize their Augustan destiny. If London is to arise from the ashes of the Great Fire "more August," vindicating its ancient name "Augusta," as Dryden prophesies it will at the climax of the poem (1177–80), it will take time and the sweat of English brows.

This double-plottedness of Augustan reference in *Astraea Redux* and *Annus Mirabilis*, Dryden's use of it to create an appearance of calm on the surface and also to plumb some troubled depths, is emblematic of the state of English culture in the early 1660s. For all but the most die-hard opponents of the Restoration, these were years of laughter and forgetting; but already there were signs that the ghosts of England's turbulent past had not yet been laid. After the publication of the Declaration of Indulgence in 1672 which suspended the penal laws against Protestant dissenters from the Church of England, but was widely interpreted as the first phase of a campaign to reintroduce Roman Catholicism, only the hardest-drinking Cavaliers could have ignored those signs. As the brittle varnish of the Restoration settlement cracked, so did that of Dryden's early Augustan mode. What had been undertones of misgiving in the Augustanism of the poems he wrote in the 1660s become overtones of disillusionment in his Augustan voice during the 1670s as tensions escalated towards the Exclusion Crisis. In *MacFlecknoe* (circulating in manuscript from 1676), the pressure which had built up in Dryden over the decade he had spent since his appointment as poet laureate struggling to keep an Augustan lid on his increasingly volatile culture exploded in a burst of mock-heroic steam. Here it is the hack-poet Richard Flecknoe, a byword since the 1650s for the uninspired and unsplendid, who presides "like Augustus" over the empire of letters (3); aureate formulations from the *Aeneid* are applied to a leaden culture characterized by smut and sensationalism (some of it, as Dryden concedes, furnished by his own sex comedies and heroic tragedies); and the "fair Augusta" which has risen from the smoking ruins of old London is a shanty town of brothels, madhouses and theatre-schools for aspiring ham actors (65–78). The poem's topsy-turvy Augustanism mostly tells of the emancipation of Dryden's powers of fantasy. But it was also a vent for the frustration and shame he felt at being in the – infrequent – pay of a monarch who fell far short of the famously high standards set by Augustus in patronage of the arts: the mock-enthronement of the playwright Thomas Shadwell as Flecknoe's successor is modeled in a number of respects on Charles II's own coronation.[8]

Absalom and Achitophel (1681) initiates a new, darker phase in the development of Dryden's Augustanism. The widening rift between the Augustan ideal and the prevailing realities of English culture is no longer a mine to be plundered for comic treasure, but a pit to be plumbed in elegiac despair. Of course, Dryden's supreme masterpiece of political satire depends on a biblical rather than an Augustan parallel. David, a good king with a wandering eye, made a more plausible type than the notoriously temperate Augustus for Charles II now that the latter's priapic exploits and their political consequences – "His sceptre and his prick are of a length," wrote Rochester, "And she may sway the one who plays with th' other"[9] – were the talk of London's coffee houses. However, Augustan allusion does spring up now and again in the poem; most thickly and tellingly in the catalogue of the anti-Exclusionists when Dryden commemorates Thomas Butler, Earl of Ossory, the eldest son of his patron the Duke of Ormonde. Ossory had died prematurely in the summer of 1680. Mourning him, Dryden's mind went back to some celebrated instances of premature death in the *Aeneid*, that of Marcellus, Augustus' stepson and designated heir, anachronistically mentioned in Book VI, and those of the precocious friends Nisus and Euryalus in Book IX. But it also went back to another Virgilian death, one which is pointedly not premature; indeed, the only death from old age in the entire *Aeneid*. For Dryden's description of Ossory as "always Mourn'd, / And always honour'd" (832–3) remembers Aeneas' words on the anniversary of the death of his father Anchises at the beginning of Book V: "already, if I am not mistaken, the day is at hand which I shall keep always as a day of grief, always as one of honour" ("semper acerbum, / semper honoratum"). It is a remarkable and revealing allusion. Comparing Ossory to Marcellus or to Nisus and Euryalus, Roman heroes-to-be cut down before they could fulfill their promise, was a grim enough prognostication for the future of Augustan culture in England. But by figuring him as Anchises, Dryden was despairing of that future in a more absolute and personal sense. Had Ossory lived, he would have become a father to Dryden, Anchises to his Aeneas, when he succeeded his own father Ormonde as the poet's patron. Instead, "snatcht in Manhood's prime" (833), Ossory has left the poet as vulnerably alone in his cultural duty as Aeneas would have been had Anchises died prematurely – with the fate of the Augustan line resting on his adolescent and fatherless shoulders. Somewhere in his mind's eye, that was how Dryden saw himself on the cusp of his fifties, two decades after he had first prophesied the coming of an Augustan age in England.

Between 1681 and 1685 Dryden's thoughts returned again and again, almost compulsively, to pathetic scenes of youthful death in the *Aeneid*. Virgil's tears for Marcellus and for Nisus and Euryalus water the roots of "To the Memory of Mr Oldham" (1684), Dryden's great funeral elegy for the poet John Oldham whose death at the age of thirty had cut short a promising career in satire and classical translation. And when Dryden began his own career as a translator of Virgilian epic a year or so later, in *Sylvae* (1685), he did so with versions of the episodes of Nisus and Euryalus, and of the Etruscan prince Lausus who dies at the hand of Aeneas while defending his father Mezentius in Book X. By now the political tide had turned against the Exclusionists, following the discovery of the Rye House Plot to assassinate the king and the Duke of York. A sunny Augustan forecast for the Stuart dynasty was in order; but Dryden failed to provide it. One of the pair of Eclogues which he translated for *Miscellany Poems* (1684), the Ninth, ends with the shepherd/poet Moeris bemoaning the loss of his voice. From his translation of the other, the Fourth, which he had now been quoting and imitating for a quarter of a century, it is clear that Dryden himself could no longer hit the high notes of Virgilian optimism:

> The last great Age foretold by sacred Rhymes
> Renews its finish'd Course; Saturnian times
> Rowl round again, and mighty years, begun
> From their first Orb, in radiant Circles run.
>
> (5–8)

There is no equivalent in Virgil of "its finished course," deflatingly positioned after "Renews," while "Rowl round again" adds a measure of world-weariness, of familiarity pregnant with contempt, to Virgil's plain "redeunt" ("return"). The rhyme of "begun" against "run" has itself rolled round again from Dryden's first re-voicing of this passage, his prophecy in *Astraea Redux* that with the Restoration "times whiter Series is begun / Which in soft Centuries shall smoothly run" (292–3), a prophecy long since debunked by history. This "last great age" is not the "conclusive" ("ultima") era of which Virgil speaks; it is just the latest in the line of recent times given a glittering Augustan reception by Dryden and other English poets but which had not turned out golden.

No longer able to foresee a grand Virgilian future for his country, Dryden turned to different areas of Augustan culture for a contrasting vision of life lived privately and contentedly in the present. At the end of the sequence of translations he contributed to *Sylvae*, as if in counterpoint against the episodes of doomed heroic ambition from the *Aeneid* which began that sequence, Dryden placed (we know that he had a say in arranging the contents of the volume) versions of a group of Horatian odes to which English poets bruised or beaten in the public arena had been resorting for consolation throughout the preceding troubled half-century. His translations of these odes are enriched by a series of echoes of Raphael's speech in *Paradise Lost* advising Adam to "be lowly wise" (VIII: 173), which suggests that Horace's vision of contented retirement had penetrated to his spiritual core. Yet he did not endorse that vision unreservedly. The counterpoint between the Virgilian and Horatian sections of Dryden's contributions to *Sylvae* cuts both ways, for the heroes of the episodes he translated from the *Aeneid* are young men "Eager of action" for whom "rest" is an "enemy" ("Nisus and Euryalus," 120), and Dryden also palpably thrilled to their civic zeal (I shall return to this point later). Even within the Horatian pieces there are hints that

Dryden recognized he was not cut out for the life of rustic retirement they recommend. The group concludes with the Second Epode, a favorite source of consolation for royalist translators like Sir Richard Fanshawe, Mildmay Fane, and Abraham Cowley during the wilderness years of the Interregnum. But unlike Cowley, for instance, Dryden did not remove the surprise ending in which it transpires that the speaker of the poem is a moneylender Alfius (re-named Morecraft by Dryden), who does not in fact go on to practice the "quiet country life! / Discharg'd of business, void of strife" which he has preached, but returns forthwith to the city and his "prevailing love of pelf" (3–4, 96–102).

Three years after his translation of the Second Epode was published, following the "Glorious" Revolution, the poem's ideal was horribly realized for Dryden. His years at the center of the "clamours of contentious law, / And court and state," of being "bribed with hopes" and running to "servile salutations," came to an end; not because he had "wisely shun[ned]" public life but because it had shunned him ("From Horace, Epod[e] 2[n]d," 14–17). Unable to find it in his heart or soul to re-convert from his Roman Catholic faith, despite the blandishments of the Williamite government, he was "Discharg'd of business" in the sense of being stripped of his public posts and salaries, and would soon discover from cruel experience that Horace's question

> How happy in his low degree,
> How rich in humble poverty is he
> Who leads a quiet country life!
>
> (1–3)

is not as rhetorical as it seems. Dryden never again translated Horace, and in later years pointed out that the Horatian ethic of rural retirement was more popular "in reversion" (that is, as a plan for the future) than "in possession" (Dedication of the *Georgics: Works* V: 141). In the last decade of his life, between 1689 and his death in 1700, Dryden's situation would resemble not that of Horace, holidaying with Augustus's blessing on his de luxe Sabine farm, but (as he told Sir William Leveson-Gower in the dedication to *Amphitryon* [1692]; see *Works* XV: 224) that of Ovid whom Augustus exiled to the freezing wastes of Tomis on the Black Sea.

Dryden translated extensively from Ovid during his "unhappy Circumstances"; not the exile poems (seventeenth-century readers tended to take Ovid's rhetorical deprecations of the *Tristia* and *Epistulae ex Ponto* as literal truth) but selections from the *Metamorphoses*, amounting to roughly one third of the poem's length. The sequence begins with a version of Book 1 in its entirety, placed at the head of Dryden's contributions to the third Tonson miscellany *Examen Poeticum* (1693), which was probably once meant to open a complete *Metamorphoses* by divers hands.[10] But the remaining ten translations from the poem which Dryden published in that volume and in *Fables Ancient and Modern* (1700) are cherries picked from whichever part of Ovid's picaresque epic took the poet's wandering fancy: private Augustan works not in the moralistic Horatian sense but in a more licentious Ovidian one. If Dryden retired to an Augustan "paradise within" after 1688, the paradise in question was not a Horatian estate of moderate self-possession, but a garden of self-gratification, an Ovidian bower of bliss. From his account of the conception of the Ovidian episodes in *Fables* it is clear that, like David's illegitimate son Absalom, they were "got . . . with a greater gust" (*Absalom and Achitophel*, 20) than Dryden's official Augustan productions:

> From translating the first of Homer's *Iliad* (which I intended as an essay to the whole work) I proceeded to the translation of the twelfth book of Ovid's *Metamorphoses*, because it contains, among other things, the causes, the beginning, and ending of the Trojan War. Here I ought in reason to have stopped, but the speeches of Ajax and Ulysses lying next in my way, I could not balk 'em. When I had compassed them, I was so taken with the former part of the fifteenth book (which is the masterpiece of the whole *Metamorphoses*) that I enjoined myself the pleasing task of rendering it into English. And now I found by the number of my verses, that they began to swell into a little volume, which gave me an occasion of looking backward on some beauties of my author in his former books. There occurred to me the *Hunting of the Boar*, *Cinyras and Myrrha*, the good-natured story of *Baucis and Philemon* and the rest.
>
> (*Works* XXI: 24)

Answerable to no-one but himself ("I enjoined myself the pleasing task . . ."), Dryden zig-zags across the *Metamorphoses* as the mood takes him (from "the *twelfth* book" on to "the *fifteenth*" and then "backward to the former books"), so losing himself in the pleasures of his Ovidian task ("I could not balk 'em") that the translations appear almost to write themselves ("And now I *found* by the number of my verses, that they began to swell into a little volume").

Without passing explicit comment on the nature of Ovid's style or concerns, Dryden proves himself in that passage a brilliantly sympathetic reader of the *Metamorphoses*. The characteristics of the passage – its transgressive energy, its quasi-sexual ("began to *swell*") attitude to the act of writing, its defiantly self-indulgent voice – are those of Ovidian narrative. They recur in the translations themselves, particularly at the crucial instants of metamorphosis; as, for instance, in "Iphis and Ianthe" (1693). Iphis and her mother have been to petition the goddess Isis for the female-to-male sex-change which would enable Iphis to marry her/his fiancée Ianthe. Outside the temple, their prayers begin to be answered, and Iphis momentarily hovers between femaleness and maleness:

> Forth went the Mother with a beating Heart,
> Not much in fear, nor fully satisfi'd;
> But Iphis follow'd with a larger stride:
> The whiteness of her Skin forsook her Face;
> Her looks embolden'd with an awful Grace;
> Her Features and her Strength together grew,
> And her long Hair to curling Locks withdrew.
> Her sparkling Eyes with manly Vigour shone,
> Big was her Voice, Audacious was her Tone.
> The latent Parts, at length reveal'd, began
> To shoot, and spread, and burnish into Man.
> (189–99)

Iphis leaves the temple with a spring in her step, and her faith wins its reward as that step, already "larger" (more confident) than her mother's, becomes "larger" (covers more ground) than those she herself had previously taken, being now the gait of a man. Likewise, the "whiteness of her skin" forsakes her face first because she no longer fears that it will be impossible for her to marry Ianthe, and then because her fearlessness is justified as her complexion darkens to a ruddy masculine tint. The rhyme "grew"/ "withdrew," correlating the diverse physical motions involved in Iphis's gender reassignment, is superbly dynamic: the verse equivalent of a computer-generated morphing sequence in a science documentary. But the coup de grâce is the crescendo "shoot, and spread, and burnish," a triple-take of increasingly proud self-examination on Iphis's part, in which the third verb is much the best endowed not only acoustically but also semantically, being used in the magnificently rare sense of "broaden" (a sense whose origins Samuel Johnson did not know and which his *Dictionary* records only Dryden using). Clearly when Iphis's "latent parts" were "at length reveal'd," they were revealed at impressive length.

Classical and Renaissance commentary on the *Metamorphoses* traditionally deplored the aspects of the poem which Dryden so exuberantly embraces in those lines: Ovid's fascination with sexual deviancy, and the related tendency of his wit to transgress boundaries of artistic and moral decorum. Ben Jonson had drawn out the political implications of those twin failings in his play *Poetaster* (1601) where Ovid is banished after being caught *in flagrante delicto* with Augustus's daughter Julia during a metamorphic masquerade in which the pair are dressed up as gods. It is not that Dryden was unaware of the view that Ovid's reckless restless wit was subversive of moral and political order; several passages in his critical essays incline toward that view (see, for instance, *Works* I: 112, XXI: 32). That he nevertheless retained – in fact accentuated – that wit in the translations from the *Metamorphoses* he made in his later years suggests that at some level he had come to consider the kaleidoscopic outlook on life it fosters appropriate to the dizzying changes and chances of human life and the world in which it is lived.[11] The Ovidian character who epitomized this elastic mode of vision for Dryden was the philosopher Pythagoras, the protagonist of Book XV. Wisps of topical reference which flit across Pythagoras' speeches in Dryden's translation, as when he says "former things / Are set aside, like abdicated kings" ("Of the Pythagorean Philosophy," 274–5: *Works* XXI: 388; William III's title to the throne officially rested on the supposition that James II had abdicated), encourage the belief – the hope – that among the vicissitudes which this newfound mode of Augustan wisdom permitted Dryden to contemplate with something approaching equanimity in his old age were the "giddy turns" of his own age and career.

The other half of Dryden's energies as a translator of Augustan verse in his "unhappy Circumstances" was devoted to Virgil. It is tempting to present *The Works of Virgil* (1697) as Dryden's penance for the pleasures of his Ovidian translations, an act of public Augustan duty by which he atoned for those interludes of private Augustan gratification. Dryden had long tended in his critical writings to present the style of Virgil as the aesthetic and moral antidote to Ovid's disease of self-indulgence: retracting an indecorously witty line from his version of "Mezentius and Lausus" in the preface to *Sylvae*, for instance, he observed that "Virgil wou'd not have said it, though Ovid wou'd" (*Works* III: 9). Virgil was for Dryden emphatically the poet of self-sacrifice or (to use the term Dryden favored) "retrenchment" (see, for instance, *Works* V: 326) in the cause of nationhood. The prime Virgilian instance of such self-sacrifice is, of course, Aeneas; and it was by analogy with Aeneas' devotion to the duty of founding Rome that Dryden construed his own labors on *The Works of Virgil*. He had not translated mere fragments of Virgil, as previous English translators (John Denham, Richard Fanshawe, Sidney Godolphin, Edmund Waller) had done, but instead taken "the weight of a whole Author on my shoulders" (*Works* V: 325–6) like Aeneas carrying his father Anchises out of the burning wreck of Troy; and he had undertaken his pilgrimage of translation, as Aeneas undertook his geographical journey from Troy to Italy, for the benefit of his nation, in the hope that "it will be judged in after-ages, and possibly in the present, to be no dishonour to my native country" ("The Postscript to the Reader"; *Works* VI: 807).

Yet the image of Dryden as Aeneas dutifully leading his nation on a Virgilian journey raises a fundamental question. Which nation exactly did he translate Virgil for? After all, whether one means by Dryden's nation England or Britain, that nation was bitterly divided in 1697: between those who acknowledged William III as their king, those (including Dryden himself) who continued to regard James II as the reigning monarch, and those who thought of themselves as subjects of neither but as citizens of a soon-to-be-reconstituted republic. Three hundred and forty-nine of Dryden's compatriots, from a range of political persuasions, sponsored the publication of the expensive folio *Works of Virgil* (1697) under the subscription arrangements put in place by Dryden and Tonson, with 101 of the wealthiest paying extra for the privilege of having their coat of arms inscribed beneath one of the illustrations.[12] But the vision of British culture marching as one to the beat of Dryden's Virgilian drum requires some qualification. Several commentators have shown that divisions within that culture register obliquely in *The Works of Virgil*; that Dryden encoded anti-government innuendoes here and there into the fit between an illustration and its subscriber, as well as into the prose dedications and the verse of the translation itself; that, on one level, Dryden was leading his readers toward an Augustan destination at which only a minority of them wished to arrive: a British Rome ruled once again by the Roman Catholic James II.[13]

Which is not to say, however, that it would be naive to credit Dryden's sense of his translation of Virgil as a work conceived and executed on a national scale. Those of the translation's subscribers who did not share Dryden's particular political views but nevertheless handed over their two or three guineas up front were not having the wool pulled over their eyes. "The nation considered its honour as interested in the event," as Samuel Johnson later observed;[14] and on the whole it was right to do so. Topical allusions palpable enough to gratify Jacobite or offend Williamite readers are few and far between in the text, whereas in the more sustained poetic and cultural properties of the translation – its voice – not just some but all of Dryden's compatriots did indeed have an interest. *The Works of Virgil* represents the culmination of Dryden's lifelong endeavor to bring over into British culture the voice of Virgil; and by contrast with other poets and critics engaged in the same endeavor in his lifetime, Dryden's conception of that voice was signally ample. He never endorsed the partisan royalist view of Virgilian style as the quintessence of civility or (to use the favored contemporary term) "smoothness," an ideal of courtly discourse toward which English culture had been progressing over the course of the seventeenth century (despite the major hiccup of the Civil War and the Interregnum) and which it had attained at the Restoration. Proponents of this view dubbed Edmund Waller "the English Virgil" because he had set new standards of phonic and metrical polish in his courtly lyrics and panegyrics.[15] But whilst Dryden certainly recognized and admired the refinement of Virgil's verse, he also found and enjoyed in it properties which for seventeenth-century readers came under the rubric not of "smoothness" but of its opposite within the contemporary critical lexicon, "strength"; forms of stylistic sublimity like hyperbole, bold metaphor, and a taste for unnaturalistic subjects (see, for instance, *Works* XI: 12, *Works* XII: 90 and *Works* XVII: 29) which for the more courtly-minded of those readers might have brought back troubling memories of the civic energies unleashed in England during the Civil War and the Interregnum. For Dryden the voice of Virgil, spanning the extremes of civic strength and civil smoothness, as his life had spanned the last years of the Roman republic and the first of the Augustan principate, was the voice not of the royalist or republican interest in British culture but, potentially, of that culture as a whole.

Realizing that potential is what, in the end, Dryden would have understood by inventing Augustan culture in Britain. But this was to prove an elusive goal, as elusive as the ghosts of Aeneas' wife and father which slip through his fingers as he tries to embrace them in Books II and VI of the *Aeneid* – the Augustan Dream, one might call it. Already by the time Dryden made his first sketches for the Virgil, in the mid-1680s, he feared that the battle to achieve an integrated Virgilian idiom was being lost; that his culture was lurching from the extreme civic strength of its chaotic past to an opposite extreme of hyper-civility. He would state this view openly some years later in a celebrated passage of "To My Dear Friend Mr Congreve" (1694): "Our Age was cultivated thus at length, / But what we gained in skill we lost in strength" (11–12). But it is latent within his despairing insistence in the preface to *Sylvae* that though Virgil "is smooth where smoothness is requir'd, yet he is so far from affecting it that he seems rather to disdain it" (*Works* III: 7). And within the triptych of poems which gloss the contemporary significances of that remark, Dryden urges the need for such "disdain" in Restoration culture: "Nisus and Euryalus" and the two original pieces from the same period which orbit it, "To the Memory of Mr Oldham" and *Threnodia Augustalis* (1685), Dryden's "Funeral-Pindarique Ode" for Charles II.

Nisus and Euryalus are strong to a fault, impetuously heroic, fatally overwhelmed by their "eagerness of blood" when they come upon the besieging Rutulian forces asleep on the plain outside the Trojan camp. Verbal parallels connect this failing in them with that of Oldham's style which Dryden had described as possessing "too much force"; and, as in Oldham, so in Nisus

and Euryalus, erring on the side of strength is for Dryden a "noble error":
he sides zestfully with the disgust of the vigilant young heroes at seeing
the Rutulians "securely drench'd in Sleep" (195; Virgil has only "soluti,"
"relaxed"), "Their watch neglect[ing]" (196; no equivalent in Virgil) and
"drunk with Wine, supinely snor[ing]" (309; Virgil says nothing of snoring).
Similar phrases then recur in the first stanza of *Threnodia Augustalis* where
the British are sleeping "securely," "out of guard" and "Supine amidst our
flowing Store" (14–17) when the catastrophe of Charles's death bursts on
them "like a hurricane on Indian seas" (24). Lacking the strength symbolized
by the now-deceased Oldham, they inhabit a "golden scene" (13) which is
a decadent travesty of that foretold in Virgil's Fourth Eclogue, a coterie of
Walleresque smoothness, and so are "unprovided for [that] sudden blow"
(6) which occurs not "by Just Degrees" (23), as transitions of mood were
supposed to in courtly recensions of Augustan poetic theory like *The Art of
Poetry* (1683), a Frenchified version of Horace's *Ars Poetica* ("Happy who
in his Verse can gently steer, From Grave to Light; from Pleasant to Severe"
[76–7; *Works* II: 126]), but with the sublime suddenness and ferocity of a
"Thunder-clap" (16).

    The Works of Virgil was produced in the aftermath of a more devastat-
ing thunder-clap – revolutions, even "Glorious" and bloodless ones, do not
happen "by Just Degrees" – and the translation is marked by Dryden's cor-
respondingly enhanced sense of the sublime strength of Virgil's voice. Virgil's
"Native Character . . . is Sublimity," he now declared at the head of the volume ("Dedication of the Pastorals": *Works* V: 4); and more clearly than ever
he now saw that sublimity as answerable to the conditions of instability under
which human civilization must be perpetuated. "Answerable" in the sense of
instantiating in small measure such instability and therefore providing protection against it. Dryden's sublime translation of Virgil aims to inoculate
its culture against the thousand natural shocks that human cultures are heir
to by dosing it with a poetic tincture of such shocks. In his versions of the
Eclogues, Dryden underscored Virgil's precocious impatience with the limi-
tations of pastoral decorum, that haste to be off to the wider pastures of civic
poetry which Dryden had discussed in the Dedication: "Virgil remember'd,
like young Manlius" – a hero, it should be noted, of the Roman republic –
"that he was forbidden to Engage; but what avails an express Command to
a youthful Courage, which presages Victory in the Attempt?"; *Works* VI: 5.
In his version of the *Georgics*, he enhanced the traces in Virgil's didactic
manner of the "masculine" prosody and "magisterial" voice of his great
predecessor in the didactic mode, Lucretius (again, a figure from the republican age of Roman history), traces Dryden had learned to recognize while
translating extracts from the *De Rerum Natura* for *Sylvae*.[16] In the *Aeneis*, he

whipped up the various forms of chaotic power in the cosmos of the poem (the winds of the storm in Book I, the flames with which the Trojan women fire their own ships in Book V, Allecto in Book VII) as well as the interior human variants of those recidivist energies (anger, madness, despair) which menace Aeneas' efforts to invent Augustan culture.

However, to talk of such properties of Dryden's Virgil as jabs of strength intended to build up British culture's resistance against the unpredictable powers which beset it from without and within is to invite a further, darker application of the image. Give a patient too strong a dose of a vaccine, and you risk infecting rather than immunizing that patient. In a remark which deserves to be better known, Samuel Johnson pointed out that Dryden, often set down as the poet of (monarchist) order, was vertiginously drawn toward poetic forms of chaos:

> Next to argument, his delight was in wild and daring sallies of sentiment, in the irregular and excentrick violence of wit. He delighted to tread upon the brink of meaning, where light and darkness begin to mingle; to approach the precipice of absurdity, and hover over the abyss of unideal vacancy.[17]

Critics who have followed up Johnson's insight have generally construed this side of Dryden's imaginative temperament as the antithesis of his veneration for the poets of Augustan Rome.[18] But in fact the brink of chaos is the home terrain of his mature Augustan vision; and not only of the Ovidian pole of that vision (Dryden's taste for the "excentrick violence of wit" and his frequenting of the hinterland "where light and darkness begin to mingle," where oppositions such as those of gender begin to break down, are perfectly exemplified in his extracts from the *Metamorphoses*) but also of its Virgilian hemisphere, even of his translation of the *Aeneid*, the poem regarded in Dryden's day as the prime testament to the Augustan world order. In Book II of that translation, as the Greeks sack Troy, Dryden's Aeneas enters the fray "Spurr'd by my Courage, by my Country fir'd" (427–8). The ambiguity in that line, momentarily equating Aeneas's celebrated devotion to his country (*pietas*) with the chaos into which that country is collapsing – it is both Aeneas and Troy who are "fir'd" – is typical of the complexion of Augustan culture, as Dryden finally invented it.

What of the afterlife of that invention? Aspects of Dryden's Augustan vision did survive and evolve in the poetic culture of early eighteenth-century Britain, most famously, of course, the mock-heroic ones can-vassed in *MacFlecknoe*. However, the more radical elements of that vision were diluted, and its complex unity was not preserved. The progressive entrenchment of party divisions during Walpole's long ascendancy killed off the nuanced mode of political Augustanism developed by Dryden in his

Restoration panegyrics. For Whigs the resemblances between Hanoverian Britain and Augustan Rome were cause for celebration; for Tories they were grounds for gloom. The masterpieces of political Augustanism in the period, Pope's *Imitations of Horace* (1733–9), blend the posture of disengagement Dryden had struck in his Horatian pieces in *Sylvae* with some powerfully oppositional impulses. Yet not even Pope could match the texture and pathos which had accumulated within Dryden's Augustan political thinking over four decades first within the establishment and then outside it. As for Dryden's influence as a mediator of Augustan poetic voices, the indefatigable Tonsons, father and son, certainly maneuvered his classical translations into a position of canonical eminence within the literary marketplace; but whether this indicates the triumph of the poetic understandings which inform those translations is open to question. None of the contributors (among them Congreve, Gay, and Pope) to the complete version of the *Metamorphoses* by divers hands (1717), which Samuel Garth assembled around the extracts translated by Dryden, shared Dryden's intelligent appetite for what Garth in his preface termed "the too frequent puerilities of [Ovid's] luxuriant fancy."[19] And Dryden's sublimely strong Virgil had even scanter posterity in an age when Virgil's poems circulated most widely as dainty morsels of quotation within periodicals like *The Tatler* and *The Spectator*, catering to the sense readers of such periodicals were being encouraged to develop of themselves as unprecedentedly polite and civilized. The one lineal heir of Dryden's Virgil, of its unsettling Augustan intuitions about the interrelatedness of culture and chaos, is an anti-*Aeneid* in which Aeneas' sublime civilizing energies are wielded by the ridiculous agents of uncivilisation: *The Dunciad in Four Books* (1742).

NOTES

1. David Norbrook, *Writing the English Republic* (Cambridge, 1999), pp. 433–95; David Womersley, ed., *Augustan Critical Writing* (Harmondsworth, 1997), pp. xi–xl; Howard D. Weinbrot, *Britannia's Issue* (Cambridge, 1993).
2. Harold Love, "Constructing Classicism: Dryden and Purcell," James A. Winn, " 'According to my Genius': Dryden's Translation of 'The First Book of Homer's *Ilias*,' " and Cedric D. Reverand III, "The Final 'Memorial of my own Principles': Dryden's Alter Egos in his Later Career," *John Dryden: Tercentenary Essays*, ed. Paul Hammond and David Hopkins (Oxford, 2000), pp. 92–112, 264–81, 282–307.
3. On classical "imitatio," see Stephen Hinds, *Allusion and Intertext: Dynamics of Appropriation in Roman Poetry* (Cambridge, 1998); on Renaissance redactions of it, see Richard S. Peterson, *Imitation and Praise in the Poems of Ben Jonson* (New Haven, 1981) and Thomas M. Greene, *The Light in Troy: Imitation and Discovery in Renaissance Poetry* (New Haven, 1982).

4. For examples of Dryden's use of Horace in a spirit of "Restoration modernism," see Paul Hammond, "Figures of Horace in Dryden's Literary Criticism," in *Horace Made New*, ed. Charles Martindale and David Hopkins (Cambridge, 1993), pp. 127–47.

5. Norbrook, *Writing the English Republic*, chapter 10, for instance, characterizes Restoration Augustanism as a vein of undiluted monarchist flattery; a modern account of the culture of Augustan Rome which resembles Dryden's in its complex variousness is G. Karl Galinsky, *Augustan Culture: An Interpretive Introduction* (Princeton, 1996).

6. Howard Erskine-Hill, *The Augustan Idea in English Literature* (1983), pp. 46–73.

7. On Dryden and contemporary theories of poetic praise, see James D. Garrison, *Dryden and the Tradition of Panegyric* (Berkeley, 1975); for more examples of the provisional character of his early Augustan panegyrics, see Paul Hammond, *Dryden and the Traces of Classical Rome* (Oxford, 1999), pp. 84–105.

8. Howard Erskine-Hill, "MacFlecknoe, Heir of Augustus," in *John Dryden: Tercentenary Essays*, ed. Paul Hammond and David Hopkins (Oxford, 2000), pp. 15–31.

9. "A Satire on Charles II," pp. 11–12; in *Restoration Literature: An Anthology*, ed. Paul Hammond (Oxford, 2002), p. 39.

10. David Hopkins, "Dryden and the Garth–Tonson *Metamorphoses*," *Review of English Studies* 38 (1988), 64–74.

11. See David Hopkins, "Dryden and Ovid's 'Wit out of Season,' " in *Ovid Renewed*, ed. Charles Martindale (Cambridge, 1988), pp. 167–90.

12. For further details about the subscribers, see John Barnard, "Dryden, Tonson, and the Patrons of *The Works of Virgil* (1697)," in *John Dryden: Tercentenary Essays*, ed. Paul Hammond and David Hopkins (Oxford, 2000), pp. 174–239.

13. Steven Zwicker, *Politics and Language in Dryden's Poetry* (Princeton, NJ, 1984), pp. 177–205; Howard Erskine-Hill, *Poetry and the Realm of Politics* (Oxford, 1996), pp. 201–15.

14. "Life of Dryden," in *Lives of the Poets*, ed. G. B. Hill, 3 vols. (Oxford, 1905), vol. I, p. 448; readers from some parts of the wider nation of Europe did too: see John Barnard, "Early Expectations of Dryden's Translation of Virgil in England and on the Continent," in *Review of English Studies* 50 (1999), 196–203.

15. Norbrook, *Writing the English Republic*, 311–15.

16. Paul Davis, " 'Dogmatical' Dryden: Translating the *Georgics* in the Age of Politeness," *Translation and Literature* 8 (1999), 28–53.

17. "Life of Dryden," in *Lives of the English Poets*, ed. Hill, vol. I, p. 460.

18. See in particular Love, "Constructing Classicism: Dryden and Purcell," in *Dryden: Tercentenary Essays*, 93–4.

19. Samuel Garth, *Ovid's Metamorphoses Translated by John Dryden and Others*, ed. Garth Tissol (Ware, 1998), p. xxxi.

6

CHRISTOPHER RICKS

Dryden's triplets

Dryden was sovereign of the heroic line and of the heroic couplet. In the *Discourse concerning the Original and Progress of Satire* with which he prefaced his translation of Juvenal (1693), he ruled that "The *English* Verse, which we call Heroique, consists of no more than Ten Syllables" (*Works* IV: 88). Not strictly true, such a syllable-count, as everyone knows who has ever felt a bit blank as to what exactly is an iambic pentameter or a line of blank verse. But what of any larger count, such as of lines? Two by two? The heroic couplet has always been recognized as both the favored means and a characteristic flavor of Dryden's art, keen as he was to pursue and to outdo the instrumental skill shown in the 1640s by Edmund Waller and by Sir John Denham. But the heroic triplet? This is neither a term that is in use nor an accomplishment that is much appreciated.

The development from couplet into triplet, or the terms at least, may be marked in the *Oxford English Dictionary*.

couplet   A pair of successive lines of verse, *esp.* when riming together and of the same length.

This, from 1580. Then:

triplet   Three successive lines of verse, esp. when riming together and of the same length.

This, not until 1656. The term "triplet" plays a part in what the Augustan poets liked to stage as the Progress of Poetry. The lexicographer proffers perhaps a nuance of lighting, given that the dictionary italicizes *esp.* for the couplet, but leaves it at merely roman dignity, "esp.," when it comes to the triplet.

Mark Van Doren – in what has proved to be the single most influential book on Dryden (influential not only, though *esp.*, because T. S. Eliot so praised it) – felt obliged to set limits to his praise for two aspects of Dryden's craft that are often complementary and that most distinguish his measures or numbers from those of his successor, Alexander Pope: triplets and alexandrines, "a line of six feet."[1] "He did not always succeed in rendering them organic to his verse structure," wrote Van Doren; "often they were excrescences."[2] But something organic may perfectly well be an excrescence (a wart, for instance), and if you undertake a portrait of Dryden's verse, do you have to paint the triplets as warts and all?

How best might a reader exercise imagination, when after a run of seventy-seven consecutive couplets[3] of *Absalom and Achitophel*, there is conjured up – as more than a detail within the portrait of the Earl of Shaftesbury in all his damaged and damaging energy – this corporeal triplet?

> A fiery Soul, which working out its way, ⎫
> Fretted the Pigmy Body to decay: ⎬
> And o'r inform'd the Tenement of Clay. ⎭
> (*Works* II: 10, lines 156–8)

Dryden's triplet animates not only a soul but a body, and then, through the body of the verse itself, it works that of which it speaks. For the soul of the lines can be seen and heard to be working out its way, out through the acknowledged restraint, even while fretting to decay the body of the couplet – more, while over-informing the tenement that is the couplet-form itself.

Such a realization of what the triplet can effect, by way here of irruption and disruption, is a powerful reminder of one form that power may take – or that may speak truth to power. In Shaftesbury there is felt the power of passionate ambition to break the social bonds of convention or tradition, this and the fierce power to break free from a bodily plight. "Organic"? But Shaftesbury's organs, for all their lapses, do not make him collapse. "Excrescence"? But his very body is an excrescence. Very small of stature, he possessed a pigmy body. But "the Pigmy Body": this turn of phrase is not to be limited to him alone, for the body is a pigmy thing compared to the soul. Like Milton's Satan, to whom *Absalom and Achitophel* often likens him, Shaftesbury is to be excoriated and resisted, but he is not to be condescended to or slighted or bantered. Fear of the Lord is the beginning of wisdom, but the second pillar of wisdom may be fear of the devil. The Duke of Monmouth staggers within Shaftesbury's coils of temptation: "Him Staggering so when Hells dire Agent found" (*Works* II: 16, line 373). And the o'er-informed verse-form, the teeming eruptive triplet, is one of the forms within which – and by which – these counter-currents of judgment upon Shaftesbury are contained.

Dryden's triplets are at once largely obvious and (critically speaking) little attended to. There is, for instance, nothing about the triplets of *Absalom and Achitophel* in Earl Miner's magisterial work, *Dryden's Poetry* (1967).

The great satire contains, within its one thousand and thirty-one lines, eight triplets. None of them is an excrescence. All of them succeed in being organic in their relation both to the tissue of the verse and to the issue of the poem: the outcome that is awaiting the illegitimate issue that is, or rather who is, the king's bastard son, the Duke of Monmouth, with his claims to succeed. Dryden's indictment not only of Monmouth (Absalom) but of his pernicious backer, Shaftesbury (Achitophel), widens from Shaftesbury's body politic to the greater body politic, larger even than England. For there ensues almost immediately a second triplet, one that celebrates the Triple Bond – the Alliance between England, the States General, and Sweden in 1668. Celebrates it while execrating Shaftesbury's part in severing the Alliance, Shaftesbury who was "Resolv'd to Ruine or to Rule the State":

> To Compass this the Triple Bond he broke;
> The Pillars of the publick Safety shook:
> And fitted *Israel* for a Foreign Yoke.
> (*Works* II: 10, lines 175–7)

This triplet enacts the triplicity of which it speaks. It expands the lines' compass, being fitted to a different yoke from that of the couplet, a yoke foreign to the usual public safety (safety as confident prediction) that is a covenanted verse-movement, the heroic couplet. Yet at the same time this triplet is a tribute to a triple bond, rhyme itself being by nature a bond, one that will either evince or resist bondage. For Milton, the decision to use blank verse in *Paradise Lost* constituted a political and social achievement as well as an artistic one:

> This neglect then of Rime so little is to be taken for a defect, though it may seem so perhaps to vulgar Readers, that it is rather to be esteem'd an example set, the first in *English*, of ancient liberty recover'd to Heroic Poem from the troublesom and modern bondage of Rimeing.
> ("The Verse," 1668 – the year, as it happened, of the Triple Bond)

For Dryden, in this intensely Miltonic poem of his, it had now become the heroic couplet that manifested an ancient liberty recovered to Heroic Poem – and a liberty recovered to the latest form that a heroic poem might take, coming to incorporate much that, while in deadly earnest, was mock-heroic. The great age of the heroic couplet is the great age of mock-heroic, from *MacFlecknoe* through to *The Rape of the Lock* and *The Dunciad*.

It is the imaginative aptness of particular triplets in Dryden, their being so variously germane, that makes good the sense of the triplet as much more than a convenience to Dryden, much more than the granting of an extension that owes its existence only to the artist's having failed to compact his thoughts and feelings into a couplet. Take the measure of Shaftesbury's seduction of Monmouth in assuring him that the king's popularity is in decline. Twenty years ago, there had been a Restoration, but now the king's fortunes are, with any luck, beyond restoration. "He is not now . . .": whereupon the couplet will have to expand into a memory of the fulsome welcome (painful for the king's enemies at the time, but now an occasion for gloating) that had overflowed once upon a time:

> He is not now, as when on *Jordan*'s Sand
> The Joyfull People throng'd to see him Land,
> Cov'ring the *Beach*, and blackning all the *Strand:*
> (*Works* II: 13, lines 270–2)

Over and above the call of duty had been the people's joy, and therefore over and above anything that the dutiful couplet could accommodate. The "full" in "Joyfull" proceeds to fill the couplet so that it has to spill over (Dryden likes having some form of *full* or *-ful* within a triplet, the couplet being full and more). The couplet is "throng'd" to the point at which the adulation has to find itself "Cov'ring" a further line. Within that extra line, the extra syllables (calling for equable elisions) can be heard in their expansive movement: "Cov'ring the *Beach*, and blackning all the *Strand*."[4] Covering, blackening: dilating and undulating and diverse.

Such an expansive welcome, as though with more than usually open arms, is no longer the king's reception, Shaftesbury is happy to report. And soon Monmouth is heard to stir up the fickle populace with the help of oratorical arts that he has learnt from Shaftesbury, arts that Dryden realizes through another triplet which goes artfully beyond bounds in asserting that the King has taken liberties – worse, has taken away your liberties:

> Now all your Liberties a spoil are made;
> *Ægypt* and *Tyrus* intercept your Trade,
> And *Jebusites* your Sacred Rites invade.
> (*Works* II: 26, lines 704–6)

Is nothing sacred? Not even the rite of the heroic couplet?

Yet in Dryden, as in Milton, there is no complacent assumption that a particular device inherently lends itself to vice, or to virtue for that matter. The very same turn that can deplore – by means of a triple bond – the destruction of the Triple Bond, or that can take the liberty of a triplet to reprimand the taking of liberties, is one that can on a different occasion practice the art not of sinking but of rising. *Absalom and Achitophel* is supreme as satire because not only its author personally but the poem impersonally can be trusted to value panegyric aright. A great age of satire is always a great age of panegyric. (Which is one reason why the way we live now is incompatible with any substantiated art of satire as against lampoon or burlesque.) Dryden goes, not out of his way, but truly by means of his way, when he incorporates within his poem a tribute, in triplet form, to the eldest son of the Duke of Ormonde, a loyal son (unlike Monmouth), and a son dead in his prime:

> always Mourn'd,
> And always honour'd, snatcht in Manhoods prime
> By'unequal Fates, and Providences crime:
> Yet not before the Goal of Honour won,
> All parts fulfill'd of Subject and of Son;
> Swift was the Race, but short the Time to run.
>
> (*Works* II: 30, lines 832–7)

Unequal Fates are one thing, but to attribute to Providence a *crime*: this risks blasphemy (as all genuine religious conviction does) while preserving decorum in that this sudden rashness is pinioned by "honour'd" and by "Honour." And it is only with "All parts fulfill'd" – *full* and *fill* again – that the couplet permits itself to enter upon the elaboration into a triplet. The further solemnity then itself embodies a paradox, in touch with the startlement of "Providences crime." For the added observation – "Swift was the Race, but short the Time to run" (a famously favorite figure of speech and of thought for Dryden) – makes the run of the lines *less* swift and *less* short than it would have been had the sentiment fulfilled itself with "All parts fulfill'd of Subject and of Son." The alliteration and internal rhyme of *Sub*ject and *Son* suggest that these duties are perfectly at one.

The triplet that is positive, then, in owning virtue, as against in disowning vice, is an indispensable counterthrust, a feat that is more than technical but never less than technically accomplished. Once again there will be the conjunction of something paradoxical with a word that invokes the full (the "faithful," this time), when Dryden's tribute to "a small but faithful Band" finds itself expanding from a small to a larger unit, as though in the confidence that the small band's being united in faith has given it a greater strength and energy than fortifies those whose faithless unity the faithful band confronts:

> These were the chief, a small but faithful Band
> Of Worthies, in the Breach who dar'd to stand,
> And tempt th' united Fury of the Land.
>
> (*Works* II: 32, lines 914–16)

The breaching of the couplet is the reaching of a larger unity, and a better unity, than possesses those who oppose fury to faith.

The last of the eight triplets in the poem (though not the last to be attended to here, since one of them is being reserved for the moment . . .) comes within the king's ample speech that closes the poem (closes it, save only for six lines of narrative that both praise and predict). The king laments that it is his duty not to turn a blind eye or the other cheek to his son's rebellious misconduct.

> Oh that my Power to Saving were confin'd:
> Why am I forc'd, like Heaven, against my mind,
> To make Examples of another Kind?
> (*Works* II: 35, lines 999–1001)

The movement of mind is doubly of another kind. First, in that, by being a triplet, it is an example of another kind, and is itself less confin'd.[5] Not uniquely of another kind, but strikingly so. Second, in that, of all the triplets, this, the conclusive one (more in sorrow than in anger, but in anger), is the only instance of there being an unremitting impetus from the second line into the third. Run through this triplet's predecessors again.

> A fiery Soul, which working out its way,
> Fretted the Pigmy Body to decay:
> And o'r inform'd the Tenement of Clay.
> (*Works* II: 10, lines 156–8)

There, the second line (the couplet-completer) is end-stopped, syntactically complete, and the move into the couplet's becoming a triplet is signaled by a beginning again: "And . . ." The same goes for the second, fourth, and sixth triplets in the poem.

> To Compass this the Triple Bond he broke;
> The Pillars of the publick Safety shook:
> And fitted *Israel* for a Foreign Yoke.
> (*Works* II: 10, lines 175–7)

> Now all your Liberties a spoil are made;
> Ægypt and *Tyrus* intercept your Trade,
> And *Jebusites* your Sacred Rites invade.
> (*Works* II: 26, lines 704–6)

> These were the chief, a small but faithful Band
> Of Worthies, in the Breach who dar'd to stand,
> And tempt th' united Fury of the Land.
> (*Works* II: 32, lines 914–16)

Two other triplets are not furnished with an "And" to re-commence in introducing their third line, but they do have the couplet that constitutes the first two lines be such as to complete the sense, or a sense:

He is not now, as when on *Jordan*'s Sand
The Joyfull People throng'd to see him Land,
Cov'ring the *Beach*, and blackning all the *Strand:* }
(*Works* II: 13, lines 270–2)

Yet not before the Goal of Honour won,
All parts fulfill'd of Subject and of Son;
Swift was the Race, but short the Time to run. }
(*Works* II: 30, lines 835–7)

It is only the final triplet, the king's lament, that cries out against any such pause of temporary completeness, with the impetus "Why am I forc'd . . . / To" incarnating an overriding duty, one that has no choice but to override the couplet:

Oh that my Power to Saving were confin'd:
Why am I forc'd, like Heaven, against my mind, }
To make Examples of another Kind?
(*Works* II: 35, lines 999–1001)

The one remaining triplet in *Absalom and Achitophel* remains in some ways the most capacious and captivating of them all. Its compacted ingenuity and congruity should widen the terms of appreciation.

For *Shimei*, though not prodigal of pelf,
Yet lov'd his wicked Neighbour as himself:
When two or three were gather'd to declaim }
Against the Monarch of *Jerusalem*,
Shimei was always in the midst of them: }
(Works II: 23, lines 599–603)

"For where two or three are gathered together in my name, there am I in the midst of them" (Matthew 18: 20). Is it sacrilege, or blasphemy, or good clean fun, for Dryden so to compromise Christ's promise? T. S. Eliot once said that it was impossible to imagine George Bernard Shaw's blaspheming (there are worse things than blasphemy, in other words, since blasphemy is only possible for one who is at least in some part a believer).[6] As it happens, Shaw, in 1906, made play with this same biblical allusion:

Weariness of the theatre is the prevailing note of London criticism. Only the best critics believe that the theatre is really important: in my time none of them would claim for it, as I claimed for it, that it is as important as the Church was in the Middle Ages and much more important than the Church was in London in the years under review. A theatre to me is a place "where two or three are gathered together." The apostolic succession from Eschylus to myself is as serious and as continuously inspired as that younger institution, the apostolic succession of the Christian Church.[7]

More is at stake for Dryden hereabouts than for Shaw. But it has to be the sheer exuberance of Dryden's ways with Christ's words, the range of the concentration within his triplet, the prodigious prodigality of it all, that can constitute – if anything can – the poet's justification for risking blasphemy, justification by works in which we can justifiably have faith.

There is, for instance, the dynamism, unparalleled elsewhere in the triplets of *Absalom and Achitophel* (their energies are different), by which, in the Shimei triplet, the first line of the couplet-that-is-to-become-a-triplet is impelled into the second line, and this then into the third. Next, there is the deliciously impertinent pertinence that has "When two or three" be the opening of a twosome that will turn out to be a threesome. Next, there is the fact that the first twenty-two verses of this chapter of Matthew do not just gather up into themselves Christ's words about "two or three," but rather have the entire tissue be an elaboration of numbers, not the Book of Numbers but the chapter of them. In sequence:

- one such little child
- one of these little ones [thrice]
- two hands or two feet
- one eye, rather than having two eyes
- an hundred sheep, and one of them be gone astray
- the ninety and nine [twice]
- take with thee one or two more, that in the mouth of two or three witnesses
- if two of you

It is only after this thoroughly patient enumeration that Christ is moved to say "For where two or three are gathered together in my name, there am I in the midst of them." And then immediately, by an extraordinary vaulting into the very next verses, there comes one of the most challenging of all the New Testament's numberings:

> Then came Peter to him, and said, Lord, how oft shall my brother sin against me, and I forgive him? till seven times? Jesus saith unto him, I say not unto thee, Until seven times: but, Until seventy times seven.

Yet all these are only part of what Dryden gathers into his triplet. Presumably it was a partial echo within Christ's words in the language of the "King James" Bible (*name / them*) – "For where two or three are gathered together in my name, there am I in the midst of them" – that prompted Dryden's auditory imagination (*declaim / Jerusalem / them*):

> When two or three were gather'd to declaim ⎫
> Against the Monarch of *Jerusalem*, ⎬
> *Shimei* was always in the midst of them: ⎭
> (Works II: 23, lines 601–3)

And then again the two Testaments are gathered together. For not only does Christ gather with Shimei, but the very sounds reach to the New from the Old:

> And when King David came to Bahurim, behold, thence came out a man of the family of the house of Saul, whose name was Shimei, the son of Gera: he came forth, and cursed still as he came. (2 Samuel 16: 5)

What is the sound that we hear declaimed by these two or three verses? The word *came*, three times, of Shimei.[8] Four times if you include "King David came," and five times if you accommodate the rhyme "name." When two or three . . . ? And even "forth" might be drafted: "he came forth." The old schoolboy joke was not mindless, though not – of course – mindful of spiritual realities: *"Come forth," and he came fifth and lost his* – what was it, exactly?

Granted, this is to allow or even encourage the numbers game to ripple out too far, but the root of all this is sound: that Dryden is not one to play emptily with "two or three" when introducing a triplet within a poem that is in couplets. It would be too much of a coincidence if every one of the eight triplets in *Absalom and Achitophel* just happened to have in it something that might bear upon the couplet/triplet and upon what, at this particular point, the poem was engaging with.

For Dryden is likely to have had something in mind when he chose, with whatever degree of full deliberated consciousness of everything that might lurk within any such decision, to introduce a triplet into the run of his couplets. "When two or three . . .": Dryden often has recourse to "two or three," with its robust approximation. "To conclude, if in two or three places I have deserted all the Commentators, 'tis because I thought they first deserted my Author."[9] There is something amiably offhand about "two or three," or not so amiably, the idiom commanding one tone that dismissiveness may take. On a faultless sonnet:

> A hundred Scribling Authors, without ground
> Believe they have this only Phœnix found:
> When yet th' exactest scarce have two or three
> Among whole Tomes, from Faults and Censure free.
> (*The Art of Poetry;*[10] *Works* II: 134, lines 321–4)

On one occasion, Dryden introduces a "two or three" that is not to be found in the original that he is translating:

PERSIUS How anxious are our Cares; and yet how vain
The bent of our desires!
FRIEND   Thy Spleen contain:
For none will read thy Satyrs.
PERSIUS   This to Me?
FRIEND None; or what's next to none; but two or three.
                    (*The First Satyr of Persius; Works* IV: 259, lines 1–6)

It is a pleasant little surprise, the thought that "what's next to none" is not *one* "but two or three." And sure enough, this touch of lugubrious comedy is not exactly to be found in the Latin, which has a different inconsequence: *nemo . . . nemo? Vel duo, vel nemo.* Literally, either two or none. "No one? well, one or two perhaps." One or two perhaps / two or none / two or three. Any advance on two or three? Such comedy starts to add up (but who's counting?) when the idiom "two or three" occurs within a couplet en route to becoming a triplet.

I have already Buried two or three
That stood betwixt a fair Estate and me, ⎬
And, Doctor, I may live to Bury thee. ⎭
                    (*The Third Satyr of Persius; Works* IV:
                    192, lines 192–4)

Dryden's energy is happy to mount a succession of tours de force, where five consecutive triplets enact, in various ways, that of which they speak. This is the momentum that is both deplored and admirably realized in *The Hind and the Panther: The First Part*, lines 361–75, when after a run of twenty couplets there comes this proclamation:

The fruit proclaims the plant; a lawless Prince
By luxury reform'd incontinence,
By ruins, charity; by riots, abstinence.[11]
Confessions, fasts and penance set aside;
Oh with what ease we follow such a guide!
Where souls are starv'd, and senses gratify'd.
Where marr'age pleasures, midnight pray'r supply,
And mattin bells (a melancholy cry)
Are tun'd to merrier notes, *encrease* and *multiply*.
Religion shows a Rosie colour'd face;
Not hatter'd out with drudging works of grace;
A down-hill Reformation rolls apace.

What flesh and bloud wou'd croud the narrow gate,
Or, till they waste their pamper'd paunches, wait?
All wou'd be happy at the cheapest rate.

$\left.\begin{array}{l}\\\\\end{array}\right\}$

(*Works* III: 133, lines 361–75)

Every one of these triplets makes a piercing point of what it is to have to reach to a triplet, because of incontinence, say, or because of a misguiding guide, or because of the urging to increase and multiply, or to roll downhill, or to crowd the narrow gate.

"What flesh and bloud wou'd croud the narrow gate": Dryden's heroic couplet may be a narrow gate, but it was wide enough to let in Samuel Johnson, who fashioned – thanks to Dryden and to Swift – the line "Unnumber'd Suppliants croud Preferment's Gate" (*The Vanity of Human Wishes* [1749], 73). Johnson is the poet-critic whose observation, with extensive view, surveys the busy scenes of Augustan verse, and in his life of Dryden he is careful, not to lay down the law, but to lay out the considerations:

> The triplet and alexandrine are not universally approved. Swift always censured them, and wrote some lines to ridicule them. In examining their propriety it is to be considered that the essence of verse is regularity, and its ornament is variety.

Johnson then follows his characteristically wise practice of setting out a strong case from which, in the end, he withdraws some of his support. Triplets are intrinsically unsatisfactory? Yes, and yet not altogether so – or they are judged less unsatisfactory than would be their banishment. The movements of mind are these:

> the English alexandrine breaks the lawful bounds, and surprises the reader with two syllables more than he expected.
>
> The effect of the triplet is the same: the ear has been accustomed to expect a new rhyme in every couplet; but is on a sudden surprised with three rhymes together, to which the reader could not accommodate his voice did he not obtain notice of the change from the braces of the margins. Surely there is something unskilful in the necessity of such mechanical direction.
>
> Considering the metrical art simply as a science, and consequently excluding all casualty, we must allow that triplets and alexandrines inserted by caprice are interruptions of that constancy to which science aspires. And though the variety which they produce may very justly be desired, yet to make our poetry exact there ought to be some stated mode of admitting them.
>
> But till some such regulation can be formed, I wish them still to be retained in their present state. They are sometimes grateful to the reader, and sometimes convenient to the poet. Fenton[12] was of opinion, that Dryden was too liberal and Pope too sparing in their use.[13]

Yet there is occasion for respectful dissent from Johnson. First, the lawful bounds of a verse-form are what is at issue. Second, there is nothing intrinsically inartistic or unavailing about surprise, twice invoked (predictably) by Johnson. His speaking twice, likewise, of expectation might remind us of the sly comedy by which Dryden can encompass a reference to expectation within a triplet, one that accommodates in its threesome the two-fold thing that is balance, alongside two worlds and two possibilities.

> Paint *Europe*'s Balance in his steady hand,
> Whilst the two Worlds in expectation stand
> Of Peace or War, that wait on his Command?
> (*The Art of Poetry; Works* II: 155, lines 1064–6)

Next, the braces of the margins are not a necessity, only a convention that may be of service (similar perhaps to such a stage direction as *Aside*, of which Johnson avails himself in his tragedy *Irene*). Fourth, considering the metrical art simply as a science is simply inapposite, since no such art can be a science, even when one allows for the different coloring of those words in 1779. It is a lapse in Johnson to be even tempted by the thought of the metrical art as consequently excluding all casualty, since it is he of all critics who most truly appreciates the "felicities" of artistic accomplishment, felicities being exactly such effects as happily befall by benign casualty. Johnson praised Pope's epitaph on Simon Harcourt:

> This epitaph is principally remarkable for the introduction of the name, which is inserted with a peculiar felicity, to which chance must concur with genius, which no man can hope to attain twice, and which cannot be copied but with servile imitation.[14]

Why, then, is the metrical art the sole aspect of the poetical art that cannot benefit from such a concurrence of chance with genius?

Finally, when Johnson presses upon us that "we must allow that triplets and alexandrines inserted by caprice are interruptions of that constancy to which science aspires," we should not allow this move of his. Not only because the aspirations of science may not be conducive to the inspirations of art, but because of the injustice of *caprice*: "Freak; fancy; whim," in Johnson's Dictionary. It is not by caprice (as the instances from *Absalom and Achitophel* show) that Dryden inserted a triplet, and "inserted" is coercive too. Moreoever, Dryden does not limit himself to adducing, he educes a triplet, and most educative the process is.

What better way could there be to see the Three Unities than under the aspect of a triplet, one that will then incorporate the word "tripled"?

> Time, Action, Place, are so preserv'd by thee ⎫
> That ev'n *Corneille*, might with envy see ⎬
> Th' Alliance of his tripled Unity. ⎭
>
>   (*To my Friend, the Author*
>   [Peter Motteux], 33–5)

And this, with the name Corneille hovering appositely between two syllables and three.

"The braces of the margins," deprecated by Johnson as an unskilful and mechanical direction to the reader, are themselves oddly suggestive when it comes to being, not at sixes and sevens, but at twos and threes. The *OED* defines this sense of *brace* as "a sign used in printing or writing, chiefly for the purpose of uniting together two or more lines, words, staves of music etc" (from 1656), but when it comes to the lines of Augustan verse, it is not a matter of two or more lines, but of three. A brace in the margin is the sign of a triplet. So there is something tauntingly convenient about the fact that the very next definition in the *OED* is a reminder that (despite the marginal brace for a threesome), on other occasions a brace is "two things taken together; a pair, a couple. Often a mere synonym for *two*." And it is in this sense, a pair, that Dryden himself uses the word "brace" in his poetry. The couplet meets the triplet (into which it expands) there in the word and the sign "brace."

Of triplets and alexandrines: "Fenton was of opinion, that Dryden was too liberal and Pope too sparing in their use." It is imaginative of Johnson that when he came to praise Dryden, it should have been by courtesy of the particular tribute that Pope paid to his predecessor, a tribute that takes the form of using the form (a triplet concluding in an alexandrine) that Pope for his own part mostly eschewed.

> What can be said of his versification will be little more than a dilatation of the praise given it by Pope:[15]
>
> > Waller was smooth; but Dryden taught to join ⎫
> > The varying verse, the full resounding line, ⎬
> > The long majestick march, and energy divine.[16] ⎭

Pope honors Dryden, first, by imitating the form that energy often took in Dryden. The wit of the triplet, in various senses of wit, is manifest, first, in the way in which "full" then prompts the overflowing into the next line, next by the extension intimated in "The long . . .," and then in the interplay of the sequences that come to constitute an alternation of twos and threes:

> varying verse / full resounding line
> long majestick march / energy divine

– yet not an alternation exactly. For this interplay takes one of the shapes that Augustan verse relished, a b b a, *chiasmus*[17] – a shaping that is in tension, very happily, with the shape of couplets themselves and the paired planks that build the platform: aa, bb, cc . . . This, with "varying verse" and "energy divine" as the couples that open and close the sentiment, and with "full resounding line" and "long majestick march" as the triplicities that resound at the heart of the lines.

If we ask what form, for both Dryden and Pope, the "energy divine" supremely took, the answer is the Trinity. The words "energy divine" here conclude the three-fold verse-form, and Pope, in paying this tribute to his predecessor (Dryden dead but still living through his art and his faith), may be recalling how Dryden himself used the triplet to incarnate the Trinity:

> Good life be now my task: my doubts are done,
> (What more could fright my faith, than Three in One?)
> Can I believe eternal God could lye
> Disguis'd in mortal mold and infancy?
> That the great maker of the world could dye?
> > (*The Hind and the Panther: The First Part;*
> > *Works* III: 125, lines 78–82)

The "majestick march," then, may honor not only kings but the King of Kings. Pope's phrase certainly honors Dryden, not least in that the word "Majesty" is the one that Dryden had chosen to celebrate the union of triplet with alexandrine ("the Pindarick line") in his artistic decision for his *Aeneis*:

> When I mention'd the Pindarick Line, I should have added, that I take another License in my Verses: for I frequently make use of Triplet Rhymes, and for the same Reason: Because they bound the Sense.[18] And therefore I generally join these two Licenses together: and make the last Verse of the Triplet a Pindarique: For besides the Majesty which it gives, it confines the sense within the barriers of three Lines, which wou'd languish if it were lengthen'd into four.
> > (Dedication)

One of the shrewd moves that Dryden makes there is his seizing an initiative, and advancing that the triplet, far from being an uneconomical couplet, is essentially two couplets economized upon.

Pope's triplet in praise of Dryden has the tone of Dryden's own high moments. But one attractive thing about a triplet is the multiplicity of tones to which it may lend itself, including delectably low ones. George Saintsbury, whose historical criticism of English prosody has been often contested and never superseded, conceded that the impulse to make use of the triplet and of the alexandrine may have begun with a poet's wish to make things easier for oneself ("The original persuasive to both is, of course, clear enough – it is simply a sense of too narrow room in the ten or twenty syllables"), but he soon moves to complicate that *simply* of his, by picking up his own word "persuasive" and then turning it to the thought of being unable to persuade, not others, but himself:

> I have never been able to persuade myself that the giving up of them was not one of those rather unreasonable, though it would seem quite inevitable, "tightenings up" of rule which have spoilt almost all games at one time or another. The triplet has no doubt a slight tendency to burlesque, and, if used often, throws the general effect out of character; but then it is the poet's business to guard against these results. Both in descriptive and argumentative verse it is of great importance, and has something of the effect of a parenthesis – that figure hated by the vulgar, and beloved by the elect.[19]

Speak for yourself. Van Doren, speaking for himself, valued in Dryden this effect of a triplet, "the supplying of a colloquial, first-hand note," adding that "The third line of a triplet in Dryden frequently represents a lowering of the voice to the level of parenthesis or innuendo."[20] A heightening of this lowering, a comic compounding of the effect, is manifested when a triplet avails itself not only of the vocal level of a parenthesis but of a parenthesis proper, or improper:

> *Hippomenes*, who ran with Noble strife   ⎫
> To win his Lady, or to loose his Life,   ⎬
> (What shift some men will make to get a Wife?) ⎭
> Threw down a Golden Apple in her way,
>   (*Amaryllis, or the Third Idyllium of Theocritus,*
>   *Paraphras'd; Works* II: 162, lines 91–4)

The energy of Hippomenes can be felt to throw down that golden apple so that it sails sheerly over the space of an entire triplet, and of the wry shift constituted by an entirely parenthetical line.

But an apt way to end this conspectus of Dryden's triplets might be with an epilogue. One of his, to furnish one for this occasion too. Comedy attended upon his decision as to how to end his *Epilogue Spoken at the Opening of the New House.* This Epilogue, a tour de force, opens with two triplets:

> Though what our Prologue said was sadly true, ⎫
> Yet, Gentlemen, our homely House is new, ⎬
> A Charm that seldom fails with, wicked, You. ⎭
> A Country Lip may have the Velvet touch, ⎫
> Tho' She's no Lady, you may think her such, ⎬
> A strong imagination may do much.   ⎭
>   (*Works* I: 150, lines 1–6)

A strong imagination will, on occasion, be one that cannot be satisfied with a couplet alone but needs an ampler field for the new. So this Epilogue is to end, likewise, with two triplets. Between opening and closing, it enjoys itself in and with more than a dozen couplets (including one that then makes play with twos and threes in yet another garb),[21] before arriving at its burly end. The California editors offer an invaluable elaboration of the line, "The best which they reserv'd they now will Play," that begins Dryden's scabrous finality:

"The best wit (plays) from the older period, their exclusive property, and hitherto unproduced in these times, the management at this theatre will now proceed to revive for your delectation, as a more than sufficient offset to the empty magnificence which is the best the other house has to offer."[22]

> The best which they reserv'd they now will Play,
> For, like kind Cuckolds, tho' we have not the way
> To please, we'l find you Abler Men who may.
> If they shou'd fail, for last recruits we breed
> A Troop of frisking Monsieurs to succeed:
> (You know the French sure cards at time of need.)
>
> (*Works* 1: 151, lines 135–40)

The conclusive triplet makes mock of French breeding, and thinks twice about what it is to succeed (always a crucial consideration in this poet who so much pondered successes and successions). Then, at the moment when it shares its confidences, it lowers its voice: "(You know the French sure cards at time of need.)"

It takes a great deal of assurance to end a poem – and this is one that is for the ear earlier than the eye, being an Epilogue – with a line that is parenthetical and yet central. (But then Dryden knew the triplet a sure help at time of need.)

Elizabeth Barrett wrote of Dryden, with doubly bitter emphasis: "He established finally the despotism of the final emphasis."[23] Not altogether so, for one of the many good things about the triplet is the way in which it resists or tempers the despotism of the couplet and of its particular finality of emphasis. Voltaire was nearer the truths when he came by his figure of speech for the poetical numbers of the two greatest Augustan poets: "Pope drives a chaise with a couple of neat trim nags but Dryden a coach and six, with postilions and all."[24] It was left to Johnson to contest this, with affectionate gruffness: "That is very well. But the truth is they ride both in coaches, only Dryden is always either galloping or stumbling; Pope even trot."[25]

NOTES

1. *OED*: "a line of six feet or twelve syllables, which is the French heroic verse, and in English is used to vary the heroic verse of five feet" (the first instance of the adjective being Puttenham, 1589, and of the noun, Dryden, 1667).

2. Mark Van Doren, *The Poetry of John Dryden* (New York, 1920), p. 77.

3. A run that is interrupted, at line 87, by "And their's the Native right – ", a turn that is denied its native right by being half a line and unrhymed. (Hence the first triplet's arriving with an odd number.)

4. A. W. Verrall, *Lectures on Dryden* (Cambridge, 1914), pp. 68–9: "The reception of Charles at Dover in May 1660 is described in the triplet, 270ff., a variation of the couplet rarely used in this poem. Some effect is here certainly both felt and meant; for note also the unique rhythm in the last line due to the two trisyallabic words 'covering,' 'blackening,' and compare with this the effect of the single trisyllabic 'lengthening' in *v.* 269: – 'The shadows *lengthening* as the vapours rise.' What is the effect intended in the triplet? Is not the picture meant to be disagreeable? – '*Covering* the beach and *blackening* all the strand.' What does it call up to us? Beetles?"

5. Dryden enjoys placing both "confin'd" and "unconfin'd" within triplets. Both are in *The First Book of Ovid's Metamorphoses*, lines 125–7, 809–11:

> E're Sails were spread, new Oceans to explore: ⎫
> And happy Mortals, unconcern'd for more, ⎬
> Confin'd their Wishes to their Native Shoar. ⎭

> No puny Pow'r, but he whose high Command ⎫
> Is unconfin'd, who rules the Seas and Land; ⎬
> And tempers Thunder in his awful hand. ⎭

6. T. S. Eliot, *After Strange Gods* (1934), p. 52: "I repeat that I am not defending blasphemy; I am reproaching a world in which blasphemy is impossible."

7. "The Author's Apology" (1906), *Our Theatres in the Nineties* (1932).

8. It is an old tradition to toll *came* three times.

> Night came, but unattended with repose, ⎫
> Alone she came, no sleep their eyes to close, ⎬
> Alone, and black she came, no friendly stars arose. ⎭
> (*The Hind and the Panther: The Third Part*, 607–9)

9. Argument of *The First Satyr of Juvenal*. Similarly, Explanatory Notes on *The Sixth Satyr of Persius* (note 4): "And since he and *Lucan* were so great Friends, I know not but *Lucan* might help him, in two or three of these Verses." Marcia Karp drew my attention to the erratum, correcting "three" to "two," in the first edition of Dryden's *Aeneis*, VI: 1131: "the two devoted *Decij.*"

10. Boileau (here translated by Dryden) ends his line with "deux ou trois entre mille," which lacks the comedy of rhyming on "three" in a couplet.

11. The California edition explains: "The four vices of Henry VIII which are named *reform'd* the Catholic vice, *incontinence*, and quelled the virtues of *charity* and *abstinence*, along with three aspects of the sacrament of penance (*Confessions, fasts and penance*)," *Works* III: 372, note to lines 361–4.

12. Elijah Fenton (1683–1730), who translated four books of the *Odyssey* for Pope.
13. *The Lives of the English Poets*, ed. George Birkbeck Hill (Oxford, 1905), vol. I,
    pp. 467–8. This preface, biographical and critical, to the works of Dryden was
    published in 1779.
14. *The Lives of the English Poets*, ed. Hill, vol. III, pp. 258–9.
15. The form *dilatation* has its pertinence when the couplet finds itself dilated into
    a triplet. *OED*: "the etymologically correct formation," still common in the
    eighteenth century although *dilation* is to be found in 1598 in Florio (where the
    word was corrected to its expansion in 1611).
16. "The First Epistle of the Second Book of Horace Imitated," lines 267–9. *The
    Lives of the English Poets*, ed. Hill, vol. I, p. 465.
17. *OED*: "A grammatical figure by which the order of words in one of two parallel
    clauses is inverted in the other." Widened, then, to larger patterns of a b b a.
18. For the word "bound" within triplets, see *The Medall*, lines 239–41:

> On utmost bounds of Loyalty they stand;
> And grin and whet like a Croatian Band,
> That waits impatient for the last Command.

Relatedly, *Lucretius: The beginning of the First Book*, lines 23–5:

> O'er barren Mountains, o're the flow'ry Plain,
> The leavy Forest, and the liquid Main
> Extends thy uncontroul'd and boundless reign.

To Sir Godfrey Kneller, lines 147–9:

> Thy Genius bounded by the Times like mine,
> Drudges on petty Draughts, nor dare design
> A more Exalted Work, and more Divine.

The triplet may again suggest the Divine. For the especial *sound* of the triplet,
after invoking the triplicity that is Heaven, Earth and Skies, there is *The Twelfth
Book of Ovid His Metamorphoses*, lines 56–60:

> Full in the midst of this Created Space,
> Betwixt Heav'n, Earth and Skies, there stands a Place,
> Confining on all three; with triple Bound;
> Whence all Things, though remote, are view'd around;
> And thither bring their Undulating Sound.

19. George Saintsbury, *A History of English Prosody* (1908, 2nd edn. 1923), vol. II,
    pp. 389–90.
20. Van Doren, *The Poetry of John Dryden*, p. 79.
21. "The Audience from worn Plays and Fustian Stuff / Of Rhyme, more nauseous
    than three Boys in Buff." It is permissible to be baffled, since even the California
    editors are. "A droll of the time, *The Three Merry Boyes*"? Not persuasive, this
    conjecture. "The line, thus, remains obscure."
22. *Works* I: 355, note to line 35.
23. "The Book of the Poets" (1842).

24. *Boswell on the Grand Tour: Germany and Switzerland*, ed. Frederick A. Pottle (1953), pp. 299–300; 27 December 1764.

25. *Boswell on the Grand Tour: Italy, Corsica, and France*, ed. Frank Brady and Frederick A. Pottle (1955), p. 281; 13 February 1766. The editors supply a few words within square brackets: "Pope [goes on at an] even trot." But the manuscript, which has its happy unevenness, does not read like a trot.

2

A LITERARY LIFE IN
RESTORATION ENGLAND

7

HAROLD LOVE

Dryden's London

Dryden's greatest subject, which occupied him all his professional life, was the emergence into history of the modern city. Much of his conduct as a writer – the forms he chose or invented, the kinds of human behavior he examined, and his choice of a poetic rhetoric – were responses to the challenges posed by that subject. Even politics, though national in its terms of reference, was generated, as he saw it, along an axis between Whitehall and Cornhill. In reflecting on the momentous changes in metropolitan organization that were taking place around him and the new kinds of sociability to which they were giving birth, he was also helping to mold and direct these things, never merely an observer. We will look first at his experience of the old metropolis, which came to a spectacular end in September 1666, then his engagement, beginning with *Annus Mirabilis*, with the new metropolis, and finally his concern, in the last decade of his life, with the relationship of the metropolis to the nation at large.

Old and new London

Dryden's first London, which he learned to know from the external perspective of Westminster School in the 1640s and as a clerk to Sir Gilbert Pickering in the 1650s, was the ancient City within the walls together with its attendant suburbs and liberties. The West End at the time was still largely fields. The built environment was dominated by medieval and Tudor structures, most notably St. Paul's and the Royal Exchange, the first serving as a social space for the transmission of news as well as a place of worship and the second as the major business center and shopping precinct. A multiplicity of parishes inside and outside the walls each still preserved the ancient churches so lovingly described by Stow in his *Survey of London*, while trade and manufacturing had their own local temples in the halls of the City companies, some of them hardly less ancient. The sociability of the metropolis was organized around these halls and their neighboring taverns, where, lacking modern office space, tradesmen would meet at established hours to settle accounts and drive bargains. Members of companies used their halls for splendid feasts as well as for the regulation of their respective mysteries, with the civic whole cohering in the annual ceremonies connected with the installation of the Lord Mayor. Many of the aristocracy still had their London houses in the City and along the Strand. Matters not directly connected with trade hung on the outskirts – the court at marshy Westminster, the lawyers in their Inns to the West and North, and the sub-headquarters of the national church on the South Bank at Lambeth, where it rubbed shoulders uneasily with the pleasure district of brothels, taverns and the by then empty shells of the pre-1642 theatres.

In these outlying segments we have a premonition of the separating out of the later, much larger, metropolis into specialized areas housing diverse, self-chosen populations; but this was not true of the ancient hub on the North Bank. Specialization there was more likely to relate to the exercise of particular trades – bankers in Lombard Street, stationers in Paul's churchyard, skinners in Dowgate – rather than differences of ideology or lifestyle. Visitors from the country on their (usually reluctant) visits to the old London had no option but to thrust themselves into its dirt, clamor and incessant bustle as they battled their way through its networks of narrow, insanitary lanes overhung by upper stories that in many cases came close to blocking out the sky:

> When I come to town, and find my self really in the Citty, I begin to think that I am at Sea the smel turns my stomack, the noise and tumult offends my head, the conversation and rudeness of the sailors, and my fellow passengers is uery importunate, and I can do nothing else but wish to see land again, that is the Country.[1]

Houses, which mostly doubled as workplaces or warehouses, were still largely wooden-framed. Even for the wealthy, accommodation was crowded and privacy at a minimum, with conversations always in danger of being overheard.[2] Sensory overload and the need to defend oneself against innumerable routine discomforts and dangers were an intrinsic part of everyday urban life. Unfortunately, the origin of one of the greatest of these dangers, disease, lay in the material structure of the City itself and could not be evaded, any more than its other great enemy and eventual nemesis, fire.

In reading Dryden's prophecy of the new post-Fire metropolis in the concluding stanzas of *Annus Mirabilis*, we should not forget the enormous desolation and sense of loss that are excluded from direct mention. During the later 1660s and early 1670s Dryden's experience of his immediate urban environment must have been similar to that of an inhabitant of Dresden or Hiroshima returning to the obliterated site in 1945: a huge area of built environment had disappeared for ever, along with the personal, cultural, and institutional associations aroused by its sights, sounds, and smells. Buildings and streetscapes had been tellers of stories, all of them now lost. This physical obliteration of the urban past seems to be reflected in Dryden's verse by a sense of time itself as only to be retained in confused, unsatisfactory snatches. Even so brief a poem as "To the memory of Mr Oldham" is packed with images of oblivion – the friend "too little and too lately" known whom he had "just begun" to value when he was snatched away, the unequal race in which "the last set out the soonest did arrive," the fruit plucked "early ripe," the glimpse of Marcellus in the underworld frozen in a tape-loop of futile celebration. None of these fragments could provide a satisfactory basis for regaining a past. Only the evocation of the Virgilian master text allows any semblance of permanence and even that is saturated with regret for the irrevocably departed.[3] The disappearance of the past also haunts Flecknoe in *MacFlecknoe*. His own mighty deeds are forgotten. "Worn out with business" he celebrates the greater achievements of his successor Shadwell but even these are preserved only in snatches – a catch-phrase from a play and the muddled recollection of a boat trip down the Thames. Shadwell himself, drugged with ale and opium, is a figure without memory. The theatre in which his coronation takes place is a "Monument of vanisht minds." In *Absalom and Achitophel* "Honest *David*" is to be put by as if he had never existed; there is a dim memory of a joyful reception on "*Jordan*'s Sand" and some "Mouldy Rolls of *Noah*'s Ark" and the rest silence. Dryden's defining post-Fire metaphor of the inherited past is of "ancient Fabricks" that "threat to fall" (*Works* II: 5–36, lines 507, 270, 302, 801). Otherwise "Fate and gloomy Night" hover ready to extinguish all things. The figuring of a textual Rome or Jerusalem as contiguous with and interpenetrating the present indicates not a living succession of time but its absence. Take away a handful of ancient stories, which are only pale simulacra of another lost past, and we are left with void.

In each of the two longer poems mentioned, the past is so unsatisfactory and the present so fugitive and unstable that the poet's attention is irresistibly carried forward to the future, whether envisaged as a consummation of heroic imbecility by Shadwell or a series of new time in which "The mighty Years" might run in "long Procession." In both *MacFlecknoe* and *Absalom and Achitophel* an urgent political concern with the problem of succession in the state echoes a larger problem of constituting a future from a damaged past. Yet, the loss of prompts to memory need not always be felt as deprivation: in some instances it might represent an escape from failure and oppression. A memory can be a rooted sorrow and its loss a liberation. Alternatively, the freedom to imagine a future may be accepted as an adequate recompense for the loss even of a loved past rather than as a poor consolation. Whatever the reason, Dryden's elegy on the old London in *Annus Mirabilis* is unexpectedly dismissive. However great the trauma, there was no conceded regret. The lost city, we find, was simply unworthy of its Platonic idea:

> Before, she like some Shepherdess did show,
>   Who sate to bathe her by a River's side:
> Not answering to her fame, but rude and low,
>   Nor taught the beauteous Arts of Modern pride.
>   (*Works* 1: 103, lines 1181–4)

The full force of that quatrain can only have revealed itself to those who, like its author, retained vivid memories of the reality of those bustling, riverside areas south-east of St. Paul's which had seen the origin and most disastrous depredations of the fire.[4] Dryden discards the London of the past in order to consider the London that was to come and which in the course of his lifetime was to assume reality:

> Now, like a Maiden Queen, she will behold,
>   From her high Turrets, hourly Sutors come:
> The East with Incense, and the West with Gold,
>   Will stand, like Suppliants, to receive her doom.
>   (*Works* 1: 104, lines 1185–8)

The loss of the old city had been a necessary sacrifice through which London had "as far as Humanity can approach" become "a great Emblem of the suffering Deity" (*Works* 1: 49) and could now anticipate a joyful resurrection.

The most important new development, inaugurated well before the Fire, which mostly spared it, was the long-delayed settling of the West End in the open spaces between the City and Westminster. James I and Charles I had discouraged building in this area because they wished to keep the landed aristocracy and gentry in the country, performing their necessary functions of local government and political control. Once the obstacle was removed, many such families did exactly what had been feared by becoming urban dwellers for substantial parts of the year, returning to their estates only in the summer. Avoiding the City, they purchased houses in the newly created squares and streets that even today, in many cases, bear the name of entrepreneurs of the reign of Charles II.[5] It is important to realise that this internal migration was an act of colonization, by the gentry, of a metropolis that had until that time been the preserve of the manufacturing and mercantile classes. Its effect was to create a second urban entity, contiguous with but distinct from the older one and outside its system of government. Dryden was himself one such colonizer. The hubs of this new metropolitan formation were the shopping precinct of the New Exchange in the Strand and the auditoria of the theatres, especially Drury Lane and Lincoln's Inn Fields. The theatres were of special importance because attendance was not solely, or even primarily, to see the show but to meet friends in a club-like atmosphere and deliberate over reputations, a process reflected in several scenes of Wycherley's *The Country-wife*.[6] When the South Bank was replaced as a theatrical precinct by the Covent Garden area, the writers came with it, gathering regularly at Will's Coffee House in Russell Street. References to the metropolis now conventionally invoke a new tri-partite classification of the Court, the City and the new entity of the "Town."[7] Dryden's primary London is the third of these entities. The Court, while needing to be flattered, was too hieratic to serve as a model for the new Town-based civility, while the City (as we will see) is its explicit enemy.

The demographics of the Town were naturally more complex than is here indicated. Peter Borsay, in *The English Urban Renaissance: Culture and Society in the Provincial Town, 1660–1700*, sees the authority of traditional civic elites as being challenged by that of provincial gentry, members of the professions, and "pseudo-gentry."[8] Nonetheless, it was the urban branch of the landed gentry that determined manners, civility, and patterns of consumption. This community of countrypersons come to London was for many years a puzzling one for new arrivals. Living the life of unaccustomed leisure outside the ambit of circumscribed and circumscribing rural hierarchies exposed its members to uncertainties of both collective and personal behavior. A country wife or husband come to live in London was not immediately certain what it was to be a Town person and how one should behave as a Town person. There is no need to discount the evidence of Restoration comedy and the Restoration Town lampoon (forbidden the press but omnipresent in manuscript) that sexual morality became far more relaxed.[9] Gentry males in the country may have been free to disport themselves with farmers' daughters (though many came from Puritan families which presumably avoided such practices) but they did not have the distraction of a huge provision of prostitutes highly skilled in enticement. Lines 189–249 of Rochester's "A Letter from Artemiza in the Towne to Chloe in the Countrey" narrate the course of one such case of fatal attraction.[10] Country daughters and wives, never having had the freedom to travel of the fox-hunting males, had also had less opportunity to become involved in sexual impropriety: folklore restricted their errancies to occasional flings with the butler or the chaplain. Relocated to London they encountered a huge increase in both temptation and opportunity. Compounding the problem for both sexes was the insistent demand that they should shed their country ways and country manners, and that to do otherwise was to condemn them to the boorishness of the raw squire of Dryden's "Prologue to *The Wild Gallant,* revived." Yet to remain in the country, according to Isabelle in the same play, was to be "like a wild beast in the wilderness" (III. i. 233–4). Once the Town became a settled society with thoroughly internalized rules and conventions, the life of pleasure could be pursued with a clear understanding of what was acceptable, what merely imprudent, and what strongly to be avoided; but between the 1660s and the 1690s, while these rules were still being negotiated, literature and drama became a principal, if not the principal, source of practical advice. While the writers of comedy and the lampooners exercised a kind of rough, vigilante justice, Dryden stood in the vanguard of a group of "polite" writers whose task was the generation of a new, Town-specific civility.

This was not so much through his comedies, which generally remain court-oriented, as through his occasional verse and above all those perfectly judged public addresses to the Town gathered in assembly, the prologues and epilogues. The poetic wit of these "stage orations" had been learned from the court but is transformed into a means of interrogating the Town. Personally Dryden seems to have been rather awkward in company but in the stage orations he was able to borrow the voices and bodies of skilled professional actors: these are performance scripts and in many ways his most effective pieces of dramatic writing. The persona he created is one vividly responsive to urban sights and sounds, which are composed into Hogarth-like vignettes of unacceptable behavior, as in the "Epilogue to the King and Queen":

> But stay: methinks some Vizard Masque I see,
> Cast out her Lure from the mid Gallery:
> About her all the flutt'ring Sparks are rang'd;
> The Noise continues though the Scene is chang'd:
> Now growling, sputtring, wauling, such a clutter,
> 'Tis just like Puss defendant in a Gutter:
> (*Works* II: 198, lines 11–16)

or this on fops, from the epilogue to *The Man of Mode*:

> His bulky folly gathers as it goes,
> And, rolling o're you, like a Snow-ball growes.
> His various modes from various Fathers follow,
> One taught the Toss, and one the new *French* Wallow.
> His Sword-knot, this; his Crevat, this design'd,
> And this, the yard long Snake he twirls behind.

From one the sacred Perriwig he gain'd,
Which Wind ne're blew, nor touch of Hat prophan'd.
Anothers diving Bow he did adore,
Which with a shog casts all the hair before:
Till he with full Decorum brings it back,
And rises with a Water Spaniel shake.

(*Works* 1: 154, lines 19–30)

In each case the peril of uncontrolled pleasure-seeking is exhibited not so much by argument (though in the first Dryden explicitly warns those who might be inclined to join puss in the gutter that "The Surgeon will be told a wofull story") as by sharp observation and the mocking elegance of couplet wit. But Dryden makes no pretense of being a reformer. Indeed, at this period and in this place, he is no enemy of hedonism, accepting a "soft" Hobbesian vision of the human being as a pleasure-seeking animal. His concern is that pleasure should be pursued in ways that were not self-destructive to individuals and that helped the Town to cohere into a community. Through the vividness of his pictures and the deftness of his ironic deflations, he provided the Town with a social memory of good and bad examples; but he was also a generalist, drawing on a model of human nature as constituted by universal "passions," to be understood theoretically from Hobbes and Descartes and empirically through day-to-day observation of the humors of others. The wit of the closed couplet allowed the general and the particular to be brought into an exceptionally happy conjunction.

Being part of the Town, as Dryden presents it in his stage orations, was in many ways an extension of being a member of the theatre audience. At one level the listener was invited to become a self-aware spectator of the life, vigor, energy, and frequent absurdity of the Town, the boorishness of the country, and the grossness of the City; at another the skill of being a critic or judge was one that should be applied to life as well as to the acted drama. One was also required to be a performer in the Town's everyday theatre, choosing the part that best suited one's capabilities. Even to be a public buffoon, like the fop in the epilogue, need not be a bad thing if one performed one's role with flair and conviction and contributed through it to communal enjoyment. To perform such a role half-heartedly would be to fail in one's duty of being a bad example to the Town. These basic instructions once conveyed, Dryden could instil more elevated ideals of intellectual clarity and personal grace, learned from ancient Rome and modern Paris. For these advanced lessons one might need to turn from the prologues and epilogues to those suave lessons in civility, his dedications. Modern readers tend to skip dedications, but we have no reason to believe that contemporaries did not value them as exemplary demonstrations of polished manners. The preface to the Juvenal of 1693, addressed to the Earl of Dorset, is remarkable not merely for the shrewdness of its reasoning but for its graceful enactment of Town civility.

Lastly, there was the challenge of making something positive out of leisure that would justify it as more than an evasion of the serious tasks of the world. At one level leisure is valued as necessary for the pursuit of pleasure, but in a nobler conception, originating with Aristotle, it is the precondition for acting disinterestedly in matters relating to the conduct of the nation. The cit who never raised his mind beyond money-grubbing was hardly to be compared (in this partisan view) to the Town-polished squire whose leisure encouraged him to enlarge his understanding of human nature. It is striking that in Dryden's prophecy in *Annus Mirabilis* of the rebirth of London, there is no concession that it would need to be the result of very hard work. Likewise, Shimei in *Absalom and Achitophel* is judged by the Town criterion of his failure to consume, not that of his real-life capacity to produce. Work, we seem meant to understand, narrowed the mind while leisure expanded it. Dryden was always aware that the Town, in being the chosen gathering-place of the nation's hereditary ruling class, was the one location in which that class might forge a distinct corporate identity, rather than being divided from itself by local and county allegiances. A parliament that was still the preserve of these lords and squires had to be taught lessons of sense, judgment, and civic purpose that would have been impossible to inculcate had this leisured, semi-permanent coming together in the metropolis never taken place.[11]

The urban other

Dryden's engagement with the City was no less dismissive than that with the country; however, in this case the relentless assertion of cultural superiority is accompanied by curiously mixed feelings of admiration and apprehension, which are never fully resolved. For all his gibes at the country Dryden, along with most of the Town, would regularly travel there for the summer. Apart from in the Dedication to *Annus Mirabilis*, the City is treated throughout his life with unwavering contempt. Bibber, the merchant tailor in *The Wild Gallant*, can be indulged because his personal values are those of a town fop; but his wife Frances's attempt to stand up for the steeple hat against the dressing-box exposes her to merciless Town ridicule (III. ii. 44–91). The prologue to *The Loyal Brother* (1682) entertains the Town assembled at Drury Lane with a vignette of the conduct of its urban other, gathered together for a Pope-burning:

Sir *Edmond-berry*, first, in woeful wise,
Leads up the show, and Milks their Maudlin eyes.
There's not a Butcher's Wife but Dribs her part,
And pities the poor Pageant from her heart;
Who, to provoke revenge, rides round the fire,
And, with a civil congee, does retire.
But guiltless blood to ground must never fall:
There's *Antichrist* behind, to pay for all.
The Punk of *Babylon* in Pomp appears,
A lewd Old Gentleman of Seventy years:
Whose Age in vain our Mercy wou'd implore;
For few take pity on an Old-cast Whore.
The Devil, who brought him to the shame, takes part;
Sits cheek by jowl, in black, to cheer his heart:
Like Theef and Parson in a Tyburn-Cart.
                    (*Works* II: 191, lines 20–34)

The lines express a political confidence which is not as assured as it pretends to be; for the City cannot be trusted:

What if some one inspir'd with Zeal, shou'd call,
Come let's go cry, God save him at *White-hall*?
His best friends wou'd not like this over-care:
Or think him e're the safer for that pray'r.
                    (*Works* II: 191, lines 46–9)

The City's ability to mobilize itself into a politically potent mob had been responsible for the overawing of the Rump and the bringing back of the king in 1660. The here evaded truth was that around 1680 that same power came close to realizing an alternative future in which Britain would have been ruled, in Dutch or US style, by an alliance of capitalists and bureaucrats rather than by its hereditary landholders. Political rivalry disguises itself as a critique of lifestyle. The topics of Dryden's anti-City rhetoric are familiar from the wider field of Restoration comedy and satire. Male cits were grasping and mercenary whereas Town wits were generous and extravagant. Cits were impotent whereas the Town wit performed prodigies of fornication. Female cits were divided between the beautiful and compliant and the ugly and aggressive – both eager for the sexual gratification which their husbands or City suitors were unable to give them. Cits were devoted to a rigid Puritanism in religion, while remaining hypocrites in their daily behavior. The Town wit supported the political cause of the Church of England but was not much concerned with niceties of doctrine or morality (a sign, in Dryden's later view, of the inferiority of their church to that of Rome). Cits were disloyal, filled with nostalgia for the great days of Oliver, while the Town wit was loyal to both the king and the duke. Cits were "greasy," the Town nymph or gallant smooth and scented. In each of these respects the values of the Town were defined in opposition to those envisaged for the cit.

But the real threat of the City was not its vestigial Puritanism, more-than-latent Whiggism, or lack of Town civility, but its control of the national economy. The fact that it hardly missed a step before setting out, like post-World-War-II Germany and Japan, to make itself more brilliant and powerful than before should have been a stunning advertisement for the power of urban, proto-capitalist futurism; but for Dryden to concede this fact would have been to consign the Town to the secondary role of a mere market for commodities which were manufactured or imported by the City. Town wealth was based on land and Town consumption was paid for by income from estates in the country. Yet such income in a period of diminishing agricultural profits – and where protectionist measures such as the Irish Cattle Bill, placing prohibitive duties on the exportation of Irish cattle to England, were necessary to maintain the position of English agriculturalists – was steadily declining. Agricultural land required expensive improvements if it was to sustain its returns, or if, as in the newly-drained fens, fresh areas were to be brought into production. Landed property also bore the main brunt of direct taxation. Increasing one's wealth required involvement in urban land speculation, stockjobbing or overseas trade, all of which could only be undertaken using the expertise of the City and through a preparedness to accommodate oneself to its cultural values. Indeed, the Town, regarded as built environment, was itself a creation of City investors. A few powerful members of landowning families had the good sense to ally themselves with City expertise in order to create fortunes which in some cases are still considerable today. In 1671 George Villiers, second Duke of Buckingham, the Zimri of *Absalom and Achitophel*, put his affairs into the hands of trustees headed by two experienced City bankers. Dryden's quip "Begger'd by Fools, whom still he found too late: / He had his Jest, and they had his Estate" is an uncomprehending reference to this transaction, which in reality was greatly to Buckingham's advantage (*Works* II: 22, lines 561–2).[12] "Alderman George," as Buckingham was called, had shown excellent financial sense in allying himself with City expertise and City sociability. Dryden had no wish to acknowledge a reality that was so much in conflict with his image of the quintessential cit, nor did he ever try to grapple, as Swift and Pope were forced to do, with the ontological conundrum of public credit.[13] His mockery of Buckingham acknowledges the power of the City-based, moneyed interest but refuses to concede that the leisured landowning class could not sustain its hegemony without coming to an accommodation with that interest or that, if it had not been for the Fire, the City rather than the Town might have been the dominant influence on a transformed national politics and culture.

The City wielded a power that was to be envied and feared and for which its transformed physical environment of serviceable brick was a better metaphor than Dryden's envisaged towers. That power became entrenched through the need of the post-Revolution government for huge sums of money which could only be provided by the City and on terms of its choice. Charles II had run the finances of the kingdom pretty much as a Town rake dealt with his tailor's bill – incurring debts and then borrowing more to pay them or, in the state bankruptcy of 1672 known as the Stop of the Exchequer, disowning them. Having exhausted all that the City was prepared to lend, he turned to his cousin Louis XIV, as one might to a generous head of family. In the closing years of his reign, commercial expansion (created by the City) offered him an enhanced yield of customs revenues, which was sufficient in times of peace to support the expenses of government. James, despite enlarging the army, did not occupy the throne long enough to exhaust the money chest left to him by his brother; but under William, committed to ongoing warfare both at home and abroad, the demands of the state escalated enormously. The 1690s were a period of astonishing fiscal adventurism as regarded revenue-raising schemes (including lotteries and taxes on chimneys and windows), state borrowing, and the management of the resulting debts, which could no longer be allowed to fail.[14] The crown, under pressure from a parliament that included many of its creditors, ceased to be a wild gallant and became a deep but responsible borrower. The effect was an enormous increase in the power of the urban other at the expense of the Town and the hereditary landowning class of which the Town was the urban manifestation. And yet that class still clung successfully to cultural authority and political power. It achieved this, as we shall see, through a new-forged alliance against the City between the Town and the previously despised country. Over the last decade of his life Dryden endeavored to enunciate the cultural terms for this alliance, but owing to his oppressed status as a Jacobite this had to be done with delicacy and through texts which are ostensibly concerned with Rome.

The English-Roman city

In the work of the Roman satirists and elegists, Dryden found reflections on the greatest of all historical cities. The Jerusalem of *Absalom and Achitophel* is a mere simulacrum of London: no-one would go to the poem for information about the historical Jerusalem. The Rome of Horace, Ovid, Persius, and Juvenal prefigured aspects of London's modernity but was also a unique historical phenomenon in its own right. Dryden clearly believed that general principles governed the behavior of human beings of all times gathered together in large cities. This happened not only because like circumstances inevitably produced like effects but because the movement of history, as he saw it, was intrinsically cyclic. The writer, through understanding these principles and cycles, had an opportunity to mitigate or even modify their workings. Moreover, because the writer on London had the enormous advantage of being able to reflect on the prior, Roman experience, this opportunity was greater in Dryden's case than it had been for the Roman satirists, who had no city of comparable wealth and power against which they might measure their experience of their own. Where they in the end had turned away from their city in contempt or despair, their English successor could see himself as possessing the intellectual tools to promote a process of urban reformation.

This relationship with the past is fundamental to the whole method of the translations, or paraphrases as Dryden preferred to call them. Comparing his version of the greatest of all city poems from the ancient world, the third satire of Juvenal, with that of his predecessor Oldham or his successor Johnson, we find it is still ostensibly about Rome and Roman life, while the other two use a Roman framework to structure an account of the poet's own world. Dryden's version has a declared archaeologizing tendency which is emphasized by its use of explanatory notes. The reader is left in no doubt that Rome was another country in which many things were done differently. Yet the sense of otherness is continually undercut by the vivid contemporaneity of the language (clothes sent to the botcher; "*Dutch Kitchins*") and the studied insertion of anachronisms. Juvenal's Umbricius includes the gladiatorial games in the colosseum among the aspects of Roman life that an exile might miss. Here Dryden offers both a modernization and an addition:

> But, cou'd you be content to bid adieu
> To the dear Play-house, and the Players too.
> (*Works* IV: 133, lines 363–4)

Not only has the playhouse replaced the arena but the allusion to the sexual availability of the performers, which has no counterpart in the Latin, betrays how closely the tone of the translation has crept to that of Dryden's stage orations. In a similar reference in the sixth satire's account of Hippia's leaving her husband for a "Brother of the Sword" –

> But, stranger yet, and harder to conceive,
> She cou'd the Play-house, and the Players leave.
> (*Works* IV: 155, lines 123–4)

– the original does give the name of a single actor, or rather pantomimist, but the "Damask Bed" she abandons to follow her lover is modern. There is also a careful pointing of urban continuities to counterpoise the evidence of difference. When a note identifies "Arturius" (also Artorius in some early editions of the Latin) as "Any debauch'd wicked Fellow who gains by the times," there is no limitation on which times those might be. The generalizing tendency of Dryden's treatment is further illustrated by his eliding Arturius/Artorius with the Asturicus/Asturius of line 212 of the Latin, whose fortunes are not merely revived but augmented by the gifts of hopeful heirs after the possibly self-instigated burning-down of his house.[15] Knavery and miraculous recovery from fire are linked in Dryden's mind by being phenomena of the City. Baffled by the fact that the fire had left the City grander and wealthier than before, Dryden might almost be suggesting that it was started for exactly that purpose. The summary at the head of the sixth satire points out that the women of Rome "*Love to speak* Greek (*which was then the Fashionable Tongue, as* French *is now with us*" (*Works* IV: 146). The women of this misogynistic rant are urban before they are Roman, with their behavior governed by a transhistorical principle under which country virtue mutates into Town libertinism which is then masked by affectation.

The Persius offers another displaced representation of Dryden's London. Yet, while the Roman foreshadows many of Dryden's misgivings regarding the urban, he advocates an extreme of rejection which Dryden, in his introductions and notes, implicitly condemns. Despite its many drawbacks (to which by this date we have to include the complicity of London in the political change of 1688), the life of the Town is still for Dryden the most desirable of all existences and its polished social values the indispensable foundation for a national culture. Persius, on the other hand, is opposed to the urban to such a degree that he has withdrawn to a private arena of narcissistic rectitude totally apart from the great world of his time. The ideal place for a philosopher in this view is to be on one's estate in the country writing about the irredeemable evils of Rome. Dryden's desire to help in the creation of a national future – doubly important now that this was a matter of political contestation between Williamite and Jacobite – means that his attitude toward his author is always a critical one. Yet Persius clearly had a point. It was only to be expected that the Whigs of the City would have rallied to William's cause, but the quiescence of the Town was something different. Perhaps the life of urban pleasure was not, after all, the best way to produce a generation of politically right-thinking Britons. Persius denounces avarice, the darling vice of the City, but he is no less severe on sloth and luxury, the prerogatives of the Town.

This critique is subjected to more of the careful distancing under which London both is and is not Rome. Differences are made explicit through the preservation of ancient names and through notes explaining archaic customs; yet stress is also laid on continuities. The fifth satire is prefaced with a comparison between Persius' relationship to Cornutus – Persius' "Master and Tutor" – and Dryden's to Richard Busby "to whom I am . . . oblig'd my self, for the best part of my own Education" (*Works* IV: 323). The attack of the first satire on "*the Noblemen and their abominable Poetry, who in the Luxury of their Fortune, set up for Wits, and Judges*" (*Works* IV: 257) can hardly not be read as applying to Dryden's own lifetime of enforced deference to such persons. Anachronisms of the kind illustrated earlier, by jerking the reader unexpectedly back to the present, underscore the artificiality of the whole posture of erudite detachment – the unwilling scholar who writes with a quill instead of a stylus, the tyrant who William-like "trembling in his Arms, takes his accomplice Wife," the dice game in which one throws "Sice" and "Ames-Ace," or the reference in the last line of the fifth satire to "a clipt Sixpence, or a Schilling *Dutch*" (*Works* IV: 343). By endorsing Casaubon's view that Persius had discovered "*some secret Vices of* Nero, *concerning his Lust, his Drunkenness, and his Effeminacy, which had not yet arriv'd to publick Notice*" (*Works* IV: 311), Dryden is able to insinuate that lines 82–8 of "The fourth satyr" should be applied to William, whom the Tory lampooners routinely accused of homosexual relationships with his Dutch favorites.[16] The pose works by imputing a naivety to the annotating translator which is totally at odds with the shrewd, politically hardened ex-laureate of real life. Once the genie of secret meanings has been let out of the bottle, statements made about Rome can hardly not be applied to London. The possibility of writing in this way is the real cause of Dryden's enthusiasm for Persius, an author for whom as a stylist and a kind of philosophical Puritan – "*our Poet was a Stoick Philosopher; and . . . all his Moral Sentences . . . are drawn from the Dogma's of that Sect*" (*Works* IV: 257) – he has mixed feelings.

These equivalences allow us to read Dryden's translations from the Roman satirists as part of his wider reflection on the nature and mutations of the urban. We know Rome through our experience of London and, if properly interrogated, the textual records of Rome will return the compliment. Yet, in the last analysis, the force of these splendid translations lies in the fact that what they represent is not Rome but London presented in Roman dress, like those royal statues and funerary monuments of the time in which Roman armor sits uneasily with the modish wig and moustache. The translations invite us to embrace a comparative understanding of the historical evolution of the two metropolises and the general principles of human behavior there revealed. The conduct of this examination leads to the conclusion of Umbricius and Persius that the metropolis, debauched in one of its divisions by greed and the other by pleasure, had lost the authority to lead the empire in Rome's case and the nation in London's, but not to their despair. The visionary future can still be sought from a foundation of achieved urban values. What has changed is that the metropolis now needs to reinvigorate those values by reacquainting itself with the severer virtue of the country. Nothing in this respect could be done for the City, but the Town, made up of still relatively recent settlers, was equipped to reactivate an older heritage of principled political action without losing the softer accomplishments celebrated in Dryden's eulogy of Ormond in the Dedication of the *Fables*.

City and country

We have seen that the Town was the country come to London and that as part of that process a newcomer was required to discard country manners and values. This contempt is vividly on display in the conversation between Artemis, Doralice, and Melantha in ii. i. of *Marriage A-la-Mode*, with its picture of country families as existing in a kind of Siberian exile from civilization, hungry for every stale scrap of information about Court and Town. And yet Town-resident members of the landowning class still spent part of the year on their estates. In summer Dryden himself liked to join them in their seclusion: much of his best work was done there. The country offered peace and health – two things in short supply in the metropolis – but it was also the nurse of political virtue and a vital training ground for the direction of the state. Insofar as ownership of land involved its productive management, the country taught the principles of business, but not to the point where they became an all-consuming obsession. Insofar as the squire was also the justice of the peace it encouraged a direct experience of the varieties of human nature which, if sharpened by books and Town conversation, gave rise to the ideal legislator. The realization is central to Dryden's late representation to the Town of the country behavior of his cousin and namesake of Chesterton:

> Just, Good, and Wise, contending Neighbours come
> From your Award to wait their final Doom;
> And, Foes before, return in Friendship home.
> (*Works* vii: lines 7–9)

Hunting, savagely mocked in *The Wild Gallant* (iii. i. 236–46), is now portrayed as a social benefit. The pursuit of the "wily Fox" is a contribution to "the Common Good," and even an act of justice in which the quarry is "made to bleed, / Like Felons, where they did the murd'rous Deed" (lines 56–7). Another quarry, the hare, teaches lessons of morality for those able to perceive them (lines 62–6). Exercise gained through the chase preserves one from the murderous attentions of the grasping apothecaries of the City.

> *Garth*, gen'rous as his Muse, prescribes and gives;
> The Shop-man sells; and by Destruction lives:
> Ungrateful Tribe! who, like the Viper's Brood,
> From Med'cine issuing, suck their Mother's Blood!
>
> (lines 107–10)

Yet health is to be valued not merely for itself but for the fact that it supports Cousin Driden through his visits to the insalubrious metropolis in order to attend parliament, which he enriches with "solid Sense" (learned from books and the bench), "spritely Wit" (surely acquired from the Town), and the country virtue of "Integrity." City values have so prevailed that even war is now fought on business principles. "*Munster* was bought" and yet "Who fights for Gain, for greater, makes his Peace" (lines 140–1). Commentary on this poem has been largely concerned with determining its political alignment, yet it also marks a development in Dryden's thought about London, in which the country, after so much earlier mockery, is enrolled as the ally of the liberal Town against the grasping City in a contest for domination of the metropolis and through it of the nation. The townee, once secure in his or her new identity, could move easily between these two worlds, enjoying the good points of both and protected from the worst. The despised "Shop-man" could never make this transition.

It is not necessary to align oneself with these prejudices to accept that they were the terms in which Dryden, at the end of his career, made sense of the emergence of the polycentric, culturally hegemonic modern metropolis into history. The central event of that emergence was the colonization of the Town by the hereditary, landed governing class with a consequent enrichment, of which Dryden himself was prophet and enabler, of both urban and national culture. The historical accident that the flood-tide of this migration coincided with the physical destruction of the part of the metropolis that housed the previously dominant, mercantile civic community left that community ill-equipped to battle for the spoils of its subsequent economic triumphs against the more politically skilled gentry and aristocracy and their clients of the robe, gown, and pen. Nicolson has pointed out that England's landowners enjoyed "the great advantage of being the national inheritors of a language of ethics developed over the preceding century to justify their ruling position."[17] Aware of a huge outpouring of social creativity in a context of incessant innovation, Dryden, himself by temperament an innovator, sought according to the terms given to him by his class and education to channel that creativity. His championing of Yorkist absolutism proved futile in the face of the brute resistance of the City but his wider project of extending polished metropolitan values to a national constituency was remarkably successful and, as much as any writer of his century, he must be allowed a primary role in the creation of the metropolitan literary culture that would sustain the British landed ruling class through two subsequent centuries of first national and then imperial political domination.

NOTES

1. "'Buckingham' commonplace book," Hertfordshire Record Office MS D/EP F37, p. 34.
2. See on this topic Laura M. Gowing, *Domestic Dangers: Women, Words and Sex in Early Modern London* (Oxford, 1996), pp. 70–1, 98–9.
3. The related idea of Dryden's *Virgil* as a "work of mourning" is developed in Julie Candler Hayes, "Temporality, Subjectivity, and Neo-classical Translation Theory: Dryden's 'Dedication of the Aeneis,'" *Restoration* 26 (2002), 97–118 but without reference to the physical loss of the London of Dryden's youth. David B. Morris, "Writing/Reading/Remembering: Dryden and the Poetics of Memory," in *Critical Essays on John Dryden* ed. James A. Winn (New York, 1997), argues that "Memory . . . *makes* the past. Writing that slips through the cracks in memory effectively ceases to exist, swallowed up by the darkness surrounding Dryden's portrait of Oldham" (p. 175). The effects of the Fire and post-Fire rebuilding on the metropolitan imagination are richly explored in Cynthia Wall, *The Literary and Cultural Spaces of Restoration London* (Cambridge, 1998).
4. Described in Neil Hanson, *The Dreadful Judgement* (London, 2001), pp. 64–5 and T. F. Reddaway, *The Rebuilding of London after the Great Fire* (London, 1951), pp. 221–2.
5. I have suggested elsewhere, drawing on Susan E. Whyman's invaluable account of the changing attitudes of one such family, the Verneys, that the newcomers also created a new mode of sociability built around the institution of the "visit." See Whyman's *Sociability and Power in Late-Stuart England: the Cultural Worlds of the Verneys 1660–1720* (Oxford, 1999), pp. 87–109; see also my "Dryden, Rochester and the Invention of the Town," in *John Dryden (1631–1700): His Politics, his Plays, and his Poets*, ed. Claude Rawson (Newark, DE, 2003), pp. 36–51.
6. For this aspect of theatregoing see my "The Theatrical Geography of *The Country Wife*," *Southern Review* (Adelaide) 16 (1983), 404–15.
7. For examples, see Love, "Dryden, Rochester and the Invention of the Town," p. 36 and n. However, "Town" is still often used in its broader sense, necessitating a further, frequently encountered distinction between "this end of the town" and "t'other end of the town."
8. Peter Borsay, *The English Urban Renaissance* (Oxford, 1989), pp. 199–212. "Pseudo-gentry" are defined as either "émigré country gentlemen" or "townspeople who lived an essentially leisured existence, succoured not by any occupation but by the lucrative returns on inherited capital." Their income came from

"money-lending and investment in urban property and the stock-market" (p. 204). The following century brought the new category of the "gentleman merchant" (p. 208), foreshadowed in John Verney.

9. For the lampoon see J. H. Wilson, *Court Satires of the Restoration* (Columbus, Ohio, 1976), and Harold Love, *English Clandestine Satire* (Oxford, 2004).

10. *The Works of John Wilmot, Earl of Rochester* (Oxford, 1999), pp. 68–70.

11. For the wider context of this revolution in manners see Borsay, *The English Urban Renaissance*, pp. 257–83.

12. See on this Frank T. Melton, "A Rake Refinanced; The Fortune of George Villiers, second Duke of Buckingham, 1671–1685," *HLQ* 51 (1998), 297–318.

13. Because it was regarded as "beyond any human control"; see Colin Nicholson, *Writing and the Rise of Finance: Capital Satires of the Early Eighteenth Century* (Cambridge, 1994), pp. 6–7 and passim.

14. See on this Andrea Finkelstein, *Harmony and Balance: An Intellectual History of Seventeenth-century English Economic Thought* (Ann Arbor, 2000), 219–22.

15. A connection had also been suggested by commentators known to Dryden. See *Works* IV: 614.

16. For the lampoon attacks, see Paul Hammond, *Figuring Sex between Men from Shakespeare to Rochester* (Oxford, 2002), pp. 172–85.

17. Nicholson, *Writing and the Rise of Finance*, p. 177.

8

PAULINA KEWES

Dryden's theatre and the passions
of politics

bear your good fortune moderately, Mr. *Poet*: for . . . if I had written
for your Party, your Pention wou'd have been cut off, as useless.
Dryden, *Vindication of the Duke of Guise* (1683)[1]

Restoration theatre was political theatre. To write for the stage or to become
involved in theatre business in the early 1660s – as did the Earl of Orrery,
Sir William Davenant, Thomas Killigrew, Sir Robert Howard, and the less
socially exalted John Dryden – was to declare one's royalist and pro-Stuart
credentials. Dryden's most substantive printed composition prior to the
return of Charles II had been *Heroique Stanzas* (1659), commemorating
Oliver Cromwell. His choice of the profitable dramatic medium signaled his
desire to make money. Yet it also reiterated his commitment, manifest in his
versified celebrations of the Restoration, to the Stuart monarchy.

What were Dryden's early allegiances – personal, political, commercial –
and how did they change over a playwriting career that spanned nearly
four decades? Dryden eulogized the king in *Astraea Redux. A Poem on the
Restoration of Charles the Second* (1660) and *To His Sacred Majesty, A
Panegyrick on His Coronation* (1661), and he made Stuart rule the stuff
of heroic poetry in *Annus Mirabilis* (1667), a Virgilian chronicle of 1666;[2]
he collaborated with Sir Robert Howard, Sir William Davenant, and the
Duke of Newcastle on *The Indian Queen* (1664), *The Tempest* (1667), and
Sir Martin Mar-All (1667) respectively; and he dedicated his published work
to a range of noble recipients. Even as he sought royal and aristocratic
patronage, he solidified his position in the theatrical marketplace. Dryden
re-invented the dramatic profession after an eighteen-year hiatus. He started
out as a freelancer but in 1668 he signed an exclusive contract with the King's
Company under the management of Thomas Killigrew, effectively becoming
a house playwright. The contract obliged Dryden to supply three scripts a
year in return for one and a quarter shares, out of twelve and three-quarters,
in the company's profits.[3]

Dryden's bid for royal favor and recognition was rewarded. He was
appointed Poet Laureate in 1668 and Historiographer Royal in 1670. With

these appointments came a change in status. Dryden was not typical of the class of professional playwrights who would dominate the period.[4] His position as shareholder and laureate afforded him, at least initially, a measure of financial security denied to those such as Thomas Shadwell, John Crowne, Elkanah Settle, Aphra Behn, Edward Ravenscroft, and Nathaniel Lee, all of whom began writing regularly for the theatre in the late 1660s or early 1670s. Dryden was, moreover, a public figure in a way those other writers were not. No longer an expression of a private individual's view, his writings came to be interpreted in the context of royal policy. Readers were reminded of Dryden's official status by the title-pages of the printed editions of his work: "Written by John Dryden. Servant to his Majesty."

How did commercial pressures and demands of public office affect Dryden's handling of politics in the plays he wrote under Charles II and James II? To what political ends did he shape the dramatic media after the Revolution of 1688–9 that deprived him of his official appointments and forced him into opposition? A number of critics have responded to these questions by emphasizing Dryden's engagement with monarchist ideology, with propaganda and foreign policy, and with the uncertainties and anxieties that attach to the representation of kingship. For others, Dryden is a player in the publicity surrounding Exclusion, or, after the Glorious Revolution, the principal of Jacobite allegory and innuendo.[5] These studies have made us more sensitive to the subtle ways in which Dryden endorses divine-right kingship and have drawn attention to the breadth of Dryden's political interests, but we still need to appreciate how varied was Dryden's response to politics and ideology across decades of changing political circumstances, and in a range of dramatic genres – heroic plays, comedies, tragedies, tragicomedies, operas, and adaptations of Shakespeare. While Dryden was the imaginative writer most closely identified with the Stuart cause both before and after the Glorious Revolution, there is no necessary order, coherence, and consistency to his theatrical work. Themes, tropes, plots, generic conventions, and methods of engagement with ideology and politics recur, shift, and alter to meet the need of the moment. Dryden is at his most accomplished and ingenious as a political dramatist at times of uncertainty or defeat – early in the Exclusion Crisis or shortly after the arrival of William and Mary – when ambiguity and teasing allusiveness replace the more transparent topicality. From a strictly literary point of view, we shall find most arresting his attempts – admittedly not always successful – to appropriate and destabilize genres, forms, and styles practiced by or associated with his opponents: Milton's republican epic and the City of London's pageantry which he transformed into royalist operas, *The State of Innocence* (1673–4, unperformed; pub. 1677) and *Albion and Albanius* (1685) respectively.

Drama and politics

The claim is heard repeatedly in prologues, epilogues, ballads, and more substantial prose and verse writings of the 1660s that two decades earlier the philistine rebels had imposed a ban on play-acting because of the drama's royalist bias; and that the return of Charles-Augustus, who lifted it, signaled a revival of arts and letters – and of public order.[6] This assumption was implicit in Dryden's *Essay of Dramatic Poesy* (pub. 1668), the most significant piece of dramatic criticism in English to that date. "[W]e have been so long together bad *Englishmen*," Dryden wrote, "that we had not leisure to be good Poets . . . as if in an Age of so much horror, wit and those milder studies of humanity, had no farther business among us" (*Works* XVII: 33–4). Set against a background of the English naval victory over the Dutch, the *Essay* mapped out a bold route for contemporary playwrights. They were called upon to surpass the achievement of the Ancients such as Sophocles, Plautus, and Terence, of Renaissance dramatists such as Shakespeare, Jonson, and Fletcher, and of French neoclassical writers, notably Corneille, and to produce patriotic drama that would glorify the future martial exploits of post-Restoration England.

The myth of the abiding royalism of pre-Civil War drama – which, as Martin Butler and others have shown, had expressed a range of anti-court opinions[7] – was convenient for aspiring playwrights. It helped cast the intervening years as an aberration, a chaotic intermezzo succeeded by the king's providential restoration. New plays (Dryden's chief among them) and revivals of old ones offered reassurance and an affirmation of continuity. Neither monarchy nor theatre, however, was what it had been before. Although its powers as embodied in the Restoration settlement were considerable, the monarchy's mystique had been damaged by the overthrow of Charles I. Under Charles II, it declined further.[8] The restored regime never commanded full ideological sway but by the late 1660s even a semblance of consensus disappeared.[9] The king's libertinism and his flirtation with Catholic France; the embarrassing circumstances surrounding the fall of Clarendon; and the humiliation of the Second Dutch War were compounded by natural disasters, the plague and the Great Fire of London, that Charles's Puritan critics interpreted as divine punishment. The drama, hitherto the province of virtually unqualified royalism, ceased to be so. In the late 1660s plays voiced criticism of the king's personal conduct and his public policy. Those concerns and the anxieties raised by the conversion to Catholicism of his brother and heir, James, Duke of York, mounted steadily throughout the 1670s. They came to a head during the Popish Plot and the Exclusion Crisis of 1678–81. The polarization of public opinion and the rise of political parties – Tories and Whigs – led to the emergence of partisan drama, both pro- and anti-government. A side-effect of the crisis was the shrinking of audiences and the demise of one of the acting companies. Following the consolidation of the Tory victory and the accession of James II in 1685, there came a lull in the production of politically charged plays. It lasted until the Revolution of 1688–9, which in turn gave rise to Williamite apologetics and long-term Jacobite polemic.[10]

These developments shaped both content and mode of political engagement of late seventeenth-century drama. Contemporary plays participated in the public debate on national politics in four ways. First, they articulated royalist ideology, increasingly signaling contradictions within it (the picture of kingship in heroic dramas by Orrery, Dryden, Settle, and later Otway and Lee); secondly, they provided topical commentary on recent or current events, often by means of parallels drawn from the native or the foreign past (Sir Robert Howard's *The Duke of Lerma*, 1668; Dryden's *The Spanish Fryar*, 1680; Otway's *Venice Preserv'd*, 1682); thirdly, they used personation to attack specific people or factions (George Villiers, Second Duke of Buckingham and Sir Robert Howard's *The Country Gentleman*, 1669; Dryden and Lee's *The Duke of Guise*, 1682; and John Crowne's *City Politiques*, 1683); and, fourthly, they deployed allegory to shadow well-known people and events (Dryden's *Albion and Albanius*, 1685). While some Restoration plays were fairly explicit about their political aims, most were not – or at least were sufficiently subtle to preclude simple analogical interpretation. In the absence of detailed reception records, we may at most speculate on applications that might be made of plays under particular circumstances by audience members of a distinctive political orientation. John M. Wallace, Robert D. Hume, and Susan J. Owen have argued that it may be unwarranted to attribute political intentions to playwrights and to assume that those intentions were conveyed in performance.[11] Yet to question whether and to what degree the author's political meanings were realized in the theatre is not to deny that plays were written to score political points as Dryden's certainly were. That would be to argue for a kind of political innocence that was surely foreign to the hyper-conscious political environment of the Restoration. It is true that, even when the prologue invited the spectators to look for an unambiguous political message, the play often disappointed such expectations. It is also true that there were malicious interpretations that deliberately ascribed views to authors which they obviously did not hold. There is no doubt, however, that Dryden and other dramatists exploited this climate of interpretative free-for-all to deny responsibility for dangerous or divisive arguments by adopting a pose of naivety.

Rebellions and restorations

The approach of drama to politics in the early years of Charles II's reign was uncomplicated in being almost exclusively backward-looking and consensual. Playwrights concentrated on the traumas of civil war and regicide, responding to them in one of two ways. They either cast the agents of rebellion as comic dupes or they reconfigured rebellion as aristocratic usurpation, its inevitable failure being followed by the return of the rightful ruler or his heir.[12] In his collaborations and solo plays, Dryden adapted these plot-lines for tragicomedy (*The Tempest*, 1667; *Marriage A-la-Mode*, 1671) and rhymed heroic drama (*The Indian Queen*, 1664; *The Indian Emperor*, 1665; *Tyrannick Love*, 1669).[13] But in these same plays he also developed strikingly new plots.

Several satiric comedies produced in the 1660s were set during the Interregnum. John Tatham's *The Rump* (1660), Abraham Cowley's *Cutter of Coleman Street* (1661), Sir Robert Howard's *The Committee* (1662), and John Lacy's *The Old Troop* (1664) re-played the conflict between the Roundheads and the Cavaliers. All these pieces conclude in the ritual humiliation of the Puritan upstarts over whom the loyalist heroes triumph in the end, although not without a fair amount of trickery and underhand dealing. None of Dryden's plays is so topical in its setting or so transparent in targeting the Puritans.

The Tempest, or The Enchanted Island, an adaptation of Shakespeare co-written with Davenant, shadows recent history. By debunking the political ambitions of low-class rebels ("I say this Island shall be under *Trincalo*, or it shall be / a Common-wealth," II. iii. 131–2), it satirizes the architects of the English Revolution. In the printed edition of the play, however, Dryden assigns the scenes in question – "[t]he Comical parts of the Saylors" – to his partner (x: 4). If the subplot of the *Tempest* provides a mocking commentary on the constitutional debates of the 1640s and 1650s, its high plot recalls the auspicious events of 1660. Dryden and Davenant strengthen Shakespeare's emphasis on the evils of usurpation by staging two restorations instead of one (Prospero's to the throne of Milan and his ward Hippolito's to that of Mantua). For all their insistence on the superiority of kingly rule to other forms of government, and for all their preoccupation with royal legitimacy, Dryden and Davenant hint at the decline in the stature of the monarchy.[14] The Restoration Prospero possesses neither the authority nor the power of his Jacobean counterpart. Both his children (he has two daughters, Miranda and Dorinda, and an adoptive son, Hippolito) and his subjects (Caliban and his sister Sycorax) defy him. Only the *deus-ex-machina* intervention of Ariel secures a happy ending. Some critics have argued that *The Tempest* goes beyond rehearsal of the recent past and extends its topical allusions to the present, casting an oblique glance at the impeachment of the Earl of Clarendon.[15] There is no evidence that any contemporary spectator made such a connection. Yet even if some members of the audience understood the Restoration *Tempest* in this way, this does not mean that the collaborators had intended their play to be so interpreted: the shaping of its two plots directs the spectators to look back to the Civil War and the subsequent reinstatement of the monarchy rather than pointing towards the murky present.

If the collaboration with Davenant gave Dryden a taste for exploiting the political potential of Shakespeare – something he would pursue single-handedly in *All for Love* (1678) and *Troilus and Cressida* (1679) – the slightly earlier cooperation with Sir Robert Howard on *The Indian Queen* (1664) had been his first foray into heroic drama, a form of which he would become chief practitioner and theorist. In *The Indian Queen* the lines of division between heroes and villains are sharply drawn. The usurping queen of Mexico, Zempoalla, whose lover had murdered the rightful king, is lustful and treacherous. Her moral and sexual corruption contrasts with the nobility and magnanimity of the king's son and heir, Montezuma, who has been brought up in obscurity but who now returns to claim the throne.

Yet even at so early a date there are intimations of two sorts of threat to political stability. The play demonstrates the pitfalls of royal highhandedness in alienating a powerful subject or ally. Before his identity is revealed, indeed before he himself is aware of his royal lineage, Montezuma impulsively changes sides in response to what he perceives as kingly ingratitude. He supports, by turns, the Inca of Peru and the Mexican usurper. His shifts of allegiance temporarily bring down both regimes: the legitimate and the illegitimate. Another danger to royal authority is posed by popular power. Montezuma's restoration is assisted by a popular rising. Although the people instinctively recognize the justice of his cause, their volatility – until now they have been loyal to the usurping queen – is an uncomfortable reminder of the equally unstable loyalties of the English. Similar reminders are issued in Dryden's *Marriage A-la-Mode* (1671) whose high plot dramatizes yet another successful restoration and, more sternly and reprovingly, in a series of anti-populist plays, from *Oedipus* (1678), *The Spanish Fryar* (1680), and *The Duke of Guise* (1682) to *Don Sebastian* (1689) and *Cleomenes* (1692).[16]

It would be misleading, however, to see Dryden's plays as the exclusive domain of domestic politics. Bridget Orr has recently called attention to the prominence of foreign affairs in late seventeenth-century drama.[17]

The theatre, Orr has shown, provided a public platform for debates about the ethics and the political and economic viability of empire. Heroic plays registered developments in Stuart foreign policy, commerce, and popular sentiment toward states suspected of reaching for universal dominion – Spain, the Dutch Republic, and France. In *The Indian Emperor* (1665), Dryden's sequel to *The Indian Queen*, the now aging Montezuma is faced with invasion from abroad and opposition at home. Written when Anglican royalists under the leadership of the Duke of York pushed for war against the Dutch whom they saw as dangerous aspirers to the universal empire of trade,[18] the play dramatizes the conquest of Mexico by England's old imperial rival, Spain. Drawing on vilifying accounts of Spain, Dryden attacks the cruelty, greed, and irreligion of the conquerors.

Spain's imperial doctrine rested on legal and religious arguments designed to justify the subjection of colonized peoples. Both are challenged here. Montezuma's verbal confrontation with the Spaniards reveals the hollowness and irrelevance to the New World of such legislation in the Old. The scene of the Mexican emperor's torture by a priest and a conquistador graphically demonstrates the mercenary motives of both. It also exposes the spuriousness of Catholic claims of superiority to paganism. Nonetheless in his portrayal of the virtuous Cortez Dryden offers a more positive rationale for empire that seems to hint at England's providential mission in the Americas. He plays with yet another imperial scenario two years later in the dedication of the play to Anne, wife to Charles II's bastard son, James, Duke of Monmouth.[19] Cast as Dryden's creative offspring, a heroic lover, and a princely victim of Spanish atrocities, Montezuma pays homage to the Duchess and thus, by implication, to the English. His tribute serves as an acknowledgment of his new masters' civility, magnanimity, and power. As we shall see, Dryden was to exploit the alliance between the indigenous population of the Spice Islands and the English, whom, in his later blood-soaked domestic-tragedy-*cum*-history-play, *Amboyna* (1672–3), he contrasts with the barbarous Dutch.

Apologies for Stuart kingship

Towards the end of the first decade of Charles II's reign the drama's royalism became muted and uncertain. Paradoxically, just as public support for the restored regime began to falter, Dryden came to occupy a position that made him a spokesman for the king. He was not – at least not then – drafting royal proclamations or policy documents but scripts for performance before paying audiences. *Tyrannick Love, or The Royal Martyr* (1669), the first play Dryden composed after the award of the laureateship, illustrates the challenge now before him. In his effort to meet royal expectations, a tension may be detected between the ideal and the real, between the heroic medium of the drama and the context of its production.

This tension lies behind the seeming contradictions in design and effect of *Tyrannick Love*. Set in imperial Rome, the tragedy pits the blasphemous and despotic usurper Maximin against the Christian martyr and saint-in-the-making, Catherine of Alexandria. The play was conceived as a compliment to Charles II's Catholic consort, the Portuguese Infanta, Catherine of Braganza, who had been regularly likened to, and represented as, St. Catherine. A medal struck in her honor in 1662, the year of her arrival in England, depicted both Catherine and, on the obverse, her saintly namesake. Edmund Waller's song "Sung by Mrs. Knight, to her Majesty, on her Birth-Day" in 1663 also exploited the parallel, as did contemporary portraiture and civic entertainments. In 1664, the Queen had been portrayed as St. Catherine with the saint's principal emblem, the broken wheel, by her favorite painter, Jacob Huysmans.[20] In John Tatham's Lord Mayor's Show for that year, *Londons Triumphs . . . Performed at the Costs and Charges of the Worshipful Company of Haberdashers*, the figure of St. Katharine – "Patronesse of the Company" – addressed the newly elected Lord Mayor and the royal couple who attended the pageant in a "Scene . . . presented as the Hyroglyphick of *Integrity*."[21] Dryden's choice of St. Catherine as his heroine was thus singularly appropriate. His tribute was also timely, for late in 1669 rumors circulated about the queen's pregnancy.[22]

In his presentation of the saint, Dryden was careful not to draw attention to St. Catherine's status as a Catholic icon. Instead, he emphasized the strength of her Christian faith in the face of the emperor's atheistic outbursts. If Dryden's solution to the confessional problem presented by his subject was, like Tatham's, effective in being non-contentious (Tatham's St. Katharine hailed true Christianity's ultimate victory over "Faction and Prophaneness," p. 10), his treatment of the politics of imperial Rome was rather less so. *Tyrannick Love* evokes a series of topical associations. At the outset, Catherine (the "*Royal Martyr*") seems to recall another Royal Martyr – Charles I; her nemesis, the usurping Maximin, is a satiric portrait of the regicidal Cromwell (Maximin had murdered the rightful emperor). Yet, as the action unfolds, those associations dissolve and shift. Maximin's adulterous propensity, for example, distances him from the Puritan Cromwell; and some spectators may have seen it as an allusion to the promiscuity of Charles II. More generally, in contrast to earlier heroic plays which routinely concluded with the reinstatement of hereditary kingship, the political resolution of *Tyrannick Love* is ambivalent. "The play closes with the tyrant's death and the election of two Emperors by the Senate."[23] This "un-English constitutional settlement" is compounded by the virtuous characters' death or retirement from political life.[24]

One of the bodies littering the stage at play's end is that of the emperor's pure and brave daughter Valeria, acted by the King's Company's chief comedienne, Nell Gwynne, who became Charles II's mistress shortly afterwards. The instant the bearers are to take her up and carry her off the stage, Valeria–Gwynne revives and cries out:

> Hold, are you mad? you damn'd confounded Dog,
> I am to rise, and speak the Epilogue . . .
> I come, kind Gentlemen, strange news to tell ye,
> I am the Ghost of poor departed *Nelly*,
> Sweet Ladies, be not frighted, I'le be civil,
> I'm what I was, a little harmless Devil . . .
>
> As for my Epitaph when I am gone,
> I'le trust no Poet, but will write my own.
> Here *Nelly* lies, who, though she liv'd a Slater'n,
> Yet dy'd a Princess, acting in S. *Cathar'n*.
>
> (lines 1–6, 27–30)

Shattering the vision of heroic Roman society poised to adopt Christianity, the Epilogue returns the audience to the unheroic social and political world of contemporary London where a slut's impersonation of a chaste princess advances her to the royal bed.

In the 1670s Dryden moved from exorcizing the past to glorification, defense, and justification of the present. He deployed historical or biblical settings to shore up the prestige of the Stuart monarchy in rhymed heroic plays (*1–2 The Conquest of Granada by the Spaniards*, 1670–1);[25] to defend the Crown's foreign policy in a sensationalist tragedy (*Amboyna*, 1672–3); to affirm the value of Carolean court culture in the operatic version of *Paradise Lost* (*The State of Innocence*, 1673–4); and to defuse concerns over the king's passion for the French Catholic Louise de Kéroualle by glorifying history's greatest illicit lovers, Antony and Cleopatra, in a blank verse tragedy based on Shakespeare (*All for Love: Or the World Well Lost*, 1677).[26] Yet Dryden was too acute a political observer and too good a dramatist to offer unqualified praise. Like his contemporaries, he was alive to the personal shortcomings of the Stuart brothers and to the growing unpopularity of the Carolean regime as well as to its inconsequentiality on the international scene. Even his most magnificent and seemingly unambiguous tribute to Stuart kingship, the two-part heroic extravaganza, *The Conquest of Granada*, registers fissures within the royalist ethos. We discern a note of guarded criticism too in his portrayal of inadequate rulers from Boabdelin in *The Conquest of Granada* to the old emperor in *Aureng-Zebe* (1675), Dryden's last effort in the heroic mode.

Written in resounding rhyming couplets, *The Conquest of Granada* is a ten-act heroic extravaganza. With its ample cast of characters and its epic setting against the background of the Spanish re-conquest of Granada torn by the tribal rivalry between the Abencerrages and the Zegrys, the play was an artistic success and a huge box-office hit. As such it became the main target of the Duke of Buckingham's and others' burlesque in *The Rehearsal*, in which its high-blown verse and its larger-than-life hero Almanzor were savagely satirized as was Dryden himself. *The Conquest* was also parodied in an intensely obscene anti-monarchical closet piece, *Sodom*, sometimes doubtfully attributed to Buckingham's political ally, the Earl of Rochester.[27]

The principle of teaching by praise animates both Dryden's play and the dedication of the printed edition to the heir apparent, James, Duke of York. "Since . . . the World is govern'd by precept and Example; and both these can onely have influence from those persons who are above us, that kind of Poesy which excites to vertue the greatest men, is of greatest use to humane kind. 'Tis from this consideration," Dryden says, "that I have presum'd to dedicate to your Royal Highness these faint representations of your own worth and valour in Heroique Poetry" (*Works* IX: 3). The duke's courage and military prowess during the Second Dutch War are highlighted in anticipation of renewed hostilities: "when our former enemies again provoke us, you will again solicite fate to provide you another Navy to overcome" (p. 5). Dryden's play had been published shortly before the king, urged on by his brother, declared war against the Dutch on 17 March 1672. Within a few months Dryden joined the anti-Dutch campaign with his *Amboyna or The Cruelties of the Dutch to the English Merchants* (1672–3), a xenophobic history play with elements of political prophecy whose title echoes Davenant's Protectorate opera, *The Cruelty of the Spaniards in Peru* (1658). Dryden chronicles the massacre of several East India Company merchants at Amboina in the Moluccas or Spice Islands (now in Indonesia) in February 1623. The events at Amboina had previously furnished subject-matter for documentary drama and painting, both commissioned by the East India Company in 1625. Those had been promptly suppressed by the Jacobean authorities keen to avoid inflaming public opinion against the Protestant Dutch, with whom England was making common cause against Catholic Spain.[28] Memories of Amboina that had flared up during successive Anglo-Dutch conflicts, the First and Second Dutch Wars in 1652–4 and 1664–7 respectively, were deliberately revived in 1672. Original pamphlet accounts of the massacre were reissued and new ones printed with pointed and timely prefatory comments.[29] There were also anti-Dutch mayoral pageants and puppet shows such as Anthony

Di Voto's "the Dutch cruelties at Amboina."[30] Dryden may have undertaken *Amboyna* at the suggestion of Thomas Clifford, Charles II's Lord Treasurer and dedicatee of the printed version.[31] Clifford had been one of the architects of the Treaty of Dover that had allied England with Catholic France and, in a secret clause, committed the king to re-Catholicizing the country. Designed to incite anti-Dutch feeling during the early stages of the Third Dutch War, the tragedy sets mercantile competition between the two nations in the context of personal rivalry between an Englishman and a Dutchman, Captain Towerson and Harman Junior, for the hand of the native Ysabinda.

Dryden works on his spectators' emotions, stirring up their indignation and rage at Harman Jr.'s brutal rape of Ysabinda and his compatriots' base torture and execution of the English traders (and their Spanish ally Perez) whose goods they greedily seize. Yet he also appeals to the viewers' rational faculties: prologue and epilogue proclaim – and dramatic dialogue and action illustrate – the innate corruption of the Dutch republican polity. Although they are both Protestant nations, Dryden insists that the English and the Dutch are natural enemies. The commonality of religion should not be used as an argument against the clash between the English monarchy and the self-styled High and Mighty United Provinces whose statehood, like that of the mid-century Puritan Commonwealth, had its origin in an ungodly rebellion against sovereign authority. Political principles rather than commercial rivalry are at the root of the Anglo-Dutch enmity. Dryden's *Amboyna* is thus more than a timely boost of the Carolean regime's foreign policy; like his earlier heroic plays, it is an affirmation of royalism made in the context of international relations and articulated through reversal of literary tropes traditionally associated with the republican ethos, notably Tarquin's rape of Lucrece and Scevola's attempted regicide. For Dryden, the republican Dutch embody the sexual and political tyranny of the Tarquins. He presents the loyalist English as rightful heirs to ancient Roman honor, heroism, and liberty.

Dryden continued his royalist program in *The State of Innocence* (1673–4) – his refashioning of *Paradise Lost*. Whereas his potboiler of a tragedy had re-staged the past, his semi-opera abbreviated Milton's epic, and in the process subjected it to a thoroughgoing ideological revision. *The State of Innocence* may have been designed to celebrate the nuptials, on 21 November 1673, of the Duke of York and Mary Beatrice d'Este of Modena, to whom the printed text was inscribed. The opera was certainly meant as a counterweight to the multimedia spectaculars that the Duke's Company had been successfully mounting at their fancy Dorset Garden Theatre. The elaborate special effects, machines, and scenery that *The State of Innocence* called for were not to be had in the King's Company's recently opened Drury Lane, described by Dryden himself as a "Plain Built House."[32] Although his opera remained unacted, its impact as a reading text must have been considerable. It circulated widely in both manuscript and print, going through nine editions in Dryden's lifetime.[33]

The State of Innocence has been dismissed by modern scholars as a woeful mangling of *Paradise Lost*. Yet most contemporaries were impressed by its artistry. That Dryden dared to turn Milton's blank verse into rhyme was a sign of creative self-confidence, even though he had obtained the older poet's permission. By the early 1670s, Dryden was the most highly acclaimed living poet. As Steven N. Zwicker has noted, it was Milton who seems to have fallen prey to anxiety of influence: he composed his brief epic, *Paradise Regained*, and his closet play, *Samson Agonistes*, both published in 1671, at least in part as refutations of the theory and practice of Dryden's heroic drama.[34] Dryden's operatic retort to the chief apologist of the English Commonwealth inverted not only the politics and religion but also the style and genre of Milton's epic.

Dryden conveys loyalism and respect for monarchical authority through the satiric language, reminiscent of the anti-republicanism of *Amboyna*, in which the infernal rebels describe their enterprise: "Most high and mighty Lords, who better fell / From Heav'n, to rise States-General of Hell" (I. i. 85–6). Although Dryden does not refer explicitly to the Puritan Revolution, Lucifer's insurgency, malice, and pride – "vain desire / of Empire, in my thoughts still shot me higher, / To mount above his sacred Head" (III. i. 5–7) – would probably have been associated with Oliver Cromwell by pro-Stuart readers who had been long accustomed to demonic portrayals of the Protector in dramatic pamphlets and royalist historiography: *Craftie Cromwell* (1648), *The Second part of Crafty Cromwell* (1648), *The Famous Tragedie of King Charles I* (1649), *Cromwell's Conspiracy* (1660), *Hells Higher Court of Justice; or, The Triall of The three Politick Ghosts, Viz. Oliver Cromwell, King of Sweden, and Cardinal Mazarine* (1661), and James Heath's *Flagellum: Or The Life and Death, Birth and Burial of Oliver Cromwel The late Usurper* (1663, in its fifth edition by 1672). In 1649, the year of the regicide, the prologue to *The Famous Tragedie* had predicted of the rebels that "*Joves* all potent thunder shall divide / Their plots, and sinke them, in their height of pride"; in 1660, the year of the Restoration, the Prologue to *Cromwell's Conspiracy* pithily summed up Cromwell's Lucifer-like rise and demise: "Long thus he domineer'd, at last he fell; / Despairing dy'd a *Sacrifice for Hell*."[35]

Dryden takes issue with Milton's religious stance. He departs from the predestinarian doctrine that animates *Paradise Lost* by conferring an anti-deterministic slant on the discussion of free will conducted by Adam, Gabriel, and Raphael (IV. i). Consonant with the notion of a "fortunate fall," his closing vision of the future is also more optimistic than Milton's: "*Here a Heaven descends, full of Angels and blessed Spirits, with soft Music, a Song and Chorus*" (V. iv). This vision was to be conjured up by music and spectacle of the kind promoted, if not financially sponsored, by the Carolean court. In 1674 the King's Company mounted Pierre Perrin's French opera *Ariane*, revised to compliment the Duke of York, with scenic sets borrowed from Whitehall.[36] Dryden thus imposed the royalist court ethos on the old regicide's Puritan epic. His admirer the young Nathaniel Lee enthused in a commendatory poem prefaced to the first edition:

> He [Milton] first beheld the beauteous rustic Maid,
> And to a place of strength the prize convey'd;
> You took her thence: to Court this Virgin brought
> Drest her with gemms, new weav'd her hard spun thought
> And softest language, sweetest manners taught.
> Till from a Comet she a star did rise,
> Not to affright, but please our wondring eyes.[37]

Dryden further signaled his loyalty to the Stuart cause in the fulsome dedication to Mary of Modena, the Duke of York's recent bride. Here Dryden seems not to have aimed either for ecumenism or for confessional reconciliation.[38] Both Mary and James were Catholic – the Duke's failure to take the Test in 1673 had made his conversion public, and it was clear that their offspring would be too. By proffering his unperformed opera to the likely future queen – "the Creator . . . has plac'd You so near a Crown" (*Works* XII: 82) – Dryden declared his firm support for Catholic succession. His dedication combines praise of the Duchess's beauty, provocatively couched in the idiom of anti-Yorkist polemic, with an extravagant encomium of the Duke. Dryden thus counters opponents of the popish successor such as Andrew Marvell, author of the inflammatory *An Account of the Growth of Popery, and Arbitrary Government in England* (1677).

The State of Innocence was published in February 1677, on the eve of a new session of Parliament. That session proved turbulent. Buckingham and Shaftesbury, leading opponents of the Crown's policy – and of Dryden's patron, the Duke of York – were sent to the Tower. The theatre was not slow in responding to the darkening of the political scene. The drama's shift in outlook from idealistic and commendatory in the early 1660s to critical or at best apologetic and justificatory in the mid-to-late 1670s is epitomized by the treatment of royal consorts and mistresses, above all the Egyptian Cleopatra. Like plays about royal favorites,[39] those about royal mistresses could reflect unease or outright disapproval of the monarch himself. In the translations of Corneille's *La Mort de Pompée* by Katherine Philips and the Court Wits, in 1663 and 1664 respectively, Cleopatra's undaunted spirit and virtue had been held up for admiration.[40] She had been portrayed as a fit consort for the victorious and equally virtuous Caesar. By the late 1670s, the focus of theatrical representations of Cleopatra's love life had changed from Julius Caesar to Mark Antony – for instance, in Sir Charles Sedley's *Antony and Cleopatra* (Duke's Company, Feb. 1677) and Dryden's *All for Love; or, The World Well Lost* (King's Company, by Dec. 1677). Were these plays innocuous meditations on private passions and public duties of kings and queens? Or did they insinuate comparisons between Antony and Cleopatra and Charles II and his then most powerful mistress, Louise de Kéroualle, Duchess of Portsmouth?

Widely despised as a Catholic and a foreigner, and condemned for her meddling in politics and costly lifestyle, Kéroualle was denounced by her enemies as a stranger and a whore: the Philistine Delilah and the Egyptian Cleopatra. We find satiric vignettes of her as the biblical spy and *femme fatale* in contemporary poetic ephemera such as *Sir Edmund Berry Godfrey's Ghost* (1679) and *Satire on Old Rowley* (1680).[41] There are no surviving visual representations of Kéroualle as Delilah or Cleopatra. *On the Dutchesse of Portsmouths Picture*, a contemporary verse encomium that likened her to Egypt's queen, may suggest, however, that such a painting had once been in existence.[42] Sedley's dramatized portrayal of the Eastern temptress drew on a rich vein of Restoration portraiture. Art historians have noted the changing iconography of Cleopatra and Antony in the Restoration. Whereas in the Renaissance Cleopatra had been typically depicted at the moment of her death, in the later seventeenth century she was most frequently shown holding or dissolving a pearl. With its emphasis on royal opulence, extravagance, and recklessness, that scene encapsulated the glamor and wastefulness associated with Charles's court.[43] In presenting Cleopatra as Antony's consort, Sedley may have alluded to the quasi-wedding ceremony staged for the king and his new mistress at Euston, the Arlingtons' country seat, in October 1671. "It was universally reported," John Evelyn recorded on 10 October 1671, "that the faire Lady – was bedded one of these nights, and the stocking flung, after the manner of a married Bride."[44] Appearing at a time when the king lavished huge sums of money on the duchess, and when her political influence stood high, Sedley's tragedy exposed Cleopatra's manipulative and exploitative nature and her responsibility for Antony's downfall. *Antony and Cleopatra* resonated with the mounting concerns about the king's private and public conduct, portraying the great Roman hero – "in love and pleasure drown'd" – torn between patriotic duty and passion for an unpopular, alien mistress.[45]

Sedley's "Antony is a critical portrayal of Charles II," Derek Hughes contends; "Actium stands for the Third Dutch War."[46] The king, we know, attended a performance of Sedley's tragedy on 12 February 1677.[47] If *Antony and Cleopatra* was an overt attack rather than a potential "application" play, why did he not suppress it? Only spectators who already strongly disapproved of Charles II's profligacy and infatuation with Kéroualle and who were also opposed to the diplomatic alliance with Catholic France and war against the Protestant Dutch, would likely have taken Sedley's play as an indictment of Charles's morals and politics.[48] Dryden's *All for Love*, by contrast, provides a moving apology for the lovers and absolves Cleopatra from charges of treason and duplicity. It also seems far removed from the public outcry over the king's sexual conduct, expenditure, and foreign policy. The modern audience, used to the infinite variety of Shakespeare's "serpent of the Nile," would be startled by Dryden's heroine's claim "Nature meant me / A Wife, a silly harmless houshold Dove, / Fond without art; and kind without deceit" (IV. i. 91–3). Innocent of exposure to Shakespeare, the Restoration spectators apparently found the portrait convincing. The disparity between Sedley's and Dryden's Cleopatras was emphasized by casting. Whereas "Sedley had contrasted a meek, self-sacrificing Octavia (Mary Betterton) with a powerful Cleopatra played by Mary Lee, a specialist in dominant, passionate women . . . Dryden's Cleopatra and Octavia were played by the small, vulnerable Elizabeth Bowtell and the strapping, forceful Katherine Corey."[49]

Dryden's version of the Antony and Cleopatra story proved more successful and more critically acclaimed than Sedley's. According to neo-Aristotelian commentators such as Charles Gildon, *All for Love*, "were it not for the false *Moral*, wou'd be a Masterpiece that few of the Ancients or Moderns ever equal'd."[50] Objecting to its glorification of illicit love, Gildon assessed the play in universalizing terms, but at least one politically attuned contemporary took Dryden's sympathetic portrayal of the Eastern queen as a point of departure for his own tribute to Charles's favorite mistress. *On the Dutchesse of Portsmouths Picture* alluded to *All for Love* in extolling both her and her royal lover:

> Hadst thou but liv'd in Cleopatra's Age,
> When Beauty did the Earths great Lord ingage;
> Britain (not Egypt) had been glorious made
> Augustus then (like Julius) had Obeyd:
> A nobler Theam had been the Poets Boast,
> That all the world for Love had been well lost.[51]

Whether passionate and treacherous or meek and faithful, Sedley's and Dryden's Cleopatras would have been viewed by the audience in the context of contemporary visual representations of the Egyptian Queen as well as poems in praise of, and attacks against, royal mistresses, especially the Duchess of Portsmouth.

All for Love is not a political allegory. Yet given the propensity of contemporary audiences to look for topical meanings, Dryden was aware that in the aftermath of Sedley's tragedy the historical figures he had chosen to represent might be associated with Charles and his French favorite. By engaging the spectators' sympathies on the side of the lovers, he challenged Sedley's cynical interpretation of the past – and, by implication, of the present. Nevertheless, in Dryden as in Sedley the political victory belongs to Octavian Caesar – the future Emperor Augustus – whom Dryden keeps off stage. Some viewers and readers of the printed text may have remembered that in his early Stuart panegyrics and in his major historical poem *Annus Mirabilis* Dryden had celebrated Charles II as Augustus. They may have therefore inferred that by aligning the king with the defeated Antony, *All for Love* conceded that that earlier, more optimistic and flattering historical analogy had lost its force.[52]

Plots, conspiracies and the politics of propaganda

Playwrights of Dryden's generation who had begun their careers in the 1660s were unequivocal in signaling their loyalist stance. Such directness was acceptable, indeed desirable, in the climate of apparent national concord and reconciliation. Yet it became progressively less so as support for the Restoration regime crumbled. The polarization of society in the turbulent years of the Popish Plot, and the ensuing parliamentary attempts at excluding James, Duke of York from succession, were mirrored in the drama. Dryden's position as official spokesman for the court was precarious. He had to serve the interests of his master, as best he could understand them, in commercially viable scripts. He had to do this without alienating too many members of his audience and without foreclosing arguments and positions that the rapidly changing political situation might lead him to adopt. How did he navigate his course between these often contradictory demands of his public and professional roles?

As the divisions within the political nation deepened, Dryden's targets became more explicit. From Creon in *Oedipus* to the rogues' gallery in *The Duke of Guise*, his stage-villains shadow leaders of the opposition, notably the Earl of Shaftesbury and the Duke of Monmouth. A product of collaboration with Nathaniel Lee (who had also co-authored *Oedipus*), *The Duke of Guise* proved the most controversial play of its time. Although partisan rhetoric, whether Whig or Tory, was a feature of many plays written between 1678 and 1683, none matched the ferocity and determination with which *The*

Duke of Guise savaged the advocates of Exclusion. The thinness of its allegory and the transparency of its historical parallels provoked angry rebuttals from the Whigs, to whom Dryden in turn responded in the *Vindication of the Duke of Guise*.[53]

On the evidence of that formidable piece of theatrical propaganda and its prose defense as well as of his political poems, *Absalom and Achitophel* and *The Medall*, Dryden stands out as a staunch Tory. But both *The Duke of Guise* and his verse satires post-date the Oxford Parliament of March 1681 that marked the turning point in the struggle between Charles II and the Whigs. Tory victory was now assured. In October 1680, when Dryden's *The Spanish Fryar; or, The Double Discovery* had reached the stage, the political situation was far less clear. The play is a tragicomedy. Its high plot focuses on the evils of usurpation but rather than suffering punishment Leonora, the female usurper and would-be regicide, is married to the son of the rightful king with whose restoration the play concludes. The low plot centers on the repeatedly thwarted attempts at adulterous coupling between Lorenzo and Elvira who ultimately turn out to be siblings. Their schemes to deceive Elvira's husband, the rich old cit Gomez, are abetted by a corrupt priest, Friar Dominick, played by one of the period's best comic actors, Antony Leigh.

Critics disagree about the politics of *The Spanish Fryar*. Judith Milhous and Robert D. Hume have read it as a piece of Tory propaganda, in which the anti-Catholic low plot is a mere sop that does not invalidate the firmly loyalist message of the high plot.[54] According to Phillip Harth, the play's anti-popery as much as the dedication addressed to a young Whig lord are indicative of Dryden's neutrality or perhaps his reluctance to make explicit his political commitment. Recently, Susan J. Owen has argued that *The Spanish Fryar* called for caution and moderation. "Dryden is adapting to apparent Whig ascendancy and royal disinclination to severity," she writes, "by reminding people of the atmosphere of 1660 and appealing for unity around the triumphant values of that time: respect for sovereignty, forgiveness of penitent transgressors and an avoidance of extremism, either radical or royalist, sectarian or papist."[55] For all his ostentatiously moderate rhetoric, Dryden's position in the autumn of 1680 was hardly moderate. He did indeed invoke the consensual, conciliatory mood of the early 1660s, not least through his tragicomic plotting: *The Spanish Fryar* paralleled Dryden's early Restoration tragicomedies and heroic dramas that had staged a series of more or less providential restorations. Yet the play was more a boost for the beleaguered Tories than a concession to the Whigs.

After *The Spanish Fryar* came Dryden's devastating attack on the opposition in *The Duke of Guise* and, with *Albion and Albanius*, an operatic celebration of the Crown's triumph over the Exclusionists. Composed in 1683–4 at the behest of Charles II and rehearsed before him in the Duchess of Portsmouth's apartments at Whitehall, the opera, set to music by the Frenchman Louis Grabu, was adjusted and finally produced after the king's death and the accession of James II. The first – and only – run was interrupted by Monmouth's rebellion in June 1685. Opening with the Restoration and closing with the apotheosis of Charles II, *Albion and Albanius* offered a partisan chronicle of the past quarter century. Through a sustained historical allegory, it targeted the Crown's enemies: Augusta (City of London), Democracy (Good Old Cause, later transformed into Whiggish Patriot), and Zealota (mid-century sectarianism, later masquerading as True Religion). Modern scholars have noted the opera's affinity with the court masque but they have paid virtually no attention to Dryden's ingenious use of civic pageantry.[56] *Albion and Albanius* relied for its iconography and allegorical plotting on Charles II's coronation entry into London in June 1661 and on successive Lord Mayor's Shows. By confidently incorporating elements of these civic forms into an all-sung royalist opera that re-enacted the defeat of the seditious metropolis, Dryden proclaimed the Crown's political and cultural dominance.

Relations between Crown and City had long been troubled. During the Popish Plot hysteria Whigs gained control over City government and juries and the king felt compelled to call the 1681 Parliament to Oxford whose royalist credentials were impeccable. Mayoral pageants and Pope-burning processions in 1679–81 reflected the City's Whiggish orientation.[57] By 1682, however, Charles had been able to ensure election of a Tory mayor and sheriffs, and by 1683 he had revoked the City's Charter.[58] No pageants accompanied mayoral inaugurations in 1682 and 1683. The incipient Toryism of those ceremonies was semi-public, being conveyed through loyal songs allegedly sung during the feasts in company halls in honor of the new incumbent. *The Lord Mayor's Show* for 1682 is a particularly striking precedent for *Albion*: like Dryden's libretto, its songs celebrated a second restoration ("Then welcome Great Monarch, welcome again . . . This day shall shew how great you reign / In spite of Faction's busie Arts") and denounced the Whigs' Commonwealth principles ("we hate all that would Monarchy depose").[59] In 1683, *The Triumphs of London* acknowledged the City's culpability: "Talking of Treason without any reason, / Hath lost the poor City's bountiful Charter."[60] By 1684, the dramatic component, now firmly loyalist, was back in place as Lord Mayor's Shows returned to their former musical and visual splendor.[61]

Dryden provided a running commentary on these developments in plays, verse satires, prologues, and epilogues. He repeatedly castigated the City's oppositional politics and sneered at its low-brow pageantry. Most objectionable to the Whigs proved his attack on the municipal authorities in *The Duke of Guise*. By drawing a tendentious parallel between contemporary London and sixteenth-century Paris, that tragedy had satirized the capital as a hotbed of sedition. Hostile pamphleteers accused the laureate of slandering the City and of advocating suppression of its liberties. "[H]is Intentions are evidently in this Play to insinuate by false Colours into the People," fumed the anonymous author of *Some Reflections* (1682), "and as much as in him lies into the *King*, a Hatred to the Capital City, and a scorn of Authority placed in the Citizens."[62] Thomas Hunt charged Dryden and his partner Lee with having "already condemned the Charter and City, and . . . executed the Magistrates in Effigie upon the Stage."[63] Having mercilessly reviled the City's champions in print in the *Vindication of the Duke of Guise*, Dryden continued the assault in *Albion and Albanius*. The opera brought on to the stage both the City and its lost charter. If Dryden shows as providential Charles II's double restoration and his and James's delivery from the Rye House Plot, he is no less adamant that the City's forfeiture of its liberties is a just punishment for its rampant democracy and pride.

Defiance, compromise, evasion?

Albion and Albanius was Dryden's last work for the theatre until after the Glorious Revolution. Faced with James II's flight and the arrival of William and Mary, the recusant laureate refused to change his religion and political allegiance. He was duly deprived of his state offices, which, in March 1689, devolved to his old enemy and Whig apologist, Thomas Shadwell.

The loss of court pension precipitated Dryden's return to the theatre. Over the next five years, he wrote *Don Sebastian* (1689), *Amphitryon* (1690), *King Arthur* (1691), *Cleomenes* (1692), and *Love Triumphant* (1694). In 1700 he contributed the *Secular Masque* for John Vanbrugh's revival of Fletcher's *The Pilgrim*. Dryden knew that audiences expected some sort of political statement from him. He gratified their appetite or perhaps mere curiosity in a series of personal-topical prologues and epilogues and in the plays themselves. Dryden's Jacobitism was a liability but it was also a commercial asset. He exploited it by wittily referring to his oppositional stance, demotion from court appointments, and consequent penury, and by including suggestive if teasingly ambivalent allusions to domestic and international affairs. Stuart loyalists sympathized with his plight and politics; Williamites, except for those few who gloated over his fall, tolerated his banter or even patronized him. The spectacle of the greatest living poet reduced in circumstances and forced to use complex rhetorical subterfuges was a more effective testimony to the new regime's power and benevolence than if Dryden had re-converted and served it with his pen. Yet to make his Jacobite sympathies too pointed was dangerous; the provocation could result in censorship or suppression of his work and loss of earnings. Dryden's prologue for the operatic adaptation of the Fletcherian *The Prophetess or, The History of Dioclesian* (1690) was banned on account of "a double Meaning . . . reflect[ing] on the Revolution";[64] and *Cleomenes* was temporarily held up.[65]

Modern scholars have proposed a variety of identifications with specific figures and events in Dryden's late plays.[66] His method there is not allegory but elusive topical allusion. To dramatize the story of King Sebastian of Portugal or of the Spartan Cleomenes, both of whom, like James II, had lost their thrones to foreign princes, was sure to whet the spectators' appetite for, and send them in search of, further connections. *Amphitryon* paraded vocabulary and ideas familiar from current parliamentary debates and polemical writings – "Prerogative," "Arbitrary Power," "absolute Dominion," "bumpkin Patriots," "Grumbletonian Morals," "Act of Settlement," "Wrongs to redress, and Tyrants to disseize," and so on.[67] Dryden's insouciantly libertine and despotic Jupiter recalled the merry monarch Charles II. Yet the play also capitalized on iconographical uses of classical mythology in revolutionary propaganda that cast William as Jupiter and James II as Saturn or Phaeton. One coronation medal depicted "two figures, identified as the two princesses Mary and Anne, [as] suppliants before the throne of Jupiter (symbolizing William of Orange), while Saturn (James II), Jupiter's father, who had conspired against his son's interests, is shown in flight, devouring an infant." Another "showed Jove thundering against Phaeton who was driving a chariot over a burning world, an image intended to say that James II had nearly destroyed the government of England and was displaced to save it."[68] William was also praised as a latter-day Hercules,[69] a trope that Jupiter's jocular prediction of Hercules' birth at the end of the play works to undo (v. i. 413–21). An anonymous supporter of the Revolution described *Don Sebastian* as being "With Bobs and Innuendo's thick, / Which Abdicated Laureat brings / In praise of Abdicated Kings."[70] This is an apt assessment not only of *Don Sebastian* but of all of Dryden's late plays. They are thick with innuendo although, as Dryden wrote of *Cleomenes*, "here is no Parallel to be found" (*Works* XVI: 79).

What had changed after 1689 were not Dryden's political views but the means and genres he deployed to express them. Under Charles and James, he had written two major types of political drama: ideological heroic plays in support of the Stuart monarchy and topical propaganda pieces such as *Amboyna*, *The Duke of Guise*, and *Albion and Albanius*. His crypto-Jacobite plays are very different from both these types. They are more allusive than his rhymed heroic dramas but they eschew the transparency and sustained parallelism characteristic of his Tory propaganda. If there is an early precedent for the ambivalent and fleeting allusiveness of *Amphitryon* or *Love Triumphant*, it is *The Spanish Fryar* that had been composed – if not in defeat, like those late plays – at least at a time of acute crisis and uncertainty when the Crown's prospects seemed bleak.

Dryden never tried to conceal his politics but late in life he became more careful to displace responsibility for political applications on to his audiences and readers. "The Fable has a Moral too, if sought," he told them in the Prologue to his last play, *Love Triumphant* (*Works* XVI: 29). Given the nature of the subjects he tackled and given contemporary habits of thought, anyone who so wished might find a political message of some kind in virtually any of his plays. As a spokesman for the court, Dryden had made no bones about what lessons his dramas were intended to teach; as a deposed laureate, he opted for ambiguity and allusion in order to ensure that no obvious parallel could be laid at his door. During the last six years of his life, when his chief effort was translation, Dryden wrote no plays. One reason for this self-imposed silence may have been the weight of theatrical censorship that was more restrictive than that of print. "How wretched is the Fate of those who write! / Brought muzzled to the Stage, for fear they bite," he complained in the Prologue to Fletcher's *The Pilgrim* (*Works* XVI: 1–2). Yet, somewhat ironically, it was in Williamite England, when those constraints were at their heaviest and perhaps because of the very presence of constraint, that Dryden produced some of his most accomplished, sophisticated, and subtle political plays.

NOTES

This essay was written during my tenure of the Benjamin N. Duke Fellowship at the National Humanities Center in North Carolina in 2002–3. I am grateful to the NHC for its generous support and to its library staff for their unfailing efficiency, courtesy, and helpfulness.

1. *Works* XVI: 346–7.
2. John Barnard, "Dryden: History and 'The Mighty Government of the Nine'", *The University of Leeds Review* 24 (1981), 13–42.
3. James Anderson Winn, *John Dryden and His World* (New Haven, 1987), p. 191. His shares unpaid, Dryden defected to the more prosperous Duke's Company in 1678 where his profit from a play amounted to the net proceeds on the third day of the first run.
4. On the professional status of playwrights in the Restoration, see Paulina Kewes, *Authorship and Appropriation: Writing for the Stage in England, 1660–1710* (Oxford, 1998), chapter 1.
5. Maguire, *Regicide and Restoration: English Tragicomedy, 1660–1671* (Cambridge, 1992), pp. 190–214; Orr, *Empire on the Restoration Stage, 1660–1714* (Cambridge, 2001) and Orr, "Poetic Plate-Fleets and Universal Monarchy:

The Heroic Plays and Empire in the Restoration," *Huntington Library Quarterly* 63 (2000), 71–97; Owen, *Restoration Theatre and Crisis* (Oxford, 1996); Harth, *Pen for a Party: Dryden's Tory Propaganda in Its Contexts* (Princeton, 1993); Bywaters, *Dryden in Revolutionary England* (Berkeley, 1991); Winn, *John Dryden.*

6. On the circumstances of the parliamentary closure of the theatres in 1642 and subsequent attempts to suppress illicit acting, see Leslie Hotson, *The Commonwealth and Restoration Stage* (Cambridge, Mass., 1928); Susan Wiseman, *Drama and Politics in the English Civil War* (Cambridge, 1998), pp. 1–16.

7. Martin Butler, *Theatre and Crisis, 1632–42* (Cambridge, 1984); Albert H. Tricomi, *Anti-Court Drama in England, 1603–1642* (Charlottesville, Va., 1989).

8. Paul Hammond, "The King's Two Bodies: Representations of Charles II," in *Culture, Politics and Society in Britain, 1660–1800*, ed. Jeremy Black and Jeremy Gregory (Manchester, 1991), pp. 13–49.

9. N. H. Keeble, *The Restoration: England in the 1660s* (Oxford, 2002).

10. Susan J. Owen, "Restoration Drama and Politics: An Overview," in *A Companion to Restoration Drama*, ed. Owen (Oxford, 2001), pp. 126–39.

11. John M. Wallace, "Dryden and History: A Problem in Allegorical Reading," *ELH*, 36 (1969), 265–90; and Wallace, "'Examples Are Best Precepts': Readers and Meanings in Seventeenth-Century Poetry," *Critical Inquiry* 1 (1974), 273–90; Robert D. Hume, "The Politics of Opera in Late Seventeenth-Century London," *Cambridge Opera Journal* 10 (1998), 15–43; Susan J. Owen, "Interpreting the Politics of Restoration Drama," *Seventeenth Century* 8 (1993), 67–97.

12. Maguire, *Regicide and Restoration*; Owen, "Restoration Drama and Politics."

13. Paulina Kewes, "Dryden and the Staging of Popular Politics," in *John Dryden: Tercentenary Essays*, ed. Paul Hammond and David Hopkins (Oxford, 2000), pp. 57–91.

14. Michael Dobson, *The Making of the National Poet: Shakespeare, Adaptation and Authorship, 1660–1769* (Oxford, 1992), pp. 38–61; and his "'Remember / First to Possess His Books': The Appropriation of *The Tempest*, 1700–1800," *Shakespeare Survey* 43 (1991), 99–107.

15. Gavin Foster, "Ignoring *The Tempest*: Pepys, Dryden, and the Politics of Spectating in 1667," *Huntington Library Quarterly* 63 (2000), 5–22.

16. Kewes, "Dryden and the Staging of Popular Politics."

17. Orr, *Empire on the Restoration Stage.*

18. Steven C. A. Pincus, *Protestantism and Patriotism: Ideologies and the Making of English Foreign Policy, 1650–1668* (Cambridge, 1996), pp. 248ff.

19. *Works* IX: 23–6; Orr, *Empire on the Restoration Stage*, p. 146.

20. The medal and the Huysmans painting are reproduced in *Painted Ladies: Women at the Court of Charles II*, ed. Catharine MacLeod and Julia Marciari Alexander (London and New Haven, 2001), pp. 86 and 88 respectively.

21. John Tatham, *Londons Triumphs* (London, 1664), pp. 6–12. For discussion, see L. J. Morrissey, "English Street Theatre: 1655–1708," *Costerus* 4 (1972), 105–37; Kenneth Richards, "The Restoration Pageants of John Tatham," in *Western Popular Theatre*, ed. David Mayer and Kenneth Richards (London, 1977), pp. 49–73; Sheila Williams, "The Lord Mayor's Show in Tudor and Stuart Times," *Guildhall Miscellany* 10 (1959), 3–35.

22. Commentary, *Works* X: 382–3.

23. Derek Hughes, *English Drama 1660–1700* (Oxford, 1996), p. 78.
24. Maguire, *Regicide and Restoration*, p. 206.
25. Susan J. Owen, "Heroic Tragi-comedy: John Dryden's *The Conquest of Granada by the Spaniards*, Parts I and II," in Owen, *Perspectives on Restoration Drama* (Manchester and New York, 2002), pp. 9–41.
26. Ann A. Huse, "Cleopatra, Queen of the Seine: The Politics of Eroticism in Dryden's *All for Love*," *Huntington Library Quarterly* 63 (2000), 23–46.
27. Owen, "Heroic Tragi-comedy."
28. *The Control and Censorship of Caroline Drama: The Records of Sir Henry Herbert, Master of the Revels 1623–73*, ed. N. W. Bawcutt (Oxford, 1996), pp. 54–5; Paulina Kewes, "Contemporary Europe in Renaissance Drama," forthcoming in *Shakespeare and Renaissance Europe*, ed. Andrew Hadfield and Paul Hammond, *Arden Critical Companions* series (London, 2004).
29. Pincus, *Protestantism and Patriotism*, pp. 59ff.
30. John Spurr, *England in the 1670s: "This Masquerading Age"* (Oxford, 2000), pp. 34–5.
31. *Works* XII: 257.
32. Dryden, *Prologue Spoken at the Opening of the New House*, in *Works* I: 148–9; Winn, *John Dryden*, pp. 262–4; Commentary, in *Works* XII: 322–5.
33. Commentary, in *Works* XII: 325.
34. "Milton, Dryden, and the Politics of Literary Controversy," in *Culture and Society in the Stuart Restoration: Literature, Drama, History*, ed. Gerald MacLean (Cambridge, 1995), pp. 137–58.
35. *The Famous Tragedie of King Charles I* (n.p., 1649), sig. A4v; *Cromwell's Conspiracy. A Tragy-Comedy, Relating to our latter Times. Beginning at the Death of King Charles the First, And ending with the happy Restauration of King Charles The Second. Written by a Person of Quality* (London, Printed for the Author in the Year, 1660), sig. A2v.
36. Pierre Danchin, "The Foundation of the Royal Academy of Music in 1674 and Pierre Perrin's *Ariane*," *Theatre Survey* 25 (1984), 55–67; Christina Bashford, "Perrin and Cambert's 'Ariane, ou le marriage de Bacchus' Re-examined," *Music and Letters* 72 (1991), 1–26.
37. "To Mr. DRYDEN, *on his* POEM *of* PARADICE," in John Dryden, *The State of Innocence, and Fall of Man: An Opera* (London, 1677), sig. A4r.
38. For a contrary point of view, see Winn, *John Dryden*, p. 289.
39. Blair Worden, "Favourites on the English Stage," in *The World of the Favourite*, ed. J. H. Elliott and L. W. B. Brockliss (New Haven and London, 1999), pp. 159–83.
40. Philips, *Pompey. A Tragoedy* (Dublin, 1663); *Pompey the Great . . . Translated out of French by Certain PERSONS OF HONOUR* (London, 1664).
41. *Poems on Affairs of State: Augustan Satirical Verse, 1660–1714*, 7 vols. (New Haven, Conn., 1963–75), vol. II: 1678–81, ed. Elias F. Mengel, Jr., pp. 7–11 (lines 30–3) and 184–8 (lines 31–4) respectively.
42. Commentary, in *Works* XIII: 373. For an overview of the Duchess's portraits, see *Painted Ladies*, ed. MacLeod and Alexander, pp. 136–51.
43. Commentary, in *Works* XIII: 372–3.
44. *The Diary of John Evelyn*, ed. E. S. de Beer, 6 vols. (Oxford, 1955), vol. III, p. 589, quoted in *Painted Ladies*, ed. MacLeod and Alexander, p. 139.

45. *Antony and Cleopatra*, in *The Poetic and Dramatic Works of Sir Charles Sedley*, ed. V. de Sola Pinto, 2 vols. (London, 1928; repr. New York, 1969), vol. I, I. i. 1–2.

46. Hughes, *English Drama*, p. 246.

47. Lord Chamberlain's warrant for payment to the Duke's Company for Sedley's play seen by the king (P.R.O. LC 5/142, p. 81), cited in Allardyce Nicoll, *A History of English Drama, 1660–1900*, 6 vols. (Cambridge, 1952–59), vol. I, p. 248.

48. The growing hostility toward France and outcry against the Third Dutch War forced the government to change its foreign policy. See Steven A. Pincus, "From Butterboxes to Wooden Shoes: The Shift in English Popular Sentiment from Anti-Dutch to Anti-French in the 1670s," *Historical Journal* 38 (1995), 333–61.

49. Hughes, *English Drama*, p. 250.

50. Charles Gildon, *Lives and Characters of the English Dramatick Poets* (London, [1699]), sig. A6v.

51. Victoria and Albert Museum MS Dyce 43, p. 278, quoted in Dryden's *Works* XIII: 373. For a reading of *All for Love* which argues that Dryden's Cleopatra was intentionally modeled on the Duchess of Portsmouth, see Huse, "Cleopatra, Queen of the Seine."

52. On the politics of theatrical representations of ancient Rome by Dryden's contemporaries, see Paulina Kewes, "Otway, Lee and the Restoration History Play," in *A Companion to Restoration Drama*, ed. Owen, pp. 355–77.

53. For accounts of the play's politics and reception, see Harth, *Pen for a Party*, pp. 188–205, Kewes, *Authorship and Appropriation*, pp. 162–76, and Kewes, "Dryden and the Staging of Popular Politics." On the changing preoccupations and tropes of Exclusion Crisis drama, see Owen, *Restoration Theatre and Crisis*.

54. Judith Milhous and Robert D. Hume, *Producible Interpretation: Eight English Plays, 1675–1707* (Carbondale, Ill., 1985), pp. 141–71.

55. Susan J. Owen, "The Politics of John Dryden's *The Spanish Fryar; or, The Double Discovery*," *English* 43 (1994), 97–113.

56. Eugene M. Waith, "Spectacles of State," *Studies in English Literature* 13 (1973), 317–30; Paul Hammond, "Dryden's *Albion and Albanius*: The Apotheosis of Charles II," in *The Court Masque*, ed. David Lindley (Manchester, 1984), pp. 169–83. L. J. Morrissey has noted Dryden's deployment of civic pageantry but he has not explored its ideological significance ("English Street Theatre," pp. 118–22).

57. Sheila Williams, "The Pope-burning Processions of 1679, 1680, and 1681," *Journal of the Warburg and Courtauld Institutes* 21 (1958), 104–18.

58. See *The Sur-Rejoinder of Mr. Attorney General to the Rejoinder Made on the behalf of the Charter Of the City of London* (London, 1682).

59. *The Lord Mayor's Show: Being a Description of the Solemnity at the Inauguration Of the truly Loyal and Right Honourable Sir William Prichard, Kt* (London, 1682), sig. A1v and p. 4 respectively.

60. *The Triumphs of London: Performed . . . for the Entertainment of the Right Honourable, and truly Noble Pattern of Prudence and Loyalty, Sir Henry Tulse, Knight* (London, 1683), p. 5.

61. See Thomas Jordan's suggestively titled *London's Royal Triumph for the City's Loyal Magistrate: In an Exact Description of several Scenes and Pageants, Adorned with many Magnificent Representations . . . At the Instalment of*

the Right Honourable Sir James Smith, Knight (London, 1684) and Matthew Taubman's *London's Annual Triumph: Performed . . . For the Entertainment of the Right Honourable Sir Robert Jeffreys, Kt* (London, 1685), which was the first mayoral pageant of James II's reign.

62. *Appendix B: Some Reflections upon the Pretended Parallel in the Play called The Duke of Guise, In a Letter to a Friend* (London, 1683), in *Works* XIV: 611–22 at p. 620.

63. Thomas Hunt, *A Defence of the Charter, and Municipal Rights of the City of London. And the Rights of other Municipal Cities and Towns of England* (London, 1682), p. 24.

64. *The Muses Mercury* for January 1707, ed. John Oldmixon, quoted in *Works* III: 508.

65. See the April and May issues of *The Gentleman's Journal: or the Monthly Miscellany*, ed. Peter Motteux (London, 1692), pp. 25 and 17 respectively, and Dryden's dedication and preface to *Cleomenes*, *Works* XVI: 73–81.

66. See esp. Bywaters, *Dryden in Revolutionary England*. For more subtle topical readings, see Steven N. Zwicker, "Representing the Revolution: *Don Sebastian* and Williamite Panegyric," in *Lines of Authority: Politics and English Literary Culture, 1649–1689* (Ithaca, NY, 1993), pp. 173–202; Richard Kroll, "The Double Logic of *Don Sebastian*," *Huntington Library Quarterly* 63 (2000), 47–69; Anne Barbeau Gardiner, "John Dryden's *Love Triumphant* and English Hostility to Foreigners, 1688–1693," *Clio* 18 (1989), 153–70, and Gardiner, "Dryden's *Cleomenes* (1692) and Contemporary Jacobite Verse," *Restoration* 12 (1988), 87–95.

67. I. i. 25; I. i. 131; I. i. 136–7; I. i. 143; I. i. 147; V. i. 374–5; V. i. 415.

68. Lois G. Schwoerer, "Images of Queen Mary II, 1689–95," *Renaissance Quarterly* 42 (1989), 717–48, at pp. 732–3 and pp. 734–5 respectively. See also Schwoerer, "The Glorious Revolution as Spectacle: A New Perspective," in *England's Rise to Greatness, 1660–1763*, ed. Stephen B. Baxter (Berkeley, 1983), pp. 109–49; Lois Potter, "Politics and Popular Culture: The Theatrical Response to the Revolution," in *The Revolution of 1688–1689: Changing Perspectives*, ed. Lois G. Schwoerer (Cambridge, 1992), 184–97.

69. Stephen B. Baxter, "William III as Hercules: The Political Implications of Court Culture," in *The Revolution of 1688–89*, ed. Schwoerer, pp. 95–106.

70. Prologue to the Players, in *The Late Revolution: Or, The Happy Change* (London, 1690), sig. I2r.

9

JOHN MULLAN

Dryden's anonymity

Dryden had good reason to know that it could be dangerous to be recognized as an author. On 18 December 1679 the Poet Laureate was attacked in Rose Alley, Covent Garden by several men and badly beaten. Accounts soon appeared in newssheets:

> Last night Mr. *Dryden*, the famous *Dramatic* Poet, going from a Coffee-house in *Covent-Garden*, was set upon by three Persons unknown to him and so rudely by them handled, that it is said, his Life is in no small danger.[1]

Dryden advertised for information about the identity of those responsible, promising any informer fifty pounds and, if necessary, immunity from prosecution. There is no evidence that he ever found a culprit. Four private accounts of the time record that the assault was provoked by Dryden's supposed authorship of *An Essay upon Satire*, an anonymous poem recently circulated in manuscript.[2] This had attacked a whole gallery of courtiers, including the Duchess of Portsmouth, one of Charles II's mistresses ("False, foolish, old, ill-natur'd and ill-bred").[3] One of the newssheet accounts concurs, reporting that Dryden's assailants "designed not to rob him but to execute on him some *Feminine*, if not *Popish* vengeance" (the duchess was a Roman Catholic).

There is no doubt that the *Essay upon Satire* was widely attributed to Dryden. Rochester, whom it also lampoons, was told and believed that Dryden was its author.[4] Some have argued that Rochester ("Mean in each motion, lewd in ev'ry limb, / Manners themselves are mischievous in him," according to the *Essay*) is indeed the likeliest instigator of the attack.[5] There is room to doubt that the duchess was behind the attack, but it seems clear that the *Essay* was the provocation. Given the range of high-ranking victims of this lampoon, observes one scholar, "our problem becomes one of choosing, rather than finding, a suspect."[6] For some contemporaries, the attack confirmed the attribution. An anonymous manuscript satire, "The visitt," written shortly afterwards describes approaching Robert Julian, the best known vendor of manuscript satires and lampoons, for a copy of the offending composition.

> Feirce Drydens satyr wee desir'd to veiw
> For wee had heard he mourn'd in Black and Blew.[7]

Dryden's bruises, it seems, only stimulated the interest of gentlemanly consumers. Reference continued to be made to Dryden as the author or co-author of *An Essay upon Satire*, especially in pieces attacking him.[8] There was considerable gloating.

In fact, Dryden had been physically endangered by a misattribution. Since the eighteenth century it has been widely accepted that the poem was by John Sheffield, Third Earl of Mulgrave, one of Dryden's most important patrons. In his *Essay upon Poetry* of 1682 Mulgrave was to refer to "The Laureate" being "prais'd and punish'd for another's Rimes" – almost certainly a reference to the attribution of the *Essay upon Satire*. In marginal notes to a 1691 edition of the same work, Mulgrave referred to this work as "A Libel" and recalled that Dryden had been "both applauded and wounded" for it, "tho entirely innocent of the whole matter."[9] The poem was published as Mulgrave's in *A New Collection of Poems Relating to State Affairs* in 1705, and included by Alexander Pope in his edition of Mulgrave's *Works* in 1723.

The whole episode demonstrates how questions of attribution that are now recondite matters of literary scholarship were once live and dangerous. The prevailing anonymity of satirical verse allowed for vituperation and vindictiveness; it also encouraged readers (and rival writers) to "discover" the authorship of authorless works. There were other cases where discovery threatened violence. According to one contemporary account, the playwright Thomas Otway challenged Elkanah Settle to a duel over the character of him in *A Session of the Poets*. Settle supposedly wrote an apology in which he admitted to his authorship, which he had previously denied strongly. "*I confess I Writ the* Session of the Poets, *and am very sorry fo't and am the Son of a Whore* for doing it."[10] More threateningly still, the state on occasion attempted to attribute a controversial work.[11] The government tried hard, for instance, to find the author (and indeed the printer) of Andrew Marvell's *Second Advice to a Painter* and *Third Advice to a Painter* (both 1667), scathing attacks on those the writer held responsible for disastrous naval actions against the Dutch. Later, a reward of £100 was offered for revealing the identity of the author of Marvell's anonymous *Account of the Growth of Popery* (1677). In a notorious case soon after Dryden's misadventure, the attribution of verse became a matter of life or death. In July 1681, Stephen College, vehement anti-Catholic and writer of political ballads, was charged with being the author of an anonymous broadside called

A Raree Show. This mockingly describes Charles II's supposedly contemptuous treatment of Parliament and his determination to deliver the country to Catholicism. At his trial in August 1681 College was accused of singing the ballad and distributing it, as well as writing it.[12] He denied authorship. Found guilty, he was hanged, drawn, and quartered on 31 August.

So we might think that Dryden's use of anonymity for some works that he certainly did write is likely to fit into the simple scheme offered in the most comprehensive guide to anonymous writings in English, Halkett and Laing's *Dictionary of Anonymous and Pseudonymous Literature of Great Britain*. "Generally the motive is some kind of timidity, such as (a) diffidence, (b) fear of consequences, and (c) shame."[13] Motive (b) is interpreted narrowly as fear of persecution, imprisonment, and the like. Yet, while satirical authors did sometimes have reason to be fearful, the most notable cases of Dryden's anonymity (*MacFlecknoe*, *Absalom and Achitophel*, *The Medal*, and *The Hind and the Panther*) hardly seem to derive from "timidity." The peculiar fact about Dryden's anonymity is how little calculated for self-protection it usually was, and how inadequate to maintain any actual secrecy. None of these four poems seems ever to have been attributed to anyone except Dryden. Over and over again, modern editors of Dryden will tell you that the authorship of one or other of them was not really a secret. When *The Medal* was published by Jacob Tonson in March 1682, its title page identified it as "By the Author of Absalom and Achitophel." Paul Hammond's note in his edition of Dryden's *Poems* observes that, though the poem remained anonymous until 1692, "by now D.'s authorship of *Absalom and Achitophel* was no secret."[14] Perhaps that title page was some declaration of authorship (though we might note that one immediate reply, *The Medal Revers'd*, did wonder whether the two authors were in fact the same).

The Mushroom, a response to *The Medal*, published no more than a week later, already confidently identified Dryden ("John Laureat," as it calls him) as its author. *The Medal Revers'd*, published little more than two weeks after *The Medal*, pins the poem on Dryden in the manner beloved by his enemies, that is by recalling Dryden's elegiac verses on Cromwell's death. The self-declared "satire against Persecution" begins by considering how "triumphant" wit can seem when it rides "in Power's chariot."

> This well the author of *The Medal* knew,
> When Oliver he for an hero drew.[15]

Two months later, *The Medal of John Bayes*, probably by Shadwell, was entirely an antagonistic portrait of Dryden, taking its title from the satirical portrait of Dryden as Bayes in Buckingham's *The Rehearsal*. It included details of the doses of venereal disease Dryden supposedly got from his

mistress, Anne Reeves, and of the self-importance of his coffee-house monologues. Naturally, in its introductory "Epistle to the Tories," it referred
to "the libel your poet was cudgell'd for" – purporting to disapprove of
Dryden's way with abuse, but in fact gleefully recalling his supposed humiliation. Its opening lines do so again.

> The fool, uncudgell'd, for one libel swells,
> Where not his wit, but sauciness excels.[16]

In his prefatory "Epistle to the Whigs," the author of *The Medal* seems
to recognize that the poem's anonymity will not protect him. He invites
responses from those "who have combated with so much success against
Absalom and Achitophel." "Raile at me abundantly; and, not to break a
Custome, do it without wit"(*Works* 11: 41); Dryden knows that anonymity,
in the case of this poem, will not remove him to a place of safety. In such
an attribution-hungry literary culture, anonymity incites name-calling. The
veil of anonymity works "more to excite and exasperate than to conceal."[17]
Attribution is often antagonistic, the tactic of an enemy keen, for instance, to
find evidence of low or mercenary literary activity. According to *The Medal
of John Bayes*, Dryden took lodgings with the bookseller Henry Herringman
at the beginning of the 1660s and

> Writ Prefaces to Books for Meat and Drink,
> And as he paid, he would both write and think.
> (129–30)[18]

Dryden's antagonist claims to know his hand in the anonymous hackwork
of his early career. Equally, attribution can be the way of undermining the
poet's achievement. *The Medal of John Bayes* claims at length to be able to
recognize in Dryden's verse the poetry plagiarized from other writers.

> How little owe we to your native store,
> Who all you write have heard or read before.
> (83–4)

Only his "libels" are impudently novel.

The satire of the 1670s and 1680s, itself invariably anonymous, gave blows
in the dark. The concealment of one author was calculated to render all the
more telling his identification of the authors of other anonymous works. The
authority of a satire was often determined not directly by whom it came *from*,
but by whom it was directed *at*. The satirical writing of this period brought to
a fevered, even dangerous pitch a timeless habit of satire: recognizing people.
Dryden learned the skill of such portraiture – the mocking depiction of an
individual who is made into a type – from Horace and Juvenal; and from

Dryden, Pope would learn this art. Satirists have always seemed to describe people whom they know (as if speaking with inside knowledge), but they also like to recognize in their victims representative characteristics. The renaming of Shaftesbury as Achitophel or Buckingham as Zimri was no kind of disguise or puzzle, but it was a way of turning the person into a malign or ridiculous epitome. This was not Dryden's discovery. Thus the tireless delight with which his enemies fixed on the character of Buckingham's playwright "Mr Bayes," shameless plagiarist and anxious sycophant, ludicrous success story of the Restoration stage. The character was Dryden, but also a damningly representative creature of the age.

Dryden wrote for readers who were used to recognizing the characters in satires. They were also habituated to recognizing their authors. Amongst the most useful evidence for the attribution of Restoration satirical verse are the names written on particular texts by their original owners. The strongest evidence, for instance, of Shadwell's authorship of *The Medal of John Bayes* is Narcissus Luttrell's annotation to his copy of the first edition of the poem: "By Thomas Shadwell. Agt Mr. Dryden. Very severe."[19] Luttrell was a collector of satire and an informed connoisseur of contemporary controversy. Another copy has a contemporary manuscript annotation "shadwell is run mad" on its title page. Owners were in the habit of writing in names in this way, as if to do so were to make oneself belong to a knowing, coterie readership. This was not only for anonymous printed texts. The manuscript poems of the period that have survived, sometimes in miscellanies made by keen contemporary collectors, often have attributions written in by their original owners. These can range from wild guesses to ascriptions that declare insider knowledge. The accuracy of the latter can suggest that the texts have been received from the author or with his approval.[20] Restoration lampoons, which mercilessly satirized particular individuals and which invariably circulated only in manuscript, particularly tempted readers into attributions. Harold Love has noted that these are not necessarily reliable. "Most are probably speculative, and it is not exceptional for the same poem to appear in different sources attributed to two or three different authors."[21] Attribution was certainly a habit of readers, but misattribution was common.

The potential attributors would usually include the main victims. Shadwell was to claim that he had "taxed" Dryden in person with being the author of *MacFlecknoe*, the poem that crowned him the monarch of "dullness" and for which *The Medal of John Bayes* was probably a belated revenge. According to Shadwell, Dryden "denied it with all the Execrations he could think of."[22] Shadwell did not indicate when the encounter took place, but it is not unbelievable. Dryden would have known that Shadwell would be one of the keenest searchers after the author of the satire. In turn, when Dryden contributed the portrait of Shadwell as Og in *The Second Part of Absalom and Achitophel* ("A Monstrous mass of foul corrupted matter, /As all the Devils had spew'd to make the batter") it was surely vengeful evidence that he attributed *The Medal of John Bayes* to Shadwell (*Works* II: 75). The Earl of Rochester told Gilbert Burnet that, in this genre of lampoons, "A man could not write with life, unless he were heated by Revenge."[23] He seems to have been imagining that his own satires would reach those whom he had mocked. Rochester attacked Dryden in his anonymous poem *An Allusion to Horace*, widely circulated in manuscript from 1675. This lordly survey of contemporary verse and drama, taking in all the major writers of the day, gives Dryden some dismissive praise ("His excellencies more than faults abound"), but mocks his "lumpish fancy" and vain aspirations to "wit."[24] Dryden was still nettled in 1678 when he replied to the attack in his preface to *All for Love*, his adaptation of Shakespeare's *Antony and Cleopatra*. Yet even here he found it convenient to pretend not to recognize the poem's authorship. As if he were detecting the author in an unusual act of poetic cowardice, he invited him to "subscribe his name to his censure" (*Works* XIII: 16–17).

This invitation, from a professional writer to an aristocratic literateur, is the more striking given that Rochester, more than any other of Dryden's contemporaries, asserted his poetic identity through anonymity. His readers were to be privileged to recognize his wit.

> He had a strange Vivacity of thought, and vigour of expression: His Wit had a subtility and sublimity both, that were scarce imitable. His Style was clear and strong: When he used Figures they were very lively, and yet far enough out of the Common Road.[25]

Robert Wolseley, in the Preface by "one of his friends" to Rochester's version of *Valentinian*, celebrates "the inimitable Turns of his Wit."[26] "Inimitable" sounds like ordinary hyperbole, but over and over again it was said that Rochester was entirely singular, truly beyond imitation. In a dedication to Rochester, who was for a time his patron, the playwright John Crowne expresses his delight "that I have seen in some little sketches of your Pen, excellent Masteries and a Spirit inimitable."[27] Though in a subservient position, Crowne has been allowed to read Rochester's manuscript verse and can claim to see in it the spirited traces of Rochester's authorship. In a culture of manuscript circulation and what has come to be called "scribal publication," this meant that Rochester's writing should be recognized, his authorship successfully guessed at:

he laid out his wit very freely in libels and satires, in which he had a peculiar talent of mixing his wit with his malice and fitting both with such apt words that men were tempted to be pleased with them: from thence his composures came to be easily known, for few had such a way of tempering those together as he had; so that when any thing extraordinary that way came out, as a child is fathered sometimes by its resemblance, so it was laid at his door as its parent and author.[28]

His productions were hotly collected.[29]

This activity of attribution was essential to the very life of Restoration manuscript culture. So common an activity was it that Rochester, with audacious self-reflexiveness, was able to make mock of it in one of his best known satires. In "Timon," the speaker is buttonholed in the Mall by some "dull dining sot" who fancies himself a connoisseur of contemporary satire. The fool assures Rochester's alter ego that he recognizes his authorship of the incompetent verses.

> He takes me in his coach, and as we go,
> Pulls out a libel of a sheet or two,
> Insipid as the praise of pious queens
> Or Shadwell's unassisted former scenes,
> Which he admired, and praised at every line;
> At last it was so sharp it must be mine.[30]

The speaker denies that he never writes more than the odd amorous song, observing with a pretense of innocence, "I vowed I was no more a wit than he" (19). But it is no good.

> He knew my style, he swore, and 'twas in vain
> Thus to deny the issue of my brain.   (25–6)

There is no choice but to leave him "to his dear mistake," and soon the dunce has spread the misattribution "o'er the whole town" (28–9).

Guessing at a particular author's style was essential to the pleasure of being a consumer. A manuscript satire of 1679–80 dramatizes the insinuating approaches of a purveyor of the latest lampoon on Charles II and one of his mistresses.

> A man can make no visitt now but his Caresse
> Is a Lewd Satyr shewn which Pray S[r]. Guess
> whose still [style] it is: good Faith S[r]. I don't care
> For truly I read none that Treasons are[31]

The loyally incurious gentleman who is supposed the speaker of this is, from all the evidence of contemporary curiosity, an unlikely fiction. The verse surely preserves a real frisson. The prospective reader, perhaps purchaser, is tempted by being asked to guess at the author of the latest satire. We might imagine that the purveyor of the piece would then offer (reliably or not) his information about its authorship.

Though Dryden was a professional writer who lived through print, he did sometimes write for manuscript circulation only.[32] It is not surprising that his own first major satire, *MacFlecknoe*, written in July–August 1676, was circulated in manuscript. This was how satirical verse lived its topical life. *MacFlecknoe* remained unpublished until a pirated edition appeared in 1682, followed by an authorized edition, anonymously, in the *Miscellany Poems* of 1684. The pirated edition attributes it to "the Author of *Absalom & Achitophel*," while Mulgrave attributes it to "The Laureat" in *An Essay upon Poetry* (1682). In *Miscellany Poems*, though appearing in the company of *Absalom and Achitophel* and *The Medal*, it remained anonymous. Dryden only publicly laid claim to it in his "Discourse concerning the Original and Progress of Satire" of 1692. Seventeen manuscript copies are known to survive. Only two of these attribute the poem to Dryden. Perhaps for many of the early readers the poem was truly, intriguingly anonymous.

Harold Love emphasizes the connection between this poem's means of circulation and its satirical animus. It is "an anti-print poem, picturing a world choked up with the mighty yet evanescent products of the press."[33] The sub-culture of libertine courtiers to which, at the time, Dryden was only awkwardly attached was inherently "scribal," preening itself on knowing compositions for limited circles of knowing readers. Yet, from the magnificently bathetic stumble as its sententious opening couplet turns into an encounter with Richard Flecknoe, prolific poetaster, a contemporary reader should have sensed an expansion of the medium.

> All humane things are subject to decay,
> And, when Fate summons, Monarchs must obey:
> This *Fleckno* found . . .   (*Works* II: 54)

Here is satire turning to a business of literary antagonism well known to lampooners of the times, yet with a grandeur of survey that is unprecedented – and the best part of the joke. When we find Flecknoe "pond'ring which of all his Sons was fit / To Reign, and wage immortal War with Wit" (11–12) we can hear Satan in *Paradise Lost*, declaring that the fallen angels can hope "To wage by force or guile eternal war / Irreconcilable, to our grand foe" (I, 121–2). So like, and so unlike. A few lines later and Flecknoe is styling himself John the Baptist to Shadwell's Christ. Satirical verse against rivals was invariably circulated anonymously; the novelty here is Dryden's use of the convention for the purposes of a loftiness at once absurd (Shadwell is to be crowned monarch of dullness) and real (this mode requires true resources of learning and poetic ambition). It really is nothing personal.

The poem's anonymity is all the more appropriate as so much of it is ostensibly dramatic. Flecknoe speaks more than half of its lines, in absurd encomium on his poetic "son." Anonymity will be comparably fitting for the dramatic monologues of *Absalom and Achitophel* and the dialogues of *The Hind and the Panther*. In *MacFlecknoe*, Dryden ironically and slyly draws attention to the uses of anonymity. For he makes the recognition of the marks of authorship – entirely negatively – one of the subjects of the poem. In Flecknoe's closing address to Shadwell, before he is sent through a trapdoor to oblivion, he wishes that all the characters of Shadwell's plays might display their author's own characteristics (155–62). Let them be Shadwell's "issue," "All full of thee, and differing but in name." Just as, in a culture of manuscript circulation, attribution might flatter both reader and writer by catching the singular grace of an author, so here, on the contrary, the qualities of an author are seen as ludicrously present in the writing.

The poem activates the rumor that portions of Shadwell's work were subcontracted. Flecknoe commands his son to be true to his own dullness and not to let a courtly helper like Sir Charles Sedley supply him with lines, as he is supposed to have done for Shadwell's play *Epsom-Wells*.

> But let no alien *S—dl—y* interpose
> To lard with wit thy hungry *Epsom* prose.
> (163–4)

Co-authorship might not be inherently shameful, but the covert acquiring of another's wit is. The implication is that the unShadwellian elements of the play were evident to the discerning. Shadwell attached an angry note to *Epsom-Wells* denying the "calumny" that "I did not write the Play."[34] Now we might recall that line in Rochester's "Timon" about the insipidity of Shadwell when he is "unassisted." This too is a barb about attribution. Flecknoe proceeds to disdain Jonson (Shadwell's professed mentor) for failing to "purloin" his scenes from Fletcher, while Shadwell "whole *Eth'rege* dost transfuse to thine" (184). The qualities of authors become nouns, recognizable to the qualified reader or spectator. Shadwell will not be allowed to change himself into another, as the gloss in the following couplet clinchingly decides:

> But so transfus'd as Oyl on Waters flow,
> His always floats above, thine sinks below.
> (185–6)

MacFlecknoe devastatingly advises Shadwell (in the voice of Flecknoe) to be himself. "Trust Nature, do not labour to be dull" (166). Sir Formal Trifle in *The Virtuoso* is Shadwell at the top of his form and his language returns upon Shadwell in his various "*Northern Dedications*" (170). It is a revenge for Shadwell saying, in the Prologue to *The Virtuoso*, that Dryden could not do wit, but can "write a Fool the best."[35] The best writers have essential qualities, their handiwork recognizable to the well-schooled. Shadwell possesses only dullness – or the lines and ideas of other writers. It is peculiar, in a culture in which translation and imitation are the honorable activities of poets, that plagiarism is such a frequent accusation. In the Duke of Buckingham's *The Rehearsal*, the dramatic satire that established Dryden as "Mr Bayes," he is made to boast of the ways in which he steals from other writers, when the mere recording of snippets of other men's witty coffee-house conversation is not sufficient.

> Why, Sir, when I have any thing to invent, I never trouble my head about it, as other men do; but presently turn over this Book, and there I have, at one view, all that *Perseus, Montaigne, Seneca's Tragedies, Horace, Juvenal, Claudian, Pliny, Plutarch's lives*, and the rest, have ever thought, upon this subject: and so, in a trice, by leaving out a few words, or putting in others of my own, the business is done.[36]

Some twenty years later, Gerard Langbaine's hostile entry on Dryden in his *Account of the English Dramatic Poets* is almost entirely an account of his concealed borrowings, a catalogue of "his Petty-Larcenies."[37]

In the field of satire, the first act of an author was often to dispossess himself of what he had written, to let it loose into the small world of a knowing readership, without a declaration of its origins. We know rather little about how successful readers were in attributing *MacFlecknoe* correctly. As well as the two attributions on manuscript copies, there is a reference in the manuscript satire *Advice to Apollo*, which probably dates from 1677, to Dryden quitting the stage "To lash the witty follies of our age."[38] This seems certain to have been a reference to *MacFlecknoe*, and suggests that Dryden's new departure – his entry into the lists of satire after years as a dramatist – was known quite widely. After the first circulation of this poem we find a number of lampoons and epigrams being misattributed to Dryden; *An Essay on Satire* is but the best known case.[39] In his dedication of *Eleonora* (1692) Dryden talks of the "mad Combat" of contemporary satirists. "They have sown the Dragons Teeth themselves; and 'tis but just they should reap each other in Lampoons" (*Works* III: 234). He wrote against lampoons in his "Discourse concerning Satire" of 1692. Yet clearly he went on taking an interest in the insider culture of verse vituperation. In the last year of his life he was sending a friend "two lampoons lately made," along with speculations about their authorship and the identities of their victims.[40] "I know not the authours; but the Town will be ghessing." It is usual to see Dryden, after 1688, withdrawn from satire and political controversy, content to insinuate his Jacobitism into some of his translations. Contemporaries were still, however, apparently willing to detect his hand in satires on political controversies of the 1690s.[41]

Yet Dryden does not exactly belong to this culture of literary anonymity. From his earliest major poetry, *Astraea Redux* and *Annus Mirabilis*, he had looked for a public voice. By about 1670, his success as a playwright made him a public figure (and therefore potential target). Anonymity is likely to be a different gesture for the poet aspiring to public, perhaps representative, status. Not for Dryden the faux testiness of Rochester about the "discovery" of his hand in some inferior authorless composition. Dryden was to use anonymity to create a strange kind of impersonality, his authorship of some of his greatest poetry a widely known yet officially unacknowledged fact. When he gathered *MacFlecknoe*, *Absalom and Achitophel* and *The Medal* for publication in Jacob Tonson's *Miscellany Poems* of 1684, he made sure that they remained anonymous (and this in a volume full of the names of its "Eminent Hands", including, elsewhere, Dryden's). The authorship of these poems was undisputed and the danger of them gone. Yet Dryden kept up the show of mystery or reticence. The sense of show was all the stronger as these are the first three items in the collection.

Dryden did occasionally attempt truly secretive, anonymous writing. In the wake of Charles II's dissolving of parliament in March 1681, and the publication of the king's *Declaration to all His living Subjects*, justifying his action, there appeared the anonymous *His Majesties Declaration Defended*. It is thought to have been, in whole or in part, by Dryden.[42] Later, anonymity almost certainly allowed him to contribute propaganda at the command of James II.[43] But these, if he was involved, were hidden tasks. The anonymity of his greatest satire was louder. Here is the reason for the careful maintenance of concealment in cases where there was no real secrecy. It was one means by which Dryden, professional writer, aspired to impersonality. Here is the point of an anonymity that cannot be preserved, that only the author himself seems to believe in.

Or perhaps not only the author. The second edition of *Absalom and Achitophel* included two anonymous commendatory poems. One was later attributed to Nathaniel Lee, with whom Dryden had collaborated on the play *Oedipus*.[44] The other, signed "R D" when the second edition was reprinted in 1682, was by Richard Duke, a protégé whom Dryden had supported and encouraged. Yet these two poems by intimates of Dryden were entitled, respectively, "To the Unknown Author of this Excellent Poem" and "To the Unknown Author of this Admirable Poem." Clearly, both were under instruction to keep the notional secret, to behave as if they were in ignorance. Yet the ignorance seems a kind of propriety. Duke in particular implies a knowledge of the author.

> Sure thou already art secure of fame,
> Nor want'st new glories to exalt thy name:
> What father else would have refused to own
> So great a son as godlike Absalon? (25–8)[45]

Anonymity is the sign in this case of a magisterial carelessness about status.

The 1682 reprint of the second edition also included a new commendatory poem by Nahum Tate, signed "N. T." Dryden had encouraged Tate, who was more than twenty years younger than himself, and in 1679 had written a Prologue to his *The Loyal General*. The two men had been co-contributors to *Ovid's Epistles* (1680). Tate's composition – "To the Concealed Author of this Incomparable Poem" – is a highly pitched celebration. *Absalom and Achitophel* is "a work to vie / With Homer's flame and Virgil's majesty" (4–5). Yet the "matchless bard" is addressed as "thou great unknown", a description that, by the time that the poem appears, is untrue as well as disingenuous. The supposedly modest poet would, says Tate, have to "shun mankind" if he wished to avoid praise of his poem. The eulogy ends by hoping that Charles II might somehow find "the unknown author" and shower favors on him. Tate must surely have supposed that the poem already had its origins in some official encouragement.[46] Yet his hope is the more peculiar for being published with the poem. It keeps up the fiction that it is of mysterious origins and not attributable to any activity of patronage or motive of service. What is more, Tate acknowledges that though readers and admirers like himself might have their hunches about the identity of "The sire to whom this lively birth we owe," they can only direct their admiration "by guess" (32–4). This is not literally true, yet perhaps it catches a truth about the poem's rhetoric. We should know by its mere quality who has written it – but we should also know that it has escaped personality.

At almost the same time, Tate supplied an anonymous commendatory poem ("Upon the Author of the following Poem") to the first edition of *The Medall*, published in March 1682.[47] This certainly sounds as though the poem's authorship is known not only to Tate, but to everyone else who matters. It refers to Dryden's belated entry into the ring.

> By art and nature for this task designed,
> Yet modestly the fight he long declined.
> (5–6)

Only when "the needful hour" came did the unnamed author let loose his satire. Dryden had published no original verse aside from prologues and epilogues to plays in between *Annus Mirabilis*, at the beginning of 1667, and *Absalom and Achitophel* in 1681 (if we discount the manuscript circulation of *MacFlecknoe*). Accompanying Tate's was another anonymous commendatory poem, attributed more than thirty years later to T. Adams. In the style of the poems attached to the second edition of *Absalom and Achitophel*, this was entitled "To the Unknown Author of the following Poem, and that of *Absalom and Achitophel*."[48] Its opening even spins a conceit out of the business of praising an unknown poet. The commender is like virtuous pagans who raised altars "to gods unknown."

> They knew not the loved deity, they knew
> Divine effects a cause divine did show.
>
> (3–4)

Commendations make much of the divine origins of Dryden's poems, for they assert a divine scheme of things against innovators and rebels. The best trick of *The Medal* is to contrast the rather different kinds of God behind, on the one hand, Shaftesbury's Whiggism and, on the other hand, the enthusiasm of his non-conformist Protestant supporters – his "canting friends." Shaftesbury's Epicurean deity must be

> A jolly God, that passes hours too well
> To promise Heav'n, or threaten us with Hell.
> (*Works* II: 51, lines 279–80)

The simple, ridiculous assonance of "jolly God" – a deity absurdly made in the image of tolerant, confident improvers – contrasts sharply with the "tyrant" who is the deity of Calvinist Protestants. They dream of a heaven which is "A Conventicle of gloomy sullen Saints" (284).

The religious subtext accounts in one way for the anonymity of *Absalom and Achitophel*. The poem's preface "To the Reader" indeed makes rhetorical play of this. "Were I the Inventour, who am only the Historian, I should certainly conclude the Piece with the Reconcilement of *Absalom* to *David*" (*Works* II: 4). The poet follows the track of a story that he has not invented. It is not his narrative. This is because he is writing about real events and relationships; he cannot decide that Monmouth and the king will become reconciled. Yet it also implies that the Bible story that is being used describes the shape of destiny. (And the reader would be expected to know the sad trajectory of the story in 2 Samuel, ending in Absalom's death.) The poet withdraws from the narrative because he is not its creator (though he has altered the details, especially of Achitophel's responsibility, to suit his purposes). It follows a providential pattern. This is all the more striking once we catch Achitophel trying to persuade Absalom into rebellion, for we hear from him that it is Fortune, not Providence, that shapes men's destinies. Fate favors the opportunist.

> Our Fortune rolls, as from a smooth Descent,
> And, from the first Impression, takes the Bent:
> But, if unseiz'd, she glides away like wind;
> And leaves repenting Folly far behind.
>
> (256–9)

The preface also talks as if the poem's anonymity displayed its disinterestedness. The poet is surrounded by antagonistic readers, yet bids for "the commendation of adversaries." To the "Common-wealths-men," die-hard republicans who cannot be swayed, even by "good verse," he turns with a reference to their own liking for anonymous, controversial publications. "You cannot be so Unconscionable, as to charge me for not Subscribing of my Name; for that woud reflect too grosly on your own Party, who never dare" (*Works* II: 4). These men will be keen to put a name to the poem, as if this might excuse them from its satire. Meanwhile, *Absalom and Achitophel* is written out of a wise reticence. "I have but laughed at some men's follies when I could have declaimed against their vices." The author has held back – held back even from declaring his identity. Dryden had no reason to fear official antagonism. He seems to have written the poem at King Charles's prompting, and to have been financially rewarded for doing so.[49] He made no realistic attempt to conceal his authorship, and yet he continued to withhold his name from succeeding editions of this, his most famous poem.

Dryden's removal of himself from the poem has its effects from the first extraordinary, poised yet risky, lines:

> In pious times, e'r Priest-craft did begin,
> Before *Polygamy* was made a sin. (1–2)

What is the tone of this? Do we hear "Priest-craft" as a word coined by radical Whigs, and used here in mockery of their scoffing habits, or as one being employed with the author's own easy irony?[50] What are we to make of the daring joke about "sin" being a matter of mere convention? For, in a narrative of temptation and fall, "sin" will also be the word for the rebellion that Absalom will embrace (372). We know, and contemporaries suspected, that the poem was written at Charles II's behest. Yet the audacity of allegorically drawing attention to both the king's promiscuity and his helpless affection for the dangerous Monmouth belies this. It is a strange kind of propaganda, seen in a disinterested perspective. It is made to seem beyond personal allegiance. We might think this impersonality especially convenient when we reach the gallery of complimentary portraits near the end of the poem, for some of these admirable characters were Dryden's own patrons – agents of his own advancement.

The drama of *Absalom and Achitophel* exploits and emphasizes its author's distance from the poem. Dangerous arguments are put in the mouths of Absalom and Achitophel and not directly contradicted by the author. With an easy turn of phrase, Achitophel tempts Absalom with the radical Whig argument that was later to be associated with John Locke's *Two Treatises of Government* (written by this time, but not published until 1689). Perhaps David will confirm him heir to the throne,

> If not; the People have a Right Supreme
> To make their Kings; for Kings are made for them.
>
> (409–10)

As Satan, "squat like a toad," used his "devilish art" to try "inspiring venom" in the thoughts of the sleeping Eve in *Paradise Lost* Book IV, so Achitophel uses "studied Arts" and "sheds his Venome" into Absalom's thoughts in the poem's temptation scene (228–9). This requires Absalom to be given strong arguments for loyalty to Charles II and respect for the succession (315–62). Untethered from its author's partisanship, an account of Charles's right to rule, and his brother's right of succession, of the former's virtues and the latter's courage, loyalty, and mercy, is put in the mouth of the would-be rebel – as if he cannot help but say so. Equally, the dramatic mode is calculated to lend authority to the concluding speech of David, the poem finally being given over to providential history.

Dryden, we might say, withholds himself, giving us over to the biblical story. Yet there is another religious narrative here, though biblical only at one remove. From line 30, when Absalom's beauty is glossed with the strange, unsettling line "And *Paradise* was open'd in his face," we start being given snatches of the Miltonic narrative of the Fall. The English who grumble against their king are "*Adam*-wits, too fortunately free." David disarms discontent for a while,

> But, when to Sin our byast Nature leans,
> The carefull Devil is still at hand with means.
>
> (79–80)

This devil will become incarnate in the poem as Achitophel, who will first help "the Croud" to the "Golden fruit" of power (202–3) and then tempt Absalom to pluck what is forbidden.

> Believe me, Royal Youth, thy Fruit must be
> Or gathered Ripe, or rot upon the Tree.
>
> (250–1)

Like Satan, Achitophel is the greatest of the fallen.

> Some had in Courts been Great, and thrown from thence,
> Like Feinds, were harden'd in Impenitence. (144–5)

Courtiers out of place become Milton's fallen angels. When Achitophel finally begins to close in on Absalom, who is ominously "Too full of Angells Metal in his Frame" (310), we see "Him Staggering so when Hell's dire Agent found" (373). The verse takes on a Miltonic syntactic inversion as it asks us to see Achitophel as Milton's Satan.

All this is more evidence of the extraordinary impact on Dryden of *Paradise Lost*. It is an ironical appropriation and homage, given that the epic of the unrepentant Republican is being revisited for the purposes of a Tory monarchist. Perhaps it is no wonder that Dryden's reverential "Lines on Milton," composed for Tonson's 1688 edition of *Paradise Lost*, should have been anonymous and have remained unavowed by their author. At a time when *Paradise Lost* was by no means the acknowledged masterwork that it would become by the early eighteenth century, the pattern of allusions in *Absalom and Achitophel* looks now like a deeply personal one. Dryden is recalling Milton's poem for himself as much as for his reader. Yet the recollection also serves to turn the personal and political into the timeless. The Whig opponents of Charles II's brother James, Duke of York, are made followers of the original rebel, the self-tormenting enemy to all "subjection". Rebellion against the king is poetically imagined as – not just said to be – rebellion against God. Psychologically speaking, Shaftesbury *is* satanic, destructively glorying in his own boldness.

"'Tis Dreydon's they say; and no doubt, upon ye presumption, somebody will fall upon him," wrote one reader only five days after its publication.[51] Only rhetorically did his enemies fall upon him, none of the many rejoinders doubting the identity of the hidden author. Soon Dryden's *Heroic Stanzas* in memory of Oliver Cromwell were being reprinted to reveal him as a mercenary changeling. Yet the poem was hugely successful and widely admired.[52] Though he took so long publicly to admit its authorship, *Absalom and Achitophel* was a poem central to Dryden's reputation in his own lifetime, as it is now. However, he could sometimes be genuinely careless about readers recognizing his "hand." Our external evidence for the attribution to Dryden of two hundred lines of *The Second Part of Absalom and Achitophel* is the testimony of its publisher, Jacob Tonson. In 1716, in *The Second Part of*

Miscellany Poems, he recalled that Dryden had been pressed to compose a continuation of *Absalom and Achitophel*. Declining the task, he had asked Nahum Tate to write it "and gave him his Advice in the Direction of it."[53] According to Tonson, Dryden did himself contribute lines 310–509, "besides some Touches in other places." The attribution became especially important to Alexander Pope, who numbered Tate ("a cold writer, of no *invention*") as one of the dunces in *The Dunciad*. In a note attached to Book I of his 1729 *Dunciad Variorum*, Pope observed that Tate "sometimes translated tolerably when befriended by Mr. *Dryden*."[54] "In his second part of *Absalom* and *Achitophel* are above two hundred admirable lines together of that great hand, which strongly shine through the insipidity of the rest."

Pope needed to use the portraits of Og (Shadwell) and Doeg (Settle) that Tonson identified as Dryden's. Dryden's Shadwell swears when drunk:

> When wine has given him courage to Blaspheme
> He Curses God, but God before Curst him.
>
> (466–7)

In Pope's final *Dunciad* of 1743, Shadwell has grown into Colly Cibber, gamester, unbeliever and dunce.

> Swearing and supperless the Hero sate,
> Blasphem'd his Gods, the Dice, and damn'd his Fate.
>
> (I, 115–16)[55]

In Book IV of this version of Pope's poem, the Queen of Dullness commands her many followers, "My Sons! be proud, be selfish, and be dull" (IV, 582). She remembers the strange birth of Og in *The Second Part of Absalom and Achitophel*.

> The midwife laid her hand on his thick skull
> With this prophetic blessing: "Be thou dull."
>
> (476–7)

Lines attached to Elkanah Settle as Doeg were also to lodge in *The Dunciad*. In Dryden's version we see how Doeg the blundering poet

> Spurred boldly on, and dashed through thick and thin,
> Through sense and nonsense, never out nor in.
>
> (414–15)

The lines had a special appeal to Pope, reappearing twice in his mock-epic of modern stupidity. The hacks invited by their Goddess to dive into the filthy Fleet Ditch are required to "prove who best can dash thro' thick and thin" (II, 264). In the four-book *Dunciad* the fatuous academic philosophers, riding their hobbyhorses, "dash'd thro' thin and thick," mounted on the works of modern logicians (IV, 197). How better to stand in awe of the energy of dunces? For Pope, being able to see Dryden's "great hand" in any otherwise indifferent poem was assurance of the wide gap between true poetry and the ephemeral manufactures of the dunces. His transfusion of some of Dryden's lines into his own poem honored and confirmed their survival, all the more striking when taken from an occasional piece about whose attribution Dryden seemed to care little.

Dryden's use, or his withholding, of his name are not just matters of interest to biographers and literary historians. Attribution shaped what his writing once meant. Take the self-awareness with which he attached his name to *Religio Laici*. To a reader now, approaching all his major poems under the heading of Dryden's name, this is likely to seem unremarkable. For a reader of the 1680s, the author's naming of himself was striking – a pointed refusal of anonymity, broached in the first sentence of the poem's Preface.

> A Poem with so bold a Title, and a Name prefix'd, from which the handling of
> so serious a Subject wou'd not be expected, may reasonably oblige the Author,
> to say somewhat in defence both of himself, and of his undertaking.
>
> (*Works* II: 98)

The title is "bold" because it implies that a layman might have the authority to deal in "speculations which belong to the profession of divinity." But bold too, apparently, is Dryden's identification of himself on the title page. The implication here is that anonymity would be the normal covering for a work of such seriousness, the natural aid to its dignity. A writer might have ways of letting readers infer his identity, but he would let the thing stand for itself. Dryden writes as if he is doing something unusual in making his vindication of Anglicanism a personal matter. "I pretend not make myself a Judge of Faith, in others, but onely to make a Confession of my own." This is a poem that rests on personal authority, without ever becoming a personal poem.

This will seem peculiar to a modern reader, taken by *Religio Laici* through a series of religious arguments – a series of "isms," indeed. Yet the poet, Dryden in propria persona, is where these arguments and isms meet. The poem finds itself in a special time and place. When it puts the Deist account, we can believe it one that Dryden has perhaps read, probably heard (in coffeehouse conversation, in familiar tones of intellectual ingenuity). Presumably when Narcissus Luttrell wrote "Atheisticall" on his copy of the poem, he was reacting to the very airtime that Dryden had given to the Deistical arguments that he was rebutting.[56] Yet the reader is required not to regard it as personal in another way: having the authority of personal insight. In the Preface, Dryden goes so far as to disown any of his opinions that cannot be commended by the Church of England. "I submit them with all reverence to my Mother Church, accounting them no further mine, than as they are Authoriz'd, or at least, uncondemn'd by her."

Dryden attaches his name to *Religio Laici* because it is a poem that searches for some kind of authoritative humility.[57] So it is written against "wit," which is arraigned at every turn for leading men into vanity and self-delusion. After he first states the Deist argument about the sufficiency of natural religion, Dryden exclaims,

> Vain, wretched Creature, how art thou misled
> To think thy Wit these God-like notions bred!
>
> (64–5)

Behind these lines is the story of the fall, where Eve was told by the serpent that she and Adam would be as gods if they ate the fruit. In *Paradise Lost*, Satan uses the very adjective ("God-like") that Dryden retrieves when, having taken Eve to the tree of knowledge, he asks,

> And what are gods that man may not become
> As they, participating godlike food?
>
> (IX, 716–17)

But also, more immediately, there is the transformation of Milton's story in *Absalom and Achitophel*, where being like a god is the prospect contemplated by Absalom, drawn to imagine usurping "Godlike *David*" (14).

> Why am I Scanted by a Niggard Birth?
> My Soul Disclaims the Kindred of her Earth:
> And made for Empire, Whispers me within;
> Desire of Greatness is a Godlike Sin.
>
> (369–72)

Wit is of course there in the most famous couplet of *Absalom and Achitophel*:

> Great Wits are sure to Madness near ally'd;
> And thin Partitions do their Bounds divide.
>
> (163–4)

The "great Wit" is that modern Satan, the Earl of Shaftesbury. "Wit" is even the possession of the gullible "Multitude" in *The Medal*, assured by Shaftesbury that the authority of a monarch is a matter of alterable convention.

> Almighty Crowd, thou shorten'st all dispute;
> Pow'r is thy Essence; Wit thy Attribute!
>
> (91–2)

"Wit" can be a value in Dryden's writing: over and over again in *MacFlecknoe*, "wit" is everything that Shadwell lacks. As the value of an age, however, it is different. "Wit seems to have lodg'd itself more Nobly in this Age, than in any of the former," he wrote in hopeful servility to Rochester in his Dedication to *Marriage A-la-Mode* of 1673 (*Works* XI: 223). This was in the process of declaring that he could never rival the young aristocrat's abilities. When he attacked Rochester in his Preface to *All for Love*, it was as the leader of a company of "witty men" and the adjective, used repeatedly, was made positively dismissive (*Works* XIII: 13). We can see the double service of the word in "To My Dear Friend Mr Congreve" (a complimentary poem prefixed to Congreve's *The Double-Dealer* in 1694), in which he refers several times, in admiration, to the young playwright's "wit." Congreve will eventually be seen "High on the Throne of Wit" (53). Yet when he talks of an "Age of Wit," in the poem's opening couplet, Dryden's tone is uncertain, perhaps ironical.

> Well then; the promised hour is come at last;
> The present Age of Wit obscures the past.
>
> (*Works* IV: 432)

At moments like this we can sense Auden's error, representative of many readers before and after him, when he said of Dryden, "His lines have no undertones, as Pope's often have: they mean exactly what, on first reading, they seem to say."[58] These lines, urbane and conversational as they purport to be, are all undertone. If we wish to listen hard enough, we can hear Dryden musing on the self-regarding self-image of an age – an age in which, as the poem goes on to observe, "Poetry is cursed" (47). The post of Historiographer Royal (once held by Dryden) has, upon the death of his old foe Thomas Shadwell, passed to a new enemy, Thomas Rhymer: "*Tom* the Second reigns like *Tom* the first" (48). What "Age of Wit" can this be? But then "wit" as a cultural value was invariably suspect in Dryden's writing. In *Religio Laici*, "wit" is responsible for some of the clever arguments of the times. A self-regarding sense of the age is implied in the lines that compare the imagined Deist with Socrates, the wise pagan.

> Hast thou a Wit so deep, or so sublime,
> Or canst thou lower dive, or higher climb?
>
> (76–7)

And "wit" becomes a term of scorn a few lines later when Dryden transforms Virgil's line from the *Aeneid* about "high-minded heroes, born in better times" (*magnanimi heroes nati melioribus annis*; *Aeneid*, Book VI, 649) into

"Those Gyant Wits, in happyer Ages born" (80). Wit is the special standard of the aristocratic manuscript culture to which Dryden never quite belongs.

Against wit Dryden sets his own modest, fearless attempts at plainness. The force that anonymity can have in this period should help us measure the power of Dryden's name, when he uses it. His stamping of *Religio Laici* with his own name is no attempt to make the poem autobiographical (indeed, given his conversion to Roman Catholicism only four years later it has been tempting to think that the poem thoroughly disguises the inner life of the poet). "Thus have I made my own Opinions clear" (451), he says at the poem's conclusions. Even the most sympathetic biographer would not think this quite true. Yet the owning of the opinions is what makes the poem work, rhetorically speaking. It is an offering of an unschooled individual's reasonings, with "little Skill" (318), against wit.

> Shall I speak plain, and in a Nation free
> Assume an honest *Layman's Liberty*?
> (316–17)

"Honest" here will sound suspicious to anyone with an idea of Dryden's religious and political progress. The poem cannot be telling us what he thought, even what he believed. Yet rhetorically the question catches why the poem has to be personal. As inexpert as experience has made him, the poet names himself to be beyond either wit or theology. He even associates the intellectual libertine with the theological precisian, by using "wit" to refer to the intellectuality of the latter. He has just said how the "unlettered Christian . . . Plods to heaven," undistracted by doctrinal niceties.

> For the *Streight-gate* wou'd be made *streighter* yet,
> Were *none* admitted there but men of *Wit*. (324–5)

Amongst biblical exegists, there are some whose accounts are "*forc'd* by *Wit* and *Eloquence*" (333).

Yet when he came to his second great poetic statement of faith (which contradicted the first), he turned back to anonymity. The anonymity of *The Hind and the Panther* seems a puzzle. The poem was written in privacy and retreat, with only a few rumors as yet attaching Dryden to Catholicism. And there it suddenly appears, fully formed, an impolitic and elaborate apologia for a faith. Its prefatory address "To the Reader" explicitly declines to give personal information, and indicates that all personal considerations have been transformed into poetic argument. "What I desire the *Reader* should know concerning me, he will find in the Body of the Poem; if he have but the patience to peruse it" (*Works* III: 119). But the lines in the poem that sound sharply autobiographical will be unsatisfying to any biographer.

"My manhood, long misled by wandering fires, / Follow'd false lights" (I, 73–4). There is some suggestion of a personal pressure in the lines about how the poet can come to accept the doctrine of transubstantiation (I, 85–6), but the point is that "my doubts are done" (I, 78). They are below the poem's horizon. There is no room here for any personal grappling with doctrine and authority. *The Hind and the Panther* is a poem of submission, in which the story of fallen angels used in *Absalom and Achitophel* is now applied to all forms of Protestantism.

> God's and kings rebels have the same good cause
> To trample down divine and humane laws.
>
> (I, 357–8)

The Anglican Church is but "the fairest of the fallen crew" (I, 450). "Rebellion equals all" (I, 456). Anybody not a Roman Catholic is a rebel.

Surely there must have been agonizing over his change of faith, but if so nothing of it remains in the poem, which triumphs over private considerations. *The Hind and the Panther* is a reversal not only of some of the arguments of *Religio Laici*, but also of its testimony from personal knowledge (or ignorance). Dryden's Roman Catholic poem is literally a work of self-abnegation. The suppression of "wit" attempted in *Religio Laici* is to be taken to its logical conclusion.

> If then our faith we for our guide admit,
> Vain is the further search of humane wit.
>
> (I, 122–3)

After its parade of beasts in Part I – the variety of characters itself evidence of the instability of all forms of Protestantism – the poem turns to dialogue. Not only does the author remove himself, he even makes the Hind, the voice of the Church of Rome, turn against him. The Hind now forbids the poet's own self-assertive or satirical instincts. Religious devotion means ignoring "humane honour" (III, 286). As if foreseeing the many scoffing responses that the poem would arouse (none of them failing to distinguish Dryden as the author), it warns against retaliation. For the will to self-vindication, the poem uses that word whose political and psychologically satanic implications Dryden explored in his satires: "rebel."

> Down then thou rebell, never more to rise,
> And what thou didst, and dost so dearly prize,
> That fame, that darling fame, make that thy sacrifice.
>
> (III, 288–90)

Dryden has written so eloquently against rebellion. Now he finds that the rebel is within him. Thus perhaps the ultimate use of anonymity for Dryden: to make a rhetoric that subjugates its maker.

It is tempting for the modern reader to ask, why anonymity? Yet in the poetry of Dryden's age, anonymity was so frequent and conventional that it might sometimes be more appropriate to ask why you would put your name to your published work.[59] In the case of *Religio Laici*, the very non-anonymity of the poem has a special voltage. Elsewhere, with Dryden's most successful satires, the question might better be, what were the uses of anonymity? Dryden had many contemporary precedents for withholding his name, whilst relying on his readers' appetite for attribution. Yet he used a literary convention that was commonly available for mischief or self-protection to confirm his status as an impersonal authority, a deus ex machina. In the last great composition of original verse before he turned to translation, anonymity again became compelling for him. This time, however, it was to perform a conquest over his own appetite for poetic power.

NOTES

1. *Mercurius Anglicus*, 17–20 December, 1679.
2. See Edward L. Saslow, "The Rose Alley Ambuscade," *Restoration* 26, 1 (Spring 2002), 27. See James M. Osborn, *John Dryden: Some Biographical Facts and Problems* (1965), pp. 144–5 for documents relating to the attack.
3. *An Essay upon Satire*, line 73, in *POAS* 1, 405.
4. See his letter to Savile, 21 November 1679, in *The Letters of John Wilmot, Earl of Rochester*, ed. J. Treglown (Oxford, 1980), 232–3.
5. *Essay upon Satire*, lines 240–1, *POAS* 1, 412.
6. Saslow, "The Rose Alley Ambuscade," p. 35.
7. Harold Love, *Scribal Publication in Seventeenth-Century England* (Oxford, 1993), p. 258.
8. See Hugh Macdonald, *John Dryden: A Bibliography of Early Editions and Drydeniana* (Oxford, 1939), p. 217.
9. Ibid., pp. 217–18.
10. See Paul Hammond's note in his edition of *The Poems of John Dryden*, vol. II (London, 1995), p. 53.
11. See *POAS* 1, Introduction, xxxv–xxxvii.
12. *POAS* 2, 425.
13. *Dictionary of Anonymous and Pseudonymous English Literature*, ed. Samuel Halkett and John Laing, enlarged James Kennedy *et al.* (1926), vol. I, p. xi.
14. Paul Hammond, ed., *The Poems of John Dryden*, vol. II, p. 7. He uses the same phrase for the authorship of *The Hind and the Panther*, *Poems*, vol. III, p. 32.
15. *POAS* 3, 61, lines 7–8.
16. Ibid., 81, lines 3–4.

17. Steven Zwicker, "The Constitution of Opinion and the Pacification of Reading," in *Reading, Society and Politics in Early Modern England*, ed. Kevin Sharpe and Steven N. Zwicker (Cambridge, 2003), p. 303.
18. For Herringman prefaces that might be by Dryden, see Osborn, *Dryden: Some Biographical Facts*, pp. 193–9.
19. In *POAS* 3, 75.
20. Love, *Scribal Publication*, p. 213.
21. Ibid., p. 236.
22. Dedication to *The Tenth Satyr of Juvenal* (1687) in *The Complete Works of Thomas Shadwell*, ed. Montagu Summers, 5 vols. (1927), vol. v, p. 292.
23. Gilbert Burnet, *Some Passages of the Life and Death of the Right Honourable John Earl of Rochester* (1680), p. 26.
24. *The Complete Poems of John Wilmot, Earl of Rochester*, ed. David M. Veith (New Haven, 1968), pp. 124–5.
25. Burnet, *Some Passages*, p. 7.
26. In *Rochester. The Critical Heritage*, ed. David Farley-Hills (1972), p. 139.
27. John Crowne, Dedication to *The History of Charles VIII of France*, in *Dramatic Works*, ed. J. Maidment and W. H. Logan (1873), vol. i, p. 127.
28. Burnet, *Some Passages*, p. 14.
29. See Love, *Scribal Publication*, p. 248, for an example from contemporary correspondence of a reader "in quest of some more of my Ld Rochesters ingenuitie."
30. Rochester, *Poems*, ed. Veith, pp. 65–6.
31. In Love, *Scribal Publication*, p. 257.
32. An early example is his poem to the king's mistress Lady Castlemaine, probably composed in 1663.
33. Love, *Scribal Publication*, p. 296.
34. *Works of Shadwell*, ed. Summers, vol. ii, p. 105.
35. Ibid., vol. iii, p. 103.
36. George Villiers, Second Duke of Buckingham, *The Rehearsal*, ed. D. E. L. Crane (Durham, 1976), p. 6.
37. Gerard Langbaine, *An Account of the English Dramatick Poets* (1691), 151.
38. *POAS*, i, 394.
39. For a list of these, see Paul Hammond, "The Circulation of Dryden's Poetry", in *Critical Essays on John Dryden*, ed. James A. Winn (1997), p. 50. Contemporaries seem sometimes to have been positively eager to detect Dryden's hand. Buckingham's *A Familiar Epistle to Mr. Julian, Secretary to the Muses*, despite containing a dismissive reference to Dryden, is attributed to him in four separate manuscript copies. See *POAS*, i, 387.
40. Letter to Mrs. Steward, 23 February 1700, in *The Letters of John Dryden*, ed. Charles E. Ward (1942), p. 133.
41. See Winn, 619, n. 56.
42. See ibid., 596, n. 24 for detailed arguments.
43. See ibid. 420 (and n. 85) on *A Defence of the Papers Written by the Late King of Blessed Memory and Duchess of York*.
44. Macdonald, *Bibliography*, p. 23.
45. The commendatory poems are reprinted in *Poems of Dryden*, ed. Hammond, vol. i, Appendix C, pp. 540–3.

46. See Wallace Maurer, "Who Prompted Dryden to Write *A&A?*" *Philological Quarterly* 40 (1961), 130–8.
47. In *Poems of Dryden*, ed. Hammond, vol. II, pp. 437–8.
48. Ibid., pp. 438–9.
49. Tonson in *The Second Part of the Miscellany Poems* (1716) reports that it was written "upon the Desire of King *Charles* the Second."
50. See Paul Hammond's note in his edition of *Poems of Dryden*, vol. I, p. 454.
51. Macdonald, *Bibliography*, p. 20.
52. For calculations of its sales, see Hammond, "The Circulation of Dryden's Poetry," p. 55.
53. *Poems Of Dryden*, ed. Hammond, vol. II, p. 38.
54. *The Poems of Alexander Pope*, ed. John Butt (1963), p. 357 (note to line 103).
55. Ibid., p. 726.
56. See Macdonald, *Bibliography*, p. 33; for a reproduction of the title-page with Luttrell's annotation see *John Dryden: Selected Poems*, ed. Steven N. Zwicker and David Bywaters (Harmondsworth, 2001), p. 163.
57. See Dustin Griffin's argument that a patronage culture made Dryden practiced at combining self-abnegation with self-assertion, *Literary Patronage in England, 1650–1800* (Cambridge, 1996), chapter 4.
58. W. H. Auden, Introduction, *A Choice of Dryden's Verse* (1973), p. 9.
59. The best overview of the uses of anonymity in Restoration poetry is Paul Hammond, "Anonymity in Restoration Poetry," *The Seventeenth Century* 8, 1 (Spring 1993), 123–42.

10

KATSUHIRO ENGETSU

Dryden and the modes of Restoration sociability

Dryden's literary life would have been completely different had it not been for the coffee houses of Restoration London. Indeed, coffee houses came to occupy a pivotal position in a series of overlapping literary spheres that swept from the elite culture of the Restoration court to the popular life of the town. Coffee houses were a new type of urban space that first appeared in Oxford in 1650 and then in London in 1652. Dryden early acknowledged as much when he addressed the audience "of Court, of Coffee-houses, or Town" in the "Epilogue" to *The Indian Emperor* (1667) (*Works* IX: 112), and Pepys records Dryden's presence in Will's Coffee House even earlier, in 1664:

> In Covent-garden tonight, going to fetch home my wife, I stopped at the great Coffee-house there, where I never was before – where Draydon the poet (I knew at Cambridge) and all the wits of the town, and Harris the player and Mr. Hoole of our college; and had I had time then, or could at other times, it will be good coming thither, for there I perceive is very witty and pleasant discourse. But I could not tarry and it was late; they were all ready to go away.[1]

Late in the seventeenth century Pope paid tribute to Dryden's dominant presence in this new culture: "It was Dryden who made Will's Coffee-House the great resort for the wits of his time."[2] Hovering over Dryden's various literary life lay a continuous commitment to the emerging idea of urban sociability as most typically seen in the rise of coffee houses in Restoration England. His involvement in urban sociability defines him as the true successor of Ben Jonson, who presided over the Sons of Ben in the Apollo Room of Devil and St. Dunstan Tavern near Temple Bar; and Dryden's patronage of a specific coffee house might identify him as the model for Samuel Johnson, who devoted himself to the meetings of the Club in the Turk's Head Coffee House at Soho. Dryden's place in the history of English literature cannot be fully understood without considering the cultural relationship between his literary activities and Restoration modes of sociability. The aim of this essay is to draw together some of the implications of sociability for Dryden's career and for Restoration literary culture.

It might be convenient to begin with a closer look at Pepys's description of Will's Coffee House in order to get a preliminary understanding of Dryden's idea of sociability. The coffee house was located between the official institution of the state and the private realm – a geography Pepys illustrates for us as he drops into the coffee house on his way "home" from the Navy Office. Following Jürgen Habermas's immensely influential work, we might well define the social space of the coffee house as a "public sphere" where private persons, free from affairs of state, voluntarily got together to form publicity.[3] The space is characterized by social fluidity; Pepys was allowed to join the company voluntarily without any special qualification or reservation, and its customers were quite miscellaneous – poet (Dryden), actor (Henry Harris), historian (William Hoole or Howell), and navy official (Pepys). Pepys's references to "Cambridge" and Magdalene "college" suggest that the intimacy at the coffee house was created as much by the mutual trust of shared social and intellectual backgrounds as by political, religious, or commercial interests. He found the "discourse" "witty and pleasant," and was as much impressed by the contents of talk as by its manner. And at the very center of the "witty and pleasant discourse" in the public sphere of Will's Coffee House was John Dryden, representing the new mode of sociability in Restoration London.

Dryden's reputation was based not only on his printed words but also on his discourse in the emerging public sphere of the late seventeenth century where oral and literate culture mingled and where a number of "sociable conversations" and fictional dialogues found their way into print, and such new genres as "humours" and "conversations" were used as vehicles to comment on urban life. *The Humours and Conversations of the Town* (1693) (published anonymously, but likely written by James Wright), for example, is a dialogue among Mr. Jovial, Mr. Pensive, and Mr. Sociable on contemporary London life. Here Mr. Pensive, who is most cautious about new urban fashions, praises "the Company of the Author of *Absalom* and *Achitophel*" because "what he says, is like what he writes." This pamphlet suggests that there is no clear boundary between printed words and spoken discourse. In his preface to *Country Conversations* (1694), Wright tells us that he imitates "*the Original Draught of Le Pere Bouneurs*,"[4] a model of the art of "witty and pleasant" conversation. His reference to Bouhours is of special significance for Dryden because Bouhours is also the author of *La Vie de Saint François Xavier* (Paris, 1682), translated by Dryden as *The Life of St. Francis Xavier* (1688). Bouhours's precepts are connected explicitly to Dryden in Wright's idea of the literary genre of "witty and pleasant" conversation, since *An Essay of Dramatic Poesy* (1668) is mentioned in the discussion on coffee houses in *Humours and Conversations of the Town*.[5] The rise of fictitious dialogues of sociable conversation suggests that the formal quality of Dryden's major critical work in a dialogue form might well be reconsidered in the context of early modern literary sociability.

An Essay of Dramatic Poesy represents Dryden's idea of "witty and pleasant" conversation in the emerging public sphere in Restoration England. The historical framework of the fictional dialogue underlines the widening separation of the early modern public sphere from affairs of state. The discourse takes place among a "company" of four characters – Eugenius, Crites, Lisideius, and Neander – as all other Londoners are attracted by "the noise of the Cannon" on 3 June 1665, the date of the naval battle off Lowestoft. The "company" take a barge and pass London Bridge in order to satisfy their "curiosity with a strict silence," followed by "those little undulations of sound, though almost vanishing before they reach'd them, yet still seeming to retain somewhat of their first horrour which they had betwixt the Fleets" (*Works* XVIII: 8–9). They try to shield their discourse from "the noise" of political and military events, although the "silence" around them is not so "strict" as they expect. The historical setting suggests a delicate relationship between the Restoration public sphere and affairs of state; the Restoration public sphere insists on its autonomy while it admits its own vulnerability to facts and events and ideologies from without. In his dedication to Lord Buckhurst (afterwards Sixth Earl of Dorset), a man actually engaged in the battle, Dryden recommends "the divertisement of the Publick" to him, drawing a suggestive parallel between "the fight of the Greeks and Trojans" and "this war of opinions." Dryden allows that the discourse in the public sphere – modeled on real battles in affairs of state – might be engaged either "by some, like Pedants, with violence of words" or "by others like Gentlemen, with candour and civility" (*Works* XVIII: 4–6). His representation of the public sphere floats, as if on "a Barge" on the Thames, between the political threat of "violence" and the gentlemanly notion of "civility."

An Essay of Dramatic Poesy is concerned with the establishment of the emerging idea of "civility" in conversation.[6] The dialogue reads like a manual of public discourse. Eugenius (likely modeled on the dedicatee of the essay) often reminds the company of their gentlemanly propriety; when Crites comes close to criticizing contemporary poets personally, the dialogue takes the following course under Eugenius's care: "Well, Gentlemen, said *Eugenius*, you may speak your pleasure of these Authors; but though I and some few more about the Town may give you a peaceable hearing, yet, assure your selves, there are multitudes who would think you malicious and them injur'd: especially him whom you first described; he is the very *Withers* of the City" (*Works* XVII: 11–12). Eugenius assures his company that it is a rule of gentlemanly conversation to give "a peaceable hearing" to speakers who are allowed to enjoy liberty of speech. But he also reminds them that their discourse is likely to be misrepresented by London "multitudes" who are so easily swayed by popular propaganda. Eugenius's contempt for the urban "multitudes" is characterized by his memory of the enthusiastic reception of George Wither, that prolific Parliamentarian and poet: "When his famous poem first came out in the year 1660, I have seen them reading it in the midst of Change-time; nay so vehement they were at it, that they lost their bargain by the Candles ends . . ." (*Works* XVIII: 12). Eugenius opposes his practice of "a peaceable hearing" in gentlemanly conversation to the popular "vehement" habit of reading that will see no distinction between private and public interests. The idea of civility in the gentlemanly conversation is represented against the background of the contemporary enthusiasm of urban "multitudes."

The ending of *An Essay of Dramatic Poesy* (*Works* XVIII: 80–1) depicts an intriguing scene in Restoration London in which popular enthusiasm has yet to be tamed and civilized. The public discourse of the company on the floating "Barge" closes with Neander – a self-parody of Dryden as the least civilized character – becoming wholly absorbed in his own private opinions: "Neander was pursuing this Discourse so eagerly, that Eugenius had call'd to him twice or thrice ere he took notice that the Barge stood still, and they were at the foot of *Somerset*-Stairs, where they had appointed it to land." Neander's enthusiasm terminates the discourse of civility. On leaving the "Barge," the company find "a crowd of *French* people who were merrily dancing in the open air." The four English gentlemen have to realize that their practice of civility is challenged by the intrusion of a popular culture which is, literally, foreign to them. They then go to a hybrid public place: "the *Piazze*." The piazza, an urban public open space on the Tuscan model in Covent Garden (where Will's Coffee House is located), was originally designed by Inigo Jones for aristocrats and gentlemen. But it has been transformed into a Bohemian and sociable neighborhood as we see in Pepys's diary entry for 2 January 1665 – the year of the Great Plague: "in the piazza in Covent-Guarding . . . I occasioned much mirth with a ballet [ballad] I brought with me . . . Here a most noble French dinner and banquet, the best I have seen these many a day, and good discourse."[7] Restoration London provided a variety of urban sociable amenities where popular culture competes with elite culture while outlandish fashions mix with national customs. Before returning to their private realm, the company of gentlemen look back "on the water" on which "the Moon-beams play'd . . . like floating quick-silver." The idea of gentlemanly conversation in the public sphere in *An Essay of*

Dramatic Poesy drifts about like a playful memory on the "floating" water, constantly adulterated by popular and foreign cultures as soon as it lands in actual society.

An Essay of Dramatic Poesy records Dryden's memory of sociable experience before the Great Plague in 1665. He wrote the critical piece "as an amusement" to him "in the Country" when "the violence of the last Plague had driven" him "from the Town" (*Works* XVII: 3). John Evelyn reminds Pepys, surveying the history of Restoration virtuoso culture in his surprisingly knowledgeable letter on the edge of the outbreak of the 1688/9 Revolution, that an "Academie," which was to draw on the French model, was planned in 1665 for "the Polishing of the English Language," involving Dryden:

> And indeede such was once design'd since the Restauration of King Charles II, and in order to it, Three, or foure Meetings were begun at Gray's Inn, by Mr Cowley, Dr Sprat, Matthew Clifford, Sir Cyrill Wych, Duke of Buckingham, Mr Dryden, and other promoters of it; But then by the Death of [incomparable] Mr Cowley, the [distance and] Inconvenience of the Place, [the contagion,] and other Circumstances [intervening], it crumbled away and came to nothing . . .[8]

A marginal note to "since the Restauration of King Charles II" reads "1665," exactly when "the contagion" of the Great Plague raged in London. Evelyn's epistolary memoir after more than two decades, though inevitably confused about minor details, hints that Dryden attended preliminary meetings of the English academy, abandoned because of the declining health of Abraham Cowley (who actually survived the Great Plague by two years), the geographical "inconvenience," and the Great Plague in 1665. Cowley must have been the *primum mobile* of the meetings because his name appears on the top of the list of the participants and his death is remembered as the principal reason for the termination of the project. As early as 1661, the elder poet had published *A Proposition for the Advancement of Experimental Philosophy* that began by suggesting "That the Philosophical Colledge be scituated within one, two, or (at farthest) three miles of *Lond[o]n*, and if it be possible to find that convenience, upon the side of the River, or very near it."[9] His interest in a new kind of academic institution was prescribed by the spatial structure of Restoration London, a city still networked by water transportation. Hence "the Inconvenience of the Place," according to Evelyn, as the second reason for abandoning the English academy. The setting of the ideal public sphere on the floating "Barge" on the Thames in *An Essay of Dramatic Poesy* represents the shared concern of Cowley's circle around the year of the Great Plague that the English academy had yet to find a fit location for gentlemanly conversation "upon the side of the River."

Cowley, whom Dryden remembered in 1693 as "the darling" of his "youth" (*Works* IV: 84), was important to the rising poet's social status in the 1660s. And the two poets shared acquaintance with another participant of the preliminary meetings of the English academy: Thomas Sprat. Dryden contributed "Heroique Stanzas to the Glorious Memory of Cromwell" to *Three Poems upon the Death of His Late Highnesse Oliver Lord Protector* (1659), a pamphlet of verse that also included elegies by Edmund Waller and Sprat. The friendship between Dryden and Sprat outlived the Restoration; John Dennis tells us that they were intimate when Cowley's *Cutter of Coleman Street* saw its first public performance – in which "Harris the player" (whose sociable relationship with Dryden at Will's Coffee House we have seen in Pepys's diary in 1664) portrayed Mr. Truman Junior – at the theatre in Lincoln's Inn Fields on 16 December 1661:

> The only Play that ever Mr *Cowley* writ, was barbarously treated the first night, as the late Mr *Dryden* has more than once informed me, who has told me that he went to see it with the famous Mr *Sprat*, now Bishop of *Rochester*, and that after the Play was done, they both made a visit to Mr *Cowley*, who the Death of his Brother had obliged to keep the House, and that Mr *Cowley* received the news of ill success, not with so much firmness, as might have been expected from so great a man.[10]

The oral history of the "ill success" of Cowley's play might be exaggerated by either Dryden the teller or Dennis the hearer because Pepys, who saw the first performance, recorded it simply as "a very good play." Putting a note in his *Roscius Anglicanus* (1708) that "This Play was not a little injurious to the Cavalier Indigent Officers," John Downes suggested that the first performance of Cowley's city comedy offended some of the Restoration audience. *Cutter of Coleman Street*, whose scene was set in London in 1658, was remade from Cowley's own earlier play, *The Guardian*, acted before Prince Charles at Trinity College, Cambridge, in 1641. The public performance of Cowley's city comedy in 1661 referred back to his own theatrical work, perhaps to blot out the lapse of twenty years by connecting the memory of the young Charles with the expected return of the royal Charles. Cowley, however, underestimated the historical memory of the Civil Wars. The poor reception of *Cutter of Coleman Street* owed to Cowley's failure to find a new voice for a new audience. Impressed with Cowley's poignant inability to satisfy the contemporary taste, Dryden and Sprat understood the urgent need to reform and civilize the culture of the English language.

In *History of the Royal Society* (1667), to which Cowley contributed a commendatory poem, Sprat praises the French Academy "to recommend the forming of such an *Assembly*" to the English "Gentlemen" because "*eloquence* ought to be banish'd out of all *civil societies*, as a thing fatal to Peace and good Manners." His idea of the gentlemanly "*Assembly*" is closely connected with the importance of urban sociability, reminding us of the preliminary meetings of the English academy by Cowley, Sprat, Dryden, and others in 1665: "it is from the frequent conversations in Cities, that the Humour, and Wit, and Variety, and Elegance of Language, are chiefly to be fetch'd." Sprat's proposal comes from the shared traumatic memory of the Civil Wars:

> In the Wars themselves (which is a time, wherein all Languages use, if ever, to increase by extraordinary degrees; for in such busie, and active times, there arise more new thoughts of men, which must be signifi'd, and varied by new expressions) then I say, it receiv'd many fantastical terms, which were introduc'd by our *Religious Sects*; a[n]d many outlandish phrases, which several *Writers*, and *Translators*, in that great hurry, brought in, and made free as they pleas'd, and with all it was inlarg'd by many sound, and necessary Forms, and Idioms, which it before wanted. And now, when mens minds are somewhat settled, their Passions allaid, and the peace of our Country gives us the opportunity of such diversions: if some sober and judicious Men, would take the whole Mass of our Language into their hands, as they find it, and would set a mark on the ill Words; correct those, which are to be retain'd; admit, and establish the good; and make some emendations in the Accent, and Grammar: I dare pronounce, that our *Speech* would quickly arrive at as much plenty, as it is capable to receive . . .[11]

Unlike Cowley, Sprat is keenly aware of the historical effects of the Civil Wars on Restoration culture. The "*Religious Sects*" in the middle of the seventeenth century have transformed English society and its languages by finding "new expressions" which signify "new thoughts"; the innovation has been accelerated by "several Writers, and Translators" who have made free use of "many outlandish phrases." Sprat proposes that the aim of the English academy as a branch of the Royal Society be to establish "Peace and Good Manners" by civilizing "conversations" in an English Restoration society that has to inherit the exciting but confusing cultural legacy of the Civil Wars.

In *An Essay of Dramatic Poesy*, Dryden – a fellow of the Royal Society since 1662 – shared Sprat's interest in the institution of the English academy. Hence Crites's critical reference, as we have seen, to Wither, "A very Leveller in Poetry," who has survived the Civil Wars (*Works* XVIII: 11). The point of the critical comment on Wither lies not so much in his Puritan ideology as in his old style since it is preceded by Lisideius's more explicit accusation of

"Clevelandism," the poetical style named after the Cavalier whose poetry, even after his death in 1658, had hardly been less popular than Wither's (*Works* XVIII: 10). Wither is juxtaposed with Cleveland; the two are diametrically opposed but they have equally abused the English language; both are to be corrected. Wither is defined as the poet who "helps out his Numbers with *For to*, and *Unto*, and all the pretty Expletives he can find" (*Works* XVIII: 11). Cleveland, on the other hand, is characterized by "*Catachresis . . .* wresting and torturing a word into another meaning" (*Works* XVIII: 1). The accusation of Clevelandism is also a courteous disguise for the critical consideration of Cowley; a decade after the publication of *An Essay of Dramatic Poesy*, Dryden quotes Cowley as well as Horace and Virgil when he admits that "catachreses and hyperboles" can sometimes be licensed "to make the figure bolder" (*Works* XII: 91–2). Politely avoiding any personal offense to Cowley, Dryden is aware that catachresis is as characteristic of Cleveland as of the central figure in the preliminary meetings of the English academy. In the gentlemanly discourse in *An Essay of Dramatic Poesy*, however, Eugenius proposes that, instead of criticizing specific modern poets, Crites "defend the general cause of the Ancients against the Moderns." According to this proposal, Crites begins his speech on behalf of the ancients with a proleptic admission that the moderns are superior to them in "the Study of Philosophy" – "Opticks, Medicine, Anatomy, Astronomy" (*Works* XVIII: 13). The idea of the Royal Society is praised even by Crites, the rigorous classicist, who is impatient with such abuse of the English language in the modern poetry of Wither or Cleveland (and Cowley) during the Civil Wars.

Dryden's developing awareness of the French Academy is hinted at in the *Essay of Dramatic Poesy* when Lisideius defines Cleveland as "one of those whom the *French* would call *un mauvais buffon*" (*Works* XVIII: 10). Dryden has already pronounced his interest in the French Academy in the dedicatory epistle to Roger Boyle, Earl of Orrery, prefixed to *The Rival Ladies* in 1664, the year of Pepys's first witness to Dryden and his friends at Will's Coffee House: "Only I am Sorry, that (Speaking so noble a Language as we do) we have not a more certain Measure of it, as they in *France*, where they have an Academy erected for that purpose, and Indow'd with large Privileges by the Present King" (*Works* VIII: 98). His plea for the English academy, though interrupted by the Great Plague and never authorized by the King, recurs in the period of the Exclusion Crisis. In the dedicatory epistle to Robert Spencer, Earl of Sunderland, prefixed to *Troilus and Cressida* in 1679, Dryden suggests that "the ornaments of peace" be displayed in England by following the French example of Richelieu, a patron of the French Academy, who encouraged the making of "a Grammar and a Dictionary" in the French language: "Propriety must first be stated, ere any measures of elegance can be taken . . . 'Twas the employment of the whole Academy for many years, for the perfect knowledge of a Tongue was never attain'd by any single person. The Court, the Colledge, and the Town, must be joyn'd in it" (*Works* XIII: 222). The tripartite structure of the literary world sweeping from the "Court" to the "Town," which we have seen in the "Epilogue" to *The Indian Emperor* in 1667, shows itself again in Dryden's discourse – now with a substitution of the "Colledge" for the pivotal position of the "Coffee-house." Dryden's idea of sociability derives from his respect for literary collaboration without which "any single person" could not achieve "the perfect knowledge of a Tongue."

Among Dryden's many collaborative works in the period of the Exclusion Crisis is *The Art of Poetry* (1683), published anonymously as a translation of Nicolas Boileau's *L'Art Poétique* (1674).[12] According to Jacob Tonson's "Advertisement" prefixed to *The Fourth Part of Miscellany Poems* (1708) where the translation was reprinted, Boileau's work was originally translated by Sir William Soames, who was "very intimately acquainted with Mr. Dryden" and "desired his Revisal of it"; the Poet Laureate spent "above Six Months" revising "the Manuscript" to put into practice his principle of translation "that it would be better to apply the Poem to English Writers, than keep to the French Names" (*Works* II: 368). Dryden's principle of applying "the Poem to English Writers" works well when *The Art of Poetry* anglicizes Boileau's text by replacing "the French Names" with English names (see lines 17–18). But Dryden's theory is deconstructed by the third poet who is newly inscribed in *The Art of Poetry*: Du Bartas (line 21). The French poet's biblical epic is transnational because seventeenth-century English readers, including Dryden, are familiar with it not so much in the French original, the *Semaines* (1578–84), as in Joshua Sylvester's popular English translation, *The Divine Weeks* (1592–1608). Invoking Du Bartas as a key figure of the literary commerce between England and France, the Soames–Dryden translation of Boileau's *L'Art Poétique* lays down the following warning:

> Nor, with *Dubartas*, bridle up the Floods,
> And Periwig with Wool the bald-pate Woods.
> Chuse a just Stile . . .   (lines 101–3)

The passage, which has no equivalent in Boileau's original, must be Dryden's addition because it includes one of his favorite lines. Dryden quotes the relevant lines from *The Divine Weeks* when he dedicates *The Spanish Friar* in 1681 to John Holles, Lord Haughton:

> I remember, when I was a boy, I thought inimitable *Spencer* a mean Poet in comparison of *Sylvester's Dubartas*; and was rapt into an ecstasie when I read these lines;
>
> > Now, when the Winter's keener breath began
> > To Chrystallize the Baltick Ocean;
> > To glaze the Lakes, to bridle up the Floods,
> > And periwig with Snow the bald-pate Woods:
>
> I am much deceiv'd if this be not abominable fustian, that is, thoughts and words ill sorted, and without the least relation to each other . . .
>
> (*Works* XVIII: 10)

The Art of Poetry incorporates Dryden's personal memory of Sylvester's "fustian" where there is no relationship between "thoughts" and "words" – "periwig with Snow [or Wool] the bald-pate Woods." The "fustian" is the more impressive to him because it is shared by Cleveland in his following lines:

> I had observ'd the Language of the dayes;
> Blasphem'd you; and then *Periwigg'd* the Phrase
> With humble Service, and such other Fustian . . .[13]

The "fustian" – the wrested usage of "periwig" – turns out to be an example of Clevelandism or catachresis that is criticized in the gentlemanly conversation of the English academy under Cowley's leadership around 1665 as imagined in *An Essay of Dramatic Poesy*. *The Art of Poetry* is a palimpsest on which we can decipher the historical layers of Dryden's transnational interest in academic collaboration to invent a right relationship between "thoughts" and "words" in the vernacular language from the 1660s to the 1680s.

Even in the midst of the turbulence of the Exclusion Crisis, in fact, Dryden never forgets his idea of an "Academy" or "Colledge" for literary collaboration. He dedicates *Absalom and Achitophel* not to an aristocratic patron but to "THE READER," and after the panegyric on the chief members of the Royal party, Dryden insists on the need of royal public institutions for the improvement of arts and learning as follows:

> The Prophets Sons by such example led,
> To Learning and to Loyalty were bred:
> For Colleges on bounteous Kings depend,
> And never Rebell was to Arts a friend.
>
> . . . .

Sharp Judging *Adriel* the Muses friend,
Himself a MuseIn—Sanhedrins debate
True to his Prince; but not a Slave of State:
. . . .
Jotham of piercing wit and pregnant thought,
Indew'd by nature, and by learning taught
To move Assemblies, who but onely try'd
The Worse awhile, then chose the better side . . .

(lines 870–85)

Adriel – John Sheffield, Third Earl of Mulgrave (afterwards First Duke of Buckingham and Normandy), to whom Dryden has dedicated *Aureng-Zebe* (1676) – is defined as "the Muses friend" whereas "never Rebell was to Arts a friend." The special emphasis on friendship conceals a self-contradiction in the politics of Dryden's discourse on "Colleges"; underscoring the inseparability of "Learning" and "Loyalty" to the king, he praises Adriel's intellectual freedom from affairs of "State." Before writing *An Essay on Poetry*, an imitation of *L'Art Poétique*, in 1682, the Earl of Mulgrave anonymously circulated manuscripts of *An Essay upon Satire*, which the Earl of Rochester furiously called "a libel," attributing it to Dryden as well as to the earl in his letter to Jotham – George Savile, Viscount (afterwards Marquis) of Halifax – on 21 November 1679. On the night of 18 December of the same year, Dryden was beaten in Rose Alley in Covent Garden, returning home from Will's Coffee House.[14] Although the details of the Rose Alley Ambush are unknown, Dryden's idea of "Coffee-houses" and "Colleges," which should join themselves with "the Court" and "Town," was fractured by the politics of faction and conspiracy in the period of the Exclusion Crisis. With an unusual aggressiveness, he dedicated *The Medal* in 1682 not to any of his patrons or "THE READER" but to his enemy: the Whigs in "Factious Clubs" (*Works* II: 39). He perilously set his public discourse against the public sphere of the Green Ribbon Club at the King's Head Tavern at Fleet Street and Chancery Lane: "Th' Appointed Clubb" (line 528) at which *The Second Part of Absalom and Achitophel* in 1682 discovers Achitophel – Anthony Ashley Cooper, First Earl of Shaftesbury – "Who yet not only on the Town depends, / For ev'n in court the faction had its friends" (lines 514–15).

In spite of the threatening political climate, Dryden joined another academy with Adriel and Jotham during the period of the Exclusion Crisis. It was assembled by Wentworth Dillon, fourth Earl of Roscommon, around 1680; its details remain as obscure as those of the Cowley meetings in 1665. All our information derives from two meager documents: an incidental reference in one of Elijah Fenton's notes in his edition of *The Works of Edmund Waller* (1729) and a couple of paragraphs on it in an unpublished manuscript biography of the Earl of Roscommon by Knightly Chetwood, who, as Dean of Gloucester as well as a friend of Roscommon's, would contribute "The Life of Pub. Virgilius Maro" and "Preface to the Pastorals" to Dryden's translation of Virgil (1697). The description in Chetwood's biography, drawing on his first-hand acquaintances with the Earl of Roscommon and Dryden, reads as follows:

> This storm blowing over, & one of these forfeited Estates being beg'd, by the most friendly Earl of Rochester, & presented to him [the Earl of Roscommon], without his knowledge; he set himselfe, to form a sort of Academy, in Imitation of that at Caen . . . During this happy, but short Interval, good Men began to know one another better, there was then Friendship, english good-nature flourish'd, every spark of wch ought to be preserv'd as the Sacred Fire was by the Jews, during ye time of y^r Captivity. Those who compos'd this little Body, were the Marquess of H; who undertook the Translation of Tacitus, an Author perfectly suited to his tast . . . The Lord Maitland was another, who then began his excellent Translation of Virgil. The E: of R. wrote his Essay on translated verse, in emulation of that finish'd Poem, An Essay upon Poetry . . . The Earle of D . . . t, one of the most accomplish'd persons of the Age, came sometimes among them, as did the Lord Candish, the Ingenious coll: Finch, Sr Charles Sc . . . gh, Mr Dryden, whom Lord Ros: look'd upon, as a naturall rather than a correct Poet, & therefore calls him somewhere, The luxurious Father of the fold.[15]

Characterized by the idea of "Friendship" and set against the backdrop of factional politics, the Earl of Roscommon's "Academy" met during the "happy, but short Interval" around 1680, when "the most friendly Earle of Rochester" died. Within the public sphere of Roscommon's academy, with its shared interests in translation, reappeared Jotham (Marquis of Halifax) and Adriel (Earl of Mulgrave and author of *An Essay on Poetry*) of *Absalom and Achitophel*.

A brief prosopographical description of Roscommon's academy suggests a close relationship between Dryden's literary and sociable activities that reaches beyond faction and ideology. While Halifax, a trimmer who sought for moderation in politics, rendered Tacitus, Richard Maitland (afterwards Fourth Duke of Lauderdale), who was to be a Jacobite exile after the 1688/9 Revolution, worked on the translation of Virgil, a manuscript of which was to be "freely granted" to Dryden (*Works* v: 336). In the subscription of his translation of Virgil in 1697, Dryden was almost impatient with Tonson's failure to leave "a place for the duke of Devonshire [Lord Cavendish]" (*Letters*, p. 78, 81). Sir Charles Scarburgh, physician to Charles II and James II, was praised by John Oldham in "The Thirteenth Satyr of Juvenal, Imitated" (line 197). And Oldham, on whose death in 1683 Dryden wrote a moving elegy, translated *Ars Poetica* in 1680. Roscommon wrote *An Essay on Translated Verse* in 1684, emulating *An Essay on Poetry* (1682) – an imitation of *L'Art Poétique* – by Mulgrave, who was to accept the dedication of the *Aeneis* from Dryden in 1697. Charles Sackville, now Sixth Earl of Dorset, who had appeared as Eugenius in the virtual public sphere in *An Essay on Dramatic Poesy* in 1667, reappeared in the real public sphere of Roscommon's academy in the early 1680s. Dryden was to dedicate to Dorset "A Discourse concerning the Original and Progress of Satire," his majestic preface to the Juvenal and Persius translation of 1693, in which the old poet, deprived of his public offices as Poet Laureate and Historiographer Royal, praised his lifelong patron: "There are no Factions, tho irreconcilable to one another, that are not united in their affection to you . . ." (*Works* IV: 3). The "friendly" relationships among members of Roscommon's academy survived both his death in 1685 and the Revolution of 1688/9.

Dryden's "friendship," as suggested by his elegy on Oldham, did not confine itself to noble patrons but extended to younger writers at Will's Coffee House; Dryden's most affectionate friendship was with William Congreve, the only figure the aging poet repeatedly and publicly addressed as his "Dear Friend." Congreve was a new friend of Dryden's from Will's Coffee House, while Walter Moyle, when away from London, sent the rising dramatist the following letter on 7 October 1695: "Would to God I could laugh with you for one hour or two at all the ridiculous things that happen'd at *Wills Coffee-House* since I left it, 'tis the merriest place in the World" where "Beasts of different kinds come to drink, mingle with one another and beget Monsters."[16] At the center of the "the merriest place in the World" was John Dryden. In "A Parallel betwixt Painting and Poetry" (1695), he acknowledged the generous help of "Mr. *Walter Moyle*, a most ingenious young Gentleman, conversant in all the Studies of Humanity, much above his years" (*Works* XX: 61).

The company at Will's Coffee House also included William Walsh – who was to be praised as "the Muse's Judge and Friend" by Pope in *An Essay on Criticism* (line 729) in 1711. Dryden had recommended Lady Chudleigh's poems to Jacob Tonson after letting Walsh read them "in the Coffee House" in 1697. Lady Chudleigh was connected by her marriage with the Clifford family. Thomas, Lord Clifford, one of the Cabal who ended his life miserably for his Catholic faith at the enforcement of the Test Act in 1673, was a patron of Dryden's "manhood" (*Works* V: 3) to whom *Amboyna* was dedicated and to whose nonjuring son, Hugh, Lord Clifford, the translation of Virgil's *Pastorals* was dedicated in 1697; Dryden compared his relationship with this noble family to the ancient Roman system of patronage in his dedication to the younger Clifford: "You are acquainted with the *Roman* History, and know without my information that Patronage and Clientship always descended from the Fathers to the Sons" (*Works* v: 7). Recommending Lady Chudleigh's poems to Tonson, however, Dryden told him not to "send them" to the printer till he heard from Lord Clifford whether she would "put her name to them or not" (*Letters*, p. 98). Dryden was concerned to adjust the courtly tradition to the commercial world of the book trade because the experienced poet was well aware that "the stigma of print"[17] died hard in early modern aristocratic culture. On the other hand, discussing the successful arrangement of the contribution from Knightly Chetwood (author of the manuscript biography of the Earl of Roscommon) to the forthcoming translation of Virgil, Dryden was proud that his *Alexander's Feast* was "esteemed the best" of all his poetry "by all the Town" (*Letters*, ibid.). Dryden was also well aware that his reputation depended on the effect of print publication on conversations in "the Town." Shadwell suggested in *The Medal of John Bayes* (1682) that Dryden had a special partnership with the bookseller Henry Herringman: "He turn'd a journey-man t'a bookseller, / Writ prefaces to books for meat and drink" (lines 128–9).[18] The sharpest rival is often the best observer. Shadwell was right, although he should have noticed his rival's new connection with Tonson after the publication of *Troilus and Cressida* (1679), in pointing out that Dryden, freed from "the stigma of print," was happy to collaborate with the most important booksellers in Restoration London, Herringman and Tonson, in order to find a literary market for his own writings by making a cultural bridge between "Court" and "Town." The sociable sphere of Will's Coffee House had became a commercial center of print publication by the end of the seventeenth century, and this transformation created a new literary world where elite and popular cultures competed and mingled with one another beyond the factional politics of the early modern book trade, a world in which the Protestant Williamite Jacob Tonson was only too happy to publish the new Virgil of the Jacobite John Dryden, a translation subscribed by professionals, gentlemen and gentlewomen, and aristocrats whose very subscription crossed social borders and party lines and in itself both mimicked and helped to create the sociable, commercial, and cultural mixtures of a new literary age.

NOTES

1. R. C. Latham and W. Matthews, eds., *The Diary of Samuel Pepys*, 11 vols. (London, 1970–83), vol. v, p. 37. For the identification of the "great Coffee-house," see Bryant Lillywhite, *London Coffee Houses: A Reference Book of Coffee Houses of the Seventeenth, Eighteenth, and Nineteenth Centuries* (London, 1963), pp. 655–9.
2. James M. Osborn, ed., *Joseph Spence: Observations, Anecdotes and Characters of Books and Men*, 2 vols. (Oxford, 1966), vol. I, pp. 25, 29; vol. II, pp. 611–12.

3. Jürgen Habermas, *The Structural Transformation of the Public Sphere: An Inquiry into a Category of Bourgeois Society*, trans. Thomas Burger with the Assistance of Frederick Lawrence (Cambridge, Mass., 1989). For a revisionist account of the politics of coffee houses in Restoration England, see Steven Pincus, "'Coffee Politicians Does Create': Coffee Houses and Restoration Political Culture," *The Journal of Modern History* 67 (1995), 807–34.

4. James Wright, *Country Conversations: Being an Account of Some Discourses That Happen'd in a Visit to the Country Last Summer, on Divers Subjects* (London, 1694), pp. [2–3]; the work of Dominique Bouhours to which he refers is *La Maniere de Bien Penser dans les Ouvrages d'Esprit* (Paris, 1687); it has been attributed to Bouhours, a Jesuit man of letters, although the attribution is probably incorrect.

5. [James Wright,] *The Humours and Conversations of the Town, Exposed in Two Dialogues* (London, 1693), pp. 73, 107.

6. For the increasing importance of "civility" in conversation in seventeenth-century English society, see Anna Bryson, *From Courtesy to Civility: Changing Codes of Conduct in Early Modern England* (Oxford, 1998), pp. 153–9; and Steven Shapin, *A Social History of Truth: Civility and Science in Seventeenth-Century England* (Chicago, 1994), pp. 114–19; cf. John E. Mason, *Gentlefolk in the Making: Studies in the History of English Courtesy Literature and Related Topics from 1531–1774* (Philadelphia, 1935).

7. *The Diary of Samuel Pepys*, vol. VI, p. 2. For Inigo Jones's design of Covent Garden, see John Summerson, *Inigo Jones* (Harmondsworth, 1966), pp. 75–89; cf. Elizabeth McKellar, *The Birth of Modern London: The Development and Design of the City 1660–1720* (Manchester, 1999), pp. 193–5.

8. John Evelyn to Samuel Pepys, 26 August 1689, in Guy de la Bédoyère, ed., *Particular Friends: The Correspondence of Samuel Pepys and John Evelyn* (Woodbridge, 1997), p. 203; see also *Critical Essays of the Seventeenth Century*, ed. J. E. Spingarn, 3 vols. (Oxford, 1908–9), vol. II, pp. 310–29.

9. Abraham Cowley, *Essays, Plays and Sundry Verses*, ed. A. R. Waller (Cambridge, 1906), p. 248.

10. Edward Niles Hooker, ed., *The Critical Works of John Dennis*, 2 vols. (Baltimore, 1939), vol. I, p. 289. See also *The Diary of Samuel Pepys*, vol. II, p. 234 and John Downes, *Roscius Anglicanus*, ed. Judith Milhous and Robert D. Hume (London, 1987), p. 57. For a brief comment on the relationship between Dryden and Sprat, see James M. Osborn, *John Dryden: Some Biographical Facts and Problems* (1940; revised edn., Gainesville, 1965), pp. 270–1. The standard account of the first performance of *Cutter of Coleman Street* can be found in Arthur H. Nethercot, *Abraham Cowley: The Muse's Hannibal* (London, 1931), pp. 200–8.

11. Thomas Sprat, *History of the Royal Society*, ed. Jackson I. Cope (St. Louis, 1958), pp. 40–2, 111. Richard Foster Jones's classical study of the cultural implication of the reformation of the vernacular language in early modern England, *The Triumph of the English Language: A Survey of Opinions Concerning the Vernacular from the Introduction of Printing to the Restoration* (Stanford, 1953), should be supplemented now by Linda C. Mitchell, *Grammar Wars: Language as Cultural Battlefield in 17th and 18th Century England* (Aldershot, 2001).

12. Boileau was regarded in Restoration England as a representative voice for the court of Louis XIV before he was admitted into the French Academy in 1684. For the reception of his transposition of Horace's *Ars Poetica*, see Paul Hammond, *John Oldham and the Renewal of Classical Culture* (Cambridge, 1983), pp. 89–93.

13. John Cleveland, "To P. Rupert," lines 15–7. The quotation is from Brian Morris and Eleanor Withington, eds., *The Poems of John Cleveland* (Oxford, 1967). The last line of the passage from *The Divine Weeks* (II. i. 4, 174–7) in Dryden's dedication to *The Spanish Friar* is a misquotation; the stuff with which to "periwig . . . the bald-pate Woods" is not "Snow" but "Wool," which correctly appears in the passage in *The Art of Poetry*.

14. Jeremy Treglown, ed., *The Letters of John Wilmot, Earl of Rochester* (Oxford, 1980), pp. 232–3. For the Rose Alley Ambush, see George deForest Lord, ed., *Poems on Affairs of State*, 7 vols. (New Haven, 1963–75), vol. I, pp. 396–413 and James Anderson Winn, *John Dryden and His World* (New Haven, 1987), pp. 325–30.

15. Quoted in Carl Niemeyer, "The Earl of Roscommon's Academy," *MLN* 49 (1934), 433–4; cf. Winn, *John Dryden and His World*, pp. 387–405.

16. John C. Hodges, ed., *William Congreve: Letters and Documents* (London, 1964), p. 192; cf. Jennifer Brady, "Dryden and Congreve's Collaboration in *The Double Dealer*," in *John Dryden: Tercentenary Essays*, ed. Paul Hammond and David Hopkins (Oxford, 2000), pp. 113–39.

17. For "the stigma of print" in early modern aristocratic culture, see J. W. Saunders, "The Stigma of Print: A Note on the Social Bases of Tudor Poetry," *Essays in Criticism* 1 (1951), 139–64; see also Harold Love, *The Culture and Commerce of Texts: Scribal Publication in Seventeenth-Century England* (Oxford, 1993), 46–54.

18. Shadwell's satirical passage on Dryden's connection with the bookseller is sensibly considered in Osborn, *Dryden: Some Biographical Facts* pp. 184–99. Herringman's obscure life is described in C. William Miller, "Henry Herringman, Restoration Bookseller-Publisher," *Papers of the Bibliographical Society of America* 42, 4 (1948), 292–306; on Tonson, see, most recently, Kathleen M. Lynch, *Jacob Tonson: Kit-Cat Publisher* (Knoxville, 1971). For the historical significance of coffee houses in the early modern book trade, see Adrian Johns, *The Nature of the Book: Print and Knowledge in the Making* (Chicago, 1989), pp. 111–13.

3

COURTING AND COMPLYING
WITH DANGER

II

JOHN BARNARD

Dryden and patronage

There mark what Ills the Scholar's Life assail,
Toil, Envy, Want, the Patron, and the Jail.[1]

Dr. Johnson's scornful equation of imprisonment and dependence on a patron ("Commonly a wretch who supports with insolence, and is paid with flattery"[2]) is shared by the modern reader, even though patronage takes different forms today. Dryden's grandiose and extended praise of patrons in his dedications appears to be egregiously dishonest (if ingenious) flattery, a view forcibly supported by Johnson. "When once he has undertaken the task of praise he no longer retains shame in himself, nor supposes it in his patron," and is "more delighted with the fertility of his invention than mortified by the prostitution of his judgement": his dedication to *The State of Innocence* is written "in a strain of flattery which disgraces genius, and . . . it was wonderful that any man that knew the meanings of his own words could use without self-detestation."[3]

Johnson's own hard-won independence, however, was only possible because by the mid-eighteenth century the book trade was beginning to support professional authors. That was not the case in Dryden's day. Although as a professional playwright and from 1668 a shareholder in the King's Company, Dryden on occasions made as much as £300 a year from his contract,[4] poetry was another matter altogether: for most of Dryden's working life any reward for poetry could only come, in one way or another, from patronage.

Literary patronage was one form of a wider system of economic and cultural exchange in a society marked by a strongly structured class hierarchy.[5] It was a complex institution: if the author might hope for cash or, better still, a post in the gift of an aristocrat or government official, the patron gained cultural standing through his or her association with the literary work. Normally, though not always, the author had some kind of relationship with the patron: it seems probable too that Dryden, unlike some authors, usually sought permission for a dedication.[6]

On occasion, the workings of patronage could be more indirect. New Year's gifts to a superior were of particular symbolic value. At the very beginning of the 1660s Dryden was courting Lady Elizabeth Howard, daughter of the ageing Earl of Berkshire, whose previous loyalty to the crown had gone unrewarded, leaving him in straitened circumstances. Dryden's "To my Lord Chancellor, presented on New-Years-Day 1662" was addressed to the most powerful man in Charles II's new government, Edward Hyde, Earl of Clarendon. Deliberately old-fashioned, it appeals for the state's support for the "Muses":

> The Nations soul (our Monarch) does dispence
> Through you to us his vital influence;
> You are the Channel where those spirits flow,
> And work them higher as to us they go.
>
> (lines 27–30)

Later that month, Clarendon, influenced by the earl's frequent petitions for places and by Dryden's poem, urged the king to give his warrant for payments of £8,000 to the earl and £3,000 to his daughter, which formed her dowry on her marriage to Dryden on 1 December 1663.[7] Patronage of a very different kind is represented by Dryden's late and remarkable panegyric, *Eleonora* (1692), an elegy commissioned by James Bertie, Earl of Abingdon, who had no previous connection with the poet, as a verse monument to his recently deceased wife. Dryden had, as he admits, never met the countess, and the thirty-nine-year-old Bertie, who rewarded the ageing poet very handsomely, was on the other side of the political divide of these years (he had given very substantial financial support for William III's invasion in 1688).[8] Two points emerge from the composition and publication of *Eleonora*. By this time in his career, the excellence of Dryden's poetry stood above politics (even though Dryden included subversive political allusions in his elegy[9]): more generally, the elegy, like most of Dryden's important poems, is occasional and public. Dryden's poetry is most often written in response to history in the making (*Absalom and Achitophel, The Medal*) or for a specific occasion like the St. Cecilia's Day celebration for which he wrote "Alexander's Feast." As Coleridge remarked, "Dryden's genius is of that sort which catches fire by its own motion; his chariot wheels *get* hot by driving fast."[10]

The visible, and most important, form of literary patronage in these years is the dedication, a genre with clear rules and expectations. Coming immediately after the title page, the dedication (sometimes accompanied by a preface) creates a liminal space before the text proper, a space in which a skillful author could declare his literary, political, and religious affiliations. Dryden's addresses to his patrons reflect his own good connections and at the same time give him a platform from which he can speak indirectly to other publics. The dedication might also give the reader a brief note of the kind of work to expect, which Dryden sometimes turns into a substantial critical essay. Dryden, that is, knows the rules but extends the boundaries of the form for his own ends. The paratextual space offered by the dedication therefore enabled Dryden to create his own public image, and, in conjunction with his accompanying prefatory essays, to define the literary standards by which he was to be read. It further allowed him to reply, often obliquely, to his literary and political opponents. In Dryden's hands, partly because he had such a long and productive career, the dedication became a public forum, though one conducted entirely on his own terms, for the instigation (or continuation) of literary debate,[11] within the changing social, political, and cultural tensions of Restoration England.

As a genre, dedications are constructed from two conventional forms, a private letter from an inferior to a social superior, and a panegyric (originally a public praise poem in ancient Greece) addressed to its recipient.[12] The pretense that a dedication was a private letter was often maintained, in print, by being set in type which was larger or differed from the text it precedes: contemporary manuals on letter-writing directed that when writing to "a *Person* of *Quality*, you are to leave a *great distance* between the *Superscription* or *first* line and the *second line* or beginning: for the *greater distance* you leave the *greater respect* you show . . ." When writing to any superior "it ought to be done with very great respect and honour; *here too much is better than too little*" (my italics): at the same time, the writer is obliged to employ brevity to a superior because "his place is of greater *concern,* or care."[13] Writing paper was expensive: it therefore showed respect to write in a large hand and leave a lot of white space. The typographic imitation of these features in a printed dedication positioned readers so that they were, so to speak, looking over the writer's shoulder at what purported to be a private letter addressed to a social superior. That made dedications a performative arena. At a minimum, it was necessary to observe the conventions of this highly formalized kind of epistle: beyond that the form encouraged writers to exhibit their superior virtuosity and ingenuity to impress their patron: at the same time, it was important to judge the dedication's likely impact on its print audience (if the dedicatee's reputation was at stake, so too was that of the writer).

A key element in this kind of letter was praise of its recipient's particular virtues, making clear their appropriateness to the particular work being offered. It was also important to show "very great respect and honour." Defending a particularly fulsome dedication addressed to the Lord Chancellor, John Evelyn claimed: "But they do not consider that greate persons, & such as are in place to doe greate & noble things, whatever their other defects may be, are to be panegyrized into the culture of those vertues, without which 'tis to be suppos'd they had never ariv'd to a power of being able to encourage them."[14] Or, as Erasmus put it more briefly, the function of panegyric is "exhorting to virtue under the pretext of praise."[15]

Panegyric, that is, whether in the form of a poem or a dedication (and Dryden was a highly skilled practitioner of both forms), was a public encouragement to virtuous action circulated in print, and was meant to persuade the recipient to fulfill the moral requirements and social duties of their position, which could amount to a warning that they should do so. Since Dryden's readers would, in varying degrees, know about the career, affiliations, and family of the dedicatee, many would have been alert to how far Dryden's praise matched reality or pointed up a potential as yet not realized. Criticism, carefully veiled, could therefore be implied, and Dryden's own position, though figured in self-dismissive and apologetic terms, be made clear. Over the years, Dryden's dedications were increasingly used to establish his own credentials as a poet, a critic, and a commentator on political and religious matters. The elaborately formal artificiality of the praise given in Dryden's dedications can only be understood within the dynamic of a hierarchical class structure, in which patronage and clientage were a necessary part of everyday social life. In addition, Dryden's ambivalent status as a gentleman, author, and working playwright further complicated the way in which he was positioned socially, with the added difficulty that during the Interregnum he had worked for, and publicly praised, Cromwell. In that context what is remarkable is less Dryden's dependence upon patronage (normal for his day) than the independence embodied in his coded dedications. They are, in consequence, a prime source for an understanding of his poetic and intellectual development over the years, and of his complex and changing relationship to the literary and political world in which he lived. More important for his poetry, eulogy is the obverse of satire: Dryden's training in panegyric, with its necessary obliquities, evasions, and fine balancings, laid the foundation for his devastating powers as a satirist.

Not surprisingly, then, Dryden, even though he evidently wrote his dedications swiftly,[16] took care over their composition. This is clear from the only manuscript draft now known of a dedication by Dryden. It is not for one of Dryden's own works, but was written on behalf of the young composer Henry Purcell, whom he greatly admired. When Purcell's *The Vocal and Instrumental Musick of the Prophetess, or The History of Dioclesian* was published in 1691, the dedication to the Duke of Somerset was signed, though not written, by the composer (Purcell no doubt had to pay the older man[17]). Dryden's manuscript,[18] which was used as printer's copy, makes minor verbal changes, but also has two substantial passages scored out, one on the parallel between poetry and painting, the other on the failure of English poets, unlike Dryden himself, to write for music. These passages were undoubtedly omitted on the grounds that they too obviously reflected Dryden's own preoccupations, not those of Purcell. The manuscript seems to be a first, and final, corrected draft and indicates the speed and practiced care with which Dryden by this time wrote his dedicatory material. Purcell's approach to the older poet for the dedication demonstrates how Dryden's own prestige and acquired cultural capital conferred credibility and status upon the younger man's work in the inter-related worlds of aristocratic patronage and the literary marketplace.[19] (Unfortunately, it is not known whether Purcell received more in cash or kind from Somerset than he paid Dryden.)

That Purcell got Dryden to write a dedication for him at all suggests how important these were for an author. One alteration Dryden made to his text indicates a key function of the patron. Where the printed text praises Somerset for encouraging the "Nobility and Gentry" through his "Illustrious Example, in the patronage of Musick," Dryden's earlier version refers to Somerset's "Protection" of music (*Works* VII: 325). Protection and patronage in this context are virtually synonymous. Even if the patron chose to give no financial reward, his or her name and social position vouched for the social and aesthetic acceptability of Purcell's music (or Dryden's poetry) to the public at large.

Protection, in a period where fierce and swiftly changing political disagreements were an integral part of literary politics, was vitally important. The severe beating given Dryden in Rose Alley in 1679, whoever was responsible, demonstrates the dangers facing a mere writer thought to have criticized his social betters. When in 1684 Dryden criticized the French historian Louis Maimbourg's dedications for their "Commendations of Men and Families" as being "superfluous," he promptly remembers his own vulnerability in this area, and says (rightly enough) that dedications of this kind are "pardonable in a man, who having created himself many Enemies, has the need of support of Friends" (*Works* VIII: 415). As Dryden knew only too well, the choice of a patron could be a hostage to fortune. In 1670 Dryden dedicated his tragedy *Tyrannick Love* to James, Duke of Monmouth: by 1681 Monmouth, in alliance with Shaftesbury, was threatening the Stuart succession, and had become a main target of *Absalom and Achitophel*. Not surprisingly, Dryden was accused of ingratitude, a charge he answered with considerable embarrassment and difficulty, though he continued the practice of choosing patrons who offered his work political cover. *The Spanish Fryar*, published the same year as *Absalom and Achitophel*, was self-protectively dedicated to the young John Holles, Lord Haughton, in order to claim the tragicomedy's credentials as "a Protestant Play," and for similar reasons *Amphitryon* (1690) was dedicated to the Whig Sir William Leveson-Gower.[20]

In this context Dryden's dedications, which necessarily emphasize his client status, are remarkable for the way they manage to exhibit his independence, and his confidence in his own abilities as a poet, critic, and man. This is evident even in his very first dedication to Roger Boyle, Earl of Orrery, prefixed to *The Rival Ladies* (1664).[21] Boyle was forty-three to Dryden's thirty-three and had composed the first heroic play in rhymed verse, *The General*, written at the suggestion of Charles II. Dryden's dedication defers to Boyle's genius and notes "the kindness your lordship has continually shown to all my writings," which he had read in Ireland, and Boyle's enjoyment of the stage performance of Dryden's play. The practicing playwright, that is, pays an elaborately turned tribute to Boyle's aristocratic abilities as a dramatist (exercised only when he was kept from state affairs by gout) while gaining prestige from the association with his patron – precisely what the form requires. Dryden, however, sandwiches a substantial defense of the "new way" of using rhyme in heroic drama in the middle of his dedication, providing precedents in *Gorbodoc* (mistakenly), Shakespeare (again mistakenly), Spanish, Italian, and contemporary French tragedy, followed by an account of the improvements in English poetic language recently effected by Waller, Denham, and Davenant. Dryden's style in the following discussion of the technicalities of rhyming in drama is deceptively conversational in tone:

> The advantages which Rhyme has over Blanck Verse, are so many, that it were lost time to name them. Sir *Philip Sidney*: in his *Defence of Poesie* gives us one, which, in my Opinion, is not the least considerable; I mean the help it brings to Memory: which Rhyme Knits up by the Affinity of Sounds, so that by remembering the last Word in one Line, we often call to Mind both the Verses. Then in the quickness of Reparties, (which in Discoursive [dialogue] Scenes fall very often) it has so particular a Grace, and is so aptly Suited to them, that the suddain Smartness of the Answer, and the Sweetness of the Rhyme, set off the Beauty of each other. But that benefit which I consider most in it, because I have not seldome found it, is, that it Bounds and Circumscribes the Fancy. For Imagination in a Poet is a faculty so Wild and Lawless, that, like an High-ranging Spaniel it must have Cloggs tied to it, least it out-run the Judgement.   (*Works* VIII: 100–1)

This is spoken by an experienced practitioner ("because I have not seldome found it"), knowledgeable about his English predecessors, and aimed at a general reader, yet the apparently everyday image of the "High-ranging Spaniel" is in fact drawn from a passage on the imagination in Hobbes's *Leviathan* (1651),[22] whose distinction between "fancy" and "judgement" is a formative influence here and on Dryden's later thinking. Dryden's critical style, polite, digressive and colloquial, but actually involved in a critical debate with classical and immediately contemporary literary theory, is already fully formed, as is his strategy of flattering both his patrons and his readers by an assumption of equality, while involving them in a coherently organized argument about immediately contemporary literary controversies.

Three years later Dryden published *Annus Mirabilis: The Year of Wonders, 1666. An Historical Poem: Containing the Progress and Various Successes of our Naval War with Holland, under the Conduct of His Highness Prince Rupert, and His Grace the Duke of Albermarle. And Describing the Fire of London.* Issued a year after the events described, the poem gave a firmly Royalist account of these events in reply to the immediate flurry of pamphlets which had attacked the conduct of the war or seen the Great Fire as God's judgment on the country's immorality. This unlikely eulogistic version of events was preceded by a dedication:

TO

THE METROPOLIS

OF

GREAT BRITAIN,

The most Renowned and late Flourishing

CITY of

LONDON,

In its

REPRESENTATIVES

The LORD MAYOR *and Court of* ALDERMEN, *the*

SHERIFS *and* COMMON COUNCIL *of it.*

Dryden claimed to be the first poet "who ever presented a work of this nature to the Metropolis of any Nation."[23] The dedication to the City's governing body is set in twenty-point roman type, whereas the rest of this octavo book is set in thirteen-point, and comes immediately after turning the elaborately worded title page. Dryden praises London as a city "which has set a pattern to all others of true Loyalty, invincible Courage, and unshaken Constancy," claims that London and Charles II "have come together a pair of matchless Lovers, through many difficulties," and concludes by saying that "your sufferings are at an end; and that one part of my Poem has not been more an History of your destruction, then the other a Prophecy of your restoration" (*Works* 1: 48–9). For a modern reader it is hard to see how anyone within court circles can have read the dedication as anything but a savagely ironic misrepresentation of the City's support of Parliament throughout the Civil Wars and its continuing position as the center of opposition to the restored monarchy. However, Dryden's panegyric, which seeks to unite the Crown and City corporation in a visionary and harmonious future, employs the same rhetorical strategy that Charles himself had earlier used in the Declaration of Breda (1660). The Declaration, as Paulina Kewes has shown, divested Parliament (and the country) of any direct responsibility for the execution of Charles I and the Civil Wars by laying blame on the guilty few who had misled both the Long Parliament and the people: more particularly, when writing to the City, Charles II wholly disregarded its seditious past, taking the allegiance of his "native city" as an undeniable fact.[24] Following Charles's example, Dryden is able to characterize monarch and city fathers as divided from one another by the machinations of others:

> Never had Prince or People more mutual reason to love one another, if suffering for each other can indear affection. You have come together a pair of matchless Lovers, through many difficulties; He, through a long Exile, various traverses of Fortune, and the interposition of many Rivals, who violently ravish'd and with-held You from Him: And certainly you have had your share in sufferings.
>
> (*Works* 1: 48)

This hyperbolic imagery is embodied in a dedication which looks to an ideal future, to the exclusion of past reality, and describes the kind of relationship which ought to exist between the King and the City of London in a time of need. If this mirrored the hopes of those who favored the stability brought by the Restoration, in the City it must have read as a reminder of its collective anti-Royalist past and a call for future good behavior.[25]

The dedication is immediately followed by twelve pages of "An account of the ensuing Poem, in a Letter to the Honourable, Sir ROBERT HOWARD" (set in smaller italic), which serves several functions, including that of a further dedication to his brother-in-law, a stockholder in the Bridges Street Theatre, and an M. P. Dryden claims that the first part of his poem, which deals with the Dutch Wars, is "but a due expiation for my not serving my King and Country in it," a duty incumbent upon all gentlemen, and, indeed, "the Commonalty of *England*." (Dryden must also have expected his readers to remember his own service under, and public praise of, Cromwell: he shares the same guilt as the City and the country at large.) Most of the rest of the letter is given over to a justification of his choice of stanza form for a historical poem and an extension of his ideas on wit and the imagination, further establishing his own, and by inference the court's, innovatory literary credentials. Into this, Dryden manages to insert a congratulatory poem to the Duchess of York on the naval victory gained by her husband, Charles II's brother, against the Dutch in 1665. Further, the publication of the poem's printed version seems to have been delayed so that Dryden could present it to the victorious James, Duke of York, as a New Year's gift.[26] Despite the gestures toward inclusiveness in the dedication and the poem's vision of a united polity, *Annus Mirabilis* clearly speaks on behalf of the court and restored monarchy.

By 1668, Dryden had, in addition to writing *Annus Mirabilis*, celebrated the king's return in *Astraea Redux*, published a panegyric on his coronation, written plays in the new style, laid the foundations of neo-classical literary criticism in his *An Essay of Dramatic Poesy* (1668), and lent the king £500 at 10 percent interest in October 1667.[27] Not surprisingly perhaps, he was rewarded with the post of Poet Laureate on the death of Davenant in 1668, and appointed Historiographer Royal two years later. Dryden was to remain true to the Stuart cause for the rest of his life, even though the payment of his official salaries was always intermittent and delayed. Royal patronage also brought duties. As Poet Laureate he was paid £100 from court sources for writing *Absalom and Achitophel* (1681), while the subject of *The Medal* (1682), for which he received a present of "a hundred broadpieces," was suggested by the king during a walk in the Mall.[28] In his role as Historiographer Royal, he probably wrote *His Majesty's Declaration Defended* (1681); in 1684 he translated, unprofitably, Maimbourg's *History of the League* and later translated Bouhours's *Life of St. Francis Xavier* for James II.

Royal patronage on its own was not enough, and in the early 1670s Dryden turned for financial support and protection to the younger wits and poets, Rochester and Sir Charles Sedley, in the event with little success. In dedicating *Marriage A-la-Mode* (1672) to Rochester, who was sixteen years younger than the poet, and *The Assignation* (1673) to Sedley, eight years younger, Dryden, by then in his forties, adopts the pose of a wit and man about town. This reads somewhat uncomfortably. The dedication to Sedley, who had earlier been the probable model for Lisideius in *An Essay of Dramatic Poesy*, is addressed "To my most Honoured Friend, Sir Charles Sedley, Baronet." Dryden was a gentleman, but he was not an aristocrat or courtier, as these two men were. It's made clear that he was on occasions in their company:

> We have, like [Roman poets in Augustus' age], our Genial Nights; where our discourse is neither too serious, nor too light; but always pleasant, and, for the most part, instructive: the raillery neither too sharp upon the present, nor too censorious on the absent; and the Cups onely such as will raise the Conversation of the Night, without disturbing the business of the Morrow . . . I have often Laugh'd at the ignorant and ridiculous Descriptions which some Pedants have given of the Wits . . . those wretches Paint leudness, Atheism, Folly, ill-Reasoning, and all manner of Extravagances amongst us, for want of understanding what we are. (*Works* XI: 321)

Dryden's self-identification with the wits allows him to make a distinction between the true gentlemanly wit and raillery and that of false wits or "pedants": it further enables him to characterize those who have attacked him as being beneath his and the wits' contempt. Dryden might hope that this idealized portrait of the notoriously hard-drinking Rochester and of Sedley, twice guilty of public nudity, as moderate, witty young men relaxing convivially, would remind his younger social superiors of the advisability of moderation, but neither Rochester or Sedley needed Dryden's flattery or protective camouflage. The older poet's mistaken attempt to identify himself with the wits back-fired badly: Rochester turned against Dryden, gave his support to Shadwell, and, with the easy superiority of a witty amateur, mercilessly mocked Dryden as a plodding mercenary in his manuscript satire "An Allusion to Horace," circulated in 1676.

Thereafter, Dryden's dedications and critical essays take on the character of an experienced poet and dramatist, addressing current literary issues authoritatively, but carrying his very considerable learning lightly. His most extraordinary dedication in this vein is that to Charles Sackville, Earl of Dorset, published in late 1692, now known as "A Discourse concerning the Original and Progress of Satire." This was prefixed to the translations of Juvenal and Persius, published as a handsome folio, dated 1693 on the title-page, by Jacob Tonson, who had become Dryden's publisher in 1679.

The choice of Dorset, a long-time supporter of Dryden, as dedicatee was highly significant. The two men had been connected since at least 1668 when Dryden dedicated *An Essay of Dramatic Poesy* to Dorset, then Lord Buckhurst, who is represented in the work as Eugenius, the advocate of the moderns. Appropriately, Dorset was himself a minor poet and satirist, a fact of which the dedication unsurprisingly makes a good deal. Altogether more important, however, was that Dryden had very good reason in 1692 to express his gratitude to Dorset, now William III's Lord Chamberlain and Dryden's chief protector under the new dispensation. Dryden's refusal to renounce his Catholicism or support for the Stuarts meant the loss of his official posts – the Laureateship went to his old enemy, Shadwell. Dryden uses the dedication to give a nostalgic account of the parallel careers of Dorset and himself, and to lament his lost opportunity to write an epic poem:

> But being encourag'd only with fair Words, by King *Charles* II, my little Sallary ill paid, and no prospect of a future Subsistance, I was then Discourag'd in the beginning of my Attempt; and now Age has overtaken me [he was sixty-one]; and Want, a more insufferable Evil, through the Change of the Times, has wholly disenabl'd me . . . since this Revolution, wherein I have suffer'd the Ruin of my small Fortune, and the loss of that poor Subsistance I had from two Kings, whom I had serv'd more Faithfully than Profitably to my self . . .
>
> (*Works* IV: 23)

It was in this situation, says Dryden, that Dorset, in an act of "pure dis-
interess'd Charity" was "pleas'd, out of no other Motive, but your own
Nobleness, without . . . the least Sollicitation from me, to make me a most
bountiful Present, which at that time . . . I was most in want of . . ." (*Works*
IV: 23).[29]

Although the "Discourse" is cast in the form of a letter, dated 18 August
1692, and its running head describes it as the "Dedication," the title page
has a note which gives the essay its now accepted title. Whether this was
the publisher's or Dryden's responsibility is unclear. In the course of writing the dedication Dryden himself refers to it variously as a "Preface," an
"Address," a "Discourse," and "this vast Preface" (*Works* IV: 4, 16, 26, 73,
86). However, he throughout maintains the formal pretense that he is writing
a letter: he apologizes to Dorset for his digressions, addresses him personally,
and imagines that his dedication is being spoken at a personal audience with
his patron, who is "already out of hearing" because of its length (*Works* IV:
86). It ends by depicting the suppliant author slipping quietly away from
Dorset's presence:

> Thus, my Lord, having troubl'd You with a tedious Visit, the best Manners
> will be shewn with the least Ceremony. I will slip away while Your Back is
> turn'd, and while You are otherwise employ'd; with great Confusion, for having
> entertain'd You so long with this Discourse . . .   (*Works* IV: 89)

Dryden's "Discourse," which grows directly out of the wide reading he
had undertaken for his translation in the two years from 1691, is a major
document of English criticism. It gives nothing less than a history of satire
from its beginnings in ancient Greece, through Rome and France up to the
present day (Dorset's and Dryden's own practice), and is the most important
statement in English by a practicing satirist about its nature. The length of the
"Discourse," together with its learning, is also an assertion of Dryden's own
importance as a writer since it invites an implicit comparison between his
long career as a poet and Dorset's political career: setting, as it does, Dryden's
literary status and career against Dorset's currently powerful political position, the "Discourse" emphasizes Dryden's own personally disadvantageous
constancy to the Stuart cause.[30]

Dryden's "Discourse" draws extensively on both ancient and modern commentators and critics; his tone and language, as he guides his reader through
his predecessors' learned commentaries, or makes his own judgments (including attacks on Shadwell, and for the first time in public admitting his authorship of *MacFlecknoe*), are relaxed, colloquial, and conversational. "For,
Indeed, when I am reading *Casaubon*, on these two Subjects [the origins
of satire in Greece and Rome], methinks I hear the same Story told twice

over with very little alteration." "I am now almost gotten into my depth; at least by the help of *Dacier*, I am swimming towards it." "But this, as we say in *English*, is only a Distinction without a Difference; for the Reason of it, is ridiculous, and absolutely false." "*Casaubon*, who is almost single, throws Dirt on *Juvenal* and *Horace*, that he may exalt *Persius*, whom he understood particularly well . . ." "Thus far, my Lord, you see it has gone very hard with *Persius*. . ." "*Horace* is always on the Amble, *Juvenal* on the Gallop: But his way is perpetually on Carpet Ground"[31] (*Works* IV: 32, 36, 45, 50, 54, 64). Dryden's authoritative summaries and adjudications, expressed in everyday language, provide an up-to-date guide through the thickets of neoclassical theory for his English readers.

Dryden's essay, that is, uses his patron's known interests to address a wider audience, as he makes explicit toward its end:

> We [the translators] write only for the Pleasure and Entertainment, of those Gentlemen and Ladies, who tho they are not Scholars, are not Ignorant: Persons of Understanding and good Sense; who not being conversant in the Original, or at least not having made *Latine* Verse, so much their business, as to be Critiques in it, wou'd be glad to find, if the Wit of our Two great Authors, be answerable to their Fame, and Reputation in the World. We have therefore endeavour'd to give the Publick all the Satisfaction we are able in this kind.
>
> (*Works* IV: 87)

This places Dryden and Dorset in a different position from the translation's audience: Dryden writes as one who is a scholarly critic of Latin (and Greek) poetry to a patron who is his equal in ability and understanding, but too busy to undertake the drudgery of scholarship. The translation's "public" (a recent noun at this time[32]) is that of the "polite" audience for translations from the classics. Dryden's phrasing is careful not to exclude university-educated men – who have not made the specialized study of classical culture and poetry necessary to navigate the claims and counter-claims made on behalf of the relative merits of Horace, Juvenal, and Persius (an issue dealt with at length in Dryden's discourse). This reflects the widening audience of readers for the classics in translation, which included women, few of whom knew Latin, and professional men. It was a new reading public whose tastes had been partly encouraged and partly created by the earlier publishing ventures, beginning in 1680, of Dryden and Tonson, his publisher.[33]

Tonson, beginning with *Ovid's Epistles* (1680), had, in addition to publishing Dryden's own works, increasingly co-operated with the older poet in setting up collaborative translations. *Plutarch's Lives* appeared in May 1683, and many of the same translators contributed to Tonson's *Miscellany Poems* (1684), which included twenty-six poems by Dryden, among them translations from Virgil and others. *Sylvae, or the Second Part of Poetical Miscellanies* appeared the following year, with a preface and further translations from the Greek and Latin classics by Dryden. The relationship between the two men, poet and publisher, was symbiotic. Dryden's literary stature and contacts, allied to his (and Tonson's) sense of a readership ready for such works, benefited both. It was in this context that Tonson began trying to set up the translation of Juvenal and Persius in 1691. When it was published in late 1692, Dryden had translated all of Persius himself, and Juvenal with a team of other writers, including the precocious twenty-two-year-old William Congreve (like Tonson, a Whig). Dryden was evidently closely involved in setting up the project, but whether or not Dryden received any payment for doing so is unclear.[34] However, in 1691 Dryden had sold his tragedy, *Cleomenes, The Spartan Hero* to Tonson for 30 guineas,[35] and from this time onwards there is firm documentary evidence of the growing importance of the publisher to Dryden's finances in the last decade of his career.

The most significant help Tonson gave Dryden was the organization of the translation of the works of Virgil (1697). This remarkable and innovative publishing venture exploited the patronage system to the full. Subscription publication, whereby a group of potential readers paid in advance for the printing of large scholarly works, otherwise commercially unviable, had developed earlier in the century, and had only recently been taken up by the book trade. Tonson had extended the practice to modern poetry with the fourth edition of Milton's *Paradise Lost* in 1688 in partnership with Richard Bentley, which established the poem's canonic status (and, in the process, the profitability of publishing an edition whose costs were already covered before publication[36]). It was Tonson who first saw the potential of using subscription publication as a way of using group patronage to support a major contemporary poetic project (thus establishing the means by which Pope was later to make his fortune through his translations of Homer in the early years of the eighteenth century[37]).

John Brewer argues that in this form of publication "the subscriber represents the patron not as the commissioner of the work, but as one of its consumers, a conspicuously identified member of the reading public."[38] In the case of the Virgil that is undoubtedly true, but even more important in the uncertain period following the Glorious Revolution of 1688, was the way in which Tonson and Dryden secured patrons representing all shades of political and religious belief: the 349 people[39] who chose, or were persuaded, to subscribe to the Virgil support Dr. Johnson's later assertion that the nation considered its honor "interested" in success of the translation.

That certainly seems true of the Virgil's three dedicatees. On 17 February 1697 Dryden wrote to Philip, Earl of Chesterfield, to ask permission to dedicate the *Georgics* to him, carefully explaining that Lord Clifford had asked for the *Pastorals* to be dedicated to him as long as "a year ago," and the Marquess of Normandy had similarly requested the dedication of the *Aeneid*. Chesterfield replied immediately, thanking Dryden for the request:

> When I consider that the greatest men are desirous of being distinguished by some mark of your esteem, I am surpris'd at the obligation you have layd upon me by intending (as you mention) to place my name before some of your works.[40]

The eagerness of these men to be associated with Dryden's project testifies to the accuracy of Johnson's report, and Chesterfield's letter shows that if the writers of dedications had to observe the genre's protocols, so too dedicatees were expected to behave with appropriate graciousness.

The organization of the Virgil's publication was based on the interplay between the commercial imperatives of its publisher, Jacob Tonson, the possibilities created by Dryden's widely acknowledged preeminence as a poet (despite his known Catholicism and Jacobite sympathies), and the cultural aspirations of the new Whig grandees. Tonson's contract with Dryden, which was signed on 15 June 1694 with Congreve acting as one of the witnesses, clearly builds on his earlier subscription edition of *Paradise Lost*, but with important differences.[41] In addition to paying Dryden for the copyright to his translation, Tonson organized two subscription lists. The first list were to pay 5 guineas, of which 3 guineas were to be paid prior to publication, for a large paper edition which would contain an engraving dedicated to them: this edition was to be limited to 100 copies (in fact there were 101), re-using the plates from Ogilby's edition of 1654. The second subscribers were to pay 2 guineas for a small paper edition, and Dryden was free to find as many of these as he could (in the event he had 250 second subscribers). These subscribers at once validated the Dryden–Tonson publication for the wider reading public, and were themselves both patrons and consumers. (The first subscribers were of particular value to Dryden since their 3 guineas came directly to him in 1695.) Congreve's role in this is worth remarking upon. The young dramatist was admired by Dryden and in turn admired the older poet: he not only witnessed the contract, but used his legal training to arbitrate between Tonson and Dryden when the two men had a violent disagreement over the interpretation of the contract in 1695: for the older and younger writer, poetry transcended politics, just as it seems to have done for the translation's supporters.

The importance of the translation for Dryden's finances, in a decade in which he had lost the posts of Poet Laureate and Historiographer Royal and was disenchanted with writing for the stage, is self-evident. Over the four-year period in which he translated Virgil, Dryden received £200 copy money in staged payment from his publisher Jacob Tonson, a further sum of nearly £300 from the part payment from his first subscribers in 1695, and further payments from the first and second subscribers when the work was published in 1697. Altogether, Dryden probably received as much as £1,057 from his publisher and subscribers: gifts from his three dedicatees brought the total up to £1,400,[42] giving him an average income of perhaps as much as £350 a year (equivalent in today's money of roughly £29,000 or $45,000) from the translation alone.

One aspect of Dryden's payment for the Virgil is curious. Dryden had contracted in 1694 to supply such notes, preface, or dedication, "as he Shall think most fitting."[43] One of the causes of his disagreement with Tonson in 1695 and 1696 was the publisher's refusal "to allow any thing towards the Notes"[44] (even though he had no contractual obligation to do so). Dryden was so annoyed that he angrily concluded a letter to Tonson in June 1695 – "The Notes & Prefaces shall be short: because you shall get the more by saving paper."[45] In fact, although Dryden apologized for the paucity of the notes for the Virgil in his "Postscript,"[46] his three dedications contain some of his most extended criticism. In particular, that to the *Aeneis* is his fullest statement on the nature of epic poetry.[47] Tonson was cunning enough to know that Dryden could not afford to miss the opportunity of three dedications, but his failure to limit the length of these, or of the other supplementary material, involved him in substantial extra charges for paper (the most expensive element in the book's manufacture): the dedications take up 14.75 sheets and the "Postscript" another 5 sheets: further supplementary material written on Dryden's behalf (the life of Virgil and essays on the "Pastorals" and "Georgics") written by others brings the total up to 28 sheets: Dryden's own prose alone accounts for well over a tenth (19.75 sheets) of the 173 sheets of printed text required for the volume. Tonson clearly believed this framing material, particularly that by Dryden, was an essential part of the Virgil's attraction for its audience, for whom Tonson's publication provided the considered views of the major living English poet on the major Roman epic author.[48]

Had Tonson known when the contract was signed whom Dryden would choose as dedicatees and what he would write in the dedications, the bookseller would have had cause for unease. The publication in 1697 of Dryden's translation of Virgil was a significant national cultural event (it even, unusually for an English poet, attracted attention on the continent).[49] Dr. Johnson rightly said that "the nation considered its honour as interested" in the event:[50] the translation's subscribers were drawn from all sections, political and religious, of the "polite" reading public in a fractured and sharply divided polity. Yet if the publication functioned as a literary project which united the nation, it was simultaneously a site of contestation.[51] This is clear from the disagreement between the poet and his publisher over who should be honored with the dedication. Tonson, a long-term Whig, wanted it dedicated to William III, which would have made clear the extent to which the Whig grandees, like Lord Somers and Charles Montagu, had supported the venture: Dryden, a Jacobite, refused point-blank. Baulked "of his design" by the translator, Tonson instead, rather desperately, sought to flatter the king by having the engravings altered wherever Aeneas appears: as Dryden gleefully reported to his sons on 3 September 1697, "in every figure of Eneas, [Tonson] has caused him to be drawn like K. William, with a hooked Nose."[52] Beneath the appearance of national unanimity which the translation embodied in its handsome illustrated folio volume, lay deep political divides.

These divides were made completely transparent by Dryden's choice of his three dedicatees. Hugh, Lord Clifford, was a Catholic, while Philip Stanhope, Earl of Chesterfield, and John Sheffield, Marquess of Normanby, had both refused to take the loyalty oaths to William III (and Dryden's letter to Chesterfield asking permission to dedicate the "Georgics" to him is openly Jacobite).[53] Even if Dryden had not slanted his translation of Virgil's epic so as to reflect obliquely his own Jacobite attitudes to the immediate political situation in the late 1690s,[54] his choice of patrons alone was sufficient to announce where he stood. The first paragraph of the opening dedication to Clifford asks the reader to compare Dryden's isolation in the late 1690s with his earlier career:

> I have found it not more difficult to Translate *Virgil*, than to find such Patrons as I desire for my Translation. For though *England* is not wanting in a Learned Nobility, yet such are my unhappy Circumstances, that they have confin'd me to a narrow choice. To the greater part, I have not the Honour to be known; and to some of them I cannot shew at present, by any publick Act, that grateful Respect which I shall ever bear them in my heart. (*Works* v: 3)

He goes on to remind Clifford that it was his father, Thomas, who had ensured the payment of his salary in 1672 and 1673 despite the stop of the Exchequer. Dryden compares the older Clifford to the Roman noble traditionally supposed to have successfully interceded with the emperor, Augustus, on Virgil's behalf:[55]

> He was the Patron of my Manhood, when I Flourish'd in the opinion of the World; though with small advantage to my Fortune, 'till he awaken'd the remembrance of my Royal Master. He was that *Pollio*, or that *Varus*, who

introduc'd me to *Augustus*: And tho' he soon dismiss'd himself from State-Affairs, yet in the short time of his Administration he shone so powerfully upon me, that like the heat of a *Russian*-Summer, he ripen'd the Fruits of Poetry in a cold Clymate; and gave me wherewithal to subsist at least, in the long Winter which succeeded.   (*Works* v: 3)

Dryden's nostalgic recall of a Golden Age of patronage is richly ironic in its allusions. By casting Charles II in the role of Augustus, patron of Virgil, Dryden reminds his readers that William III's court was uninterested in the patronage of literature, but he also makes it clear that even Charles II had been remiss in paying his laureate his due, and needed reminding. Clifford's son, and many of Dryden's readers, would also have recalled that Clifford was only briefly Lord Treasurer (which had enabled him help the laureate) – he was forced to resign because of his Catholicism, and hanged himself only two months later.[56] The Cliffords, like Dryden, had suffered for their religion, but remained true to their faith. More than that, Dryden's dedication to Clifford's son is a mark of his own faithful gratitude to his former benefactor, and assumes that true patronage, as in Rome, is a family matter. Dryden allies himself and the Cliffords with the virtues of constancy and generosity in a world, it is implied, marked by neither.

The use made by Dryden of the Virgil's dedications and Postscript is paradoxical. One of his, and Tonson's, aims was to unify the nation in a common cultural project, and in the Postscript Dryden is careful to thank those who have helped "one of a different Perswasion."[57] At the same time, he uses the prose surrounding his translation to fashion his own self-image, and gives, within the book itself, a self-reflexive narrative of his own career, and of the translation's gestation and completion, which has the effect of revealing the multiple political rifts amongst Dryden's patrons. The example of the *Virgil* shows how Dryden was able to assert his independence in the complex public arena created by the differences and similarities between his own views and those of his subscribers, his publisher, and his dedicatees. Here, as elsewhere, what is striking is his control of tone and his carefully calculated use of indirection to stake out clearly his own position and to assert his independence.

On one occasion, however, Dryden breaks the conventions and reveals his immediate feelings with extraordinary candor. This is in the dedication to Edward, Lord Radcliffe, he wrote for *Examen Poeticum* in 1693. The dedication has been described as "full of the self-pity that characterized the ageing poet after his dismissal from Court favour [and offices] in 1689."[58] This seems mistaken, but demonstrates the frequent difficulties for the modern reader in judging the tone of Dryden's dedications. Radcliffe, a thirty-eight-year-old Catholic nobleman who had himself contributed poetry to *Examen Poeticum*, had agreed that the volume should be dedicated to him, and had, with his wife, heard Dryden read from his translation of Ovid. Dryden must have felt that he could be franker with a co-religionist and fellow-poet about his true feelings than would otherwise be the case. He was also writing quickly – Dryden says he has been "summon'd by the Press to send away this Dedication" before it was finished, and he apologizes for failing in consequence to include "a Compliment in the close" (*Works* IV: 372, 374).

The following passage is certainly ironic and scornful, but taken as part of a swiftly written letter to a sympathetic reader who knew Dryden's actual position, and who himself suffered under the same disadvantages as a Catholic, what it reveals is not self-pity but Dryden's angry and defiant belief in his own worth:

> For what other Reason have I spent my Life in so unprofitable a Study? Why am I grown Old, in seeking so barren a Reward as Fame? The same Parts and Application which have made me a Poet might have rais'd me to any Honours of the Gown, which are often given to Men of as little Learning and less Honesty than my self. No Government has ever been, or ever can be, wherein Time-servers and Blockheads will not be uppermost. The Persons are only chang'd, but the same juglings in State, the same Hypocrisie in Religion, the same Self-Interest and Mis-mannagement, will remain for ever.
>
> (*Works* IV: 363)

It is not surprising that in August Dryden heard from a friend (probably Dorset) that the Queen had been informed that he "had abus'd her Government, (those were the words) in my Epistle to Lord Radclyffe; & that thereupon, she had commanded her Historiographer [Thomas] Rymer to fall upon my Playes . . ."[59] Although the attack never materialized, Dryden was right to fear that he had gone too far. Nor should he have been surprised that a dedication, which so far defied the generic rules of the form, attracted no financial reward from its recipient.[60]

Dryden's dedications, written in a period which placed a premium on a man's personal honor, far from "no longer retaining shame in himself," insist, sometimes to the point of foolhardiness, on the continuity of his career and on the integrity of his achievements as a writer and poet. Dryden believed in the enduring value of poetry: at once modest and confident of his own achievements, he writes in the dedication to Radcliffe – "Neither do I know why the Name of Poet should be Dishonourable to me: if I am truly one, as

I hope I am; for I will never do any thing, that shall dishonour it" (*Works* IV: 364).

NOTES

1. "The Vanity of Human Wishes" (1749), lines 159–60.
2. *Dictionary*, first published 1755.
3. "Life of Dryden", *Lives of the English Poets*, ed. George Birkbeck Hill (Oxford, 1905), vol. I, pp. 399, 400, 359.
4. James A. Winn, *John Dryden and his World* (New Haven, 1987), pp. 191, 574. A condition of the contract required Dryden to write three plays a year, something he never managed.
5. See Dustin Griffin, *Literary Patronage in England, 1650–1800* (Cambridge, 1996), especially chapter 4 on Dryden (pp. 70–98). See also the pioneering article by Paul Korshin, "Types of Eighteenth-Century Literary Patronage," *Eighteenth-Century Studies* 7 (1974), 453–73, esp. 466–8.
6. Two examples from late in Dryden's career suggest that this was the case: Dryden's letter to the Earl of Chesterfield asking permission for a dedication in 1697 and the earl's reply are cited below (pp. 209–10): in 1694 Dryden's dedication of *Examen Poeticum* to Lord Radcliffe says that the miscellany of poems is by "many Titles yours. The first they claim from your acceptance of my Promise to present them to you" (*Works* IV: 363). It is unclear what the general practice was. However, the case of the minor writer Richard Robinson shows that authors did not always seek permission. His "Eupolemia" (1603) gives a uniquely detailed account of those to whom he dedicated his publications and of the meagre returns he made: on one occasion, Sir Thomas Egerton, the new Lord Keeper, refused to give him anything because Robinson had failed to "make him privy to yt" beforehand, and on another the Bishop of London's secretary rejected his approaches because in dedicating to both the Bishop and the Lord Mayor Robinson had "praeferred his Lordes name . . . before the Lord Maiors name" (George McGill Voigt, "Richard Robinson's *Eupolemia* (1603)," *Studies in Philology* 21 [1924], 629–48, at pp. 644–5). H. R. Woudhuysen has discovered that Robinson was a professional scribe and responsible for the manuscript of the *Old Arcadia*: see *Sir Philip Sidney and the Circulation of Manuscripts 1558–1640* (Oxford, 1996), pp. 195–203, pl. v.
7. Winn, *John Dryden*, p. 127.
8. Ibid., pp. 545–7. A late but unsubstantiated tradition reports that Bertie gave Dryden the remarkably large sum of 500 guineas (p. 620).
9. Ibid., pp. 455–8.
10. *Table Talk*, ed. Carl Woodring (1990), *The Collected Works of Samuel Taylor Coleridge* (Princeton, 1970–2001), vol. I, p. 449.
11. For Dryden's unusually early use of the noun "public" in its modern sense, see the quotation from "A Discourse Concerning the Original and Progress of Satire" (1693) cited below, p. 208 and n. 32.
12. James D. Garrison, *Dryden and the Tradition of Panegyric* (Berkeley, 1975).
13. Angel Day, *The English Secretary or Method of Writing Epistles and Letters . . . (1599)*, ed. Robert O. Evans (Gainesville, 1967), pp. 47, 60, 52. Day's work,

which gives detailed instructions on the parts of a letter along with examples, was frequently reprinted in the seventeenth century.

14. Evelyn to Pepys, 12 August 1689, cited by Geoffrey Keynes, *John Evelyn: A Study in Bibliophily with a Bibliography of his Writings*, 2nd edn. (Oxford, 1968), pp. 104–5.

15. Erasmus to the orator of Louvain, cited by Winn, *John Dryden*, p. 107 from *The Epistles of Erasmus*, tr. F. M. Nichols (London, 1901), vol. I, p. 366. See also Garrison, *Dryden and the Tradition of Panegyric* pp. 20–2.

16. In addition to this example, see his dedication to Lord Radcliffe for *Examen Poeticum* (1693) cited below (p. 214).

17. In 1682 Dryden had put up his price for writing a prologue from 4 to 6 guineas: this was for *The Loyal Brother* by Thomas Southerne, whose work he admired (Winn, *John Dryden*, p. 310).

18. For the published text and manuscript version (with a photographic reproduction) see *Works* XVII: 324–6, 482–3.

19. On the idea of cultural capital see Pierre Bourdieu, *The Field of Cultural Production: Essays on Art and Literature*, ed. and introd. Randal Johnson (Cambridge, 1993); see also John Guillory, *Cultural Capital: The Problem of Literary Canon Formation* (Chicago, 1993).

20. Further, see Winn, *John Dryden*, pp. 325, 593–4 (Rose Alley affair), 385–6 (Duke of Monmouth), 334 (Lord Haughton), 444 (Sir William Leveson-Gower).

21. On this occasion the dedication is set in italic, but its type size is the same as that of the text.

22. "Sometimes a man knows a place determinate, within the compass whereof he is to seek; and then his thoughts run over all the parts thereof, in the same manner, as one would sweep a room, to find a jewell; or as a Spaniel ranges the field, till he find a s[c]ent . . ." (*Leviathan* [1651], I. iii, p. 10). Dryden also draws in this passage on Hobbes's ideas on poetic creation set out in his *Answer to Davenant* (1650) (*Critical Essays of the Seventeenth Century*, ed. J. E. Spingarn [Oxford, 1908–9], vol. II, p. 59).

23. It may have been the first "work of this nature" dedicated to London, but Franklin B. Williams, Jr., *Index of Dedications and Commendatory Verses in English Books before 1641* (London, 1962) identifies eleven printed works dedicated to the city up to 1640 (STC 4648, 4853, 4971, 7537, 10688, 11935, 14968, 15439, 19884, 21091 and 23705).

24. Paulina Kewes, "Acts of Oblivion, Acts of Remembrance: Rhetoric, Law, and National Memory in Restoration England," in *Ritual, Routine, and Regime: Institutions of Repetition in Euro-American Cultures 1650–1832*, ed. Lorna Clymer (Toronto, forthcoming).

25. This is a more nuanced reading of the dedication than that in my "Dryden: History and the 'Mighty Government of the Nine,'" *University of Leeds Review* 24 (1981), 18–22 (reprinted in *English*, 32 [1983]).

26. See the letter from Sir Allen Brodrick to the Duke of Ormonde, 29 December 1666, cited in *The Poems of John Dryden*, vol. I, ed. Paul Hammond (London and New York, 1995), p. 106.

27. Winn, *John Dryden*, p. 186.

28. As reported by Pope in 1736, Joseph Spence, *Observations, Anecdotes and Characters of Book and Men*, ed. James M. Osborn (Oxford, 1966), vol. I, pp. 28–9.

29. It is not known what this present was, but Dryden's financial situation was in a desperate state by January 1692 (Winn, *John Dryden*, p. 452).

30. Anne Cotterill, "The Politics and Aesthetics of Digression: Dryden's 'Discourse Concerning the Original and Progress of Satire,'" *Studies in Philology* 91 (1994), 465–95, argues that the "Discourse" reflects tensions, even hostility, in Dryden's relations with Dorset. Edward L. Saslow, "The Rose Alley Ambuscade," *Restoration* 26 (2002), 27–49, argues that Dorset was the instigator of the Rose Alley attack in 1679: while this seems unlikely it nevertheless suggests that the client–patron relationship between the two men may have had its complications.

31. That is, smooth ground (the image seems developed from Horace's "sermo pedestris").

32. The *OED* gives its first example from Robert Boyle in this sense from 1665: it dates "public" as meaning a particular section, group or portion of mankind from 1711. Earlier the word referred to the nation or state as a whole ("res publica").

33. There is relatively limited evidence about who bought these translations but the 349 subscribers to Dryden's 1697 translation of Virgil include, in addition to aristocrats and MPs, substantial groups of professional men along with a significant number of women (John Barnard, "Dryden, Tonson, and the Patrons of *The Works of Virgil* (1697)," in *John Dryden: Tercentenary Essays*, ed. Paul Hammond and David Hopkins [Oxford, 2000], pp. 174–239 [at pp. 182–3, 193–5, and 197–200, 213–15]).

34. Dryden seems to have approached Sedley with no success (*Works* IV: 145–6): Sedley's refusal of "so ungrateful an employment" suggests that he was offered too little money or none at all.

35. Winn, *John Dryden*, p. 451.

36. See John Barnard, "The Large- and Small- Paper Copies of Dryden's *The Works of Virgil* (1697): Jacob Tonson's Investment and Profits and the Example of *Paradise Lost* (1688)," *Papers of the Bibliographical Society of America* 92 (1998), 259–71.

37. Maynard Mack, *Alexander Pope: A Life* (New Haven and London, 1985), pp. 266–8.

38. John Brewer, *The Pleasures of the Imagination: English Culture in the Eighteenth Century* (London, 1997), p. 166.

39. In all 351 copies were subscribed for but Hugh, Lord Clifford, and Robert Harley were both first and second subscribers.

40. *The Letters of John Dryden*, ed. Charles Ward (Durham, NC, 1942), pp. 86–7. Chesterfield replied on 18 February. Dryden had prepared carefully for his approach to Chesterfield. As early as 29 October 1695 he had been asking Tonson to ensure that Chesterfield had his place among the first subscribers (*Letters*, pp. 78, 81). Dryden's dedication reminds Chesterfield that he had given permission (*Works* V: 137).

41. The contract is in the British Library (Add. MS. 36,933 and Add. Charter 8,429): a transcript of this and related documents is printed in *Works* VI: 1179–83.

42. Figures based on "Dryden, Tonson, and Subscriptions for the 1697 *Virgil*," *Papers of the Bibliographical Society of America* 57 (1963), 129–51, esp. pp. 130–1, 133–40. Dustin Griffin rightly challenges the argument put forward there that the *Virgil* was predominantly a commercial venture since the subscriptions were

a form of patronage: see "The Beginnings of Modern Authorship: Milton and Dryden," *Milton Quarterly* 24 (1990), 1–7.

43. *Works* VI: 1179.
44. *Letters*, p. 80 (late 1695 or early 1696).
45. Ibid., p. 78 (29 October 1695).
46. *Works* VI: 810.
47. The dedication has attracted discussion in its own right: see, most recently, Julie Chandler Hayes, "Temporality, Subjectivity, and Neoclassical Translation Theory: Dryden's Dedication of the *Aeneis*," *Restoration* 26 (2002), 97–118.
48. Dr. Johnson thought that Dryden wrote his prefatory material for money: "To increase the value of his copies he often accompanied his work with a preface of criticism then almost new in the English language . . ." (*Lives of the English Poets*, vol. I, p. 366). There is no firm evidence that this was the case, though it might be thought probable.
49. John Barnard, "Early Expectations of Dryden's Translation of Virgil (1697) in England and on the Continent," *Review of English Studies* n.s. 50 (1999), 196–203.
50. Johnson, *Lives of the English Poets*, vol. I, p. 448.
51. For a fuller analysis of these features of the translation's publication, see Barnard, "Dryden, Tonson, and the Patrons of *The Works of Virgil* (1697)."
52. *Letters*, p. 93.
53. Dryden wrote to Chesterfield on 17 February 1697, "My translation of Virgil is already in the Press . . . I have hinder'd it thus long in hopes of his return, for whom, and for my Conscience I have suffered . . . But now finding that Gods time for ending our miseries is not yet, I have been advis'd to make three severall Dedications . . ." (*Letters*, pp. 85–6).
54. Not just in the translation but also by the placing of his patrons' plates: see *Works* VI: 870–6 and Steven N. Zwicker, *Politics and Language in Dryden's Poetry: The Arts of Disguise* (Princeton, 1984), chapter 6, "Politics and Translation," pp. 177–205.
55. Either Asinius Pollio or Alfenus Varro were believed to have been instrumental in having Virgil's Mantuan home restored to the poet: the tradition is now doubted. See *Works* VI: 891.
56. Winn, *John Dryden*, pp. 232, 240–2.
57. *Works* VI: 808.
58. *John Dryden: "Of Dramatic Poesy" and Other Essays*, ed. George Watson (London and New York, 1962), vol. II, p. 156.
59. *Letters*, p. 59 (30 August 1693).
60. Ibid., p. 58.

12

ANNABEL PATTERSON

Dryden and political allegiance

The facts are these: Dryden opened his career as a writer by defining himself as a supporter of Oliver Cromwell, in a volume of poems honoring the Protector after his death in September 1658. A short time later, he reappeared on the literary scene as a celebrant of the Restoration. At the time of the Second Dutch War, when the first enthusiasm for Charles II had been considerably tarnished by events and his own behavior, Dryden came to the king's defense indirectly. By 1672, however, in expectation of the Third Dutch War, Dryden could be seen in print as a devoted servant of James, Duke of York, a loyalty he retained long past the point where it ceased to be helpful to him. After the Glorious Revolution, and the arrival of William III, Dryden remained a Jacobite, refusing to dedicate his great translation of Virgil to the new king.

The facts have involved generations of Dryden commentators in an evaluative struggle over whether Dryden was a turn-coat, a time-server, or a man who finally found the leader whose laureate he could sincerely be, in good fortune and bad. The point of this chapter is not, however, to renew the old arguments about principle versus interest, conviction versus prudential adaptability, which can never be resolved to the satisfaction of all of Dryden's readers, who are not themselves unbiased. I begin instead with the observation that it was scarcely necessary for Dryden to advertise his political allegiances, and their shifts, in such a definitive way. Having done it once, however, he had to keep doing it. History, having pushed him into the public sphere, would change its own direction so many times during his lifetime that he was constantly playing catch-up. Secondly, I want to reconsider the relation between Dryden's positioning of himself on the political spectrum, and his theories of language and genre. One could see this two ways. Having to restate his allegiances meant having to recast his literary theory so that it seemed to support, if not to require, the larger political change. Alternatively, one could argue a more bizarre thesis: that the literary theory, and the ambitions behind it, drove the political affiliations.

Most of this has to do, obviously, with Dryden's idea of the heroic, as something that writers, especially if they have the laureateship in mind, must redefine for their own place and time. Did Dryden already have such a goal in mind when, at the age of twenty-seven, he moved to London and accepted a minor clerical position in the Protector's civil service, thanks to the help of his cousin, Gilbert Pickering, who was Cromwell's Lord Chamberlain? Or was it Pickering who suggested he contribute a funeral elegy for the Protector? When Cromwell died, and Pickering was in charge of funeral arrangements, Dryden marched in the funeral cortege, along with Milton and Marvell, as "Secretarys of the ffrench and Latin Toungs," having like them been provided with official mourning. Whatever the incentive, Dryden clearly conceived of this, his first entry into the public sphere, properly speaking, as a species of epic or heroic poetry; but this was heroic poetry as that redefined by William Davenant in his weird long poem, *Gondibert* (1650).

Dryden, as everyone knows, chose to write in what would immediately be recognized as the "Gondibert" stanza. By choosing this stanza, Dryden also affiliated himself with the even more peculiar "Preface to Gondibert," which not only contains an advertisement for this stanza, but, if one struggles with it long enough, reveals itself as a conservative theory of government, and a defense of poetry's civic function, in an era when "we have . . . observ'd the Four chief aids of Government, Religion, Armes, Policy, and Law, defectively apply'd" (p. 44).[1] If it was peculiar, and often self-contradictory, Davenant's "Preface" was also quite circumspect. As his prejudices seeped through his baroque prose, Davenant had identified himself indirectly as what he was, a royalist appalled even more by the class implications of the Civil Wars than by the wars themselves; "the most necessary men are those who become principall by prerogative of blood . . . or by greatnesse of minde, which in exact definition is Vertue. The common Crowd, of whom we are hope-lesse, we desert."[2] And the drift of the embryonic political theory of the piece is ultimately Hobbesian, as indeed it was addressed to and answered by Thomas Hobbes. Thus the educational power of poetry, especially the heroic, will contribute to obedience, for "knowledge will soon put into one Scale the weight of oppression, and in the other the heavy burden which Disobedience lays on us in the effects of civil War; and then even Tyranny will seem much lighter, when the hand of supreme Power binds up our Load and lays it artfully on us, then Disobedience, the Parent of Confusion, when we all load one another, in which every one irregularly increases his fellows burden to lessen his own."[3] This position was compatible with Davenant's campaign to adapt himself as a poet to the Protectorate, and by 1656, newly released from the Tower, he was permitted to begin staging musical events and operas.

This position also seems to have been acceptable to Dryden. That is to say, the *Heroique Stanzas* adopt the general position that Cromwell's government has been better for the country, especially in terms of foreign policy, than the republican one that preceded it, and implicitly better than the insular and pacific reign of Charles I; but they also make sure to strike the same notes as did Davenant in his preface. Thus Cromwell is defined as one of those whose natural greatness of mind renders him at least equal and perhaps superior to kings, and sets him definitively above the common man:

> 6.
>
> His *Grandeur* he deriv'd from Heav'n alone,
> For he was great e're Fortune made him so;
> And Warr's like mists that rise against the Sunne
> Made him but greater seem, not greater grow.
>
> 9.
>
> He, private, mark'd the faults of others sway,
> And set as *Sea-mark's* for himself to shun;
> Not like rash *Monarch's* who their youth betray
> By Acts their Age too late would wish undone.
>
> 27.
>
> When such *Heroique Vertue* Heav'n sets out,
> The Starrs like *Commons* sullenly obey;
> Because it draines them when it comes about,
> And therefore is a taxe they seldome pay.
>> (*Works* 1: 6, lines 21–4; 12, lines 33–6; 14,
>> lines 105–8)

The last stanza is particularly odd, seeming to glance at Cromwell's early difficulties with Parliament, just as the reference to the unweighted palms of *this* reign (lines 57–8) seem to repudiate those weighted palms, emblematic of the sufferings of Charles I, so visible in the frontispiece of Charles's *Eikon Basilike*.

James Winn thinks that Dryden tried not to go too far in offending the royalists, and therefore deleted the qualifier "and happy" from the "Glorious . . . Memory" in question before he published the poem.[4] But he still published it, even though the wilier Marvell had withdrawn *his* elegy from the volume registered to Henry Herringman on 20 January 1659. By 11 February 1659, Marvell was already reporting to George Downing the strenuous efforts in Parliament to prevent Richard Cromwell succeeding to the Protectorate,[5] and it would not have been prudent of him to publish a poem that ended by threatening the opposition:

> Cease now our griefs, calme peace succeeds a war,
> Rainbows to storms, Richard to Oliver.
> Tempt not his clemency to try his pow'r,
> He threats no deluge, yet foretells a showre.[6]

Herringman himself abandoned his claim to William Wilson, who brought out the planned volume later in the year, with Marvell's poem replaced by a previously published poem by Waller. Thus Marvell, whose *Horatian Ode* had never been published, and whose *First Anniversary on the Government of O.C.* had been published anonymously, could move forward into the Restoration with no poetic blot in his copy-book; while Dryden's poem would be republished by his Whig enemies in 1681, with the title *An Elegy on the Usurper O.C. by the Author of Absalom and Achitophel, published to shew the Loyalty and Integrity of the Poet.*

Why was Dryden, for all his equivocal phrasing within the *Heroique Stanzas*, so lacking in foresight? Because, I believe, the death of Cromwell offered him a subject for public poetry that he could legitimately claim as "heroic," already his grand ambition. And possibly because he was already jealous of Marvell. It is hard not to believe that Dryden had read the unpublished *Horatian Ode* when his own poem begins "And now 'tis time," surely an allusion to Marvell's celebration of the opening of the Cromwellian era as one of military accomplishment: "'Tis time to leave the Books in dust, / And oyl th'unused Armours rust" (1: 91). Where Marvell came in at the beginning, Dryden came in at the end, using the same conceits: admiration of the "private" Cromwell, his speed of action, and his subtlety.

With the collapse of Richard Cromwell's Protectorate, and during the chaos and uncertainty of 1659, until General Monck made his intentions plain to bring back the king in exile, Dryden had nothing to do, or, rather, nothing to say in public. He waited until mid-June 1660 to announce his change of allegiance to Charles II, who had entered London on 29 May. When *Astraea Redux* was advertised in *Mercurius Publicus* for 21–28 June, Dryden was rather bringing up the rear in the torrent of accolades that had begun to appear in mid-May. He responded to this competition by writing a very long poem, over 300 lines, whereas the *Heroique Stanzas* had been short of 150: by packing it with Biblical and classical allusions; by filling it with a vague history of the republican and Cromwellian era that represented Charles as a David suffering in exile for the sins of his nation; by redefining the Protectorate as the period when "Faction seiz'd the Throne"; and by doing his best to resolve the war/peace dichotomy by claiming *both* that Charles II would restore the Caroline ethos of feminine sweetness ("By that same mildness which your Fathers Crown / Before did ravish, [you] shall secure your own," lines 258–9) *and* that he would continue the aggressive foreign policy of Cromwell, who is of course never mentioned:

> Tremble ye Nations who secure before
> Laught at those Armes that 'gainst our selves we bore;
> Rous'd by the lash of his own stubborn tail
> Our Lyon now will forraign Foes assail.
> (*Works* 1: 25, lines 115–18)

These lines calmly revoke the matching point in *Heroique Stanzas*:

> He made us *Freemen* of the *Continent*
> Whom Nature did like Captives treat before,
> To nobler pray's the *English Lyon* sent,
> And taught him first in *Belgian walks* to rore.
> (*Works* 1: 15, lines 112–15)

But nothing in either the tone of *Astraea Redux* or its direct statements suggest that Dryden now saw the Restoration as the rebirth of a heroic era. On the contrary, the genre implied is tragicomedy; and the *Panegyrick on his Coronation*, addressed to his "sacred Maiesty," is unequivocally written in the mode of amorous romance: soft western winds, flowers and blossoms, the wings of Incense, fragrant scents, richer dew, Summer evenings, the potential queen's chaste womb – the entire vocabulary embraces the king's early self-definition as a man of pleasure. Indeed, the phrase "Rivalls in your bed" is one of the first of Dryden's double-edged compliments to Charles's virility. The coronation took place on 23 April 1661, by which time Barbara Villiers had already been installed as public mistress No. 1. Amazingly, Dryden argues that the new ethos of public voluptuousness will keep the nation safe:

> ev'n your pleasures serve for our defence.
> Beyond your Court flows in th'admitted tide,
> Where in new depths the wondring fishes glide:
> Here in a Royal bed the waters sleep,
> When tir'd at Sea within this bay they creep.
> (*Works* 1: 36, lines 110–14)

Perhaps Marvell deliberately recalled these foolish lines when in 1667 he described how "up the stream the *Belgick* Navy glides," and how the Dutch admiral De Ruyter is overcome with amorous pleasure when he sails up the Thames and Medway to destroy or take captive the English fleet.

The year 1667 saw Dryden and Marvell take opposite sides on the issue of the wisdom and conduct of the Second Dutch War. On 10 November 1666, Dryden had just or almost finished *Annus Mirabilis*, for he dated his prefatory letter to Sir Robert Howard announcing the poem's program

10 November 1666. It was not, however, entered in the Stationers' Register until 21 January 1667, perhaps because Howard really was, as Dryden claimed in his letter, making some friendly corrections. In the *Second* and *Third Advice to the Painter*, Marvell had already, anonymously, declared the Dutch War an anti-heroic endeavor, marked by British cowardice and mismanagement. At the end of the *Third Advice*, whose main topic was the unwise division of the command of the fleet between Prince Rupert and General Monck, he had briefly referred to the Fire of London, which by implication makes London look like a second Troy. Whether or not Dryden had any inkling who was responsible for these poems, his reaction was to write an answer that, without identifying the provocation, was intended to rescue Restoration England from the sardonic mock-heroic view of the satirist, and to recast it in the aura of the heroic.

While his approach to his subject in the poem is not visibly apologetic, the Letter, in the context of the satirical *Advices*, certainly is. "I have chosen," Dryden wrote, "the motives, the beginning, progress and successes of a most just and necessary War; in it, the care, management and prudence of our King; the conduct and valour of a Royal Admiral, and of two incomparable Generals; the invincible courage of our Captains and Sea-men, and three glorious Victories, the result of all" (*Works* 1: 50). This in the face of the *Second Advice*'s conclusion, "Thus having fought we know not why, as yet / W'have done we know not what, nor what we get." This in the face of the *Third Advice*'s opening description of Prince Rupert and George Monck, "United Gen'ralls," as "ratling far / Within one box, like the two Dice of War," and its prognosis that they, "though shell'd in treble Oake / Will prove an addle Egge with double Yolke."

To counter this comic deflation, Dryden reinstated the "Gondibert" stanza that he had set aside for the more fulsome compliments on the king's return, reminding his audience, via the letter to Howard, that this stanza was inherently "more noble, and of greater dignity" than any other meter, but especially more than the couplet (which was what the *Advices* had selected):

> In this necessity of our Rhymes, I have always found the couplet Verse most easie, (though not so proper for this occasion) for there the work is sooner at an end, every two lines concluding the labor of the Poet: but in Quattrains he is to carry it farther on; and not onely so, but to bear along in his head the troublesome sense of four lines together.   (*Works* 1: 51)

This odd account of poetry-writing as the labor of completing the rhyme, and of sublimity as delaying the completion, ends with a reminder that the

"Gondibert" stanza "is much better defended in the Preface to *Gondibert*" (*Works* 1: 51), a reminder to his audience that they would do well to reread that document.

If they did, however, they would discover that Dryden had in everything else broken with Davenant's theory of heroic poetry. Dryden's claim to have, in the battle of 1666 and the Fire that followed, "chosen the most heroick Subject which any Poet could desire" (Works 1: 50) flew in the face of Davenant's recommendations in his *Preface* that the heroic poet avoid writing about his own time or his own country. Dryden's poem is not only topical, it is historical and historiographical. Where Davenant had dismissed "their improper examinations, who know not the requisites of a Poem, nor how much pleasure they lose . . . who take away the liberty of a Poet, and fetter his feet in the shackles of an Historian,"[7] Dryden is candid. "I have call'd my poem *Historical*, not *Epick*," he continues, ". . . since the Action is not properly one, nor that accomplish'd in the last successes" (*Works* 1: 50). That is to say, in its denial of the unities, the double subject, war and fire, is un-Aristotelian.

This is not the place to provide yet another account of *Annus Mirabilis*, which is a very effective poem, and actually gains a good deal from its double subject, allowing the reader to forget that at the end of 1666 the Dutch War is by no means over, and that the Chatham disaster of 1667 is still to come. But for the purposes of my argument, one feature requires special comment. Dryden here develops a new strategy (which will later have ramifications for *The Hind and the Panther*). He creates a heroic bestiary, whereby the attention of the audience to the actual costs of a naval battle is deflected by metaphors taken from a world in which conflict is taken as "natural." Thus the English fleet surrounded and outnumbered is "like the Sword-fish in the Whale," Prince Rupert's arrival to rescue Monck is "as an Eagle" whose young have been carried off from the nest, however implausible is the thought that she could actually retrieve them. More telling, however, is Dryden's recall of the lion motif he had used in both the *Heroique Stanzas* and in *Astraea Redux*. In fact, the reprise looks like a conversation between those earlier poems and the one in hand. When at the beginning of the second day's battle the Dutch reinforcements arrive, they "in their colours *Belgian* Lions Bear" (*Works* 1: 70, line 288). Later "their Fire-ships, like *Jackals*, appear, / Who on their Lions for the prey attend" (*Works* 1: 72, lines 327–8). But this most heroic of metaphors is then rescued from the Dutch and attached to Monck, whose inactivity, Dryden imagines, terrifies the Dutch into keeping their distance:

96.

So *Lybian* Huntsmen, on some sandy plain,
From shady coverts rouz'd, the Lion chace:
The Kingly beast roars out with loud disdain,
And slowly moves, unknowing to give place.

97.

But if some one approach to dare his force,
He swings his tail, and swiftly turns him round:
With one paw seizes on his trembling Horse,
And with the other tears him to the ground.

(*Works* 1: 74, lines 381–8)

Let us return to that phrase, "the most heroick Subject which any Poet could desire"; this seems to me revealing of other issues than Dryden's departure from Davenant's advice, or the need to counter political criticism. Dryden has *needed* events like these. The defense of naval policy was perhaps secondary as a motive to the more personal need for a grand occasion on which to display one's abilities. Dryden sounds oddly gratified by what Fortune has thrown his way:

> though the trouble I had in writing it was great, it was more than recompens'd by the pleasure; I found myself so warm in celebrating the praises of military men, two such especially as the *Prince* and the *General*, that it is no wonder if they inspir'd me with thoughts above my ordinary level. And I am well satisfi'd, that as they are incomparably the best subject I have ever had, excepting only the *Royal Family*; so also, that this I have written of them is much better than what I have perform'd on any other. I have been forc'd to help out other Arguments, but this has been bountiful to me . . . I have had a large, a fair and pleasant field, so fertile, that without my cultivating, it has given me two Harvests in a Summer . . . All other greatness in subjects is onely counterfeit, it will not endure the test of danger; the greatness of Arms is onely real.
>
> (*Works* 1: 52)

This is an amazing confession; all the more so for the awkward "excepting" of "onely the *Royal Family.*" Dryden gets "pleasure," grows "warm" at his task, and feels that the war has been "bountiful" to him – the Fire too, if we are to interpret literally the "two Harvests in a Summer." The Fire broke out on 2 September 1666, precisely in harvest time. If, as Dryden's editors admit, "It is difficult to avoid the suspicion that *Annus Mirabilis* was a major factor in Dryden's appointment, little more than a year after the publication of the poem, as poet laureate" (*Works* 1: 259), then we also have to admit that he throve on what was disastrous to others.[8] This was true in the most obvious way if we remember that the laureateship came open when Davenant died, on 7 April 1668.

We now move forward a couple of years, years during which Dryden established himself as the purveyor of a new form of "heroic" writing designed not for the reader but for the stage. This was the public sphere in at least two senses. The most ambitious example of the new genre was *The Conquest of Granada*, which opened in December 1670. In December 1671, George Villiers, Second Duke of Buckingham, would skewer both Dryden and his new theatre in the satirical play *The Rehearsal*, where Dryden appears as the hopelessly incompetent playwright Bayes. The *Rehearsal's* performance, and even more its printing the next summer, marked the moment when the Restoration war between the theatres took a far more interesting and intellectual turn than mere rivalry between the King's and the Duke's companies, or the staged exchange of insults between rival playwrights. The turn was to a debate on styles of theatre, of performance and representation, to a metacriticism that was, simultaneously, a political battle over what sort of literature, what sort of church, and what sort of government was possible, desirable, or necessary in the 1670s.

Dryden himself had initiated the conflation of style and political stance. While the *Rehearsal* had been begun in the late 1660s as a spoof on heroic drama generally, and included in its parodic sweep the work of Davenant, Killigrew, Edward Howard, and others, its most immediate provocation and the cause of its updating was the recent runaway success of the two-part *Conquest of Granada*. Set in fifteenth-century Spain, its ostensible topic the reclamation of Granada for the Catholic monarchs Ferdinand and Isabella, the *Conquest* celebrated the obsolete values of personal military heroism and virtuous romantic love, a very different kind of the heroic than the one he had defined and defended in the Letter announcing *Annus Mirabilis*. But beyond this, Dryden had dedicated the printed text of his play, published in late February 1672, to James, Duke of York, a manifesto that rendered the play retroactively topical. (Though this printed dedication followed the production of *The Rehearsal*, it preceded its printing, and it is, of course, only the printed version we have to go on.) Beginning with the statement that "Heroique poesie has alwayes been sacred to princes and to heroes" (*Works* XI: 3), Dryden proceeded to praise his "Royal Highness" exorbitantly as the military hero of the era, from his early engagements in Europe through the first year of the Second Dutch War, before he was withdrawn from the naval command for his own safety. Before the dedication was over, Dryden had implied that the nation needed to wipe out of the historical record the "surprise" of the last stage of the Second Dutch War, when De Ruyter's fleet sailed up the Thames and Medway and burned the English fleet at Chatham, and shockingly, he implied that the consequences of Charles's negotiations with Louis XIV would be a Third Dutch War, actually declared in March 1672. As Dryden put it, "when our former enemies again provoke us, you will again solicite fate to provide you another Navy to overcome, and another Admiral to be slain. You will, then, lead forth a Nation eager to revenge their past injuries" (*Works* XI: 5). The result will be a bonus for the poet, who in August 1670 had been appointed Historiographer Royal in addition to Poet Laureate: the new war will provide him with "abundant matter to fill the Annals of a glorious Reign," allowing him to "perform the part of a just Historian to my Royal Master" (*Works* XI: 6). Given that Charles had recalled Parliament on 4 February 1672, precisely in order to request the funds for the war, the publication of Dryden's dedication in the same month could have been seen as an attempt to influence the parliamentarians to vote the king a war-chest. In other words, Dryden had not only preselected James as his hero for the Third Dutch War, about which he was evidently cognizant long before it was declared, but was effectively giving political advice to the nation.

At this point, however, the gap between the literary theory implied in the Dedication and the plays so dedicated must have become visible to Dryden. In the essay "Of Heroique Playes" that followed the Dedication, Dryden tried to smooth over the contradictions between them. For this new, essentially Restoration genre he created a partial precedent, tracing it back to Davenant and the closing of the theatres during the Commonwealth period. "It being forbidden him in the Rebellious times," wrote Dryden,

> to act Tragedies and Comedies, because they contain'd some matter of Scandal to those good people, who could more easily disposses their lawful Sovereign than endure a wanton jeast; he was forc'd to turn his thoughts another way: and to introduce the examples of moral vertue, writ in verse, and perform'd in Recitative Musique. (*Works* XI: 9)

This laid the groundwork for Dryden's new invention, the rhymed heroic play, but it did not go far enough. Having been mightily impressed by the opening lines of Ariosto's *Orlando Furioso*, Dryden had concluded, he tells us, that "an heroic play ought to be an imitation, in little of an Heroique Poem" (*Works* XI: 10), that is (although Dryden did not put it like this) a much talkier version of the Italian romantic epic. Tasso seems to have been as important an influence as Ariosto. Davenant's two *negative* principles, Love and Ambition, whose excesses the heroic poet ought to demonstrate, now become Dryden's two positive principles, Love and Valor, whose excesses and impossible demands the *Rehearsal* would restage in the register of the absurd.

If we are looking for a provocation in Dryden's manifesto that certainly caught Buckingham's attention, we should note Dryden's defense of the amount of stage fighting his heroic plays call for. Somewhat inconsistently, given his attack on his predecessor playwrights, Dryden justifies his "frequent use of Drums and Trumpets; and my representations of Battels" on the grounds that Shakespeare used them frequently:

> But, I add farther; that these warlike Instruments, and, even the representation of fighting on the Stage, are no more than necessary to produce the effects of an Heroick Play; that is, to raise the imagination of the Audience, and to perswade them, for the time, that what they behold on the Theatre is really perform'd. The Poet is, then, to endeavour an absolute dominion over the minds of the Spectators. (*Works* XI: 13–14)

The "representation of fighting on the Stage," then, is necessary to hoodwink the audience into belief that a real battle is taking place. Forgetting, apparently, Shakespeare's consummate warnings by the Chorus in *Henry V* that, particularly in the case of battles, imagination must supply the inevitable gap between representation and reality, Dryden lapses into a peculiar form of naive realism. In the *Rehearsal*, this conceptual error is corrected in the opposite direction – by having Bayes *refuse* to stage a realistic fight, replacing it with a musical duel. Because it would be indecorous, he claims, to have "men run their Swords through one another" before a female audience, he plans to show the "whole battel in the representation of two persons only, no more: and yet so lively, that . . . you would swear ten thousand men were at it, really engag'd." The two fighters will appear, "in Armor, Cap-a-pea, with their Swords drawn, and hung with a scarlet Ribbon at their wrists, (which, you know, represents fighting enough) each of 'em holding a Lute in his hand," and they will "play the battel in *Recitativo*," each man alternating between singing and waving his sword. "Recitativo" seems a clear echo of Dryden's reference to Davenant's operas as his precedent. And Johnson complains: "But, Mr. Bayes, might not we have a little fighting for I love those Plays, where they cut and slash one another, upon the Stage, for a whole hour together." Thus Buckingham not only mocks the bellicosity of Dryden's plays, but the confusions of his introductory, theoretical matter.

But the *Rehearsal*'s primary focus, I assert, is not just the *Conquest of Granada*, its primary motive not personal enmity. Its suspicions go considerably deeper, if in rather a scattered way. Twice, Bayes explains that he does not write according to "the old plain way," the second time because he does not write "to please the Country . . . but . . . for some persons of Quality." The Court/country divide is invoked against the latter by Bayes, against the former by Buckingham. That Bayes is involved in political secrets is posited. The inaudible whispers of the two old intriguers are explained as follows: "Why, Sir, (besides that it is new, as I told you before) because they are suppos'd to be Polititians; and matters of State ought not to be divulg'd." And the central premise of the two kings of Brentford (supposed, by the 1704 Key, "to be the two Brothers, the King and the Duke") was a none-too-subtle complaint that Charles, by effectively leaving his brother as his only heir, had divided the sovereignty and hence the loyalties of his people. As Bayes puts it, drawing attention to the discomfort in the political climate:

> Why, look you, sir (nay, I beseech you, be a little curious in taking notice of this, or else you'll never understand my notion of the thing), the people being embarrassed by their equal ties to both, and the sovereigns concerned in a reciprocal regard, as well to their own interest as the good of the people, may make a certain kind of – you understand me – upon which there does arise several disputes, turmoils, heart-burnings, and all that.   (1: ii)

If anyone had contributed to the tensions and ambivalences of public opinion, however, it was John Dryden, whose effusions of praise for the Duke of York had been unusually conspicuous, long before the Exclusion crisis, long before such expressions of loyalty might have been thought of as necessary.

Dryden had effectively transferred his allegiance *already* from Charles II to the man who, he was reasonably sure, would shortly become James II. This, as it turned out, was incomplete political forecasting. More interesting, the shift in allegiance was curiously related to Dryden's theory of the heroic, which was itself undergoing a transformation of its own. Clearly, the turn from contemporary military history to Love and Valor in the romantic past was independent of Dryden's attachment to James, however much he could assert that the duke might see himself in Almanzor. But the clash between the Dedication and the Essay (and who can guess which was written first?) was enough to suggest that Dryden was experiencing some discomfort in the gap between the real world of international politics and the fantasy world of the heroic play, where inevitably, even given his preference for weapons on stage, there was more high-flown talk than action.

Between *The Conquest of Granada* and Dryden's next overt political statement much would happen to complicate still further the relation between literature and events. The Exclusion Crisis, still a useful term despite the arguments of certain historians, began in 1679 with a wave of anti-Catholic panic, and was not fully over until the Whigs, who had exploited that panic for their own ends but had failed to carry a parliamentary exclusion of the duke from the succession, were in exile, or in prison, or dead. Dryden had, of course, assisted in their defeat by the brilliance of his satire *Absalom and Achitophel*, but writing that emphatically mock-heroic poem must have brought home to him the continuing absence of the truly heroic subject matter he had wanted for so long – that is, one that could express current or recent history as a military conflict in which right would also be might.

The Exclusion Crisis might have seemed to consign Dryden to writing satires instead of heroic poetry. In the dedication of *Plutarchs Lives*, a collaborative project in translation, of which the first volume appeared in 1683, Dryden said as much: "'Tis an Age indeed, which is only fit for Satyr, and the sharpest I have shall never be wanting to launce its Villanies, and its ingratitude to the Government." And when James quietly succeeded his brother in 1685, Dryden's painfully acquired zest for satire, for a good fight in print, had not been quenched, though now it ran athwart another project, that of reconciling the country to the new and aggressively Roman Catholic king, whose policy of appointing Catholics to positions of influence was already causing both fear and anger. Although he had advertised his support of James more than a decade earlier, once Dryden himself had converted to Rome, a change that occurred inconveniently close to James's accession, he opened himself once more to the charge of prudential inconsistency.

The result was *The Hind and the Panther* (1687), a poem whose genre recalls the metaphoric beasts of *Annus Mirabilis*, now metamorphosed into the protagonists of a very different kind of poem, a dialogue couched as an overgrown Aesopian fable. Dryden's *Preface* presents the moment as one of polemical warfare: "The Nation is in too high a Ferment, for me to expect either fair War, or even so much as fair Quarter from a *Reader* of the opposite Party" (*Works* IV: 119, line 103). The opposite party, in this case, was the Anglican church that Dryden had so recently extolled in *Religio Laici*. He wanted to avoid, therefore, seeming bellicose himself (though he cannot help referring to his role in the battle over the papers of the previous Duchess of York), and the *Preface* can be seen as a retraction of epic ambitions in favor of a new ethos, James's "Kindness" as expressed in his Declaration of Indulgence of 4 April 1687. The poem presents Dryden as a peace-maker, as his protagonist, the harmless Hind, stands for the hitherto persecuted Catholics of England. In Milton's terms, Dryden had made the move from the classical epic of war, and the romantic epic of Love and Valor, to the concept of passive fortitude. Dryden, too, was no longer

> sedulous to indite
> Wars, hitherto the only argument
> Heroic deemed, chief mast'ry to dissect
> With long and tedious havoc fabled knights
> In battles feigned; the better fortitude
> Of patience and heroic martyrdom
> Unsung.[9]

But why choose a beast fable as the vehicle of this message? I wonder whether Dryden looked back once more to Davenant's *Preface*, where he would have found this solution recommended for dangerous political moments:

> It appears that Poesy hath for its natural prevailings over the Understandings of Men (sometimes making her conquests with easy plainnesse, like native country Beauty) been very successful in the most grave and important occasions that the necessities of States or Mankinde have produc'd. For it may be said that *Demosthenes* sav'd the *Athenians* by the Fable or Parable of the Doggs and Wolves, in answer to King *Philip's* Proposition; And that *Menenius Agrippa* sav'd the Senate, if not *Rome*, by that of the Belly and the Hands.[10]

At any rate, he manifested Davenant's "easy plainnesse" both in the general form of the three-part poem, and thematically in the values it promotes. The final fable-within-the fable offers the tale of the "Plain good Man" (Part III, line 906) who expects the birds in his farmyard to learn peaceful coexistence, and who stands for James II as the proponent of religious toleration. In fact, Dryden uses this unassuming term three times in the thirty lines that express this farmer's character ("unsuspected plainness" in others, though pretended, can deceive him, but nevertheless "it looks as Fate with Nature's Law would strive, / To shew Plain dealing once an age may thrive"). And Dryden's new church, the Hind, is not only innocent, but herself a country person, offering to the Panther at the end of the second part both shelter and "what plain fare her cottage cou'd afford."

But the move to simple good nature was both less and more than Dryden needed at this time to express his own emotions. Nature red in tooth and claw (including the satirist's claw) is still in evidence in Part I, in Dryden's relentless survey of the various forms of Protestantism represented as beasts of prey. That ferocious satire contained its own lion, in the form of Henry VIII, "A Lyon old, obscene, and furious made by lust" (*Works* IV: 133, line 351), the originating cause of the English Reformation. One might guess from this that the poem would move decisively from lions to husbandmen, and from satire to pastoral. But Dryden could not help himself stating in the preface that he had "endeavour'd to raise" the first part of the poem, "and give it the Majestick Turn of Heroick Poesie" (*Works* IV: 122, lines 14–15). And he cannot resist allowing James a leonine character as well as a pastoral one. In the third part of the poem, the Hind defends James's policies in those terms. "The *Lyon* buys no Converts, if he did, / Beasts would be sold as fast as he cou'd bid" (*Works* IV: 167, lines 225–6), she insists, and the Catholics "pay small attendance at the *Lyon's* court . . . / Preferment is bestow'd that comes unsought" (*Works* IV: 168, lines 236, 239). Most revealingly, perhaps, at the moment when the Hind sees herself to be winning the argument with the Panther, she is suddenly, by metaphor, metamorphosed into a lion, and hence into James himself:

> Her panting foes she saw before her lye,
> And back she drew the shining weapon dry:
> As when the gen'rous *Lyon* has insight
> His equal match, he rouses for the fight;
> But when his foe lyes prostrate on the plain,
> He sheathes his paws, uncurls his angry mane;
> And, pleas'd with bloudless honours of the day,
> Walks over, and disdains th'inglorious Prey.
> So *JAMES*, if great with less we may compare,
> Arrests his rowling thunder-bolts in air;
> And grants ungratefull friends a lengthn'd space,
> T' implore the remnants of long suff'ring grace.
> (*Works* IV: 169, lines 265–76)

A magnanimous lion, however, is still a lion. And however his poet might persuade one to the contrary, James's *enforcement* of the Declaration of Indulgence, and the trial of the seven bishops who refused to promote it from the pulpits, encouraged his subjects to band together across party lines, and bring in a second William the Conqueror. If lions were inevitable, they preferred a Protestant one.

The last phase of Dryden's career as a would-be heroic poet, after the Glorious Revolution which was far from glorious for him, can only be a postscript here. Keeping the faith with the exiled James meant, for Dryden, a disappearance from the public sphere, the loss of his laureateship, and if not ignominy, certainly a long period of lying low. It has often been said that the greatest of Dryden's literary ambitions was recast into his translation of Virgil's *Aeneid*, a work he completed in 1696, at the age of sixty-six. Refusing to dedicate this grand project to William, despite the urgings of his bookseller Jacob Tonson, was in its own way an act of heroism. It was also quite brave to dedicate the *Aeneis*, as Dryden chose to call it, to John Sheffield, third Earl of Mulgrave and Marquess of Normanby, who, as Dryden's editors remind us, despite having voted in 1688 to have William share the throne with Mary, had just, in 1696, the year before the *Aeneis* appeared in print, refused to take an anti-Jacobite oath, and been dismissed from the Privy Council.[11] But when it came to *theorizing* his last great work, Dryden, it seems to me, ran out of energy. Many, surely one must feel too many, pages he wrote to usher the *Aeneis* into public view. Yet the account he now gives of the heroic poem is pure neoclassical dogma, neo-Aristotelian in its insistence on unity, and also in its rejection of Ariosto and the other moderns whom Davenant had seen as his forerunners. Much of it is taken wholesale from the preface provided by Jean Regnault de Segrais for his own 1668 translation of Virgil. The challenge of writing an epic poem for and of his time goes unmentioned. The fire is out.

NOTES

1. Sir William Davenant, *Preface to Gondibert, an Heroick Poem* (1650), in *Critical Essays of the Seventeenth Century*, ed. J. E. Spingarn, 3 vols. (Oxford, 1908–9), vol. II, p. 44.
2. Ibid., p. 14.
3. Ibid., p. 47.
4. James A. Winn, *John Dryden and his World* (New Haven, 1987), pp. 88–9.
5. *The Poems and Letters of Andrew Marvell*, ed. H. M. Margoliouth, rev. Pierre Legouis (Oxford, 1971), vol. II, pp. 307–8.
6. Ibid., vol. I, p. 137.
7. *Critical Essays*, ed. Spingarn, vol. II, pp. 10–11.
8. "Disastrous" is, of course, a value judgment. The *Third Advice* made the Battle of Lowestoft into more of a defeat for the English than was actually the case, as Dryden made it more of a victory, and less of an embarrassment. Moreover, Dryden's poem deals, as the *Advices* do not, with the second engagement of 1666, which took place on 25 July and in which the Dutch were reduced to flight. Nobody could doubt that the Fire was a disaster, but Dryden, in envisaging how it made possible a new, more elegant and more prosperous city, would be vindicated by architectural history.
9. *Paradise Lost*, IX: 27–33.
10. *Critical Essays*, ed. Spingarn, vol. II, p. 49.
11. *Works* VI: 873.

13

JOHN SPURR

The piety of John Dryden

John Dryden's reticence about religion is one of the most surprising and perplexing of the many ways in which he challenges readers and scholars. As a public poet, Dryden offered weighty statements of religious principle on several occasions, but the variety of voices that he used and his own literary and public persona, as ironic, witty, anti-clerical, and detached, often played against the gravity of his claims. And Dryden's very public path as an individual from scion of the Puritan gentry via sardonic Anglican apologist to Roman Catholic convert was mysterious. This, plainly, was no pilgrim's progress. Although his writings on religion frequently deploy images of travel and trouble, of walking, wandering, of being foot-sore and weary, lost or plodding on, there is little evidence to suggest that Dryden's own journey to the Church of Rome was protracted or difficult. Indeed religion was perhaps of only intermittent interest to Dryden, and then only on his own terms. Yet this is precisely what makes his writings on religion and his own piety so intriguing. To explore them in their historical context is to grapple with an exceptional case, with a writer, thinker, and individual who could see further than the confines of the bitter religious divisions of the seventeenth century and who could marshal imaginative and cultural resources that were beyond the grasp of many of his contemporaries.

Even to think about the material for Dryden's religious life is a rather different enterprise from engaging with the religious lives of his fellow Englishmen and women. Historians of seventeenth-century English religion are spoiled for sources. Religious publications, such as sermons, catechisms, pamphlets, and theology, dwarf other categories of printed output and we consequently know a great deal about the religious *opinions* of both the orthodox and the heterodox. From the introspective diaries of Puritans and the sectarian narratives of suffering and conversion, we know something of the religious *experience* of individuals. Thanks to his compulsive note-taking, we can share the mentality of a melancholic Puritan wood-turner from Eastcheap in London; with the benefit of the diary that he kept for forty years, we can eavesdrop on the humdrum concerns of Ralph Josselin, a Puritan cleric in Essex.[1] Higher up the social scale, we encounter one of Dryden's acquaintances, John Evelyn, diarist and virtuoso, whose surviving papers allow us to reconstruct the piety of a notable lay Anglican and his circle.[2] Yet Dryden's own life and religion are not accessible to us in quite the same way.

There are practical differences. Apart from a few letters, Dryden's writings were for public consumption. He was a playwright and a poet of public affairs, not a confessional writer in either sense of that word. He did not write to share his own spiritual joys and despair with his readers; the rare moments of apparent self-revelation "suggest above all an awareness of his own capacity for error."[3] Dryden's cast of mind was skeptical and inquiring. His imagination was suited to dialogues and debates, to the exploration of arguments, images, characters, and voices rather than to the exposition of a single authoritative point of view. But then, if it had been otherwise, he would have been a very different kind of author. For it was the job of preachers, not playwrights and poets, to speak definitively in the later seventeenth century, and Dryden was assuredly no preacher. It also has to be recognized that Dryden did not lack self-belief and could be as secure in his own certainties, even if they were a refusal of simple-minded truths, as many a divine. His contemporaries knew him as a proud and assertive man beneath his nervous public demeanor. As an artist, Dryden had a mind stocked with a classical heritage and a cosmopolitan range of reference that went far beyond the usual mental horizons of his neighbors. To have imaginatively explored the worlds of the reconquista, the conquistadores, Mughal India, pagan Rome, and early Christianity, to know and have translated Virgil, Ovid, Horace, Epicurus, and Lucretius, to have engaged with Hobbes and French literary theory, to have written "bawdy" and panegyric, all helped to shape Dryden's religious sensibilities. His intellect struck sparks off the world around him, and his literary talents allowed him to distil a thought, argument, or posture with unaffected eloquence. To take the measure of Dryden as a writer on religious themes and as a spiritual being, we must first set him against the religious context of his stormy century.

God's pampered people

> The Jews, a Headstrong, Moody, Murmuring race,
> As ever try'd th' extent and stretch of grace;
> God's pamper'd people whom, debauch'd with ease,
> No King could govern, nor no God could please;
> (Gods they had tri'd of every shape and size
> That God-smiths could produce, or Priests devise:)
> (*Absalom and Achitophel*, lines 45–50)

Dryden's portrait of the English as a "headstrong" race dates from 1681, but it encapsulated much of his own personal experience and his family history. The English were confident that they enjoyed a special relationship with God, but unfortunately they differed among themselves over the terms of that affinity. In the sixteenth century Tudor monarchs and their preachers encouraged the English to believe that they had been chosen for a leading role in the Reformation. Designed as a compromise and promoted as a national asset, the new Church of England inevitably suited some more than others. Although the church's supreme governor was now the monarch rather than the pope, bishops and other traditional forms of government had been retained; worship, liturgy, and vestments were anglicized, but remained reminiscent of their medieval antecedents; and the official doctrines of the church were Protestant, but only vaguely so. The more aggressively Protestant elements, the "godly" or "Puritans" as they became known, believed, quite rightly, that there was a long way to go before the English church was shorn of its "popish" remnants and fully "reformed" along the lines of other Protestant churches. The Catholic minority kept their heads down for the most part and preserved the "true religion" until better days might come. The Church of England, meanwhile, based its position squarely on scripture and rejoiced in its "middle way" between "popish superstition" and the disorder of those churches that followed Calvin or Luther.[4]

Dryden's family had identified themselves with the values and agenda of the Puritans within the Church of England. His grandfather Sir Erasmus Dryden, who was imprisoned under James I for Puritan petitioning, sheltered the fiery preacher John Dod in his own house. John Dryden's upbringing in the godly atmosphere of the Dryden household at Titchmarsh and the Pickering home at Aldwinckle, where his uncle was vicar, exposed him to the liturgy of the Church of England, to the Bible, probably in King James's Authorized version of 1611, and to the deeply rooted English tradition of "anti-popery." His childhood coincided with the dark years of the 1630s, when godly hopes were dashed by the overbearing policies of Charles I and Archbishop Laud, who seemed intent on taking the English church back toward Rome. The godly gentry, for all their conservative social and political instincts, were deeply suspicious of Charles I. Some stood up for their principles: Dryden's maternal grandfather, John Pickering, died after spending a year in prison for opposing the king's "forced loan." So it was with a familial heritage of principled activism and godly values that Dryden was packed off to school at Westminster during the 1640s.

At Westminster Dryden received a rigorous classical education and encountered the royalism of the school's headmaster and many of its pupils. He must also have experienced at least some of the turmoil of civil war London. Dryden's subsequent undergraduate career at Cambridge did nothing to deepen his Puritan attachments. He would have maintained the conventional regime of chapel, prayers and Bible-reading alongside his studies, but he would also have been aware of the religious radicalism sweeping the country. In the 1640s the Presbyterians, the traditionalist wing of the Puritan movement, had assumed control of the universities, but by the following decade their radical rivals, the Independents, had achieved national political ascendancy and were clamoring for change. They were hostile to the ethos of the universities and questioned the value of those arcane studies in dead languages by which Dryden and his tutors set such store. For a bookish young man like Dryden, a career as an academic or clergyman was the obvious path, but there was little to tempt him along that route when he graduated in 1654. It was an unpropitious time to enter the ministry. Oliver Cromwell, now Lord Protector, maintained an uneasy religious peace, allowing a variety of divines, Presbyterians, Independents, and even former Anglicans, to serve as parish ministers, but he had done little to stem the rising tide of religious radicals such as the millenarian Fifth Monarchy men or the nascent Quaker movement. We know so little of Dryden's views in the 1650s, especially in the religious sphere, that we can only surmise that he found Presbyterianism unappealing and that he was – as he remained throughout his life – deeply antagonistic to anarchic, anti-intellectual, sectarianism. On leaving Cambridge, Dryden exploited a family connection to gain a clerk's job in the Cromwellian administration and began to set up as a poet.

The return of the monarchy in 1660 brought the aspiring poet opportunities to practice his skills in panegyric. He lauded the coronation of Charles II by the Anglican bishops, "How justly from the Church that Crown is due, / Preserv'd from ruine and restor'd by you!" (*To his Sacred Majesty*, lines 47–8). In fact Charles had not as yet restored the Church of England. The complex process that led to the 1662 Act of Uniformity involved factious Puritans, devious politicians, and scheming bishops. It resulted in the return of the Church of England as it had been before the Civil Wars and the creation of a new minority, the "Nonconformists," which included learned ministers and "enthusiastic" sectaries, Presbyterians and Independents, Quakers and Baptists. This hybrid Nonconformity was then subjected to a series of punitive laws known as the "Clarendon Code." Yet strange to tell, the position of the Church of England, for all its legal privileges, was far from robust. The church's political backers, especially Charles II, were unreliable and popular support was muted. Although as a known quantity the church was a valuable force for social and spiritual stability, the majority of the population did not relish the pretensions of the bishops, the persecution of fellow Protestants by the "penal laws," and the strident political tone of the new generation of Anglican clergy. Most strikingly, the Church of England's authority over the consciences of the English people was now cruelly exposed as resting on legislation rather than the church's intrinsic moral and theological authority.

These religious factors informed but did not dominate Dryden's life and writing in the 1660s and 1670s. He was too busy becoming a fashionable and successful playwright, joining all the right institutions, such as the Royal Society, and moving in the witty, libertine, court circle of the Duke of Buckingham, Sir Charles Sedley and the Earl of Rochester. His conformity to the Church of England was unremarkable and, one suspects, lukewarm. His references to the church are few and far between, and occasionally barbed; for example, he commends "the religion which I profess, to which all men who desire to be esteemed good and honest are obliged" – note the evident cynicism in the choice of the word "esteemed" as if Anglicanism guaranteed the appearance rather than the reality of virtue.[5] His mind and art ranged well beyond the boundaries of Anglican orthodoxy. When a series of disasters – defeat at the hands of the Dutch, the Plague and the Fire of London – set preachers and people asking why God was pouring out his wrath against the English, Dryden also took up the question. His historical poem *Annus Mirabilis, The Year of Wonder, 1666* tapped into conventional Anglican concern with providence and prophecy. It endorsed the commonplace views that universal sin is a provocation of God, that Cromwell was a divine scourge, and that a devout monarch could aspire to protect his people to some extent, but it also drew upon classical, especially Virgilian, ideas about submission to providence and pious dedication to one's country. Dryden's view of divine providence was altogether more complex and resonant than that retailed from the Church of England's pulpits.

Annus Mirabilis was written at Charlton, the Wiltshire house of Thomas Howard, Earl of Berkshire and Dryden's father-in-law. When Dryden married Elizabeth Howard in 1663, he established an intimate connection with a branch of one of England's great aristocratic families. Moreover he acquired an entrée into the English Catholic community since many of the Howards were Roman Catholics or sympathetic to Rome. While Dryden's father- and mother-in-law may well have been Catholics, his brother-in-law Charles, later the second Earl of Berkshire, was a "recusant," an open Catholic, and it is quite possible that Elizabeth Dryden herself was a clandestine Catholic.

Among the extended Howard family was Philip, later Cardinal Howard, who was to be a patron to one of Dryden's sons in Rome in the 1690s. Cosmopolitan and aristocratic, the English Catholic community was also politically quiescent and careful, for Roman Catholicism was no mere private matter in Restoration England.

Even the most restrained of the English were convinced that "popery" was a threat to "liberty, property and religion," namely parliamentary monarchy, the common law, low taxation, and Protestantism. "Popery" signified an international conspiracy of Jesuits, orchestrated by the papacy and inspired by the doctrine that no loyalty was owed to heretical rulers. For decades the Spanish monarchy had been the leading secular representative of popery, but of recent years Spain had been eclipsed by Louis XIV. Powerful, bellicose, Catholic, and too close for comfort, Louis was also a cousin to and, many feared, a role model for Charles II and his heir and brother James, Duke of York. By the early 1670s, such forebodings were proving correct. In 1672 Charles went to war, in alliance with Louis, against the Protestant Netherlands. To pave the way for war he unilaterally declared an "indulgence" or religious toleration that allowed Catholics freedom of private worship and Protestant Dissenters liberty of licensed public worship. This suspended the operation of all the "penal laws," some of which dated back to the days of Elizabeth I, against Catholic and Protestant dissidents from the Church of England. Both Dryden's Northamptonshire Nonconformist relatives and his Catholic Howard relations would have benefited from the "indulgence." Predictably, given the strength of anti-popery, many Protestants resented any unconstitutional improvement in the position of Catholics even if it benefited fellow Protestants. It now also became public knowledge that the Duke of York was a Catholic. Parliament expressed its displeasure by passing the Test Act (1673) to ban "papists" from public office. Public anxieties swirled around several issues. The growing influence of "popery," in the shape of French mistresses and Catholic priests, and the danger of "arbitrary government," represented by Charles's minister Danby, a tame parliament, and an authoritarian Church of England, made for an uneasy decade.

Dryden's devotion to the theatre did not prevent him from commenting on public affairs and literary matters, if more rarely on religion. In the 1660s *The Indian Emperor* discussed some fundamental questions: Montezuma laments that, unsure of religious truth, "human kind must wander in the dark"; the Catholic priest acknowledges that reason points to the existence of a deity to be adored, but divine revelation tells us more; and then he urges the pagans to accept the infallible Roman Catholic church, "renounce that carnal reason, and believe" (v. ii. lines 58, 71–2, 91). In *Tyrannic Love*,

St. Catherine the Christian martyr counsels that "faith's necessary Rules are plain and few," and if we give way to needless speculation then "faith from our hearts into our heads we drive" (IV. i. 548, 550). In the 1670s, *The Conquest of Granada* and *Aureng-Zebe* reflected upon problems of political leadership and moral authority and revealed Dryden's interest in Hobbesian psychology. Dryden was also digesting the achievement of Milton's *Paradise Lost*, which he was to versify as *The State of Innocence*. A striking characteristic of Dryden's religious comments in this period is a disdain for the clergy. Sometimes embodied in a character – as in *The Spanish Friar* – and sometimes delivered in a glancing blow: plays could offer examples of piety, he asserted in one preface, "for to leave the employment altogether to the Clergie, were to forget that Religion was first taught in Verse (which the laziness or dulness of succeeding Priesthood, turned afterwards into Prose)." Dryden exhibited little doubt that "Priests of all Religions are the same," venal, self-seeking, and hypocritical.[6]

In 1678 England succumbed to a complex three-year political crisis. Suspicion that Charles and Danby were eroding parliamentary independence and pursuing client status with Louis XIV was one strand. Hostility to the Duke of York's eventual succession to the throne was a second. And the third was a hysteria about a popish plot to murder Charles in order to ease James's way to the crown (or, in some versions, to murder both brothers), fire the City of London, massacre the Protestant innocents, and roll back 150 years of Reformation. From the political chaos there emerged two political labels, Whig and Tory, the former associated with the demand to exclude James from the succession and to ease the position of Protestant Nonconformists and the latter with a defense of traditional hereditary monarchy and the exclusive claims of the Church of England. Dryden's satirical poem *Absalom and Achitophel* memorably opens with the anticlerical gibe, "in pious times, e'r Priestcraft did begin," before launching a devastating attack on the Whig leaders and their allies.[7] The poem makes play with the divisions of the English by creating a kind of parallel universe from the biblical account of Absalom's rebellion against King David (2 Samuel: 13–18). Dryden's poem is only one of the many contemporary applications of the scripture story to current politics, and is, of course, a reminder of just how conversant Dryden and his readers were with the Bible. Dryden catalogues the religious propensities of the English and reveals the dangers the nation faces. The "Jebusites" or Catholics are derided for doctrines such as transubstantiation – "such savory Deities must needs be good, / As serv'd at once for Worship and for Food" (lines 120–1) – and their clergy are castigated for fomenting plots. At the other, Protestant, extreme are the "dreaming Saints" and the "old Enthusiastick breed" whose aim is to destroy all order and trust only in divine inspiration (lines 529–30). The "Hot Levites" or Nonconformists

> Resum'd their Cant, and with a Zealous Cry,
> Pursu'd their old belov'd Theocracy.
> Where Sanhedrin and Priest inslav'd the Nation
> And justifi'd their Spoils by Inspiration.
>
> (lines 521–4)

The danger of anarchy is not to be laid solely at the door of the sects and tub-thumping "fanatic" preachers, it was also the responsibility of the thought-less masses: "But far more numerous was the herd of such / Who think too little, and who talk too much" (lines 533–4).

In the 1680s, Dryden was turning to poetry and translation, and he began to address some major religious questions directly and at length. In *Religio Laici* he chose a supposedly "unpolished, rugg'd Verse . . . as fittest for Discourse, and nearest Prose" (lines 453–4) to make a reasoned defense of the Church of England's view of reason and revelation against the doubts of "deists" and Catholics. Confident and measured, this poem of November 1682 reads like the testimony of a layman who has worked through the arguments for himself and has reached an intellectually and emotionally satisfying position. Yet in January 1685 attentive readers of *Sylvae*, a miscellany of translations in which Dryden's was the guiding hand, would have spotted that he was now exploring questions about the limits of human reason and the nature of faith through the prism of Lucretius' poems. In March Dryden's elegy for Charles II, *Threnodia Augustalis*, appeared, not only full of praise for the new Catholic James II, but also revealing traces of Roman Catholic devotion such as the invocation of saints.[8] In all probability it was at some stage in 1685 that Dryden converted to Roman Catholicism. On 19 January 1686, John Evelyn recorded the rumour that "Dryden the famous play-poet & his two sonns, & Mrs Nelle [Gwyn] . . . were said to go to Masse; & such purchases were no great losse to the Church."[9]

Dryden's conversion was a gift to his literary enemies and his Protestant critics. It looked to all the world as though the Poet Laureate had simply adopted the religion of the new monarch to feather his own nest. But there is no evidence that Dryden profited from his change of religion or contributed much more than a little propaganda work to help James II re-convert the nation.[10] In a jocular letter to Etherege of February 1687, Dryden claimed to have seen James only once in seven months. He lamented the King's break with his Anglican allies – "he will not much advance his affaires by Stirring" – and suggested that he would do better to emulate his predecessor's "noble idleness."[11] The talk of the town in 1686 and 1687 repeatedly associated

Dryden's name with prestigious university posts such as head of Trinity College, Dublin, Eton, All Souls or Magdalen College, Oxford. Yet he was technically unqualified as "he had not actually put himself into Holy Orders, which was a great oversight" and it seems unlikely that as a Catholic layman he would now seek Anglican ordination.[12] Of course, college statutes were not insuperable and even if Dryden was "very pensive and melancholy" at not winning the Presidency of Magdalen, he could take heart from seeing his young Catholic son, John, imposed upon the college as a fellow in 1688.[13] At the Glorious Revolution, Dryden's religious and political allegiances cost him his position as Poet Laureate and left him marginalized and even suspect in the eyes of the authorities. Yet Dryden never reneged on his conversion to Roman Catholicism.

In 1687 Dryden's curious poem *The Hind and the Panther* had celebrated his new church. Thereafter his writing followed a different direction. The poetry and translations of his last decade tend to present Dryden as hemmed in by domesticity and age, exploring themes of exile and wandering, family and inheritance. He was, of course, still attending dinner parties, sitting for his portrait, haggling with Tonson, and working; "I am still drudging on: always a Poet, and never a good one."[14] Among these last poems was the verse epistle to his cousin John Driden of Chesterton, a poem which sees him reflecting on rustic serenity and political involvement, enduring literary fame and the inevitable decay of human beings – "a pamper'd Race of Men" (line 90) – and the upheavals of the century and his family's part in them. The poem links these two John Drydens, one a staunch Protestant patriot and the other, of course, a Jacobite and Catholic – "One to perform, another to record" (line 203) – and seeks to associate the poet's current suffering with his family's tradition of courageous and loyal opposition under the first Stuarts.[15]

A certain kind of noble pride?

Dryden did not reveal much of himself in his writings. Tempting though it is to regard some of his lines as pregnant with autobiography – "anxious Thoughts in endless Circles roul / Without a Centre where to fix the Soul" (*Religio Laici*, lines 36–7) – we have no warrant to apply individual lines or images to his religious life. He wrote about religion, virtue, and piety in many different guises and he also had his own, quite distinct, interior life. Yet it would be as much a mistake to isolate his writing from his spirituality as it would be to conflate them with each other. There are questions of temperament to consider. "If I am not mistaken, the distinguishing Character of Lucretius; (I mean of his Soul and Genius) is a certain kind of noble pride, and positive assertion of his Opinions," wrote Dryden in the preface to *Sylvae*. "From his time to ours, I know none so like him, as our Poet and Philosopher of Malmesbury." The "Dogmatical way" of a Lucretius or a Hobbes intrigued Dryden, not least because such "sublime and daring Genius" was allied to powerful poetic gifts. And for all Dryden's repeated claims of "natural Diffidence and Scepticism," for all the disingenuousness ("if I am not mistaken"), and the very real chasm between the principles of the poet and those of Lucretius or Hobbes, was he not also drawn to Lucretius who "is everywhere confident of his own reason" (*Works* II: 10–11)? Discernible throughout Dryden's writing is a personal determination to follow conscience and reason, to exercise moral and intellectual responsibility, and to confront ethical questions on terms that went well beyond the conventional Christian formulations.

Dryden was heir to a tradition of western philosophical and literary exploration of human happiness which turned on such issues as overcoming the fear of death and loss, accepting the vicissitudes of life and love, defining pleasure and virtue, and choosing between care and ease, the active and the contemplative life. Christianity, on the other hand, does not even expect human happiness. As sinners, human beings can do no more than submit to the will of God in this life and anticipate true happiness in the next. *Religio Laici* is condescending toward the pagan philosophers:

> But least of all could their Endeavours find
> What most concern'd the good of Humane kind:
> For Happiness was never to be found;
> But vanish'd from 'em, like Enchanted ground.
>
> (lines 25–8)

Yet the Christian seventeenth century did not generally dismiss its classical heritage quite this easily. The Stoics, Epicureans, and Aristotelians who are the subject of Dryden's facile lines provided a rich vein of ethical debate and a constant questioning of Christian assumptions which worked to open up discussion among seventeenth-century intellectuals.

Materialism, in the sense that the world is a random creation of material particles, was one of the most obvious challenges facing religion in the seventeenth century. The revival of ancient theories of materialism, such as those of Democritus and Epicurus, and the new materialism of Gassendi or Hobbes, confronted basic Christian beliefs about the existence of non-material entities such as souls or spirits, the purposeful creation of the world, divine oversight or providence of earthly affairs, the possibility of a "future state" or life after death, and even the existence of God.[16] The fascination exerted by such ideas is evident from the strange spell cast by *De rerum natura*, the Latin poet

Lucretius' exposition of Epicurean teachings. The Puritan Lucy Hutchinson "translated it only out of a youthful curiosity to understand things I heard so much discussion of at second hand." The atheism and arrogance of "this dog" only revealed to her "the insufficiency of human reason (how great an idol soever it is now become among the gown-men) to arrive to any pure and simple truth, with all its helps of art and study."[17] In repentance she composed a poem on Genesis "to wash out all ugly wild impressions, and fortifie my mind with a strong antidote against all the poison of humane Wit and Wisdome that I have been dabbling withal."[18] John Evelyn, a steadfast Anglican, had gone so far as to publish his translation of Book 1 of Lucretius, only to make amends with a massive manuscript *Rational Account of the True Religion Asserting the most Antient to be the Best.*[19] Dryden, who had considered translating Lucretius since the 1660s, was neither so cautious nor so apologetic as some of his predecessors. His preface to *Sylvae* pronounced Lucretius' teachings of the soul's mortality as "so absurd that I cannot if I would believe them. I think a future state demonstrable even by natural arguments." He then translated Lucretius on the fear of death, the nature of love and of the physical world, without casting a glance in the direction of Christian orthodoxy. At about this time, he also wrote the bleak poem *To the Memory of Mr Oldham*, which is utterly devoid of any Christian consolation: "Thy Brows with Ivy, and with Laurels bound; / But Fate and gloomy Night encompass thee around" (lines 24–5). In his poetry, at least, Dryden could contemplate a universe without the comforts of revealed religion.

Revealed religion was under attack from other quarters besides the atheists, Epicureans and Hobbesians. "Anti-scripturists" or "deists" questioned the need for a revelation of the divine will. Lord Herbert of Cherbury had famously proposed five principles which were accessible to all human beings by the use of their reason and which were adequate for salvation. These are the existence of a God, a duty to worship God, a recognition that virtue is the fundamental duty, a need to repent of vice, and the existence of rewards and punishments after this life. From yet another direction came Roman Catholic criticism of the Bible as a sufficient "rule of faith." Rome taught that the church, meaning the papacy and general councils of the bishops, was an unerring guide in matters of faith. By comparison to the infallibility of the church, the Bible was an unreliable source of Christian teaching. This was in part because individuals interpret the scriptures differently, but also because the text of the Bible had become corrupt. In 1678 Richard Simon, a French Catholic priest, published a controversial *Critical History of the Old Testament* which demonstrated the errors that had crept into the text over the centuries. The translation of Simon's book into English in 1682 was the ostensible occasion for Dryden's *Religio Laici*.

From the epigraph to its concluding lines, *Religio Laici* proclaims itself an explanation, a discourse, an attempt to "reason men into truth," but we would do well to remember that it is a poem not a tract. The poem falls into two halves addressing first the deist case and then the Catholic arguments of Father Simon. Dryden asserts the need for a revelation of God's will and offers evidence that this revelation is contained in the scriptures. A "general Law," objects the deist, "must to all, and every where be known" (lines 170–1), or, in other words, the gospel could not be necessary because God had not given the people of America or pre-Christian Greece a chance to hear it. Dryden answered that we must leave this to God and "the secret paths of Providence" (line 187): "It has always been my thought, that Heathens, who never did, nor without Miracle cou'd hear of the name of Christ were yet in a possibility of Salvation" (Preface). Turning to Simon's book, he first praises the translation but then turns the tables on its argument about textual corruption; "if written words from time are not secur'd, / How can we think have oral Sounds endur'd?" (lines 270–1). He misrepresents papal infallibility as a claim to be "omniscient" and jeers at the medieval priests' "gainful Trade" of keeping the laity ignorant (lines 282, 371ff.). The Bible, claims Dryden, is clear on all necessary points and any interpretation required should come from the "unsuspected Ancients" (line 436), the early fathers of the church, not the modern papacy. He readily admits that recent history shows the dangers that flow from allowing everyone to interpret scripture:

> The Book thus put in every vulgar hand,
> Which each presum'd he best cou'd understand,
> The Common Rule was made the common Prey,
> And at the mercy of the Rabble lay.
>
> (lines 400–3)

The only solution is to avoid each extreme, to remember that "Faith is not built on disquisitions vain; / The things we must believe, are few, and plain"; in the end private interpretations must always bow to the over-riding claim of the "Common quiet" (lines 430–1, 450). A familiar image once again comes to mind: "Th' unletter'd Christian, who believes in gross, / Plods on to Heaven; and ne'er is at a loss" (lines 322–3).

Religio Laici has been combed for clues to Dryden's sources and adversaries and for signs of his early inclination toward Rome. Such scholarship has confirmed the conventionality of Dryden's arguments. The preface acknowledges his dependence on Anglican writings and his consultation of a friend who is widely believed to have been John Tillotson, a future archbishop. The pivot of Dryden's case was the reliance on human reason to comprehend only as much as was necessary. Poetically figured in the opening image of the dim light of reason serving as the "moon and stars" to guide weary travelers, then "pale grows Reason at Religions sight; / So dyes, and so dissolves in Supernatural Light" (lines 10–11). The century's long and repetitive debate between Anglicans and Catholics over the guide or "rule of faith" had produced classic statements from Hales, Laud, Stillingfleet, and Tillotson, among others, about the role of reason. William Chillingworth explained that the Church of England did expect individuals "in the choice of their way to happiness" to follow "right reason grounded on divine revelation, and common notions written by God in the hearts of all men, and deducing, according to the never failing rules of logic, consequent deductions from them."[20] Anglicans were confident that necessary truths were few and plain, that some truths would be above human reason but none would be contrary to it.[21] Or, in Dryden's words,

> Let us be content at last to know God by his own methods, at least so much of him as he is pleased to reveal to us in the sacred scriptures; to apprehend them to be the word of God is all our reason has to do, for all beyond it is the work of faith, which is the seal of heaven impressed upon our human understanding.
> (*Religio Laici*, Preface)

Reason helps us to begin the journey toward God, but it does not conclude it: "They who would prove religion by reason do but weaken the cause which they endeavour to support" (Preface).

Within a few years, Dryden had dramatically changed his view and embraced the Roman Catholic church as the "one unerring guide." There is nothing to tell us how and why he took this step in 1685, although later poems and letters may contain clues. There was, of course, a context to his conversion which is relevant, but which is unlikely to have determined the decision made by a man so intent on measuring matters for himself. Dryden's monarch, James II, and his own sons were Roman Catholics. It was also revealed that Charles II had undergone a deathbed conversion to Rome in February 1685. Although it is implausible that Dryden took his cue from the royal brothers, the propaganda with which James II publicized the late king's conversion reveals some of the conventional arguments that Dryden was later to use in his own poetry.

It was claimed that Charles II had left a manuscript justification of his conversion. These "strongbox papers" were disseminated by James II, at first privately: he showed them, for instance, to Pepys who in turn rushed to share them with his friend Evelyn; but the pious Evelyn characteristically both brushed them off as the "usual Topics" and looked out tracts to rebut them. Later James had the papers published, along with an account of the conversion of his own first wife, Anne Hyde, Duchess of York, who had died as a Catholic in 1670. Dryden played a minor part in the defense of these papers against Anglican pamphleteers and clashed with Edward Stillingfleet over the Protestants' lack of insight into the virtue of humility. Whether many of the population could still be shocked by the behavior and views of their late monarch is debatable, but the furore aired some of the standard Catholic objections against the Protestant churches. The papers exposed, for example, what to Catholic eyes was the Church of England's dilemma over personal judgment:

> Every man thinks himself as competent a Judge of the Scriptures as the very Apostles themselves; and 'tis no wonder that it should be so, since that part of the Nation, which looks most like a Church, dares not bring the true Arguments against the other Sects, for fear they should be turned against themselves, and confuted by their own Arguments.[22]

These were arguments that Dryden was familiar with long before his conversion, and it would be naive to assume that religious apologetic was in itself a decisive factor in his or, indeed, anyone else's choice of church in the reign of James II. One of the most subtle studies of conversion in the seventeenth century has suggested that this was a process which in many cases might combine an experience of grace, a desire to protect one's person, family, and property, a compulsion to demonstrate political loyalty, and other motives, rather than a simple once-and-for-all change of institutional membership.[23] Certainly when he discussed Anne Hyde's conversion Dryden chose to emphasize the emotional impact upon her of the Christian lives of Roman Catholics, especially their devotion, austerity, charity, and humility.[24]

In May 1687 Dryden published his enigmatic 2,500-line beast fable *The Hind and the Panther*. To Etherege it showed Dryden's "noble Ambition to restaur Poetry to it's auncient dignitie in wrapping up the Misteries of Religion in verse."[25] It has intrigued and puzzled literary scholars: Dryden's modern biographer judges it to be a "fascinating risk-taking failure."[26] What was Dryden up to with this poem? "I was always in some hope, that the Church of England might have been perswaded to have taken off the Penal Lawes and the Test, which was one Design of the Poem when I propos'd to my self the writing of it," he claimed in the preface (*Works* III: 121). This emphasis on the poem as a personal rather than a commissioned project is significant. If Dryden really aspired to persuade the Anglicans to cooperate in lifting the laws which discriminated against Catholics and Nonconformists, he was distinctly out of touch with royal policy. Just two weeks after the poem was finished, James II issued a Declaration of Indulgence that unilaterally extended freedom of worship to Catholics and Nonconformists. In doing so

James made it plain that he had no intention of working with the Church of England and its political allies. Although a major poem by Dryden had to be construed as an intervention in public debate, this work, with its mysterious symbols and shifting fables, and its apparent political misjudgment, is not the work of a pen writing for a party.

The Hind and the Panther is in three parts. The first introduces the Hind which represents the Church of Rome, the Panther which figures the Church of England, and the beasts of the forest, the bears, apes, boars, foxes, and wolves, who stand for the various other sects and denominations. Since it consists "mostly in general Character and Narration," Dryden claims to have written this in the style of "Heroick Poesie." Part II, a theological exchange between Hind and Panther, "being Matter of Dispute, and chiefly concerning Church Authority, I was oblig'd to make as plain and perspicuous as I possibly cou'd." The third part Dryden might claim to be akin to "Domestick Conversation" and thus "more free and familiar" in its language, but it is the longest and most difficult section of the poem (*Works* III: 122). The Hind and Panther each recount a fable. The Hind "mark'd the malice of the tale" told by the Panther (line 640). A far from veiled warning, it tells of swallows persuaded to stay beyond the end of summer by a martin, who seems to represent one of James II's advisers, Father Petre, and their subsequent suffering when the winter snows return. The Hind's fable is of a farmyard, presided over by "a Plain Good man" (or James), into which the doves (or Anglican clergy) invite a buzzard to overawe the poultry (or Roman Catholic clergy). Inevitably the buzzard establishes a tyranny that oppresses all of the denizens of the farmyard.

The arguments of the first two parts are commonplace, albeit that Dryden now speaks from the Catholic benches. The anomalous nature of the Church of England, so similar to Rome in structure and yet so different in tenets, remains a central issue: its bishops and government "shew'd affectation of an ancient line," but its alleged Calvinism is a blot (Part I, line 397). "Least deform'd, because reform'd the least," the English church is "the fairest of the fallen crew" (lines 409, 450). Yet it was "neither lov'd nor fear'd" by other Protestant denominations (line 497). The Hind alleges that the Reformation was founded in greed and self-indulgence and that the English church evaded "the main question" of the real presence in the eucharist (Part II, line 28). And now under James II, Anglican claims of political loyalty have been exposed as sham. Above all, the Church of England lacked "innate auctority" (Part I, line 453). Having unleashed private conscience, the Protestant church is unable or unwilling to reassert authority: "shall she command, who has herself rebell'd?" (Part II, line 279). Without authority, interpretation of scripture will go unchecked: "the word's a weathercock for every wind" and that way lies damnation (Part I, line 462). The Church of Rome, however, was ready to shoulder the burden of being an infallible guide. The Hind proclaims herself in the words of Christ, "She whom ye seek am I." Taking the "marks" of a true church from the Nicene Creed, the Church of Rome announces its authority:

> One in herself not rent by schism, but sound,
> Entire, one solid shining Diamond,
> Not sparkles shatter'd into sects like you,
> One is the church, and must be to be true:
> One central principle of unity.
> As undivided, so from errours free,
> As one in faith, so one in sanctity.
>
> (Part II, lines 526–32)

This poem is more than an argument. It is a "mysterious writ" (Part III, line 2), deliberately allusive, ambiguous, even esoteric, in its language and emblems. Its literary techniques may aspire to the sublime.[27] Its figures have been related to those in other sources: the Hind has been associated with the persecuted roe or hind in chapters 8 and 11 of the Book of Daniel. For some critics, the poem is a response to charges of Catholic idolatry and a reaffirmation of "the poetry of Roman Catholic iconic worship in a prophecy of inevitable English reconversion to the true faith";[28] others have traced elaborate parallels with the imagery, characters, and narrative of the Song of Songs and drawn attention to the sexualized language and apocalyptic overtones of the poem.[29] This is not the place to judge the aesthetic power and coherence of this carefully wrought text, nor should we regard it necessarily as a summative statement of Dryden's own religious experience. Yet even in this elaborate work Dryden stages moments of apparent personal disclosure. The authorial voice accepts the need for an unerring guide and prays "O teach me to believe Thee thus conceal'd / And search no farther than thy self reveal'd." Earlier he had "follow'd false lights" and then "My pride struck out new sparkles of her own. / Such was I, such by nature still I am, / Be thine the glory, and be mine the shame" (Part I, lines 68–9, 74–7). Against this self-abnegation we might weigh some later lines from a digression refuting allegations that Dryden had converted for his own gain: in "suff'ring from ill tongues he bears no more / Than what his Sovereign bears, and what his Saviour bore" (Part III, lines 304–5). Does Dryden's apparently unwitting equation of his own suffering with that of Christ betray a real struggle with pride? There is much about Dryden that suggests his search for religious truth was based on a pride in his own intellect, especially when compared to that of clergymen, but there is also a constant admission that the light of reason is puny before the glory of God. To the end of Dryden's life, this characteristic combination of humility before God and personal pride remains visible. "I can never go an Inch beyond my Conscience and my Honour" in matters of religion and politics, he wrote to Mrs. Steward in 1699.

> I can . . . not forsake my Religion, because I know not what Church to go to, if I leave the Catholique; they are all so divided amongst them selves in matters of faith, necessary to Salvation: & yet all assumeing the name of Protestants. May God be pleasd to open your Eyes, as he has opend mine: Truth is but one; & they who have once heard of it, can plead no Excuse, if they do not embrace it.[30]

Piety and poetry

There was a strained relationship between Dryden's religious positions and his standing in his own day as a poet and, particularly, a religious poet. Time and time again Dryden explicitly raised the question of whether as a poet and a layman he was qualified to discuss religion, the province of the divine, before he went on to do just that. Not all of his readers were as convinced as Dryden of his suitability for the job. "Let me tell you, Mr. Bayes, your best Friends declare you a more competent Judge of some sort of Wit and Delight, than of Religion, or any Controversie about it," wrote Martin Clifford, who was no friend of Dryden.[31]

Legion though they were, the literary enmities surrounding Dryden need not detain us. It was his reputation as a mocker of religion, an inveterate anti-clerical, and a cynical professional writer that had a negative influence on the reception of his religious writings. He complained bitterly of being wrong-fully accused – "my Sense wire-drawn into Blasphemy and Bawdry" – when Jeremy Collier catalogued his atheism, anti-clericalism and blasphemy.[32] His play-writing was ridiculed: a Dryden figure advises a novice playwright, "mark it for infallible, in all you write reflect upon religion and the Clergy; you can't imagine how it tickles."[33] Similar fun was made of his alleged for-mula for writing a religious poem. Another "Mr. Bayes" opined that "'tis the advantage of our Coffee-house, that from their talk one may write a very good polemical discourse, without ever troubling ones head with the Books of Controversie. For I can take the slightest of their Arguments, and clap 'em pertly into four Verses, which shall stare any London divine in the face."[34] Dryden's hypocrisy stuck in the throats of his critics. "How ridiculously doth he appear in Print for any Religion, who hath made it his business to laugh at all!" jeered Clifford. "How can he stand up for any mode of Worship, who hath been accustomed to bite, and spit his venom against the very Name thereof?"[35] Dryden's readers vented their spleen on his poems directly. "The Poet an Atheist exceeding Lucretius," wrote one reader on his copy of *Absalom*. "There are no Pagan Divinities in the Scheme" of *Absalom*, complained Collier, "so that all the Atheistick Raillery must point upon the true God." "Atheisticall," scrawled Luttrell on his copy of *Religio Laici*. Henry Care, the Whig journalist, lambasted the "Obscure and Atheistical Sheets" of "a certain mercenary Versificator."[36] Another pamphleteer complained of Dryden's "Atheism and Impiety" and asserted that *Religio Laici* is "Befooling Religion by impious and inept Rhymes."[37] We should note that how Dryden wrote about religion was no less significant than what he said. "Inept rhymes" would damn him just as quickly as atheism in the eyes of his adversaries.

When Dryden chose to write a poem rather than a pamphlet on a religious subject, he presumably hoped to move and delight his readers as well as convince them. His repeated discussion of the very language that he was using in these pieces is a sign that it was important to the effect and not just the argument of the poems. In the mid-1670s he took from Longinus the notion of "imaging" as the essence of poetry: it is "a Discourse, which, by a kind of Enthusiasm, or extraordinary emotion of the Soul, makes it seem to us that we behold those things which the Poet paints, so as to be pleas'd with them, and to admire them" (*Works* XII: 94). So the imaging of journeys and light, of beasts and conversations, mattered deeply to the poetic enterprise, as did the language and verse. Yet the critical reaction was mixed. "Great King of verse," Thomas Creech addressed Dryden in a commendatory poem to *Religio Laici*; "Thy judgement is correct, thy fancy young, / Thy numbers, as thy generous faith, are strong." The Earl of Roscommon was just as laudatory:

> Let free, impartial men from Dryden learn
> Mysterious secrets of a high concern,
> And weighty truths, solid convincing sense,
> Explained by unaffected eloquence.[38]

But the prominent clergyman Gilbert Burnet was disappointed by *Religio Laici*: "Mr Dryden's 'Religion of a Layman' is farre below what might have been expected of him on such a subject." The tenor of his letter suggests that he found the poem insufficiently exalted.[39] *The Hind and the Panther* was always going to have a rough ride in a predominantly Protestant country, but critics had a field day with its obscurity. Dryden had supposed his subject "too great for Prose; for he is too proud, to creep servilly after sense; so that in his Verse, he soares high above the reach of it; to do this, there is no need of Brain; 'tis but scanning right; the labour is in the Finger, not the Head."[40] Others complained that the poem broke the conventions of fable with the beasts changing personae and acting out of character: "If you say he means the Church, how does the Church feed on lawns, or range in the Forest? Let it always be a Church, or always the cloven-footed Beast, for we cannot bear his shifting the scene every Line."[41]

Dryden did not play the game. Whether in terms of fable or seventeenth-century religious categories, he was idiosyncratic, even unorthodox, in his approach. In a century when one was supposed to wear one's religion on one's sleeve, Dryden donned a series of different coats. On occasion we may glimpse something approaching a conventional, even platitudinous, defense of his life: God had opened his eyes to the realization that truth is but one, he told Mrs Steward in 1699. "For my principles of Religion, I will not justifie them to you. I know yours are far different," he wrote to John Dennis in 1693. "For the same Reason I shall say nothing of my Principles of State. I believe you in yours follow the Dictates of your Reason, as I in mine do those of my Conscience. If I thought myself in an Error, I would retract it; I am sure that I suffer for them; and Milton makes even the Devil say, That no Creature is in love with Pain."[42] Here Dryden is constructing the persona of an individual who had reached a conscientious decision, one which had cost him dearly, and from which he would not waver. This was an undeniable component of his religious position in his last years, but so too were his abiding anticlericalism, his fascination with antiquity, and his awareness of the weight of history.

Dryden's poetry erected façade after façade to mask his own private religion. Indeed "religion" may be the wrong term to describe the amalgam of associations and values to which Dryden held, and we may need a broader notion that is more in tune with his instincts and culture. *Pietas* is an obvious contender for that role. The word is inadequately translated by the anaemic Christian "piety": as Dryden himself remarked, "the word in Latin is more full than it can possibly be exprest in any Modern Language; for there it comprehends not only Devotion to the Gods, but Filial Love and tender Affection to Relations of all sorts" (*Works* v: 286). As Dryden's writing took a more "religious" turn in the last two decades of his life, it became as concerned with virtue, loyalty, security, and serenity as with the finer points of ecclesiastical allegiance. His interest in virtue rather than mere religious "truth" is nicely caught in some lines that he translated from Lucretius. The Latin poet writes of the happiness of those who remain aloof from the follies of the world, who observe rather than suffer turmoil and pain:

> But much more sweet thy lab'ring steps to guide,
> To Vertues heights, with wisdom well supply'd,
> And all the Magazins of Learning fortifi'd:
> From thence to look below on humane kind,
> Bewilder'd in the Maze of Life, and blind. [43]

Here, Paul Hammond observes, Dryden has subtly changed the original's emphasis by adding the phrase about "labouring steps" and alluding to the heights of "virtue" rather than truth or knowledge.[44] Truth may reside in churches, but virtue has to be sought and fostered. The ageing Catholic remained as suspicious of the clergy as the younger Anglican had been. As far as Dryden was concerned, the unlettered could "plod" to heaven while the priests disputed the finer points of theology. "A Satyrical Poet is the Check of the Laymen, on bad Priests," he commented on Chaucer. He had "enlarg'd" on Chaucer's holy priest "with some Pleasure, reserving to my self the Right, if I shall think fit hereafter, to describe another sort of Priests, such as are more easily to be found than the Good Parson; such as have given the last Blow to Christianity in this Age, by a Practice so contrary to their Doctrine" (*Works* VII: 35, 36–7). It was Pepys who suggested Chaucer's *Priest's Tale* to Dryden, but in the 1690s the poet was constantly re-examining the past of his own family and country, turning over the legacy of English and other vernacular literatures, and coming back again and again to his classical heritage. This was part of the climb to virtue's heights. And for Dryden, virtue begins and ends in piety. "Piety alone comprehends the whole Duty of Man towards the Gods; towards his Country, and towards his Relations" (*Works* V: 288).[45]

NOTES

1. P. Seaver, *Wallington's World: A Puritan Artisan in Seventeenth-century London* (London, 1970); A. Macfarlane, ed., *The Diary of Ralph Josselin 1616–1683* (London, 1976). Another approach to the religion of "ordinary people" is represented by M. Spufford, ed., *The World of Rural Dissenters, 1520–1725* (Cambridge, 1995).
2. F. Harris, *Transformations of Love: The Friendship of John Evelyn and Margaret Godolphin* (Oxford, 2002); F. Harris and M. Hunter, eds., *John Evelyn and his Milieu* (London, 2003).
3. P. Hammond and D. Hopkins, eds., *John Dryden: Tercentenary Essays* (Oxford, 2002), p. 9.
4. There is no single study of English religion during Dryden's lifetime, but for a starting point see the essays by Webster, Hughes and Spurr in *A Companion to Stuart Britain*, ed. B. Coward (Oxford, 2003); K. C. Fincham, ed., *The Early Stuart Church, 1603–42* (Basingstoke, 1993); J. Spurr, *English Puritanism, 1603–1689* (Basingstoke, 1998); and B. Worden, "The Question of Secularization," in *A Nation Transformed – England after the Restoration*, ed. A. Houston and S. Pincus (Cambridge, 2001).
5. *Tyrannic Love*, Preface (*Works* X: 111).
6. Ibid. (*Works* X: 109); *Absalom and Achitophel*, line 99.
7. Also see Mark Goldie, "Priestcraft and the Birth of Whiggism," in *Political Discourse in Early Modern Britain*, ed. N. Phillipson and Q. Skinner (Cambridge, 1993), p. 218.

8. James A. Winn, *John Dryden and his World* (New Haven, 1987), p. 414.
9. *The Diary of John Evelyn*, ed. E. S. de Beer, 6 vols. (Oxford, 1955), vol. IV, p. 497.
10. Dryden wrote a part of the defense of the papers published by James II to reveal the Roman Catholic principles of his first wife and of Charles II (see *Works* XVII: 291–326). The poetic response to his conversion can be sampled in *Poems on Affairs of State*: vol. VI *1685–1688*, ed. G. M. Crump (New Haven, 1968), pp. 74–90.
11. *The Letters of John Dryden*, ed. Charles Ward (Durham, NC, 1942), pp. 26–7.
12. Doctor Williams's Library, London, Morrice Entering Book Q, fo. 49, also see fos. 44 and 93 and Entering Book P, fos. 568 and 590.
13. Morrice Entering Book Q, fo. 93; S. Zwicker, "The Paradoxes of Tender Conscience," *ELH* 63 (1996); L. Brockliss, G. Harriss and A. Macintyre, *Magdalen College and the Crown* (Oxford, 1988), p. 87 and *passim*.
14. *Letters*, p. 109.
15. See A. Cotterill, "'Rebakah's Heir': Dryden's Late Mystery of Genealogy," *HLQ* 2001.
16. See H. Jones, *The Epicurean Tradition* (London, 1989); P. Hammond, *Dryden and the Traces of Classical Rome* (Oxford, 1999), pp. 156–70; P. Davis, "Dryden and the Consolations of Philosophy," *The Seventeenth Century* 17 (2002).
17. BL, Add. MS 19333, fos. 2v, 4v.
18. See P. Hammond, "Dryden, Milton, and Lucretius," *The Seventeenth Century* 16 (2001), esp. p. 166.
19. BL, Add. MS 78298, fos. 69, 76, 78, 85–6; Add. MSS 78353–6 are the working papers on Lucretius; and Add. MS 78367 is the volume on true religion.
20. William Chillingworth, *The Religion of Protestants* (London, 1846), p. 8. On Dryden and deism see P. Harth, *Contexts of Dryden's Thought* (Chicago, 1968), esp. pp. 127–31; and on the "rule of faith" controversy see G. R. Cragg, *Freedom and Authority: A Study of English Thought in the Early Seventeenth Century* (Philadelphia, 1975); G. Reedy, *The Bible and Reason: Anglicans and Scripture in Late Seventeenth-Century England* (Philadelphia, 1985); and L. I. Bredvold, *The Intellectual Milieu of John Dryden* (Ann Arbor, 1934; 2nd edn. 1956).
21. The youthful John Locke argued that scripture "contains within it the profound mysteries of divine matters which utterly transcend the human intellect" in his essay on infallibility of 1661–2; see *Locke – Political Essays*, ed. M. Goldie (Cambridge, 1997), pp. 207–8.
22. *Copies of Two Papers Written by the late King Charles II* (London, 1686), p. 7.
23. See M. C. Questier, *Conversion, Politics, and Religion in England, 1580–1625* (Cambridge, 1996).
24. *Works* XVII: 301.
25. F. Bracher, ed., *The Letters of Sir George Etherege* (Berkeley, 1974), p. 129.
26. Winn, *Dryden*, p. 423.
27. Ibid., p. 424.
28. S. Budick, *Dryden and the Abyss of Light* (New Haven, 1970), p. 214 and chapter 9 *passim*.
29. A. B. Gardiner, *Ancient Faith and Modern Freedom in John Dryden's "The Hind and the Panther"* (Washington DC, 1998); also see George Myerson, *The Argumentative Imagination: Wordsworth, Dryden, Religious Dialogues* (Manchester, 1992).

30. *Letters*, p. 123.

31. Martin Clifford, *Notes upon Mr Dryden's Poems in Four Letters* (London, 1687), p. 34.

32. *Works* VII: 28; Jeremy Collier, *A Short View of the Immorality and Profaneness of the English Stage* (London, 1698), pp. 98–100, 103–8, 177–95.

33. Joseph Arrowsmith, *The Reformation* (1679: Augustan Society Reprint 237–8, Los Angeles, 1986), p. 18.

34. [Matthew Prior and Charles Montague], *The Hind and the Panther Transvers'd* (London, 1687), p. 17.

35. Clifford, *Notes*, p. 18.

36. P. Hammond, *John Dryden – A Literary Life* (Basingstoke, 1991), p. 114; Collier, *Short View*, p. 183; *Poems of Dryden*, ed. Hammond, I. 448–9; II. 85, 100.

37. Winn, *Dryden*, p. 384.

38. *The Poems of Dryden*, ed. Paul Hammond (London, 1995), vol. II, p. 442.

39. Hammond and Hopkins, eds., *John Dryden: Tercentenary Essays*, p. 371.

40. Clifford, *Notes*, p. 18.

41. *The Hind and the Panther Transvers'd*, sig. A3v.

42. *Letters*, pp. 72–3.

43. *Works* III: 46.

44. Hammond, *Dryden and the Traces of Classical Rome*, p. 161.

45. Here Dryden is alluding to a central topos of Anglicanism, the "whole duty of man" (Ecclesiastes 12: 13); see J. Spurr, *The Restoration Church of England, 1646–1689* (New Haven and London, 1991), chapter 6.

14

ANNE COTTERILL

Dryden's *Fables* and the judgment of art

I pass my time sometimes with Ovid, and sometimes with our old
English poet, Chaucer; translating such stories as best please my
fancy; and intend besides them to add somewhat of my own: so that
it is not impossible, but ere the summer be pass'd, I may come down
to you with a volume in my hand, like a dog out of the water, with a
duck in his mouth.[1]

Dryden's *Fables Ancient and Modern; Translated into Verse, From Homer,
Ovid, Boccacce, & Chaucer: with Original Poems* appeared less than two
months before his death on 1 May 1700. This personal miscellany closed a
prolific career shaped by contention and contest in what Dryden had come
increasingly to call "this bad Age." The volume also marked the end of a
decade, and of a century, of intense print quarrels. The two central debates
of the 1690s, to which *Fables* responds, are the controversy between the
ancients and the moderns and, more urgently and the subject of this chapter,
the Collier controversy over the morals and purposes of theatre. The nonjuring clergyman Jeremy Collier and Sir Richard Blackmore, the physician-
poet, were two of a wave of controversialists attacking Restoration theatre as
libertine and atheistic. Their critique of the theatre of Dryden and his satanic
"fraternity" and their defense of home, marriage, and Christian sensibility
were part of a public campaign against vice and in defense of the sanctity of
family, a campaign led by the government of the Dutch-speaking king who
himself had seemed to abandon home for war.[2] In this his final work, Dryden
appears to be elevated above the fray, absorbed by new literary interests, by
frail health, and at home among literary friends and relations. Yet in *Fables*
he refuses to sidestep the print quarrels; rather, Dryden complicates their
dichotomies and underscores the constant round of battle, predation, and
judgment.

In "Theodore and Honoria," his translation of Boccaccio's tale of "Nasta-
gio degli Onesti" (*The Decameron* v: 8) where more than half the lines are
Dryden's addition, ghostly hell-hounds are transformed into a masque-like
emblem of the central themes of *Fables*: vengeance and justice, mankind bare
and powerless, forever unsatisfied, and the endless cycle of chase. The stern
vision brings proud Honoria to her knees; as an alternative Dryden's Preface

introduces us to his imaginative estate and to the chase of the mind's plenty: "such a Variety of Game springing up before me that I am distracted in my Choice, and know not which to follow" (*Works* VII: 37). In fact he chooses his game easily and judges with instructive point; throughout these fables Dryden offers his readers the prospect of moral sociability, domestic solitude, and passionate imagination.

The Preface insists that passion, not unrequited love, shaped this volume, that the poet was led by affection and delight to wander from text to text. The poets he chooses are poetic relations distinguished by their abundance and by their independence. At the end of the Preface, after briefly addressing his critics, Dryden claims to "abandon my own Defence," for "being a Party, I am not to erect my self into a Judge"; yet as if to emphasize his freedom, the former laureate and now translator of Virgil has just pronounced Virgil too "quiet and sedate," too "confined" in invention; he has made the "violent," "impetuous" Homer his presiding spirit.[3] Under attack from moralists like Collier, Dryden translates Ovid and Chaucer, known for their ribaldry, and introduced as "well-bred, well-natur'd, amorous, and Libertine," the very portrait of a Restoration rake – "at least in their Writings, it may also be in their Lives," he adds. More subtly, the Preface opens with a disarming evocation of the poet as a modest, unpredictable builder who keeps changing his original plan and who by miraculous chance, despite impulsive additions, has been successful:

> 'Tis with a Poet, as with a Man who designs to build, and is very exact, as he supposes, in casting up the Cost beforehand: But, generally speaking, he is mistaken in his Account, and reckons short of the Expence he first intended: He alters his Mind as the Work proceeds, and will have this or that Convenience more, of which he had not thought when he began. So has it hapned to me; I have built a House, where I intended but a Lodge: Yet with better Success than a certain Nobleman, who beginning with a Dog-kennel, never liv'd to finish the Palace he had contriv'd. (*Works* VII: 24)

The narrative voice, both passive and active, says "it" mysteriously happened "to me" that "I . . . built . . ." Drawing on the commonplace of life as merely an inn or lodge on the road to hereafter, Dryden yet claims to have built a house where he will live – and not for a short while.

The final lines triumphantly allude to Christ's parable of the foolish builder unable to finish (Luke 14: 28–30), a warning to the half-hearted disciple – here, a reminder that Dryden's theatre had enemies long before Collier. Dryden reopens and closes once more his thirty-year-old rivalry with the late Duke of Buckingham, already immortalized as Zimri in *Absalom and Achitophel*, and swipes at the Duke's "folly" – his country house, Cliveden, described by Evelyn as "of extraordinary expense," by Brian Fairfax as the attempt at "a new way of expence in building, in that sort of architecture which Cicero calls, *Insanae substructiones.*"[4] Dryden also borrows a common analogy from Renaissance aesthetics, grounded in the biblical wisdom that God framed the universe in six days "in measure, number, and weight" (Wisdom 11: 21), which compares a poet to a builder who requires an exact design and a plan of costs before starting. He invokes this classic dictum about moral and aesthetic integrity only to overturn it and in the process to overturn much more.

The Preface opens by altering the traditional analogy between architecture and plotting or literature that, for example, introduces Geoffrey of Vinsauf's thirteenth-century art of poetry, *Poetria Nova* (1200–16), later quoted by Chaucer, and that permeates Jonson's work.[5] The first epigraph to Jonson's *Timber, or Discoveries* (1640–1) introduces Persius' figure of the mind or self as a house ("Live in your own house, and recognize how poorly it is furnished"); later Jonson defines fable as "the imitation of one entire and perfect action, whose parts are so joined and knit together as nothing in the structure can be changed or taken away without impairing or troubling the whole" and continues:[6]

> As (for example) if a man would build a house he would first appoint a place to build it in, which he would define within certain bounds; so in the constitution of a poem, the action is aimed at by the poet, which answers place in a building; and that action hath his largeness, compass, and proportion.[7]

Jonson repeats Geoffrey's advice about drawing the limits of a work first with the mind's inner compass, while Dryden's house grows by another rule. The poet is only "very exact, as he supposes" in his preliminary design.

In the second paragraph of the Preface to *Fables*, Geoffrey's inner compass becomes a verb ("When I had compassed them") to mean that Dryden has accomplished his translation of the speeches of Ajax and Ulysses; "I could not balk 'em," he explains. "I ought in reason to have stopped," continues the poet, with the translation of the twelfth book of the *Metamorphoses*, which followed his translation of the first book of Homer's *Iliad*. Why "reason" would dictate he stop after these two works is not obvious, unless Dryden means that he should have pursued instead an intention, confined within parentheses in the first sentence of the second paragraph, to translate "the whole work" of the *Iliad*, rather than continue with fragments from different whole works: "From translating the first of Homer's *Iliad* (which I intended as an essay to the whole work) . . . I proceeded to the translation of the twelfth book of Ovid's *Metamorphoses*"; then came the speeches of Ajax and Ulysses because they appear immediately at the beginning of the thirteenth book of the *Metamorphoses*, after which "I was so taken with the former part of the fifteenth book . . . that I enjoined myself the pleasing task of rendering it into English." If no compass of reason circumscribes this whole, directing him to stop and translate "the whole work" of the *Iliad*, a plumb line of pleasure ("I could not balk 'em") drops. The model of a whole is not the divine engineer's circle but the organic model of human desire producing a swelling growth: although aged and "for Ladies Love unfit," he has produced an unexpected birth – verses "began to swell into a little volume." Despite his original intention, the poet's pleasure led him to build another structure than Homer's. The volume's first fable is the Preface, which concerns the mature poet's freedom to be at home with the passions, including the passion of judgment.

Fables begins then with Dryden's metamorphosis of his final miscellany into a country house and a company of kindred spirits. Earlier in *Eleonora* (1692), he had used the image of a country house for a heart where kindred souls, like "Kings in Progress," can retire. Eight years later, the image of his own imaginative house, built far from courts, reflects his own heart's delight and initiates his final response to critics of his art and morals, transforming this last "Book of Miscellanyes" into an art of poetry that brings moral and aesthetic authority under one roof.[8]

In "To My Dear Friend Mr Congreve" (1694), Dryden hails the young poet not only as literary heir and harbinger of a new age of English wit but as our "best Vitruvius," the Roman architect synonymous in the Renaissance with proportion, symmetry, and balance. Congreve's strength of wit allows the present age to match and exceed the dramatic building of Shakespeare's "giant race" of genius "before the Flood" (*Works* IV: 432). Within *Fables*, however, Dryden recasts "strength" as Homeric speed, "vehemence," and "copiousness," and central to that "vehemence" is the capacity to choose and reject. With these youthful, pointedly "masculine" qualities, Dryden also recasts his laureate's career from prey of critics' eager hunt to hunter who chooses his game and whose fabular house will not fall to illness and death. The recurring rhymes with "prey" (not "pray") and with "chase" and "run" become echoing mnemonic threads that bind together the various pieces and replace the stately "Dorique Pillars" and "Corinthian Crowns" – the classical strength and grace – of Congreve's genius.

Dryden's image of a country house built to accommodate the owner's exercise of taste and pleasure performs several interrelated, crucial metamorphoses at once, and they are central to the achievement of *Fables*. After a career experimenting with digression and with formal and generic mixture, Dryden opens his Preface with a paragraph of effortless economy in which he dismisses preconceived ideas of beauty and morality as organizing principles for art, and for lives, and substitutes the passionate mind and temper of the mature poet for whom literary relations and coherence have become second nature.

Paul Hammond has observed that, for Dryden, translation became "the inescapable condition of the world, the shifting ground on which forms of singleness and stability could be fashioned."[9] Along with the central mutability of all things human and non-human in *Fables*, he notes that Dryden turns to images of life's "round" run, not only by a single man's lifetime but also by nature's re-circulation of life. Earlier, in his translation of the Third Book of Lucretius' *De Rerum Natura* (1685), the Latin text and author synonymous with "Irreligion," Dryden had added an image of Nature's round.[10] He expanded two of Lucretius' lines (944–5) into an English triplet (138–40) whose final Alexandrine substituted, for the "stasis" of "eadem sunt omnia semper" ("everything is always the same"), the long rolling perspective of Nature's claim that she had invented her full abundance and can only "run the round again, the round I ran before."[11] In *Fables* the natural, abundant round run "again" becomes the re-invention and re-circulation of translation as well as a frankly predatory chase that participates in the "chase of wit" Dryden once called "the greatest pleasure of the Audience" in comedy.[12]

Images of circling and circularity appear repeatedly in *Fables*, often highlighted by an echoing triplet, Dryden's flagship of rhyme – memorably, for example, the "Etherial Race" and circular dance of the stars (21–5) in "To Her Grace the Duchess of Ormond" and the wandering hare, "Emblem of Humane Life, who runs the Round" (63–6) in "To My Honour'd Kinsman." These images conflate the hunt with the Pythagorean vision of a universe endlessly re-circulating matter and spirit, themes that Dryden handles in his translation of Ovid's digression in Book xv of the *Metamorphoses*, and themes that suggest the retrospective poet who conjoins past and present to envision the natural coherence of his career and his homecoming in this miscellany. Dryden's textual country house is full of predators and prey, and Cousin Driden's real home, hunt, and circling hare circle back to a "nimble Spaniel" of imagination and another country house from November 1666. At Charlton, the Wiltshire estate of Dryden's father-in-law, the Earl of Berkshire, Dryden had written his prefatory letter to *Annus Mirabilis*, addressed to his brother-in-law, Sir Robert Howard. His image there of the writer's faculty of wit or imagination, that, "like a nimble Spaniel, beats over and ranges through the field of Memory, till it springs the Quarry it hunted after," is an early appearance of his extended figure in *Fables* for creative thought as a hunt within the well-stocked mind of the poet.[13] In the passage from a 1699 letter to Mrs. Steward, which appears as an epigraph to this chapter, the poet playfully has become that spaniel and the book his duck. In *Fables'* "To My Honour'd Kinsman," the imagination's spaniel and hunt, transformed into Cousin Driden's "well-breath'd Beagles" (52) and the wandering hare, constitute a figure for the poet's work as an independent alternative to, and metamorphosis of, Boccaccio's fearful hell-hounds of passion that painfully circumscribe men's lives.

Chapters 2–5 of six in Jeremy Collier's *A Short View of the Immorality and Profaneness of the English Stage* (1698) splice together, with cries of censure, examples of illicit passion and irreverent language from Restoration theatre. Dryden offers a competitive view of the human chase. Although only one of Dryden's tales is a beast fable – his translation of Chaucer's "Nun's Priest Tale" – Collier's horror at Restoration drama's representation of the beastliness of both sexes, especially that of women, and at the unstable line between man and beast places metamorphosis at the heart of Collier's attack and of Dryden's response. Eight of the seventeen translated tales are from Ovid.

Dryden's *Fables* constitutes a delayed but exuberant response less to the individual charges and hurtful misreadings by Collier and Blackmore than to their vision of a polite society and church which Dryden and his fellow playwrights had corrupted: a reformed world of domesticity and marriage, of manners, sentimentality, and civil contracts, which William and Mary endorsed in "the moral revolution of 1688."[14] While Dryden presents *Fables* as a private, self-indulgent miscellany, he also acknowledges his enemies and the field of contest. He formally answers attacks from 1695 and 1698 by Blackmore, Collier, and Luke Milbourne in a "corollary" to the Preface, rebukes Collier, that "severe divine," in the "Poeta loquitur" before the final tale, and defends his friend Samuel Garth and shoots at "Maurus" (Blackmore) in "To My Honour'd Kinsman." Throughout, Dryden steadily undercuts the military with its standing armies and heroism, that province so dear to William III and to the volume's dedicatee, the Duke of Ormond. More subtly, every gesture of *Fables* reinterprets Collier's and Blackmore's clarion call for art as instruction in the distinction between virtue and vice. Dryden's art challenges these critics' vision of the instructable human condition, of the firm differences between the sexes and particularly the delicacy of the female sex, of the sacred institution of marriage, and of the spirituality of the clergy. Yet the revolutionary elements in Dryden's volume are so diffused and quietly embedded throughout such a dazzling fabric of metamorphoses that *Fables* leads the critic hungry for distinctions and order in a merry chase.

After the Glorious Revolution both Dryden and Jeremy Collier underwent a metamorphosis. A nonjuror and, like Dryden, an advocate of Stuart monarchy, Collier had been imprisoned for his politics and, in 1696, along with two other nonjurors, he dared to minister at the scaffold to men condemned for their role in a plot to assassinate William. The other clerics were indicted, found guilty, and released, but Collier who refused to deliver himself up was outlawed. His zealous attack on the immorality of the theatre, however, swung public and royal opinion to his side: William stopped legal proceedings against him – Collier had atoned for his past conduct.[15] Although a Jacobite and political outcast, Collier earned public favor as a defender of the faith and of Christian womanhood. Dryden and Congreve were Collier's chief targets in the hunt after immorality and atheism. Collier attacked the laureate's plays but also addressed himself to *Absalom and Achitophel*, the Juvenal translations, and the miscellanies which he found "horribly licentious . . . some-times Collections from Antiquity, and often the Worst Parts of the worst poets. And to mend the Matter, the Christian Translation is more nauseous than the Pagan Original" (Collier, *A Short View*, 55).

In February 1695, when Dryden was deep at work on his *Virgil*, Sir Richard Blackmore launched an attack on Restoration theatre and on the literary culture of wit in the Preface to his "Heroick" poem, *Prince Arthur*, and, within the poem, on Dryden, without mentioning his debt to Dryden for the idea of an English epic on King Arthur.[16] Blackmore's military imagery for the relationship between stage and church is striking: although the stage was once "an Outwork or Fort rais'd" by the state "for the Protection and Security of the Temple," poets now have "discharg'd all their Artillery against the Place their Duty was to defend." Blackmore, the physician, also specializes in images of pleasure as contagious infection. "Ladies" and young gentlemen appear to be the consumers of verse and in most danger of the contamination from poets, and he is appalled that poetical miscellanies, "monstrous leud and irreligious Books of Poems, as they are call'd" are "publish'd, and . . . receiv'd in a Civiliz'd and Christian Kingdom, with Applause and Reputation. . . . The Sweetness of the Wit, makes the Poison go down with Pleasure, and the Contagion spreads without Opposition." In his next paragraph, he characterizes the Muses as females in need of rescue "out of the hands of these Ravishers, to restore them to their sweet and chast Mansions."[17] Although Dryden's *Fables* is hardly a "sweet and chast" mansion, the poet reported triumphantly to Mrs. Steward that "The Ladies of the Town . . . like my last Book of Poems, better than any thing they have formerly seen of mine."[18]

While Blackmore does not name Dryden in the Preface, the poem attacks him under the thin disguise of "Laurus," "An old, revolted, unbelieving Bard."[19] Dryden did not respond. In the spring of 1698 the first of Collier's four tracts against the theatre appeared.[20] In his *Short View of the Immorality and Profaneness of the English Stage*, Collier attacked the profanity and abuse of the clergy in the theatre and such abuse applauded as wit. He was especially horrified by the theatrical representation of women and of aggressive female sexuality: "Now to bring women into such misbehavior is violence to their native modesty, and a misrepresentation of their sex. For modesty, as Mr. Rapin observes, is the character of women. To represent them without this quality is to make monsters of them, and throw them out of their kind." As public defender of well-bred sensibilities, he deplored that profanity in Thomas D'Urfey's *Don Quixote* leveled all to low-class beasts:

> Beastliness in Behaviour, gives a disparaging Idea of Humane Nature, and almost makes us sorry we are of the same Kind. For these reasons 'tis a Maxim in Good Breeding never to shock the Senses, or Imagination. This Rule holds strongest before Women, and especially when they come to be entertain'd . . . To treat Persons of Condition like the Mob, is to degrade their Birth, and affront their Breeding. It levels them with the lowest Education.
>
> (*A Short View*, 205)

Easy metamorphosis of man to beast reflects Collier's anxiety over the leveling of virtue and vice, and of class and gender. He characterizes the "very Legible Distinctions" in virtue and vice in strikingly gendered terms: virtue "has all the Sweetness, Charms, and Graces imaginable," while vice is unmistakably phallic with "the Air of a Post ill Carved into a Monster, and looks both foolish and Frightful together. These are the Native appearances of Good and Evil: And they that endeavour to blot the Distinctions . . . are extreamly to blame" (*A Short View*, 140). Scandalous stage entertainment "does in effect degrade human nature; sinks reason into appetite, and breaks down the distinction between man and beast. Goats and monkeys, if they would speak, would express their brutality in such language as this" (*A Short View*, 6). Of Dryden's descriptive language in *The Conquest of Granada*, he finds "This litter of epithets makes the poem look like a bitch over-stocked with puppies, and sucks the sense almost to skin and bone" (*A Short View*, 34). On the excesses of Dryden's *Amphytrion*, he writes, "But Mr. Dryden has not so much as a Heathen President for his Singularities . . . To draw a Monkey in Royal Robes, and a Prince in Antick, would be Farce upon Colours, entertain like a Monster, and please only upon the score of Deformity" (*A Short View*, 182).

Collier's *Short View* was announced in the spring of 1698, and that June, Peter Motteux's *Beauty in Distress*, prefaced by Dryden's verse epistle, "To My Friend, the Author [Peter Motteux]" was published.[21] The poet addresses his fellow playwright, " 'Tis hard, my Friend, to write in such an Age / As damns not only Poets, but the Stage" (1–2), and uses the next twenty-eight lines to respond to their recent critics. He concedes, "What I have loosly, or profanely writ, / Let them to Fires (their due desert) commit" (15–16); the crime of profanity, however, shrinks beside that of Blackmore's and Collier's reduction to the most literal moral instruction of the solemn and "sacred" delights of poetry for whose traditions of beauty, law, and erotic delight Dryden returns to the Bible:

> That sacred Art, by Heav'n it self infus'd,
> Which Moses, David, Salomon have us'd,
> Is now to be no more: The Muses foes
> Wou'd sink their Maker's Praises into Prose.
>
> (3–6)

Their frenzy to see filth and create evil by distorting "words to blasphemy" against common sense aligns Collier and Blackmore with the Puritan zealots and with plots of the 1640s. Dryden turns back on the moralists their own satanic language about the stage, suggesting that the zealous Protestant pulpit had first, and now for long, contrived the most deadly theatre of war:

> Rebellion, worse than Witchcraft, they pursu'd;
> The Pulpit preach'd the Crime; the People ru'd.
> The Stage was silenc'd: for the Saints wou'd see
> In fields perform'd their plotted Tragedy.
>
> (19–22)

To pay his compliments to Motteux's tragedy, Dryden leaves his enemies with a bow of humility that highlights their "lofty" pride associated with high precepts and "lofty" teaching far removed from the humble realities of daily practice (23–8).

Dryden's "Character of a Good Parson" in *Fables*, translated and enlarged from Chaucer's "povre persoun of a toun," continues the criticism begun in "To My Friend, the Author [Peter Motteux]." The saintly Good Parson is the model of a charitable, cheerfully impoverished, and self-denying nonjuror who "charm'd" (and Dryden repeats the word) his listeners' ears "With Eloquence innate" and with music. He has inherited David's beautiful sound, "For David left him, when he went to rest, / His Lyre; and after him, he sung the best" [23–4]. The portrait identifies the charms of poetry and song, or poetry as song, with the Bible, not the brothel, and drives home their defense in "Peter Motteux" against Collier's outbursts against music, not only in random comments, such as that "an atheistical Rant is as good as a flourish of trumpets," but specifically at the end of his tract where he addresses music in the theatre (*A Short View*, 65). There Collier twins the dangers of music and gunpowder to the nation's social and political fabric: "Music is almost as dangerous as Gunpowder; And it requires looking after no less than the

Press, or the Mint" (*A Short View*, 279). On the authority of Cicero, he claims that "the Lacedemonians fixt the number of Strings for the Harp, by express Law. And afterwards silenc'd Timotheus, and seiz'd his Harp, for having One String above publick Allowance" (*A Short View*, 279–80).

In "Of Musick," in Part II of *Essays Upon Several Moral Subjects* (1697), Collier recalled the "Minstrelsy" of the Greek musician, Timotheus, to manipulate the passions of Alexander, a story "well known to all men conversant among Authors," according to Abraham Cowley in 1656.[22] Specifically, Collier contrasts the lightning control of the musician with the labor to persuade of Demosthenes, the orator, who "would have been Flourishing about such a Business a long Hour, and may be not have done it neither. But Timotheus had a nearer Cut to the Soul: He could Neck a Passion at a Stroke, and lay it asleep."[23] Dryden's St. Cecilia's Day ode, "Alexander's Feast," appeared in the same year as Collier's "Of Musick" and celebrates the power of Timotheus' music to manipulate the great Macedonian.[24] The poem, "esteemed the best of all my poetry, by all the Town," Dryden wrote to Tonson in December 1697, reduces Alexander's heroism to a puppet's twitch by the musician's harp strings. Dryden's ode, however, subtly reverses Collier's judgment against Demosthenes by demonstrating the powers of poetry to evoke music and sexual feeling. Indeed the musician Timotheus and the prostitute Thais appear to be linked ambiguously, not only as Alexander overcome by music and drink collapses like a child on her breast but as he is first whipped by Timotheus into "Zeal to destroy" Persepolis, then led by the courtesan "To light him to his Prey" like the torch he has seized.[25] Dryden reprinted the ode in *Fables*, placing it between "The Flower and the Leaf" and Book XII of Ovid's *Metamorphoses*, where "Alexander's Feast" recalls the unreasonable passions of the military heroes in Homer's *Iliad* and anticipates the two final texts on martial rage, Ovid's Book XII followed by "The Speeches of Ajax and Ulysses" from Ovid's Book XIII. In the latter, not music but eloquence representative of arts and learning overcomes brute strength.

The first thirty lines in "To My Friend, the Author [Peter Motteux]," then, are Dryden's only public response to his critics before he names and addresses them in the Preface to *Fables*. Congreve, Dennis, and Vanbrugh had also been attacked, and they promptly answered Collier. George Farquhar's play, *Love and a Bottle*, parodying the contemporary love comedy and scorning Collier's moralizations, appeared in November 1698.[26] Addison's satiric "The Play-House," issued early in 1699 (probably after he had seen Farquhar's play), underscored such sentiments. And in May 1699, a year after Samuel Garth, Dryden's friend and physician, opened a free out-patient clinic at the Royal

College of Physicians against the opposition of doctors and apothecaries led by Blackmore, Garth published *The Dispensary*, a mock-epic poem which ridiculed Blackmore and his verse. Predictably Blackmore countered with "A Satyr Against Wit," published 23 November 1699 when *Fables* must have been near completion. Blackmore's principal target is that deadly "infection" of obscene wit spread by Dryden who first appears in the "Satyr Against Wit" as the presiding eminence over "the leud Crew" at Wills "where first this Plague [of Wit] begun" and then as the rabid dog that bites unsuspecting men of sense. Parnassus has been overrun by "rank Weeds and pois'nous Plants" that "Fitter to be for Witches a Retreat / Owls, Satyrs, Monkies, than the Muses Seat" (284–6).[27] Dryden did not reply, but other wits buzzed forward: in *The Post-Man* of 16–19 December an advertisement appeared for the first response to Blackmore's poem with a second response circulated in manuscript and a major counter-blast launched by Charles Boyle, Sir Christopher Codrington, and Tom Brown in February 1700, the month in which Defoe published "The Pacificator" that mocked all of the factions and paper wars as a battle between the Men of Sense (Collier and Blackmore) and their targets, the Men of Wit. The King also entered the fray, as Dryden noted skeptically in a letter of 14 December 1699 to Mrs. Steward: "The King's Proclamation against vice and profaneness is issued out in print: but a deep disease is not to be cur'd with a slight Medicine. The parsons who must read it, will find as little effect from it, as from their dull Sermons: tis a Scare-Crow, wch will not fright many birds from preying on the fields & orchards."[28] Ineffective clergy and birds of prey are a familiar presence in *Fables*, in press at the letter's writing.

Collier opens *A Short View*, and Blackmore his Preface to *Prince Arthur*, with the identical premise that the primary business of verse and stage is to instruct by exposing vice and recommending virtue. Man's fallen appetite for pleasure, they acknowledge, requires that instruction be disguised as entertainment, but pleasure, which was the most political of experiences in the 1650s and 1660s, is so again in the 1690s: "Indeed to make Delight the main business of Comedy is an unreasonable and dangerous Principle," argues Collier against Dryden's early critical claims for delight as the chief end of comedy. Laughter "opens the way to all Licentiousness, and Confounds the distinction between Mirth and Madness" (*A Short View*, 161). He exclaims in disgust, "And when People are sick, are they not to be Humour'd? In fine, we must make them Laugh, right or wrong, for Delight is the Chief end of Comedy. Delight! He should have said Debauchery: That's the English of the Word, and the Consequence of the Practice" (*A Short View*, 163). In *Fables* Dryden asserts delight and pleasure as the uninhibited exercise of his own judgment in the evocation of a disjunctive, Ovidian world of endless coupling and uncoupling, of men and women driven by sexuality and often indistinguishable in that obsession. The lines between male and female, and between mankind and beasts, which Collier fears are blurred so irreverently in Restoration drama are virtually and triumphantly dissolved in *Fables*. In the headnote to the Twelfth Book of the *Metamorphoses* where Dryden praises the battle of the centaurs and Lapithae he adds mischievously, "the loves and death of Cyllarus and Hylonome, the male and female centaur, are wonderfully moving." Half-human, half-beast, these centaurs seem a grotesquely comic emblem of the human condition in *Fables*, where men and women turn into animals or other natural phenomena under the pressure of passion in a way that highlights the fragility of man's familiar form and of his firmly elevated place as a reasonable creature in a hierarchy of nature.

Sean Walsh has drawn attention to how Dryden's "Sigismonda and Guiscardo," a translation into verse of Boccaccio's prose tale about Guiscardo and Ghismonda (*The Decameron* IV: I), reflects the interest of Dryden's late work "in finding a way of talking about desire and sex that subscribes to neither prudery nor lechery. The Boccaccio translation expresses Dryden's mature interest in the mechanics and ethics of passion, also evident in the translation of Lucretius."[29] But the effects of passion and mutability on private and public lives, and their representation by poetry, had been Dryden's subject at least since *An Essay of Dramatic Poesy* (1668) where Lisideius proposes a "Description" of a play as "A just and lively Image of Humane Nature, representing its Passions and Humours, and the Changes of Fortune to which it is subject; for the Delight and Instruction of Mankind," and later Neander reiterates that poetry is the "Imitation of Humour and Passions" and will argue for mingling mirth with tragedy, for the pleasure and refreshment offered by variety, including swift-moving repartee, "more apt to move the passions" than the long discourses of the French stage whose actors "speak by the Hour-glass, as our Parsons do" (*Works* XVII: 15, 44, 48). In "The Authors Apology for Heroique Poetry; and Poetique License," prefixed to *The State of Innocence* (1677), Dryden again emphasizes the role of poetry to "sound the depth of all the Passions; what they are in themselves, and how they are to be provok'd" (*Works* XII: 91).

In *Fables* sex may bring temporary bliss but becomes inevitably a source of pain, violence, and entrapment. Think of Myrrha's agonized imprisonment within her guilty lust for her father, a hell only relieved by release into metamorphosis. And as Emily prays to Diana for release from the necessity to marry in "Palamon and Arcite," Dryden adds:

> Like Death, thou know'st, I loathe the Nuptial State,
> And Man, the Tyrant of our Sex, I hate,
> A lowly Servant, but a lofty Mate;
> Where Love is Duty on the Female Side,
> On theirs meer sensual Gust, and sought with surly Pride.
>
> (227–31)

And when she asks that, if she must take one, let it be the one who loves her best, Dryden has her add, "But oh! ev'n that avert! I chuse it not, / But take it as the least unhappy Lot" (242–3). Like Chaucer's Emilia she begs Diana to allow her still to "thy chast Will obey," but in Dryden's text she adds, "And only make the Beasts of Chace my Prey!" (246–7). Even in the exquisite first poem, the verse epistle "To the Duchess of Ormond," we might note the voyeuristic and invasive, even sexual, description of the disease which has entered and preyed on the Duchess of Ormond's sacred, yet "soft," body. We enter that body, too, through the narrator's imagination as he wonders "How those malignant Atoms forc'd their Way, / What in the faultless Frame they found to make their Prey" (113–14). The image of disease as a low-class sexual predator on an aristocratic woman ("Ev'n to your Breast the Sickness durst aspire") subtly links the associations of monstrous sexuality and infectious disease that fill the imaginations of Collier and Blackmore to the poet's Ovidian vision of love, sex, and death as a feverish hunt for game.[30]

With the simultaneous appearance in 1651 of Hobbes's *Leviathan* and the first of John Ogilby's five Restoration editions of Aesop, the human beast appeared to require firm control and instruction. Fable literature flourished after mid-century until Dryden convulsed the public with his mysterious poetic monster, *The Hind and the Panther* (1687), which reflected his absorption and manipulation of the whole tradition of English fable. He broke generic bounds and provoked a flood of parodies; after 1688 Jacobite and anti-Jacobite fable and Aesopian literature increased to a "rash" in the final decade.[31] In his Preface to *Prince Arthur*, Blackmore defended fable's instructive tradition, tracing the first attempts to civilize barbarians back to wise men in the East who "found this way of Fables especially in Verse, to be mighty Acceptable to the People," especially "the ruder and more unpolish'd Part of Mankind," for instruction in Religion and "Moral and Political Virtues." "They could learn them perfectly, and repeat them often, by which means the Instructions of Virtue covertly contain'd in them, were inculcated on their Minds."[32] But what "Instructions of Virtue" did Dryden's fables of 1687 and of 1700 contain?

"To the Reader" of *The Hind and the Panther* promises that "There are in it two Episodes, or Fables, which are interwoven with the main Design; so that they are properly parts of it, though they are also distinct Stories of themselves." Dryden says nothing about their instruction except that they contain "Common Places of Satyr"; the beasts' bird fables end mysteriously with unspecified threats (*Works* III: 122). In 1700, he assures the reader that an abundance of morals like plentiful deer will leap into view in the pleasurable hunt of reading: "I have endeavoured to choose such fables, both ancient and modern, as contain in each of them some instructive moral, which I could prove by induction, but the way is tedious; and they leap foremost into sight, without the reader's trouble of looking after them." In the only moral Dryden appends to one of his fables, which he lifts from Chaucer for "The Cock and the Fox," he omits Chaucer's reference to St. Paul and Romans 15: 4, a crucial verse about texts and their hopefulness of instruction ("For whatsoever things were written aforetime were written for our learning, that we through patience and comfort of the scriptures might have hope"), while he substitutes a confusing allusion apparently to Christ – "Who spoke in parables, I dare not say; / But sure he knew it was a pleasing way." Yet the matter conveyed is not "the moralite," Chaucer's word, but "sound sense" which has a more secular ring. Christ's presence is qualified further by the final triplet, "And in a heathen author we may find, / That pleasure with instruction should be join'd: / So take the Corn, and leave the Chaff behind" (819–21), where it is not clear what exactly is "the corn," what "the chaff." Chaucer's final address to God, evocation of the Lord's Prayer, wish for Christian bliss, and "Amen," are all missing. Similarly, after repeatedly heightening the sensual pleasures of Boccaccio's lovers in "Sigismonda and Guiscardo," Dryden adds a spare, apparently instructive end. Yet the repeated "justly" rings as mechanical and forced as the metrics:

> Thus She for Disobedience justly dy'd;
> The Sire was justly punish'd for his Pride:
> The Youth, least guilty, suffer'd for th' Offence
> Of Duty violated to his Prince. (750–3)

The swift succession of verbs – "dy'd," "punish'd," followed by "suffer'd," "decreed," "Intomb'd," "inscrib'd" – hammer the tale shut like the lovers' monumental tomb, and the hammering captures the crudity of human justice.

The virtuous man or woman whose reason governs his or her passions, familiar to Collier, Blackmore, and Locke (like Blackmore, published by A. & J. Churchill), is rarely glimpsed in *Fables*. Those serene souls who exercise self-government are persons who do not reproduce themselves: faithful

Baucis and Philemon so poor they have only an "infant fire" (51) they "feed" for their guests' pleasure; the two unmarried and sexually inactive men, John Driden of Chesterton and the Good Parson; plus the "Fair Maiden Lady" buried at Bath who died before she could lose her virginity. Ceyx and Alcyone begin to produce young only when they have been translated into birds. These virtuous souls appear to have distanced themselves from the restless chase of sexuality and hence become credible voices of morality and charity, of harmony and balance – John Driden in the secular spheres of government and law, the Parson in the spiritual life of his flock. "Mild was his Accent, and his Action free" describes the Parson but also Cousin Driden, like the Parson "uncumber'd with a Wife." Among stories that depict the natural round run by the human beast blinded with passion, these characters in their relative balance quietly stand out. With their serene perspective "uncumber'd" by sexual desire and the rage of hostility, the poet appears to align *Fables'* deepest imaginative vision. Part of the complex self-image he constructs in the Preface allows him to resemble these virtuous loners – as a harmless old gentleman, "a cripple in my limbs," a long- and hard-working poet who now reads and writes only to please himself and to preserve the fame of his virtuous unmarried relations like cousin Driden and Mary Frampton, the "Fair Maiden Lady, Who dy'd at Bath." He also aligns himself temperamentally, however, with fiery Homer and Homeric Achilles, "hot, impatient, revengeful."

In the poet's address to the reader before the last tale, Boccaccio's "Cymon and Iphigenia," Dryden urges the broadly civilizing effects of love and beauty. Yet in Boccaccio's tale "Beauty fires the Blood" with little evidence that love "exalts the Mind." The story concerns the transformation of a noble but retarded eldest son into the roughest hodge and his miraculous rebirth as a cultivated gentleman. But Dryden's additions to this tale, as to most of the tales, heighten violence and passion and the characters' pleasures of both. Dryden's version emphasizes the amoral hunt of sex yoked to violence, mocks the sacrament of marriage, and winks at even the well-born female's "willing" pleasure to be that prey. Cousin Driden, who chose to hunt the hare instead of women, avoided the humiliating conflict of Lysimachus, ruler of Rhodes, now a slave to love, between being "Man" and "Magistrate" (463), and the narrator adds twelve lines which begin a series of additions that underline how in this world not only "Love never fails to master what he finds" but might makes right, and "The Great, it seems, are priviledg'd alone / To punish all Injustice but their own" (471–2).

Although the domestic sanctuary is what Collier and Blackmore accused Dryden's plays of debauching, *Fables* begins and ends in the private pleasures of home. The Preface in which the poet announces his text as a house and a literary family is echoed by the conclusion of "Cymon and Iphigenia": "And happy each at Home, enjoys his Love" (*Works* VII: 523). At the end, however, the "each" at home with "his love" refers to Cymon, the "Man-Beast" (147), and Lysimachus who have illicitly stolen "their destin'd Prey" – women who shortly before had been married to our heroes' rivals now brutally murdered. As the "Ravishers" "redeem the Prey" with gleaming swords, irrepressible Dryden adds to Boccaccio "sprinkled Gore" that "Besmears the Walls, and floats the Marble Floor" (607), while the oars of the merry victors' ship hasting home sensuously "brush the buxom Sea" (613). Furthermore, unlike Ovid who in his epilogue to *Metamorphoses* confidently anticipates his text's immortality, or Chaucer who at the end of *The Canterbury Tales* makes a solemn prayer for his soul, or Boccaccio who concludes *The Decameron* by defending the morality and pleasures of his collection to fair female readers, Dryden takes no formal leave of his reader or work but allows Boccaccio's young lovers to usher us out the door.

The Preface to *Fables* juxtaposes at least two stories about its own distracted movement. One concerns the pleasurable spectacle of a rich, overstocked mind reveling in its own plenty, the celebration of imaginative "game"; another is a harsher story about the trial of writers and the judgment of readers. No less than Dryden's other prefaces, his last is riddled with the language of civil law and courts of judgment, of self-defense, jury, and mercy. Dryden puts Ovid's and Chaucer's "Merits to the Trial" by translating both so that "a certain Judgment may be made betwixt them, by the Reader"; "the Readers are the Jury" and if not satisfied may bring the case "to another Hearing before some other court." Later, defending his decision to translate Chaucer, he concludes, "in this I may be partial to my self; let the Reader judge, and I submit to his Decision," although he energetically continues his defense. As to assessing the worth of his original poems, "I leave them wholly to the Mercy of the Reader: I will hope the best, that they will not be condemn'd," although he immediately draws a self-portrait that emphasizes that his "Judgment" has never been sharper and his professional skills never more accomplished. Against the "Vulgar Judges, which are Nine Parts in Ten of all Nations" he defends the thoughtfulness of Chaucer over Ovid: "I have thus far, to the best of my Knowledge, been an upright Judge betwixt the Parties in Competition." In defending the morality of his fables, he adds, "Thus far, I hope, I am right in court, without renouncing to my other right of self-defence where I have been wrongfully accused and my sense wire-drawn into blasphemy or bawdry, as it has often been by a religious lawyer in a late pleading against the stage." Later in a digression in which he defends literary satire of the clergy, he swipes at Collier,

"I must needs say, that when a Priest provokes me without any Occasion given him, I have no Reason, unless it be the Charity of a Christian, to forgive him: *Prior laesit* [he hit first] is Justification sufficient in the Civil Law."

Finally the builder-poet who claims to write what he pleases and who emphasizes his "manly" imaginative fertility and professional ease drops in judgment a soft feminine mantle on the shoulders of his critics. The Preface ends with the final lines of Horace's Tenth Satire of his First Book, where Horace defends his literary ideals against "popular scribblers" and dismisses Demetrius, a trainer of actresses, and Tigellius, a popular singer and musician whom Horace loathed: "You, Demetrius, and you, Tigellius, I bid you go whine amidst the easy chairs of your pupils in petticoats!"[33] Dryden banishes his critics to the domestic cushions of the well-bred females whose virtue Collier and Blackmore have rushed to defend. Despite elaborate protestations that the reader is the judge, Dryden is the first judge and recreational hunter of this country seat. Courts of judgment, like that of Theseus, of Cousin Driden, or of this miscellany, become necessary in a Lucretian world of "jarring Seeds" in order to compose strife ("To My Honour'd Kinsman," 8).

Earlier I observed that the Preface's opening paragraph challenges a traditional parallel between the divine architect and the poet, who order chaos through ideas of measure, proportion, and unity. Dryden also challenges in that paragraph, and with the whole of *Fables*, the famous opening of Horace's *Ars poetica* where Horace draws an analogy of poetry to painting and mocks a painter's indecorous mixture of aesthetic elements as a grotesque conjunction of beast and human:

> If a painter chose to join a human head to the neck of a horse, and to spread feathers of many a hue over limbs picked up now here now there, so that what at the top is a beautiful woman ends below in a black and ugly fish, could you, my friends, if favoured with a private view, refrain from laughing? Believe me, dear Pisos, quite like such pictures would be a book, whose idle fancies shall be shaped like a sick man's dreams, so that neither head nor foot can be assigned to a single shape.[34]

Fables leads us to think anew about pieces, wholes, and beauty, about the conjunction of beauty and ugliness in both men and women and the conjunction of human and beast. In Dryden's translation and expansion of Chaucer's "The Wife of Bath's Tale," the Hag in her pillow lecture to her reluctant bedfellow alludes to Horace's woman-fish as she argues that what begins in humans as a line of beauty and nobility due to a grace of mind derived originally from God can descend over generations to brutishness:

> Thus in a Brute, their ancient Honour ends,
> And the fair Mermaid in a Fish descends:
> The Line is gone; no longer Duke or Earl;
> But by himself degraded turns a Churl.
>
> (435–8)

"Chance gave us being, and by Chance we live" (421), she observes, and the chance of human generation begins in the sexual conjunction and chance mix of seed, some good and some bad.

By following "The Wife of Bath Her Tale" with Ovid's digression "Of the Pythagorean Philosophy," Dryden hints that the world of *Fables* is not only one of constant metamorphosis between human and animal, good seed and bad, living and dead, but that what appears to leave the main line as an illegitimate digression may emerge as a long lost line of nobility. Dryden's interest in literary kinship and filial inheritance had long been evident, and as late as the *Aeneis*, he evokes the sanctity of lineal descent to praise Stuart legitimacy. But in *Fables* the problems of mixture and pleasure, of leveling and mingling, can be everywhere discerned. Swift and later the Third Earl of Shaftesbury would equate the licentious mixture of the literary miscellany with hapless bastard children that must use novelty as defense. Dryden's references to the translator and poet as home builder and to a line of literary relations from Homer to Chaucer, Spenser, Milton, and Dryden hint that this final miscellany of voices enfolding his three original poems, two addressed to relations, constitute not only a legitimate family but also a legitimate art: the personal miscellany becomes a model for digressive relations of ancients to moderns and of parts to a whole.

Dryden's headnote to his translation "Of the Pythagorean Philosophy" observes that Ovid, in Book xv of the *Metamorphoses*, "makes a Digression to the Moral and Natural Philosophy of Pythagoras: On both which our Author enlarges; and which are, the most learned and beautiful Parts of the whole *Metamorphoses*"; in the Preface he refers to the digression as Ovid's "masterpiece." In this and other headnotes, Dryden's running commentary on Ovid's modes of loose connection among tales suggests that the room opened by such digressions, including Dryden's own discursive style which, he says, he learned from Montaigne – "the nature of a Preface is rambling, never wholly out of the way, nor in it" – is a crucial space for beauty and the moral imagination (*Works* VII: 31). Digressions had played an important role in Dryden's art at least since the prerogative of that "nimble Spaniel" to range for game; and in "The Life of Plutarch" (1683), he links Plutarch, through his digressions, to Montaigne, and connects their digressions with the pleasurable and instructive and wandering ways of reading, thinking, and writing. Dryden confesses "to my shame, that I never read any thing but for pleasure," and history "has alwayes been the most delightful Entertainment of my life" as well as "the most pleasant School of wisdom" (*Works* VII: 270). Plutarch's blend of biography, history, and moral philosophy becomes a distinguished precedent for Dryden's fabular "School of wisdom" with its digressions and literary mixture.

Fables's exuberantly unsentimental vision of humanity's range reflects Dryden's life-long meditations on the imagination's delighted chase for game and the metamorphic powers of language. His answer to his last but hardly worst critic in a lifetime of critics pushes back against more immediate physical threats to imaginative and artistic freedom and perhaps against public expectations for the old Jacobite, the "pen for a party," to show his colors and trudge predictably to battle. The image of this miscellany as a house of fables is a much more provocatively complex gesture of self-protection and coming home than has been realized. What appears a private self-portrait redrawn along fiery, Homeric lines also glances at Collier's and at William III's moral sensibility. As retrospection over his critical and imaginative work, both anchored in key metaphors of the chase and the hunt, Dryden's final preface shapes his last miscellany into an imaginative home, a literary genealogy, and – not surprising for the chief critical voice of his age – an art of poetry. Dryden transforms the Vitruvian and biblical builder in order to celebrate the professional poet's expansiveness and vast furnishings of mind as the moral, heroic, and healthy domesticity of one.

NOTES

1. John Dryden, *The Letters of John Dryden*, ed. Charles Ward (Durham, NC, 1942), p. 109.
2. For reference to Dryden and his "Fraternity," see Jeremy Collier, *A Short View of the Immorality and Profaneness of the English Stage: Together with the Sense of Antiquity Upon this Argument*, 3rd edn. (1698; New York, 1974), 182. All further citation of Collier's *Short View* will be to this edition and appear parenthetically in my text.
3. To redraw his self-portrait was to modify the persona created by his lifelong engagement with Virgil, along with the accommodations that Virgil had come to represent. See Steven Zwicker, "Mastering Virgil," paper delivered at Dryden: An International Conference at Yale University, 6–7 October 2000.
4. Fairfax's memoir of 1758 is reproduced in Edward Arber's edition of Buckingham's *The Rehearsal* (1902), where the quotation appears on p. 8. The quotation is cited in *Works* VII: 611.
5. Chaucer repeats Geoffrey's opening lines (43–5 in the original Latin) in *Troilus and Criseyde* near the end of Book I (1065–9), a work Dryden names in his Preface.

6. Ben Jonson, *Ben Jonson*, ed. Ian Donaldson (Oxford and New York, 1985), 763, the editor's translation of "Tecum habita, ut noris quam sit tibi curta supellex." Persius, *Satires* IV: 52.

7. *Ben Jonson*, ed. Donaldson, 591 (lines 2703–17).

8. See Dryden's letter to Mrs. Steward, dated 4 March 1698 [/99] in *Letters*, p. 113.

9. Paul Hammond, *Dryden and the Traces of Classical Rome* (Oxford, 1999), p. 150.

10. Sir Richard Blackmore, *Prince Arthur* (London, 1695), Preface, v2.

11. Hammond, *Dryden and the Traces of Classical Rome*, pp. 166–7.

12. *An Essay of Dramatic Poesy* (1668), *Works* XVII: 48.

13. *Works* I: 53. See also in his dedication of *The Rival Ladies* (1664) (*Works* VIII: 101), "Imagination in a Poet is a faculty so Wild and Lawless, that, like an High-ranging Spaniel it must have Cloggs tied to it, least it out-run the Judgment."

14. D. W. R. Bahlmann, *The Moral Revolution of 1688* (New Haven, 1957).

15. See Robert D. Hume, "Jeremy Collier and the Future of the London Theatre in 1698," *Studies in Philology* 96, 4 (Fall 1999), 480–511, 490.

16. In his *Discourse Concerning the Original and Progress of Satire* (1693), Dryden suggests his plan for a national epic on the subject of King Arthur, "But being encourag'd only with fair Words, by King Charles II, my little Sallary ill paid, and no prospect of a future Subsistance, I was then Discourag'd in the beginning of my Attempt; and now Age has overtaken me; and Want . . . through the Change of the Times, has wholly disenabl'd me." *Works* IV: 22–3.

17. *Critical Essays of the Seventeenth Century*, ed. J. E. Spingarn, 3 vols. (Oxford, 1908), vol. III, pp. 232–4.

18. *Letters*, p. 135.

19. See James Anderson Winn, *John Dryden and His World* (New Haven, 1987), p. 477.

20. In response to his numerous responders, Collier produced *A Second Defense of the Short View* (1700), *A Dissuasive from the Playhouse* (1703), and *A Farther Vindication of the Short View* (1707).

21. Earlier, in February 1698, Dryden's verse epistle appeared, introducing the first published version of George Glanville's tragedy, *Heroick Love*; there Dryden commented on the declining stage about to be "reduc'd to second Infancy."

22. The phrase, "a little Minstrelsy" comes from "Of Musick" where Collier warns that the senses' and soul's susceptibility to music's power is only one example of man's fragile hold on reason that alone separates him from the monstrous; Collier, *Essays Upon Several Moral Subjects*, Part II, 2nd edn. (London, 1697), p. 24. For Cowley's remark, see *Works* VII: 559.

23. Collier, "Of Musick," p. 22.

24. *Letters*, p. 98. See commentary on "Alexander's Feast" in *Works* VII: 558–60, for a discussion of Dryden's sources.

25. James Anderson Winn, *"When Beauty Fires the Blood": Love and the Arts in the Age of Dryden* (Ann Arbor, 1992), p. 132.

26. See *Poems on Affairs of State: Augustan Satirical Verse, 1660–1714*, vol. VI: 1697–1704, ed. Frank H. Ellis (New Haven and London, 1970), pp. 29–30.

27. Ibid., p. 149.

28. *Letters*, p. 131.

29. Sean Walsh, "'Our Lineal Descents and Clans': Dryden's *Fables Ancient and Modern* and Cultural Politics in the 1690s," *Huntington Library Quarterly* 63, 1–2 (2000), 175–200, 191.

30. For a related discussion of Dryden's verse epistle to the duchess, see Steven N. Zwicker, "Dryden and the Dissolution of Things," in *John Dryden: Tercentenary Essays*, ed. Paul Hammond and David Hopkins (Oxford, 2000), pp. 308–29.

31. See Tomoko Hanazaki, "A New Parliament of Birds: Aesop, Fiction, and Jacobite Rhetoric," *Eighteenth-Century Studies* 27, 2 (1993–4), 235–54, 239. On English fable literature in this period, see also Mark Loveridge, *A History of Augustan Fable* (Cambridge, 1998) and Jayne Lewis, *The English Fable: Aesop and Literary Culture, 1651–1740* (Cambridge, 1996).

32. Spingarn, ed., *Critical Essays*, vol. III, pp. 235–6.

33. Horace, *Satires, Epistles, Ars Poetica*, ed. H. R. Fairclough for Loeb Classical Library (Cambridge, MA and London, 1991), pp. 113, 123.

34. Ibid., p. 451.

15

STEVEN N. ZWICKER

Dryden and the problem of literary modernity: epilogue

Near the beginning of his elegy for Yeats, Auden imagines the poet now "scattered among a hundred cities / And wholly given over to unfamiliar affections."[1] The image wonderfully conjures the transformation of the poet in the lives of readers far beyond original geographies, intentions, and ways of feeling. So it has been for Dryden, except that in Dryden's case it has not been only "unfamiliar affections" to which the poet was given over. There was the immediate and there has been the lasting affection of poets – Congreve, Pope, Scott, Byron, and Hopkins; T. S. Eliot, Auden himself, and most recently Geoffrey Hill. But in his own time, and thereafter, Dryden was also "given over" to enmity, rivalry, and suspicion. And there has been a related question, from his time to ours, of location: to whom and in whose company does Dryden belong?

Should we, for example, see him among the ancients or the moderns? For us this hardly seems a question at all. On first impression, and on many subsequent visits, Dryden's classicism overwhelms our attention: his indebtedness to Latin literature; his ability to see and hear in Restoration London the images and idioms of Rome; and the absorbing project of his last decade, *The Works of Virgil in English*. He is the great classicist standing midway in the line of poets that reaches from Ben Jonson to Alexander Pope. Nor is classicism only the effect of our distance; no theme was sounded more often or more eloquently in the elegies that commemorated Dryden's death than his intimacy with the ancients. He is the living Virgil, the British Ovid, the English Homer; he improved on Lucretius, revived Juvenal, made clear the crabbed Persius, weaving ancient wit "richer in the British Loom," refining antiquity in verse that joins "manly strength with Modern softness."

And there, in the last image, we discover a new note: Dryden is the classicist whose style joins the vigor of ancient idioms with "Modern softness." The collocation of soft and modern surprises, but so too does the whole idea of Dryden's modernity. The term would not however have surprised Dryden's contemporaries who were keenly aware of his advocacy of innovation, his patronage of new forms and modern writers. Nor would Dryden's modernity have been a surprise to his detractors. Indeed, modernity is the key term of abuse for his most brilliant critic, Jonathan Swift.

Swift's attack on Dryden is part of the most important aesthetic debate of the 1690s. The quarrel between the ancients and the moderns began when Swift's patron, Sir William Temple, got into a wrangle with Richard Bentley over the authenticity and dating of the supposedly ancient *Epistles of Phalaris*. Temple had mistakenly identified this forgery as a touchstone of the taste and style of the ancients; Bentley and others demolished Temple's case. Swift came to Temple's rescue in *The Battle of the Books*, but Swift reached beyond patronage, editing, and philology to give the debate a broader turn, assaulting the moderns not only for the niggling self-satisfaction with which they had dismissed Temple, but for all the excesses, blindness, stupidity, and self-promotion of contemporary writers: their "Noise and Impudence, Dullness and Vanity, Positiveness, Pedantry, and Ill-Manners."[2] Swift's satiric address is incomparable, *The Battle of the Books* a perfect mixture of hilarity, sorrow, and disgust. But Swift's recruitment of writers to the ranks of the offending moderns is neither so clear nor inevitable as his allegory: yes, Withers, Wesley, Davenant, L'Estrange, certainly Ogilby and Blackmore, perhaps Denham and Cowley, but why Tasso and Milton? And why Dryden?

Of all of Swift's moderns, it is Dryden who commands his most mocking and venomous attention. But who among the moderns had done so much as Dryden to carry across the glories of literary antiquity – the writings of Virgil, Horace, Ovid, Juvenal, Persius, Tacitus, Homer, Lucretius? Who had more energetically combated hacks like Withers and Wild, or engaged with greater point, and good humor, the likes of Ogilby and Blackmore whom Swift wickedly associates with Dryden among the offending moderns? Who had more exactly conjured the sophistication and equipoise of Augustan letters – the great original of aristocratic patronage and state panegyric? Properly to address Swift's enmity is less to engage aesthetics and learning than Swift's complex rivalry with Dryden as translator of antiquity and master of all the subtle registers of irony and scorn so fundamental to Swift's own art. But Swift's attack is not simply a piece of incoherence, or ill-suppressed envy and competition. Among the overt targets of Swift's attack are the modern habits of slavish dedication, self-indulgent preface and self-promoting critical essay – habits Dryden had perfected. And what especially outrages Swift is Dryden's acquisition of Virgil to his own cause and genius, and Swift's portrait of Dryden in *The Battle of the Books* ends with a hilarious and demeaning account of Dryden and Virgil on the battlefield: Dryden dressing in armor borrowed from Virgil, the poets exchanging horses, and in the end the laureate "afraid, and utterly unable to mount."[3]

Perhaps too Swift was annoyed with Dryden's long career of promoting and celebrating not simply his own inventions and innovations but the writing of his younger contemporaries. What Swift saw in Dryden was an ambivalent and opportunistic play across his critical divide. Given the personal animus and the schematizing drive of the *Battle of the Books*, it is hardly surprising that Swift chose to narrow Dryden's position through mockery and ridicule to a kind of egotistical presentism, but Swift was not wrong to locate Dryden among the moderns – he belonged there. But he was as well a champion of the ancients. Swift's brilliant reductions and exaggerations should serve to remind us of the complexity of Dryden's relations with both antiquity and modernity: his mobility, his protean critical stance, the flexibility of his temperament, and the complex and, at points, contradictory arc of his development.

Dryden's own silence in the debate between the ancients and moderns has puzzled scholars. Dryden knew the combatants, and as early as the 1660s he had directly addressed, and at length, its central critical concerns. It is difficult to argue with certainty that Dryden's silence in the 1690s constitutes a position in this debate, but I suspect that he simply could not come down on one side or the other, that he felt himself advocate of ancients and moderns, embracing the past while promoting the wit and invention of the present. Over and again in essays and letters, in prologues and epilogues, in literary satire and in his poetry of commendation, Dryden offered a vigorous defense of modern letters, and not least of his own position – early on at the vanguard of theatrical innovation, at the end of his life as an intimate of the ancients, rummaging among his favorite classical texts to turn them into modern poetry.

At the beginning of his career Dryden is all for a new drama, casting aside the oppressive shadow of the forefathers; at the end he is patron of youth and innovation: Congreve, Southerne, Granville, Walsh, Motteux. And yet he remains the admiring student and nimble proponent of antiquity: borrowing, alluding, some said plagiarizing, adapting, paraphrasing, translating, reviving classical antiquity. That the complexity of Dryden's own self-imagining and self-presentation and of the twinned project of inventing new literary forms and positioning those in relation to literary antiquity and the vernacular past – Shakespeare, Jonson, Fletcher – should have perplexed and galled Swift, as it did a number of Dryden's immediate contemporaries and rivals, should come as no surprise, for what Dryden seems to have done is to have worked both sides of the fence, and always to his own advantage. That others benefited from this imaginative imperialism and generosity was no saving grace for Swift; he felt crowded by the expansive and opportunistic critical and imaginative project, by Dryden's acts of ventriloquism, by his ease in simultaneously occupying more than one place and position, and by his ability to hold divided opinions and without apparent discomfort. Swift's way of dismissing Dryden was to identify him exclusively with the moderns, but Dryden's own career and temperament tell a more complex story. This is not wholly to discount Swift's attack, but to position its argument within a spectrum of responses that Dryden's work excited and to acknowledge the force of its locating of Dryden among the moderns, though not for the polemical reasons that Swift educes.

To whom then does Dryden belong? Should we identify him with the ancients or the moderns? And this question points to merely one ambivalence in what turns out to be a career of puzzles and complications of identity. The poet was born and grew up in a country village, but his writing reflects little interest in or intimacy with nature. He was raised in a Puritan household and his university education was supervised by Puritan divines, but almost continuously over the course of a long career, Dryden displayed his contempt for Puritans and for dissenting spirituality. His family were minor gentry; he received a gentleman's education; he inherited land, associated with courtiers and aristocrats, and married an earl's daughter, but he drove his career relentlessly on the tracks of professional advancement and commercial profit. Dryden was a gentleman writing among courtiers and aristocratic poets who disdained print, yet he seems wholly unembarrassed by pursuit of the literary market with its contracts and negotiations, marketing devices and subscription publications. He was a man of the theatre writing in an age of intense theatricality, and yet nothing of Dryden's public reputation suggests either fluency of personal manner or success in adopting the accents and postures of public life: he was apparently hesitant of speech, poor at telling jokes, awkward in reading his own scripts – an object of theatrical ridicule. Indeed, Dryden was the target of literary envy and personal and political malice for most of his career – he generated more attacks, libels, gossip, and scorn than any other writer of his age, perhaps than any other writer, period – and yet he was widely admired as poet and playwright, generally acknowledged, and rewarded, as the greatest literary talent of his age, and, at the end of his life, deeply esteemed by a generation of younger writers.

Near that time, Gerrard Langbaine set down these words on the paradoxes of his great contemporary:

> John Dryden, Esq., A Person whose Writings have made him remarkable to all sorts of men, as being for a long time much read, and in great Vogue. It is no wonder that the Characters given of him, by such as are, or would be thought Wits, are various; since even those, who are generally allow'd to be such, are not yet agreed in their Verdicts. And as their Judgments are different,

as to his Writings; so are their Censures no less repugnant to the Managery of his Life, some excusing what these condemn, and some exploding what those commend. So that we can scarce find them agreed in any One thing, save this, that he was Poet Laureat and Historiographer to His late Majesty.[4]

Remarkable and various, much read and in great vogue, yet we can scarcely find his contemporaries "agreed in any One thing, save this, that he was Poet Laureat and Historiographer to His late Majesty." There is something deeply suggestive about Langbaine's image of Dryden's ubiquity and scarcity. The poet had spent his last years cultivating translation – an art of disappearing – but in fact Dryden's disappearances had begun long before these translations. He had formed a literary career in an extraordinarily difficult political culture, one premised not merely on acts of oblivion but on the relentless cultivation of irony and deceit. Dryden's great literary and intellectual contemporaries appeal to us, in part, because of their resistance to the modes of public life of the Restoration: Milton was not to be quelled in the bold assertion of his person and talent; the Earl of Rochester could scarcely be bothered with concealment or disguise; and while John Locke and Isaac Newton were deeply secretive about their professional lives, their correspondence has allowed modern biographers to write in great and revealing detail about their personal and intellectual lives.

This is hardly the case with John Dryden. The personal and professional letters are scarce and scarcely revealing; the life is present in the work, but in a complex and hidden manner. While Dryden was much written about by his contemporaries, the biographical tradition has refused to make use of that perspective, choosing rather to defend Dryden from his often abusive contemporaries than to discover how both admiration and scandal cast light on Dryden's person and career. "Unfixt in Principles and Place" – Dryden made this scornful epithet for the Earl of Shaftesbury, but if we take away its immediate sting of inconstancy and think of the mobile, experimental, contingent poet and playwright inventing himself and a generation of writing in the 1660s, then modeling himself after the fashion of a bold, witty, pornographic court, then as a party player, a religious writer, a confessing Catholic, and finally a Jacobite and something of an internal exile, we might acquire some sympathy for enigma and mobility in a world that was extraordinarily difficult to negotiate.

We began with the puzzle of Dryden's classicism and modernism, the ways in which his work points us at once to his deep indebtedness to the classical past and to his vigorous advocacy of innovation. But even as we resolve that seeming contradiction, we become aware of deeper ambivalences and instabilities, of paradoxes and ironies that constitute the personality, the career, and finally the art of the greatest writer of the later seventeenth century. We used to think of great writers as the instrument that most perfectly expresses the temper of their time, and surely a case could be made for Dryden's writing as the very model of his wicked and turbulent age. But it is also tempting to reverse the formula, to think of the Restoration as somehow inventing and expressing Dryden, to see that age in all of its complexity and ambivalence, its false nostalgia, its social innovations, its embrace of contingency, its cool, almost Lucretian spiritual temper, its political angers and insecurities as the very origins and engine of the poet, the very thing that formed, might we say, the soul of the poet. Or perhaps we ought to see the relations between Dryden and his age as a perfect collusion: the political moment, the social structure, and Dryden's art forming an elaborate, opportunistic, and incredibly productive collaboration.

NOTES

1. *Collected Poems*, ed. Edward Mendelson (New York, 1991), p. 247.
2. *The Prose Works of Jonathan Swift*, ed. Herbert Davis, 14 vols. (Oxford, 1939), vol. 1, pp. 153–4.
3. *The Prose Works of Jonathan Swift*, vol. 1, p. 158.
4. *An Account of the English Dramatic Poets* (Oxford, 1691), p. 30.

FURTHER READING

Editions, reference, and bibliography

The Critical and Miscellaneous Prose Works of John Dryden, ed. Edmond Malone, 3 vols. (London, 1800).

The Works of John Dryden, ed. Walter Scott, 18 vols. (Edinburgh, 1808), rev. George Saintsbury (Edinburgh, 1882–93).

The Essays of John Dryden, ed. W. P. Ker (Oxford, 1900).

Critical Essay of the Seventeenth Century, ed. J. E. Spingarn, 3 vols. (Oxford, 1908–9).

The Songs of John Dryden, ed. Cyrus L. Day (New York, 1932).

Hugh Macdonald, *John Dryden: A Bibliography of Early Editions and of Drydeniana* (Oxford, 1939).

The Letters of John Dryden, ed. Charles Ward (Durham, NC, 1942).

The Poetical Works of Dryden, ed. George R. Noyes (Boston, 1909; rev. edn., 1950).

The Works of John Dryden, ed. E. N. Hooker and H. T. Swedenberg, Jr., et al., 20 vols. (Berkeley and Los Angeles, 1956–2002).

The Poems of John Dryden, ed. James Kinsley, 4 vols. (Oxford, 1958).

Of Dramatic Poesy and Other Critical Essays, ed. George Watson, 2 vols. (London, 1962).

John M. Aden, *The Critical Opinions of John Dryden* (Nashville, Tenn., 1963).

Poems on Affairs of State: Augustan Satirical Verse, 1660–1714, ed. George deF. Lord et al., 7 vols. (New Haven, Conn., 1963–75).

Dryden: The Critical Heritage, ed. James and Helen Kinsley (London, 1971).

The Prologues and Epilogues of the Restoration, ed. Pierre Danchin, 4 vols. in 7 (Nancy, 1981–8).

The Poems of John Dryden, vols. I–II, ed. Paul Hammond, vols. III–IV, ed. Paul Hammond and David Hopkins (London, 1995–).

John Dryden: Selected Poems, ed. Steven N. Zwicker and David Bywaters (Harmondsworth, 2001).

Biography

Samuel Johnson, "Life of Dryden," *Lives of the English Poets*, ed. G. B. Hill, 3 vols. (Oxford, 1905).

Sir Walter Scott, *The Life of John Dryden*, in volume I of *The Works*, ed. Scott.

Charles E. Ward, *The Life of John Dryden* (Chapel Hill, NC, 1961).

James M. Osborn, *John Dryden: Some Biographical Facts and Problems* (New York, 1940; rev. edn., 1965).

James A. Winn, *John Dryden and his World* (New Haven, 1987).

Paul Hammond, *John Dryden: A Literary Life* (New York, 1991).

History

K. H. D. Haley, *The First Earl of Shaftesbury* (Oxford, 1968).

John Kenyon, *The Popish Plot* (Cambridge, 1972).

John Miller, *Popery and Politics in England, 1660–1688* (Cambridge, 1973).

J. R. Jones, *Country and Court: England, 1658–1714* (Cambridge, Mass., 1978).

Gary Stuart De Kray, *A Fractured Society: The Politics of London in the First Age of Party* (Cambridge, 1985).

Ronald Hutton, *The Restoration: A Political and Religious History of England and Wales, 1658–1667* (Oxford, 1985).

Tim Harris, *London Crowds in the Reign of Charles II: Propaganda and Politics from the Restoration until the Exclusion Crisis* (Cambridge, 1987).

Ronald Hutton, *Charles the Second: King of England, Scotland, and Ireland* (Oxford, 1989).

The Politics of Religion in Restoration England, ed. Tim Harris, Paul Seaward, and Mark Goldie (Oxford, 1990).

Jonathan Scott, *Algernon Sidney and the Restoration Crisis* (Cambridge, 1991).

Paul Seaward, *The Restoration 1660–1688* (London, 1991).

John Spurr, *The Restoration Church of England, 1649–1689* (New Haven, 1991).

Tim Harris, *Politics Under the Later Stuarts: Party Conflict in a Divided Society, 1660–1715* (New York, 1993).

Mark Knights, *Politics and Opinion in Crisis, 1678–1681* (Cambridge, 1994).

Alan Marshall, *Intelligence and Espionage in the Reign of Charles II* (Cambridge, 1994).

Steven Pincus, *Protestantism and Patriotism: Ideologies and the Making of English Foreign Policy, 1650–1668* (Cambridge, 1996).

The Stuart Court and Europe: Essays in Politics and Political Culture, ed. R. Malcolm Smuts (Cambridge, 1996).

John Spurr, *England in the 1670s: "This Masquerading Age"* (Oxford, 2000).

Neil H. Keeble, *The Restoration: England in the 1660s* (Oxford, 2002).

Criticism and critical context

A. W. Verrall, *Lectures on Dryden* (Cambridge, 1914).

Mark Van Doren, *The Poetry of John Dryden* (New York, 1920).

T. S. Eliot, *Homage to John Dryden* (London, 1924).

Ruben Brower, *Alexander Pope: Poetry of Allusion* (Oxford, 1959).

Bernard Schilling, *Dryden and the Conservative Myth: A Reading of "Absalom and Achitophel"* (New Haven, 1961).

Alvin B. Kernan, *The Plot of Satire* (New Haven, 1965).

Arthur C. Kirsch, *Dryden's Heroic Drama* (Princeton, 1965).

Alan Roper, *Dryden's Poetic Kingdoms* (New York, 1965).

Earl Miner, *Dryden's Poetry* (Bloomington, 1967).

Ronald Paulson, *The Fictions of Satire* (Baltimore, 1967).

Sandford Budick, *Dryden and the Abyss of Light* (New Haven, 1970).

Robert D. Hume, *Dryden's Criticism* (Ithaca, 1970).

Michael McKeon, *Politics and Poetry in Restoration England: The Case of Dryden's Annus Mirabilis* (Cambridge, Mass., 1975).

Robert Hume, *The Development of English Drama in the Late Seventeenth Century* (Oxford, 1976).

George MacFadden, *Dryden the Public Writer: 1660–1685* (Princeton, 1978).

Howard Weinbrot, *Augustus Caesar in "Augustan" England* (Princeton, 1978).

Laura Brown, *English Dramatic Form, 1660–1740* (New Haven, 1981).

Derek Hughes, *Dryden's Heroic Plays* (London, 1981).

Steven N. Zwicker, *Dryden's Political Poetry: The Arts of Disguise* (Princeton, 1983).

David Hopkins, *John Dryden* (Cambridge, 1986).

David Bywaters, *Dryden in Revolutionary England* (Berkeley and Los Angeles, 1991).

Geoffrey Hill, *The Enemy's Country* (Stanford, 1991).

Richard Kroll, *The Material Word: Literate Culture in the Restoration and Early Eighteenth Century* (Baltimore, 1991).

Nancy Klein Maguire, *Regicide and Restoration: English Tragicomedy 1660–1671* (Cambridge, 1992).

Phillip Harth, *Pen for a Party: Dryden's Tory Propaganda in Its Contexts* (Princeton, 1993).

Harold Love, *Scribal Publication in Seventeenth-Century England* (Oxford, 1993).

Howard D. Weinbrot, *Britannia's Issue: The Rise of British Literature from Dryden to Ossian* (Cambridge, 1993).

David Bruce Kramer, *The Imperial Dryden: The Poetics of Appropriation in Seventeenth-Century England* (Athens, Ga., 1994).

Culture and Society in the Stuart Restoration, ed. Gerald MacLean (Cambridge, 1995).

Howard Erskine-Hill, *Poetry and the Realm of Politics: Shakespeare to Dryden* (Oxford, 1996).

Derek Hughes, *English Drama 1660–1700* (Oxford, 1996).

Dustin Griffin, *Literary Patronage in England, 1650–1740* (Cambridge, 1996).

Susan Owen, *Restoration Theater and Crisis* (Oxford, 1996).

Critical Essays on John Dryden, ed. James A. Winn (New York, 1997).

Paulina Kewes, *Authorship and Appropriation: Writing for the Stage in England, 1660–1710* (Oxford, 1998).

Michael Gelber, *The Just and the Lively: The Literary Criticism of John Dryden* (Manchester, 1999).

Paul Hammond, *Dryden and the Traces of Classical Rome* (Oxford, 1999).

Joseph Levine, *Between the Ancients and the Moderns: Baroque Culture in Restoration England* (New Haven, 1999).

Tanya Caldwell, *Time to Begin Anew: Dryden's Georgics and Aeneis* (Lewisburg, Pa., 2000).

John Dryden: Tercentenary Essays, ed. Paul Hammond and David Hopkins (Oxford, 2000).

John Dryden: A Tercentenary Miscellany, ed. Susan Green and Steven N. Zwicker (San Marino, CA, 2001).

Bridget Orr, *Empire on the English Stage: 1660–1714* (Cambridge, 2001).

Marcie Frank, *Gender, Theater, and the Origins of Criticism from Dryden to Manley* (Cambridge, 2002).

Blair Hoxby, *Literature and Economics in the Age of Milton* (New Haven, 2002).

Christopher Ricks, *Allusion to the Poets* (Oxford, 2002).

Joad Raymond, *Pamphlet and Pamphleteering in Early Modern Britain* (Cambridge, 2003).

INDEX

Absalom and Achitophel, 40, 48
    anonymity of, 166–167
    and Augustan culture, 79–80
    biblical allusions in, 98–100
    commemoration of Ossory, 80
    and English academy, 190–191
    influence of Paradise Lost, 170–171
    and post-Fire London, 115
    and religious conflict, 243–244
    religious subtext and anonymity, 168–171
    and shaping of literary life, 8
    use of triplets, 93–100
academy, see English academy; French
        academy; sociability
Addison, Joseph, 68
adultery, 23–25, 27–28
Aeneid, 41, 80–82, 235–236
Albion and Albanius, 147–149
Alexander's Feast, 54
All For Love; or, The World Well Lost,
        29–30
    and elegy, 54–55
    and influence of politics on theatre,
        145–146
    self-recognition as theme, 30
Allusion to Horace, 45
Amboyna or The Cruelties of the Dutch to
        the English Merchants, 140–141,
        142
Amphitryon; or the Two Socias, 27–28
    adultery, 27–28
    and influence of politics on theatre, 150
analogies, 42, 43
ancients, see classicism
Anglicanism, 240–241
    in Annus Mirabilis, 241
    comparison to Catholicism of The Hind
        and the Panther, 176

in Religio Laici, 9–10, 173–174, 176,
        247–249
    see also Church of England
Anglo-Dutch Wars, 140–141
    see also Annus Mirabilis. The Year of
        Wonders, 1666
Annus Mirabilis. The Year of Wonders,
        1666, 42–43, 62–63
    and allegiance to Charles II, 225–229
    and Anglican doctrine, 241
    and Augustan culture, 78–79
    criticism of Dutch trade monopoly, 64–65
    dedications, 205–207
    elegy on old London, 116
    heroic bestiary, 227–228
    ideology, 63–68
    and imperial imagination, 63–73
    and post-Fire London, 114–115
    and shaping of literary life, 6
anonymity, 156–178
    Absalom and Achitophel, 166–167,
        168–171
    accusations of plagiarism, 164–165
    attribution to Thomas Shadwell, 160–161
    commendatory poems of Nahum Tate,
        167–168
    The Dunciad, 172–173
    An Essay upon Satire, 156–157
    execution of Stephen College, 157–158
    versus identification in Religio Laici,
        173–174, 176
    and impersonality, 166–167, 168–171
    MacFlecknoe, 163–165
    The Medal, 158–159, 168
    motives for, 157–158, 166–167, 178
    and political propaganda, 166
    and Roman Catholicism, 176–178
    and satire, 159–160

290

CAMBRIDGE COMPANIONS TO LITERATURE

CAMBRIDGE COMPANIONS TO CULTURE